D1083425

480729

The Search for Social Peace

SUNY Series on Modern European Social History
Leo A. Loubère, Editor

The Search for Social Peace

Reform Legislation in France, 1890–1914

JUDITH F. STONE

State University of New York Press

To Stanley

Published by
State University of New York Press, Albany

For information, address State University of New York
Press, State University Plaza, Albany, N.Y., 12246

Library of Congress Cataloging in Publication Data

Stone, Judith F., 1946–
    The search for social peace.

    1. Social legislation—France—History. 2. France—
Social conditions—19th century. I. Title.
LAW   344.44   84-20531
ISBN 0-88706-022-6   344.404
ISBN 0-88706-023-4 (pbk.)

10 9 8 7 6 5 4 3 2 1

Contents

Acknowledgments

This study benefited greatly from the guidance, support, and encouragement of teachers, colleagues, and friends. Although none of the people whom I wish to thank are responsible for the faults of this work, they each in various ways enabled me to complete a more effective and more cogent text.

I must first express my deep appreciation to my advisor, Professor Richard F. Kuisel of the State University of New York at Stony Brook, who guided me from the inception of this project through its dissertation stage and thereafter. Professor Kuisel's insistence that I ground theory in fact, write with greater clarity, and always reexamine my assumptions was of incalculable importance to my work. I am also appreciative of the support and advice of Professors Herman Lebovics and Werner T. Angress. Professor Leo Loubère of the State University of New York at Buffalo offered valuable suggestions for the revision of the text.

Colleagues at The State University of New York's Empire State College greatly aided this endeavor. Steven Tischler's insightful and useful criticism of the revised manuscript was most important. The confidence shown by James Robinson in my effort was an ongoing source of support. My fellow teachers and students at the Center for Labor Studies taught me much about labor relations, enabling me to see the French case more clearly.

Many friends provided me with encouragement and an intellectual community during this long enterprise. In particular, I must express my deep appreciation to Diane Camilleri who gave me invaluable help through her lucidity, refusal to flatter, and force of example. This work could not have been completed without the advice and support of Stanley Stamm who gave his time, energy, and optimism unstintingly.

I am grateful to my father, who fostered my interest in France. And finally I must thank my mother, who was my earliest and most influential teacher of history.

Introduction

During the last one hundred years social legislation has been the foremost domestic issue of all industrial states. The term "social reform" has come to include a large number of sometimes apparently disparate proposals and laws. All social reform legislation has had among its objectives the material improvement of workers' conditions at the workplace, in the community, and within the family. Through either direct or indirect intervention by the state, the aim has been to lessen the devastation of unemployment and to improve the workers' bargaining position with respect to their employers. Social insurance programs now provide partial protection for working-class incomes during periods of unemployment caused by accidents, old age, sickness, or even temporary job loss. The regulation of such working conditions as hours, the workweek, sanitation, and, most important, wages, has served to create a minimum standard below which neither the employer nor the business cycle can depress workers' income. Finally, state protection has been conferred on workers' collective efforts to enhance their conditions and wages through the legal regulation of unions, conciliation and arbitration procedures, and contract negotiation.

Social reformers since the 1890s have thus created the welfare states of western Europe and the social contract between labor and capital in the United States. Especially in the decades following the Second World War, programmatic social legislation became an essential economic and social component of advanced capitalist nations. Henry Hatzfeld in his important analysis of the social security system in France has concluded that that system is "one of the mechanisms which assures the functioning of the entire capitalist economy as it exists today.... [Social security] demonstrates the adaptability of capitalism." [1]

Historians in the last decades of the twentieth century have a particularly good vantage point from which to examine the origins of systematic reform legislation. Social legislation, its cost and its impact on the labor market and labor relations have once again become political issues generating intense debate in some countries.[2] Programmatic reform no longer seems quite as inevitable nor as permanent a policy of advanced capitalist regimes as it did a decade ago. The present political controversy enables us to appreciate more fully the origins of the reform effort, its early supporters, their goals and their opponents, all of which are the subject of this study.

I have examined the early development of social reform in France because the tensions which made the "social question" an important political issue there were so finely balanced during the period 1890–1914. The interrelations of an industrializing society, a parliamentary state, and a popular egalitarian ideology created the context in which reform legislation was proposed and debated. During the first half of the Third Republic, the institutions of universal male suffrage and republicanism were tested by the emergence of an increasingly articulate and organized working class. Social reform was one response to this new reality. In order to pursue this strategy, French reformers reexamined their conceptions of republicanism, liberalism, and political economy. Seeking to base their call for social peace on empirical evidence, republican academics and academic reformers were instrumental in the development of modern sociology. This new social science placed the working class and other social classes in the larger category of society, and "scientifically" demonstrated the social value of stability.

The examination of social reform in pre-World War I France, however, is not merely a useful case study of the emergence of modern social policy. In locating the origins of reform in France, we also find a new perspective from which to analyze several of the major historical questions of the Third Republic. The goals of the working-class movement, the importance of the Radical Party, the significance of republicanism, the politics of the petite bourgeoisie, the unity and diversity of the bourgeoisie, and the conditions of the "stalemate" society—all these issues impinge on the social reform question in France.

Any explanation of reform policy must begin with the role of working-class activism in initiating the entire debate. By focusing on rank and file activity, point of production issues, and strikes, recent labor historians have demonstrated the vitality and range of the French working-class movement prior to the First World War. Several of these historians mention, in passing, the interaction between workers' organizations and nonsocialist republican politicians.[3] Bernard Moss, for example, in his study of revolutionary syndicalism notes the important but often contradictory relationship between the working class and the "republican movement."[4] Michelle Perrot in her definitive study of strike activity during the opening decades of the Third Republic suggests that by 1914 a "third party" had emerged "which was going to modify the conditions of confrontation between labor and capital."[5] The present work seeks to identify the members of that "third party," to gauge the degree to which they actually stood between labor and capital, and to evaluate their success in modifying labor relations.

Following the suggestions touched upon in these histories, I will argue that the reform movement was led by republican politicans in order to fulfill the fundamentally bourgeois objective of social peace. Many of those involved in the campaign for social legislation were leaders of the Radical Party. Although another significant group, led by Alexandre Millerand, called themselves socialists, their socialism was always one of reform and class collaboration.[6] Regardless of their party labels, the active parliamentary leaders who sought reform pursued the goals of class harmony and social peace.

Central to this study of social reform is a reexamination of the politics, politicians, and legislative activity of the Third Republic. The Radical Party was the quintessence of Belle Epoque politics and, as I will demonstrate, at the heart of the reform debate. However, despite its importance, and the numerous histories of the party,[7] its character still remains elusive. Conventional descriptions of the Radicals persist in locating them "on the right because of their attachment to property, but on the left because of their anti-clericalism."[8] Even Theodore Zeldin in his rich description of French politics occasionally characterizes them as "sterile" and "stuck in the past."[9] Such views have depicted the Radicals' failure to deliver on the promise of social reform as inevitable, and further investigation on this question as unnecessary. A more fruitful overview of radicalism and the Third Republic is offered in Madeleine Rebérioux's *La République Radicale?* She questions such basic assumptions as Radical control of the government after 1902, as implied in the title itself, and emphasizes the diversity, fluidity, and conflict within the party.[10] She also stresses the transformation which the Radicals and republicanism experienced in this critical period.[11]

I have tried to view the Radicals with as few preconceptions as possible in order not to prejudge their social program. During the years 1896–1906 there were several real alternatives open to Radical politicans. Important leaders within the party actively and consistently pursued reform. The ultimate defeat by 1910 of their social policy was not predetermined, as will be seen, but rather the final act in a series of struggles within the party and among republicans over the "social question."

To study the entire reform movement and the role of the Radicals within it from a new perspective, I have examined the ideology of republicanism, the emergence of a new political elite, and the structure of the French bourgeoisie. Any discussion of republicanism at the end of the nineteenth century must include an analysis of *solidarité* and its formulation by Léon Bourgeois. Important work has already been done in this area by J.E.S. Hayward,[12] who primarily explores the intellectual and philosophical dimensions of *solidarité*. Hayward's analysis, written in the early 1960s, often assumes much too direct a progression between Bourgeois' *solidarité* and the 20th century welfare state.[13] Theodore Zeldin in *Politics and Ambition*, on the other hand, presents Bourgeois' *solidarité* as ultimately conservative.[14] For a fuller understanding of *solidarité* and the general reform ideology one must evaluate the dual thrust toward social control and social change contained in the reformers' justifications and aims. *Solidaristes*, like all reformers, intended to preserve the social order. Yet their legislative proposals to achieve that end genuinely terrified employers and many property owners. Unlike most works in this field, this book examines the consequences of these contradictory objectives of reform. My study concludes that in the specific political and social climate of the first decade of the 20th century, reformers could not convince their constituents that social legislation would guarantee social peace.

One of the most useful analyses of the ideology of social

peace in general can be found in Sanford Elwitt's important work on the early Third Republic.[15] Elwitt examines one set of political and economic compromises finally elaborated during the 1880s. He is especially illuminating on the complex cluster of social and ideological contradictions that underlie the republican state. Among the most significant of Elwitt's contributions is his insistence that ideological and political issues be linked to socioeconomic structures. Here too he stresses the contradictions which beset the republican alliance of petty producers and the industrial bourgeoisie.[16] At the heart of these contradictions lies the confrontation between the democratic tradition and bourgeois rule, between republican egalitarianism and property.[17] Elwitt portrays early versions of *solidarité* as an attempt to hold together these disparate realities and to dampen any possible class conflict. Most important for Elwitt, *solidarité* represents a persistent effort to secure the loyalty of the working class to the Republic.[18] He views the combination of railroad construction, educational reform, tariffs, and colonial expansion as a temporary resolution of social tensions by the mid-1880s.

While Elwitt's work is essential reading for any understanding of the Third Republic, he underestimates the continuing struggle between classes and within the bourgeoisie to maintain the "resolutions" of the early 1880s. His emphasis on the balance and stalemate among different bourgeois forces leaves little room for the actual conflict and crises which occurred during the 1890s and the first fifteen years of the twentieth century. Elwitt's claim that the bourgeoisie closed ranks at the beginning of the 1890s[19] relegates the later bourgeois reformers to an insignificance which they do not deserve. I argue that the political and ideological divisions within the bourgeoisie persisted. The contradictions identified by Elwitt in the 1880s reappeared in subsequent decades under altered conditions. If anything, these divisions became especially sharp in the late 1890s, when republicans had to respond to an articulate and organizing working class. In fact, republican politicians rededicated themselves to the bourgeois ideal of *solidarité* during almost every decade of the Republic's existence. I intend to demonstrate that between 1895 and 1909 this process fostered a distinctly new vision of social peace which centered on reform legislation as the means to create an environment where workers could attain security.

I locate the development of this new reform strategy in the social context of the republican political elite. The structure of this elite was shaped, in part, by the politicians' petite bourgeois and bourgeois constituents. It was also significantly affected by the specific Parisian parliamentary and university milieu inhabited by the members of this elite. I have given special emphasis to the role of these men and their views on republicanism, the nation and class solidarity. Within this elite the Radicals' special commitment to the state and national unity led them, for a time, to call most consistently and ardently for reforms to ensure social stability and the defense of the Republic.

Fortunately there seems to be a new interest in the republican elite of the prewar era. The works of Terry Clark on Durkheim's sociology, Robert Smith on the Ecole Normale Supérieur, Katherine Auspitz on the Ligue de l'Enseignement, and George Weisz on the entire university system[20] provide the context of institutions, intellectuals, and academics within which to place the social reform issue. Several of the central figures in each of these studies reappear in my work, demonstrating the importance and cohesion of this new university-trained bourgeois republican elite. Katherine Auspitz, in particular, cogently argues for the special need to reexamine the Radicals and their role in this elite, affording them the significance they warrant.

While this elite plays a leading role in my study, I have also examined how its interests coincide with those of several strata within the bourgeoisie. The issues, debates, and the ultimate conclusion of the reform question were determined by the diversity of bourgeois interests and the essential class unity of the French bourgeoisie. The work of Leo Loubère[21] on the Radical party, petty producers, and the working class provides important insights into the relation between bourgeois interests and politics. Loubère has established that the Radical Party had an authentic left-wing, which sought to give a social dimension to the principle of equality. Even more significantly, he demonstrates the complex economic, social, and political concerns of vintners in the Midi which linked them for a time to this Radical left wing.[22] Loubère's conclusions support my claim that the Radical Party's eventual retreat from social reform was not inevitable. Furthermore, Loubère demonstrates the complex and shifting attitude of the petite bourgeoisie toward social reform.[23] While all strata of the bourgeoisie demanded the protection of property and the establishment of social peace, very different strategies to these ends were endorsed by southern winegrowers, Parisian retailers, paternalist textile manufacturers, and steel magnates. The competition among these various strategies for social peace is one of the major developments examined in my study.

The ideological, political, and social dimensions of the reform debate are significant, but I have also analyzed the legislative history and the actual implementation of reform laws. These aspects of the "social question" have often been neglected. As a result, our knowledge is less than complete about the debate and its outcome. Different problems, solutions, and compromises emerged during the long, often exhausting discussions on each proposal which took place in the Chamber and the Senate and in their respective committees. Most important is the issue of implementation. I have tried to evaluate the degree to which the laws actually affected working-class life. Unlike older histories on the subject,[24] which viewed the enactment of legislation as a victory, I argue that while political advances were made with the passage of each law, the reform objectives were essentially defeated because of the profound failure to implement uniform national laws.

In the area of French social reform legislation we are fortunate to have one model analysis, Henry Hatzfeld's *Du Pauperisme à la sécurité sociale en France*. Hatzfeld has studied the development of social security from its theoretical origins in the 1840s to the elaboration of the welfare state in the aftermath of the Second World War. In his examination of the period 1890 to 1914, Hatzfeld concludes that the main obstacle to the old age pensions were small entrepreneurs. In addition, he views social security legislation as an extension of private insurance programs established in some large industries by 1900. I have reached different conclusions about the opponents to social reform. Large industrialists opposed reform legislations as much as the petite bourgeoisie, although their opposition was not as publicly political as that of the *petit patron*. On the critical question of state intervention, large industry was more unanimous in its opposition than the petite bourgeoisie.[25] While this difference is an important one,

Hatzfeld's work is, nonetheless, an exemplary study of reform legislation, placing it at the center of a process which transformed the state, republicanism, and the bourgeoisie.

This study of social reform attempts to contribute further to our understanding of social and political stalemate during the Third Republic, which Stanley Hoffman was among the first to analyze. The efforts of the bourgeoisie to find an appropriate response to an organizing working class in the context of a republican state were essential factors in that stalemate. The bourgeois search for social peace generated several competing strategies; one of these was social legislation. The failure to implement this strategy before the First World War was a triumph of the larger bourgeois goal to maintain social peace most economically and without serious disruption to any one stratum within the bourgeosie. Perhaps this quintessential bourgeois quest for social peace, which is the major theme of my study, is synonymous with what social scientists have characterized as the stalemate society. Nonetheless, whether it is called "peace" or stalemate, it is important to recognize that these "resolutions" were the results of often intense class and intraclass conflicts. Furthermore, the stalemate or social "peace" achieved was temporary and regularly upset by the assertions of the working class and the divisions within the bourgeoisie.

In examining the origins of social reform in France, I have had to consider areas of inquiry which historians too often isolate from one another. My subject required that I analyze ideological, political, social, and economic facets of the Third Republic. I have also explored such traditional concerns as party programs and parliamentary debates. This intersection of politics, the state, and social structures is essential to understanding the effort to enact reform legislation. Contemporary history has recently suffered from a neglect of politics and state policy. Our pursuit of a too narrowly defined social history has often led us to ignore the role of the modern state. The assumption that the state can and should improve social reality is, in fact, the key to the reform enterprise. French reformers, like those elsewhere, claimed that the state can and must intervene in the social and economic conditions of its citizens. If it failed to do so, disorder and possibly even revolution might ensue. Historians must explore this contention. We must investigate the degree to which the state, or more accurately the consequences of political decisions, have affected society. In turn, we must identify the limits which social and economic relations place on legislative intervention. The analysis which follows is an effort to contribute to that larger task.

CHAPTER 1

The "Social Question"

The "social question," a polite euphemism for what to do about and for the working class, has been one of the principal political issues of the twentieth century. It first commanded consistent attention and programmatic responses in the industrial states of western Europe and North America during the period 1890–1914. Enfranchised and organizing workers forced politicians and their bourgeois constituents to address the causes and consequences of poverty in parliamentary regimes. Intense and complex conroversies surrounded all proposals to resolve or mitigate the "social question." Increasingly the political debate came to focus on the legitimacy and viability of legislation to improve working-class conditions. Those who supported reform identified economic insecurity as the major dilemma facing workers, a dilemma which amplified instability throughout society. In an effort to limit the intensifying class conflict of the period, a minority of politicians and theorists were willing to accept state intervention in the labor market and in labor relations. Beginning in the 1890s and with increasing regularity, reformers submitted plans for compulsory insurance, regulation of workers' hours and conditions, and official mechanisms for collective bargaining. While no industrial state had a fully developed or implemented social policy by 1914, the ideological and administrative foundations for the more systematic welfare legislation of the twentieth century were established during the prewar period.

The political debate engendered by proposed legislation to improve workers' conditions was protracted and bitter. In defending such reform, politicians and intellectuals were often led to reexamine conventional nineteenth-century views of the economy, class relations, and the functions of the state. Supported by the evidence of the new social sciences, reformers argued that the extreme fluctuations of the labor market and the business cycle had to be mitigated. Employers and their representatives, on the other hand, resisted any interference with well-established prerogatives of property ownership. Industrialists and the affluent feared that any tampering with the "natural" social and economic order would upset their hard-won authority, comfort, and privilege. Despite their differences, however, reformers and their opponents agreed as the twentieth century began on the urgent need to insure social peace.

This mounting anxiety, which affected all strata of the bourgeoisie in every industrial state, reflected the new militancy of the working class. Workers in France, Great Britain, Germany, and the United States, from at least the 1890s to the eve of the First World War, were transforming labor relations and politics. Throughout the industrial world, there was a marked increase in the number of strikes and strikers. This significant increase in labor disputes peaked in the European countries around 1906 and again in 1901–1911.[1]

The new working-class activism, however, was not simply a matter of expanding numbers seeking improved wages and hours. Strikes took on a new aggressiveness. A significant minority of workers consciously viewed their actions as part of a larger international class struggle to abolish the capitalist system. The combativeness of Parisian construction workers in the first decade of the twentieth century, as just one example, was justified by the revolutionary syndicalism which had come to dominate the French labor movement.[2] A similar aggressiveness characterized the actions of British, German, and American workers. To varying degrees these workers too expressed an interest in, if not an allegiance to, revolutionary syndicalism. The new industrial unionism of the London dockers, for example, exhibited a militancy and radicalism which matched their French counterparts.[3] Major strike waves led by the Ruhr miners galvanized even the staid German unions.[4] In the United States, where working-class organizations were least developed, strikes frequently ended in armed class war. Colorado metal miners, attracted to an American version of revolutionary syndicalism, battled private armies and federal troops between 1903 and 1905.[5]

While confrontations between strikers and the military dramatically illustrate the intensity of class conflict in those decades, the new political direction of the labor movement had even more far-reaching consequences. By the 1890s, some form of universal male suffrage existed in all major industrial nations. Mechanisms of popular representation served to legitimate the actions of the state. Working-class organizations successfully used the representative parliamentary system to address a national working-class audience and to enter the national political arena. Independent working-class parties began to form. These socialist and labor parties enthusiastically engaged in electoral contests, and their support among the electorate grew. Working-class constituents were now sending representatives to municipal councils, city halls, local assemblies, and national parliaments. These representatives not only voiced the grievances of specific groups of workers, but as members of socialist parties they claimed to speak for the entire working class. Furthermore, these national parties encouraged and criticized one another in the recently established Second International. The new industrial activism and particularly the new political efforts of workers spurred on the debate over the "social question." The reform strategy was one response to the demands of militant working class organizations.

Politicians, intellectuals, and academics who debated the "social question" understood very clearly the fundamental developments that had exacerbated and transformed the problems of poverty by the end of the nineteenth century. In 1900, Alexandre Millerand, then the French Minister of Commerce, claimed that social reform was inevitable. According to this independent reform socialist, such inevitability was the result of "two major facts, each belonging to a different order, which dominate contemporary French society: the theoretical sovereignty of the most numerous based on universal suffrage, and the increasingly intense concentration of labor [and] capital."[6] Industrialization and democracy, then, made reforms inescapable.

Politicians committed to the parliamentary regime feared that workers would rebel against the contradiction of being economically dependent while in theory being politically free. One French republican Deputy observed, "It is this profound discord between the political and economic systems . . . which gives the 'social question' its bitter and distressing character."[7] Reform politicians recognized that workers who voted and were politically active could no longer be ignored. The employers' traditional views of the worker as a child at best, or, more commonly, as a "greedy, drunken liar" by nature,[8] did not easily coexist with the ideal of the citizen. New union organizations, the workers' recent enfranchisement, the changing position of the working class in an expanding economy, and the presence of its representatives in legislative chambers had redefined the century-old bourgeois concern about maintaining social peace and stability.[9]

Workers and employers, socialists and liberals, reformers and their opponents, all agreed that the material insecurity of the working class posed actual or potential dangers to existing society. Arguing that workers' economic insecurity bred disorder, reformers called for legislation that would reduce such conditions and create social peace. Just as working-class activism occurred simultaneously in most industrial states, so too did the reform response. A new generation of bourgeois politicians and intellectuals developed the argument that the state must participate in securing minimal protection for workers against economic precariousness. While their influence and success varied, proponents of reform had clearly emerged in France, Great Britain, Germany, and the United States by the 1890s, if not earlier. Reform politicians, administrators and social theorists were very much aware of the activities of their counterparts in other countries. They sought one another's support in building international associations dedicated to reform.[10] They used the accomplishments of reformers in other nations as models to be emulated in their own.

Significantly, the earliest advances in the theoretical underpinnings of reform, as well as passage of the first insurance legislation, occurred in the newly invented German Empire. The new theories of society which came to support social legislation were first discussed in the German universities. A reassessment of classical liberalism giving greater attention to collective rather than individual forces, encountered fewer obstacles in German intellectual circles than elsewhere.[11] As early as the 1870s, two economists, Gustave Schmoller and Lujo Brentano, formed a historical school of economic analysis. Rejecting the abstractions of classical political economy, the German school called for a new pragmatism. Economics, they claimed, must "respect the economic fact," emphasize the evolutionary, historical nature of economies, analyze "*all* facets of economic behavior,"[12] and discard any generalizations.

Related to this historical view of the economy, and even more important for the social reform debate, was the establishment of the Verein für Sozialpolitik in 1873. The historical economists of the Verein intended their empirical research of contemporary conditions to lead to reform.[13] The most illustrious member of the group was Max Weber. He developed much of his new sociological method in his articles for the Verein.[14] Sociology provided a new conceptual framework important in the social reform effort. Not only in Germany, but in Great Britain, the United States,[15] and especially France,[16] sociology created the language and theory to justify reform. The issues and the goals of the Verein, in particular, became a model for reform-minded intellectuals and academics throughout the industrial world. The German theorists were among the first to replace the older problem of pauperism with an analysis of working-class insecurity. They were instrumental in creating the international organizations where like-minded scholars and administrators exchanged ideas.[17] These pioneer sociologists sought to explain the contradictions of industrialization and to mitigate their consequences without disrupting the social order.

Equally innovative major reform legislation was enacted by the German Reichstag in the 1880s. Compulsory insurance for workers' sickness was passed in 1883, and compulsory employers' insurance for work place accidents in 1884. In 1889 an old age pension, financed by employer, worker, and, most significantly, state contributions, became law.[18] This Bismarckian achievement, called by a French observer "one of the most important political events in the history of contemporary Europe,"[19] became a powerful model for all later social reformers. In Great Britain, the United States, and France, reform politicians explained how they would both duplicate and differ from the German advance. Insurance programs, however, were only half of Bismarck's social policy. The Chancellor easily obtained the support of the compliant Reichstag not only for reform, but also for the repression of independent working-class political activity. The legal suppression of the German Social Democratic Party from 1878 to 1890 was the second half of a social policy that linked repression and reform. Coached by the Chancellor, the German Emperor stated in 1881, "The cure for social ills must be sought not exclusively in the repression of Social Democratic excesses, but simultaneously in the positive advancement of the welfare of the working classes."[20]

As we shall see, repression continued to be viewed as an important and legitimate response to working class "excesses." In fact, the demand for repression would intensify at the same time that the pressure for reform became stronger.[21] Bismarck, however, was somewhat unusual among politicians in his early effort to combine these two strategies. In Great Britain, the United States, and France, reform politicians were usually the opponents, albeit not always successful ones, of such repression. Bismarck, on the other hand, had been able to forge this dual response to working-class mobilization by the 1880s. His easy success reflected the degree to which universal male suffrage had been sabotaged within the German state. The popular vote and working-class political participation had much less influence on reform in Imperial Germany than it did in the more representative regimes of Great Britain, the United States, and France.

Bismarck's success, however, should not be overstated. His social policy had a limited impact, both in its repressive and reformist intent. Despite the praise of later historians, the architects of the German social insurance programs viewed them as failures. The laws had not convinced the working class to abandon the Social Democratic Party. Furthermore, the much-lauded old age pension had little real effect on the working class. Since the eligibility age was 70, few German workers ever received their pensions. Although Bismarck had been willing to accept some state supervision of insurance programs and even state participation in the old age pension, his reform program was extremely limited. He adamantly rejected state intrusion into labor relations. His refusal to discuss any regulation of hours or wages was one element, although a small one, in his conflict with the new Kaiser, Wilhelm II.[22] Following Bismarck's forced resignation in 1890, Wilhelm hoped to direct a "new course" which was to include further labor reforms. However, social reform without the extension of authentic political representation was not possible. By the mid-1890s the German ruling elite, opposed only by the S.P.D., sought to resolve its "social question" through a policy of *Weltpolitik*—increased agrarian protection, military and commercial expansion, and colonialism.[23]

Unlike Imperial Germany, where no viable parliamentary reform coalition emerged after 1890,[24] the reform issue became an intensely partisan political question in the three states where universal male suffrage had been more firmly established. There are striking parallels in the chronology, personnel, and content of this debate in Great Britain, the United States, and France. The first decade of the twentieth century was pivotal for reform in all three nations. In 1906, the same year that French Radicals with Socialist support gained control of the Chamber of Deputies, a reinvigorated British Liberal Party, in alliance with the new Labour Party, became the majority in the House of Commons. Two years earlier, in the United States, Theodore Roosevelt had been elected president as a Progressive Republican pledged to curtail the abuses of big capital and protect the little man. American Progressives shared with the French Radicals a similar constituency among residents of provincial small towns, small propertied farmers, and new professionals.[25] The leaders of the French Radicals, the British Liberals and the American Progressives, all were acutely aware of working-class political organizations, the intensification of class conflict, the limitations of liberal orthodoxy, and the bourgeois desire for social peace.

The American and British reform effort had a much more lasting effect on political institutions and industrial conditions than the French did. The American and the British reformers were able to limit obstructionist conservative forces lodged in the upper chamber of Congress and Parliament. British Liberals, in particular, under the leadership of David Lloyd George, were able to do what French Radicals failed to accomplish. In 1909 they broke the resistance of the House of Lords had proceeded to reorganize the finances of the British state.[26] Following this critical breakthrough, and under the pressure of economic change and working-class agitation,[27] the Liberals secured the most successful and far-reaching reforms of the period—the old age pension of 1908 and the National Health Insurance Act of 1911. Although American Progressives were unable to enact national labor or social legislation, they did fundamentally reorient the industrial, commercial, and foreign policies of the state during the administrations of Roosevelt, Taft, and Wilson.[28] The Progressives also established the theoretical and administrative foundations for later programmatic social reform.

Despite the substantial British legislative advances and the important American political victories, it can be argued that the social reform effort floundered and slowed in Great Britain and the United States, much as it did in France, after 1910. Neither British Liberals nor American Progressives nor French Radicals were able to convince their bourgeois colleagues that reform ensured social peace. In the United States much of the reform effort was deflected toward federal regulation that supported increasing corporate concentration. State laws to improve working-class conditions were weak and often not implemented. In practice, large industrialists and smaller manufacturers remained even more bitterly opposed to working-class organizations than their French counterparts.[29] The Progressives, like the French Radicals, were unable to reduce the intensity of class conflict in the United States where its scope and violence went far beyond anything in industrial Europe.[30] In Great Britain the very success of the new Liberal reforms may have alienated portions of the traditional Liberal middle-class constituency. Liberal voters questioned the efficacy of reforms which did not reduce the constantly increasing number of strikes nor the radicalism of the new trade unions.[31] Such a reassessment of the reform position must be included among the causes of the rapid demise of British Liberalism so soon after its stunning victories.

Certainly legislative efforts to improve working-class conditions had occurred earlier in the century, notably in Great Britain.[32] However, it was during the last quarter of the nineteenth century that social reform as a response to working-class activism, itself generated by the dual pressures of expanding industrialization and universal male suffrage, became a systematic political strategy. In all industrial states, reformers had complementary concerns, political goals, and ideologies. The "social question" became particularly sharp from 1900 to 1906. In these same years some bourgeois politicians made efforts to create reform parties and enact reform legislation. Who the reformers were, the precise nature of their proposals, the extent of their success, and the composition of their opposition depended, in each of the industrialized nations, on the structure of the economy, the system of politics, the role of the state, and the interrelations of these three factors.

The emergence of a modern social reform program in France during the period 1890 to 1914 is a particularly instructive instance of this general development in all industrialized states. The fact that French reformers could not secure legislation to equal the scope of the German and British laws offers us an opportunity to examine the entire range of forces which supported and opposed social legislation. The specifically French version of the "social question" was shaped by the almost simultaneous developments of universal male suffrage and industrializaton. Parliamentary democracy was introduced with the Third Republic in 1871. While economic expansion had already occurred in the 1850s and 1860s, the widespread growth of industry and the factory system took place during the first decades of the Third Republic. The new systems of politics and production had profoundly different consequences for various sectors of the population. Furthermore, the scope of the electoral system and the distribution of French industry were very dissimilar. The institutions of universal male suffrage affected, in law at least, all Frenchmen; industrialization, and particularly the concentration of labor, was not a national experience. The factory system was unevenly distributed in France. Within industrialized regions, the organization and scope of industries varied considerably. As we shall see, this asymmetry between political and economic structures seriously inhibited the development of systematic reform proposals and greatly complicated the implementation of legislated reforms.

The parliamentary system, republicanism, and the centralized state, the last inherited from previous regimes, were key elements in creating national unity. Since local institutions of any real political influence had been severely restricted throughout the nineteenth century, the national legislative body in Paris held a near-monopoly on political debate. Universal male suffrage made it possible for the often geographically concentrated working class to elect representatives to the Chamber of Deputies, which had been evolving toward a more consistent republicanism since the 1880s. By the end of that decade the republican system was securely established. Accompanying the republicans' ideological and political victory was an important change in the personnel of the expanding state bureaucracy. A significant number of men, and a much smaller number of women, were being drawn from the "*nouvelles couches sociales*" to fill lower positions in the Ministries of Interior, Commerce, Justice, and Education. The middle and lower ranks of the bourgeoisie were now replacing an older, more affluent, more liberal generation of politicians, administrators, and civil servants. Many of these new arrivals were committed to propagating and enforcing the republican ideology and system that had made their social mobility possible.

Nowhere was that sentiment stronger than in the Ministry of Education and among the growing ranks of republican educators. The most significant and permanent reform of the Third Republic was the educational policy of the 1880s.[33] Under the leadership of the moderate republican Jules Ferry, the French parliament created the only state-run, compulsory, secular primary school system in the world. Elementary education was significantly reorganized, and reforms were also applied to the university.[34] The men and women who staffed the expanding educational system were the crucial cadre for republicanism in all its varieties. As we shall see, they provided both leaders and constituents for the social debate of the next two decades. Most important, the republican educators were to imbue their students with patriotic values that equated national loyalty with republicanism. This effort to bind together "all sons of the revolution" was supported by a renewed interest in national history. The Assembly designated "La Marseillaise" as the national anthem, and the 14th of July a national holiday to commemorate the storming of the Bastille.[35]

Although republicanism, centralization, and national unity were the dominant characteristics of the Third Republic, there were institutions within the state itself which limited these forces. In the 1880s, hoping to preserve political stability, republicans decided that the smallest administrative unit, the *arrondissement*, would serve as the electoral district in national campaigns.[36] Given the extreme weakness of all local political institutions, even the most parochial issues could only be resolved in Paris. Either these issues were ignored or they were debated in the national legislature. Deputies in the Chamber, willingly or unwillingly, perceived that their principal responsibility was to satisfy the most immediate and circumscribed needs of their constituents. National questions were often buried under the mass of local problems. This electoral system also tended to overrepresent rural jurisdictions, reducing the effect of universal male suffrage and particularly blunting the impact of the urban working-class vote.[37]

In addition, an upper chamber, the Senate, had been created in 1875 as a conservative brake on republicanism and popular suffrage. Departmental electoral colleges, composed of municipal delegates and deputies, elected senators, who were required to be forty or older. These mature men inevitably reflected the views of the provincial notables, owners of significant property in agriculture, banking and industry.[38] The French Senate, like the German Bundesrat, the British House of Lords, and the U.S. Senate, often blocked, delayed, and amended social legislation. The French upper house did not have the overwhelming power of its German counterpart, but it was certainly much more successful in preserving its influence than the British House of Lords. While the state system contained several institutions, structures, and practices that reinforced the conservatives' political power and maintained provincial elites, the official republicanism of the regime and its legitimation through the Jacobin tradition permitted political discussion to occur which would have been unheard of in almost any other parliamentary system. At the end of the nineteenth century, the very existence of the Third Republic was still considered a radical experiment in many circles.

If the political regime could be characterized as predominantly national and centralized, the economy could not. Industrialization, which together with democracy had produced the social question, was a relatively recent and still regional phenomenon in France. Responding to the state-organized expansion of the rail system in the 1880s[39] and the general international economic recovery of the late 1890s, large industry and the factory system became a more significant and common element in the French economy.[40] It coexisted, however, with other forms of production throughout the prewar decades.

By the 1880s the large agricultural sector of the economy had slowly begun to contract under the pressure of international competition, natural disaster, and overpopulation. French growers, in an effort to remain competitive with American, Canadian, and Russian imports, had been forced to reduce the market price of wheat. Rural land values followed the decline in wheat prices, dragging peasant communities into deepening poverty.[41] Winegrowers, leaders in the market-oriented sector of agriculture, had been decimated by the blight of phylloxera in the 1870s. Immediately after the turn of the century, they then experienced the contrary disaster of overproduction and plummeting prices.[42] In the face of such mounting and cumulative difficulties, the rural population did not abandon the countryside *en masse*. There was a slow drift of peasants' children to provincial towns and then to Paris, a movement which increased from the late 1880s on.[43] Despite this migration, France retained one of the largest rural populations among the industrialized states. During the first decade of the Third Republic, 51 percent of the active population was engaged in agricultural production. By 1914, slightly more than 40 percent of the labor force still worked in the primary sector.[44] The abrupt shift of rural to urban populations which had heralded and accompanied industrialization in Great Britain did not occur in France. The large French agricultural work force which persisted to the eve of the First World War contrasted strikingly to the 9 percent of the population actively engaged in agriculture in Great Britain.[45] Furthermore, agricultural production constituted 40 percent of the French gross national income in 1914.[46] The existence of this large and relatively stable rural population colored all aspects of French life. Economically declining peasants, precariously tied to small farms, permitted the continuation and even expansion of supposedly archaic forms of productions. Such modern technology as electricity ensured that traditional rural manufacturing, a twentieth-century version of the putting-out system, would persist and be profitable.[47]

Nonetheless, in this society of peasants and small-scale manufacturing an important industrial sector was emerging. The factory system was securely established in three regions: the north, the Paris basin, and the Rhône-Saône valley. The factories, mines, safety hazards, grime, and wealth of the Nord and the Pas-de-Calais could match those of the Ruhr, the Midlands, or Chicago and its suburbs. The northern triangle of Lille, Roubaix, and Tourcoing was the sturdy base of French industrial strength. While the long-established textile industry still held a leading place in the industrial production of the north, the extractive and capital goods-producing industries were of equal significance.[48] In Paris itself, small-scale production was well entrenched, and the luxury *articles de Paris* continued to be a major French export. As in other major administrative, financial, and cultural centers, the craft-dominated construction trades remained an important source of employment. However, ringing Paris proper, an important industrial zone with its own working-class towns was well established by 1900. Here the new chemical, metallurgical, bicycle, and auto industries were located. Large-scale heavy industry surrounded the Paris of luxury goods produced by sweated labor. While the export of silk was still important in the Lyons–St.-Etienne region, the southeast also produced cement, chemicals, and metals. By 1900, Marseilles was a major international port.

From the mid-1890s to the eve of the First World War, an increasing tempo of production and expanding economic activity set the pace in these industrialized regions. In the most mechanized industries, one economic historian has calculated a growth rate of 3.4 percent annually in the period 1885 to 1904.[49] Another analyst has identified the years 1905 to 1909 as those of significantly accelerated expansion, at an annual rate of 3.56 percent.[50] This same analyst demonstrates that French industrial production doubled during the decades 1880 to 1913.[51] Yet even with this expansion French industrialists could not begin to match the coal, steel, and textile output of their British, German, and American counterparts.[52]

The tempo of growth appears somewhat slower when viewed in the context of the entire French economy. Production continued to be primarily carried on in small enterprises. The 1901 census indicated that the overwhelming majority (85 percent) of firms engaged in industry and transportation (excluding railroads) had one to four employees, a percentage that had not changed since 1896.[53] However, these workers comprised only 21 percent of the labor force. In 1907, 42 percent of all manufacturing and industrial workers were employed in enterprises of fifty or more employees, but these firms represented only 1.3 percent of all French manufacturing and industrial establishments.[54] Clearly then, more and more French workers were being hired by large mechanized enterprises, organized with factory discipline. Nonetheless a massive number of small firms continued to flourish. Their significance was even greater in the commercial sector, where enterprises of less than five workers constituted 89 percent of the total.[55] As late as the 1910 census, one out of six Frenchmen declared themselves as either self-employed or an employer.[56] While the persistence of small-scale, often artisanal, production was not unique to France, the large and stable percentage of total production done under those conditions was specifically French.

By the mid-1890s industrialization and the extension of the factory system had quickened, particularly in the north, the Paris suburbs, and the Rhône-Saône valley. This development, however, did not create any severe disruption of the extensive domestic manufacturing system or the large number of small-scale producers. French capitalism was neither thoroughly nor uniformly industrialized in the last decade of the nineteenth century.

Industrialization, which was regional and uneven, and male suffrage, which was national, transformed both the working class and the bourgeoisie. The impact of industrialization and democracy on these two classes, however, was significantly different. It was these developments and their consequences for workers, employers, and property owners which engendered the national debate over the "social question." In effect, the emergence of the "social question" as a political issue resulted from the rising number and increasing intensity of confrontations between workers and their employers. Parliamentarianism and industrialization encouraged a more articulate and organized working class, willing to challenge the *patron* and his total control of the work place, and also willing to challenge the bourgeois monopoly on politics.

The material conditions of the working class had improved during the last quarter of the nineteenth century. The increase in real wages which had begun in the 1870s continued to 1914, although consumer prices rose more rapidly after 1900 than before, reducing earlier gains.[57] Furthermore, throughout the period wage increases never matched the rise in profits. While improvements had occurred, French working conditions continued to be particularly oppressive. Most workers labored in small shops, under the paternalistic or authoritarian control of the *patron*. But in the largest factories of the most mechanized industries, workers often experienced the worst conditions. For example, in 1900 the ten-and-a-half-hour day was the norm for most workers, but operatives in the northern textile mills often worked twelve hours.[58] For the entire work force anything less than a full six-day week was unheard of and seven days were not uncommon in periods of high demand. Most workers could count on at least a month and a half of unemployment annually, a figure that increased for the seasonally sensitive building trades.[59] The persistent insecurity of French workers was both an obstacle and an incentive for industrial and political organizing.

Under these changing economic conditions, workers were joining trade unions and identifying with specifically working-class and socialist parties. Union membership jumped from an insignificant 139,000 in 1890 to slightly over one million in 1913. On the eve of the war, union members equaled almost 12 percent of the work force.[60] From this strengthened material and organizational position, French workers were more willing to engage in strike activity. In 1890, the first national May Day strikes and protests, demanding an eight-hour day, took place. These initial demonstrations of new working-class militancy were marked by violent confrontations in Fourmies, a textile manufacturing city of the north, where soldiers shot and killed nine workers. Yet workers did make gains during the decade, winning 26 percent of all strikes.[61] These victories sometimes came at the end of protracted and bitter struggles, such as that of the Carmaux glassblowers, which lasted almost a year.[62] By 1895 this activity had contributed to the creation of a national organization of trade unions, the Cenfédération Générale du Travail.

The C.G.T., however, represented only a portion of organized workers and within the national federation there were strongly conflicting tendencies.. The leadership denounced electoral politics and steadily identified the federation with revolutionary syndicalism, an identification strongly endorsed by the metalurgy and building trades' unions. Simultaneously, a minority of antirevolutionary, reformist unions, such as the printers led by Auguste Keufer, continued to operate within the C.G.T. Several large and important unions never affiliated at all with this syndicalist federation. The miners, a strong early union, pursued an independent reformist political strategy until 1908. Members of the miners union in the Pas-de-Calais elected their leader, Emile Basly, to the Chamber of Deputies in 1893. Major unions of northern textile workers rejected the C.G.T. and continued their close association with the Marxist party, the Parti Ouvrier Français.

Paralleling the development of the trade unions was an equally rapid growth of working-class and socialist political parties. These parties were divided on a number of issues: the relation of revolutionary political organizations to the Republic, the importance of political activity as opposed to industrial action, the role of elected representatives in a socialist party, and the party's organizational structure. By the 1890s, three major theoretical and organizational divisions existed among French socialists. The Marxists had their well-established party, the P.O.F., led by Paul Lafargue and Jules Guesde. Urban workers, steeped in the Jacobin tradition but now organizing for a thorough social revolution, often joined the Parti Socialist Révolutionnaire led by Edouard Vaillant.[63] The third group was a loose coalition of independent socialist deputies who emphasized electoral and parliamentary politics. Until 1905, when a unified Socialist Party emerged, these contending political groups represented both the dynamic assertiveness of the working class and the profoundly divergent conditions under which French workers labored and lived.

From at least 1890 on, the socialists were increasing their representation in municipal and national politics. Despite differences, the socialists often functioned as a coherent and growing group of deputies on the extreme left of the Chamber. In 1891, Paul Lafargue was elected Deputy from Lille. During the municipal elections in 1892, the socialist presence on local councils, especially in the industrial cities of the north, increased significantly. In 1893, fifty socialists were elected to the Chamber.[64] Among them were Jules Guesde for Roubaix, and the leading independents, Alexandre Millerand for the Parisian twelfth *arrondissement* and Jean Jaurès for Carmaux in the Midi. These socialists challenged republican politicians on the issue of reform.

All socialists were staunch advocates of legislation which would improve conditions for workers. As early as the 1880s, the Marxist P.O.F. had proposed a minimal electoral program that included legislative reforms—the eight-hour day, the six-day week, abolition of child labor, a minimum wage, and employers' responsibility for accidents.[65] In the next twenty years, republicans would call for similar-sounding reforms.

Yet, as we shall see, fundamental differences existed between the socialist proposals and those put forward by republicans and other bourgeois politicians. The Guesdists and all socialists regarded reforms as concessions won from the bourgeois state by the power of an organized proletariat. To the socialists, such reforms represented a partial restitution of exploited labor and would prepare for the transition to the future collectivist society. Such assumptions were categorically rejected by all nonsocialists. Important workers' demands, such as the eight-hour day, were dismissed by the majority of the Chamber as utopian or dangerously revolutionary. Furthermore, the socialists, even after the unification of 1905, never had the political power to enact their reforms or lead a viable reform coalition. Socialist deputies frequently found themselves half-heartedly supporting proposals which were drastically revised versions of their own transitional program. The activism of the working class had transformed workers' conditions into a political issue, but it was *not* the workers' parties which led the reform debate in the pre-World War I era.

The bourgeoisie—made up of property owners of all varieties—was anxious to find a solution to the "social question" which would end worker militancy and the dangerous talk of revolution. The consequences of industrialization, universal male suffrage, and an organizing working class had alarmed all bourgeois strata. A call for the restoration or creation of social peace was made by the entire bourgeoisie. In this search for an appropriate and successful strategy to establish social peace, the diversity and tensions within the bourgeoisie were revealed. Three bourgeois groups played an important role in the attempt to resolve the "social question": large industrialists, the petite bourgeoisie, and the republican political elite.

By the 1890s, large industrialists were more frequently asserting their economic and social power in the national political arena through interest-group lobbying.[66] Chambers of Commerce that had been primarily concerned with local issues began to examine national questions affecting business. In 1899, a central, Paris-based organization of presidents of Chambers of Commerce was formed. Even more aggressive than the Chambers were the new employer associations, *syndicats patronaux*, which multiplied in the 1890s. The most successful was the iron and steel manufacturers' association, the Comité des Forges.[67] In the first decade of the twentieth century, the Comité sought to set prices, affect tariffs, influence budget decisions on military spending, and limit the scope of legislation affecting old age pensions, the working day, and labor relations.[68]

In addition to greater organizational strength and political concern, members of the *patronat* were themselves being elected to the Chamber of Deputies. The powerful industrialist, Eugène Motte, a third-generation Roubaix cotton mill owner, entered the Chamber in 1898 after having defeated Jules Guesde in a bitter contest.[69] Motte was joined that year by another cotton textile manufacturer from the Nord, Jules Dansette, who represented a district in Lille. Dansette identified himself with the moderate Catholics, who had many big-business ties. Motte, on the other hand, became an active member of the *Progressiste* group. These moderate republicans, who coalesced in the mid-1890s, were the staunchest defenders of big business. Most notable among these big-business politicians was Jules Méline. Elected from a textile manufacturing area, Méline created an important coalition between textile and metallurgy interests and large land-owners[70] who were willing to ally themselves with the Catholics.

Except for a few remarkable individuals, most prominent industrialists, their professional organizations, and their political representatives urged the preservation of social peace *and* the rejection of any legislation which would limit their prerogatives in the marketplace and the factory. Many industrialists were sincerely convinced that the social peace they sought would be as beneficial to their workers as to their own profit margins. Particularly among textile manufacturers and mine owners of the north and northeast, the tradition of *patronage*, a religiously imbued paternalism, remained strong and even found renewed vitality in the 1890s.

The legacy of the Catholic sociologist Frédéric Le Play continued to be very influential. Le Play had feared the destabilizing impact of industrialization. During the Second Empire he had urged large industrialists and landowners to maintain and extend their authority over workers and tenants. Social control through the family, religion, and sharply hierarchical class arrangements were central in the Le Playist vision of good society.[71] This strict authoritarianism was slightly mitigated by a few members of the Catholic gentry, such as René de la Tour du Pin and Albert de Mun, who hoped to reinforce social stability with reforms of working conditions, especially the length of the working day and week. This new Catholic interest in the working class was supported by the papal encyclical of 1891, *Rerum Novarum*, encouraging Catholics to distance themselves from the most exploitative aspects of industrial capitalism. This revised traditionalism projected a society organized around class hierarchy, employer authority, the Catholic church, and the patriarchal family. This cumulative authority would be tempered by Christian morality and social responsibility. Indeed, one traditionalist journalist berated the French bourgeoisie for having abandoned the "sentiments of mutual goodwill and charity."[72] The bourgeoisie itself was responsible for the present dangerous state of social conflict. They "had excited popular passions by spreading the absurd and leveling concept of equality which is contrary to the natural order."[73] Some industrialists, such as the mining magnate Eugène Schneider, the textile manufacturer Léon Harmel, and the aristocratic owner of the Baccarat crystal works, the Count de Chambrun,[74] eagerly embraced the rhetoric of *patronage* which legitimated their control of production and the work force, rejected state intervention, and condemned anticlerical republicanism and its egalitarian ideals. The impact of Le Play and social Catholicism should not be overstated, however. Most bourgeois French Catholics abandoned neither their royalism nor their economic liberalism.[75]

The second important bourgeois stratum that had a major impact on the social reform issue was that large amorphous category variously labeled the petite bourgeoisie, small property owners, the lower middle class, or, perhaps most aptly, *la bourgeoisie populaire*.[76] The existence of this numerically significant group of small manufacturers, retailers, *rentiers*, provincial professionals, small land owners enabled one out of every six French citizens to claim the status of self-employed or employer.[77] This element of the bourgeoisie was comfortably established in provincial towns, often retaining ties with peasant relatives. Although written during the Second Empire, Flaubert's portrait of M. Homais, the pharmacist in *Madame Bovary*, conveys the limited but real power of the successful petit bourgeois in claustrophobic small towns.[78] It is a bitter portrait of a social group which would later be praised as *"les couches nouvelles."* With the creation of the Third Republic and the general economic expansion of the prewar decades, the *petites propriétaires* became confident enough of their own social position to assert an ideology of autonomy, independence, individualism, and self-reliance—an integral republicanism. It was this stratum in alliance with the peasantry who republican-ized the Republic, voting first for Gambetta's Opportunists and then, by the mid-1890s, supporting the Radicals.

For all groups within the bourgeoisie, property ownership sharply separated them from the working class. Property ownership was particularly important to the petite bour-geoisie, who often had only recently acquired their status and whose possessions were relatively modest. Furthermore, property guaranteed security, an essential quality of bourgeois life. The small property owners were inevitably more sensitive to threats to their security, since their hold on such security was often precarious. Immediately before the First World War, retailers, particularly in Paris, were becoming increasingly defensive about their social position. A portion were attracted to nationalist politics that promised to defend France and Frenchmen against Jews and socialists.[79] A larger group participated in the growing number of new organizations lobbying for the economic interests and rights of the *classes moyennes*.[80] The attachment to personal property drove some petits bourgeois to a more conservative stand. Personal property remained the source of economic independence and leisure. As such, it was also the basis of autonomy and individual liberty, which enabled one to be an authentic republican citizen and formed the material basis of justice and equality.

Because of the economic, political, and moral values that personal property represented for the petite bourgeoisie, they were especially horrified by the propertyless condition of many workers. Those without property were feared as a profound source of disruption to society and the state, but they were also to be pitied as men and women without any protection, entirely helpless and vulnerable. The complex attitude of the petite bourgeoisie toward the worker frequently appeared in the novels of Emile Zola. His gruesome portrait of Parisian working-class life in the 1870s, *L'Assomoir*, begins and ends with bleak, detailed descriptions of propertylessness. The final descent of the heroine into total penury constitutes a destruction of her humanity.

> She called it her mattress, but really it was only a heap of straw in a corner. Bit by bit their bedding had found its way to the various second-hand shops round about. At first, when money had run out, she had unsewn the mattress and taken out handfuls of wool . . . which she had sold for ten sous. . . . The pillows had followed, and then the bolster. That left the bedstead itself. . . . On the ten francs from this clean-up they had a good blow-out for three days. Wasn't the straw good enough? . . . So they finished eating their sleeping arrangements by getting indigestion on bread after a fast of twenty-four hours. They pushed the straw together with a broom, but the dust always came back, and it wasn't any dirtier than anything else.[81]

The fear that such conditions endangered property and security tied the petite bourgeoisie to all property owners. And they, like all elements of the bourgeoisie, demanded that the state ensure social peace. Yet their vision of social peace differed from that of large employers or the very wealthy. Some among the petite bourgeoisie viewed large capital as an obstacle to the proliferation of small property owners. Many in urban centers had family and neighborhood ties to workers. In the rural south, the wine trade bound small local merchants to the politically progressive vintners. Until at least 1900, if not later, many urban retailers and small manufacturers considered themselves, along with workers and peasants, as part of *le peuple*, "the people," that evocative Jacobin political-social category.

The effort to legislate programmatic reforms corresponded, for almost a decade, with a petit bourgeois hope that security and property would somehow be extended to the working class under the auspices of the republican state. This hope coexisted with a fervent defense of the privileges of the property owner. The petite bourgeoisie maintained a constant ambivalence toward security, property, independence, and state intervention. It became extremely difficult for this stratum of the bourgeoisie and its political representatives in the Radical Party to support a consistent position on the issue of social legislation. Social reform required the endorsement of this key social and political force. Yet, as we shall see, at critical moments the petite bourgeoisie and its political representatives faltered.

The third stratum of the bourgeoisie engaged in the debate on the "social question" was the most important, since the reformers emerged directly from its ranks. Bourgeois social reformers were members of the republican political elite that coalesced on a national level during the first decades of the Third Republic. Most of the men of this elite had been born in the 1840s to families of the middle or lower bourgeoisie. As students in Paris they had criticized or opposed the regime of Louis Napoleon. They had been trained as lawyers, doctors, journalists, and academicians. The establishment of the Third Republic opened administrative and academic posts to these republicans. Their education, politics, and, for a significant portion, their Freemasonry and liberal Protestantism, provided them with the qualifications and connections to be appointed to important bureaucratic and academic positions. Many became professional politicians. This new national elite of professors, deputies, and *fonctionnaires* was fiercely committed to the Republican state that had made possible their upward social mobility, affluence, and security. The legislative chambers, the ministries, and the lecture halls of Paris formed their daily reality. They regarded the "social question" as a threat to republicanism that they had struggled to establish in the 1870s and to extend by educational reform in the 1880s. Many still recalled with horror the consequences of the Commune. In their view, the only appropriate solution to the dilemmas of the working class was the creation of genuine liberty and equality to reinforce social stability.

Moderate republicans such as René Waldeck-Rousseau had been promoting various forms of workers' self-help associations since the 1870s as a means to alleviate the precarious economic conditions of the proletariat.[82] Cooperatives, mutual aid insurance societies—*mutualités*—and unions were regarded as organizations which would enable them to become independent producers. The republican supporters of workers' associations, particularly the *mutualités*, viewed them as offering workers an avenue to the most cherished bourgeois virtues: "saving, foresight, the conquest of a small bit of security, and a guarantee of independence for those dear ones who will follow."[83] Although the *mutualistes* increasingly relied on state subsidies to support their various insurance programs, they and the moderate republicans (the *Progressistes* of the 1890s) continued to claim that private solutions were the most legitimate approach to the "social question." It was becoming obvious, however, that these private organizations could not begin to cope with working-class insecurity.

Reformers drawn from the national political elite eventually came to identify the republican state as the mechanism to provide security for the entire working class, protecting all of society. They insisted that the state could and must encourage access to new forms of property—insurance funds and the benefits of collective bargaining. Workers would then be less vulnerable to the viscissitudes of the labor market, more secure and better able to participate as republican citizens. This vision was central to the creation of the social reform programs of the Radical Party and the independent politicians. These political groups, supported by republican social scientists, developed, presented, and fought for the reform legislation of the prewar era.

Security, "that supreme good,"[84] was the central objective which drew all sectors of the bourgeoisie together. All agreed that their security could be jeopardized by the new conditions of an industrializing society and the new, militant demands of an enfranchised working class. Important members of the national republican elite began to suggest that only by extending material security to workers would the bourgeoisie be safe. It was the elaboration of this position and the attempt to convince large industrialists, small property owners, and their political representatives of its validity which constituted the social reform debate.

CHAPTER 2

The Ideologies of Social Reform

The success of social reform depended on the ability of its promoters to convince a significant number of bourgeois politicians and their constituents that legislation improving working-class conditions was legitimate and in the best interest of all French citizens. In an effort to justify these claims, conventional ideas about property, the labor contract, the state, and equality had to be transformed. A loosely defined, often shifting group within the republican elite—politicians, administrators, and academics—took up this task. No single uniform ideology encompassed all the views of these diverse reformers. Nonetheless, by the first years of the twentieth century, the bourgeois public was presented with a new analysis of the "social question" and a new set of solutions. Two theories dominated the new concepts of social reform, *solidarisme*, and state intervention. *Solidaristes* and interventionists often shared the same general premises about what constituted the "good" society, and they agreed on many fundamental elements of the reform program. Members of these two groups overlapped, easily adopting one another's analyses and positions.[1]

The appearance of these social reformers and their formulation of the "social question" coincided with, and was part of, a broader reassessment of classical liberalism. All French reformers, and sometimes their opponents, began with the premise that liberalism had failed to describe society fully or to prescribe satisfactory policies for the maintenance of social order. After the experience of economic dislocation in the 1880s and faced with continued social conflict in the 1890s, reformers began to question an array of liberal tenets. Free trade, domestic laissez-faire (particularly as it applied to the labor market), the noninterventionist state, and individualism became issues of debate among bourgeois intellectuals. The reexamination of classical liberalism, the repudiation, in some cases, of orthodox political economy, and the wide interest that these controversies aroused did not indicate that either liberalism or the social structures that had supported it were dead.[2] Rather, the question of social reform engendered a confrontation between the orthodox liberal view of social relations, and the often eclectic views of younger theorists, trying to adjust social policy to changing realities. While French liberalism remained very much intact both as theory and practice, liberals of the immediate pre-World War I period perceived their situation as threatened. An important liberal economist, Emile Levasseur, observed in 1907, "Liberalism, especially economic liberalism, is no longer in favor in France. . . . Interventionism is the master of the political terrain."[3]

The reformers linked their dissatisfaction with liberalism to a call for a positive reform program. Their new perspective on social and economic issues often brought them, with some reluctance, to rely on the legal power of the state. They came to insist that legislated policies would reduce the mounting conflict between workers and employers, as well as diminish the growing political force of socialism. They spoke proudly of the sacrifices that employers and the affluent would have to make. These sacrifices would establish a new understanding between classes and bring social peace. The aims of *solidarisme* were characterized by one important advocate as the attenuation of "social inequalities, as far as that attenuation is consistent with the maintenance of the actual social order and with respect for individual private property."[4]

Social peace was the overriding goal of the *solidariste* philosophy elaborated by Léon Bourgeois in the 1890s. The formulation and propagation of *solidarisme* were largely associated with this Radical politician. Bourgeois, whose career spanned most of the Third Republic, was the paradigm of a successful member of the republican political elite. The son of a Parisian watchmaker, he completed a doctorate in law and entered the government in 1876 as subdirector of litigation in the Ministry of Public Works. In the next ten years he moved on to increasingly more responsible positions in the prefectorial ranks and in the Ministry of the Interior. Predictably, Bourgeois ran for election to the Chamber of Deputies, first in an 1888 by-election, and then in the national elections of 1889.

His victories were part of the republican triumph over General Boulanger. From his first legislative session to the end of his career, Bourgeois remained one of those highly ministerial deputies. He became a necessary fixture in every government of republicans. By 1914, he had held almost every cabinet position. Bourgeois sat on the left of the Chamber and soon became a leader of the less intransigent Radical deputies. Two connected events gave him national prominence, or notoriety. He headed the first homogeneous Radical government from November 1895 to April 1896.[5] In the spring of 1895, the *Nouvelle Revue* published his theory of *solidarisme*. Much of Bourgeois' political activity was devoted to the "social question." His friend, the Sorbonne historian Ernest Lavisse, summarized his aims: "The essential ambition of Léon Bourgeois' life has been to establish a doctrine of social action and to put it into practice."[6] *Solidarisme* was that doctrine, an effort to demonstrate that social legislation was a logical extension of republican principles and a necessary element of the republican state.

The crux of the theory was *solidarité*, the mutual dependence that existed among individuals and social classes. *Solidarité* also had a historical dimension. Each generation built upon the achievements of the previous one. Most importantly, *solidarité* proved that the survival of the individual or a group required the cooperation of all members of society. *Solidarité* had two manifestations. The first was "objective and scientific, . . . a fact, the relation of interdependence between certain phenomena."[7] The second form of *solidarité* was a moral imperative, "a duty to be observed by all men toward one another. . . . It has the character of a social obligation such that society might be able to prescribe it and sanction its implementation."[8] Inevitable social interdependence, natural *solidarité*, was a negative condition, the "*solidarité* of master and slave,"[9] or that of "contagious diseases."[10] Moral *solidarité* could only be achieved by human intervention and action. This higher form of *solidarité* did not simply occur; it had to be created.[11]

Solidarité revealed that each member of society was indebted to all others. Self-interest and self-preservation required that individuals fulfill "social duties" for one another.[12] "Man living in society and being unable to live without it, is at all times a *debtor* toward society."[13] However, in the condition

of natural *solidarité*, the assignment of social debts and credits
was unequal. Justice, which moral *solidarité* aimed to establish,
called for a more equitable distribution of the benefits and
responsibilities of society.[14] Behind the abstract analysis of
individuals and society lay Bourgeois' fears about social order
in his own society. He was convinced that if economic
inequalities were not reduced and if the demands of the least
privileged continued to be ignored, French society would be
endangered. Bourgeois constantly underscored the concrete
benefits of *solidarisme*, the end of class conflict. National unity
itself necessitated a reduction of domestic strife.[15] *Solidariste*
reform was the only strategy for social preservation and
protection against violence.

> Men who are deprived of most of society's advantages sense the
> credit owed them. They suffer, they are frustrated, they demand
> their share. But not being able to measure exactly the indemnity
> due them or to calculate the just object of their demand, they
> become angry. They lose themselves in violence.[16]

The theory of *solidarité*, then, exposed a great backlog of
previously unacknowledged social debts and credits, encumbering all individuals in their social transactions. However, the
outstanding social debts that were potentially the most explosive were those owed by employers to their workers. One
important *solidariste* asked, "Who would dare today to propose
that employer and employee are always two free and equal
individuals?"[17] While Bourgeois and his supporters had no
intention of repudiating the "free" labor contract, they did
aim to create a social situation in which workers and employers
might exchange labor and wages on a more equitable basis.
This could occur once outstanding social debts and credits had
been cleared.

Bourgeois employed a variety of not always consistent
justifications for his theory. *Solidaristes* seemed to be constantly
in search of yet another more convincing source of legitimation. The claim that *solidarité* required restructuring of class
relations was strengthened by the legalistic notion of the quasi-
contract. Found in that venerable guardian of private property, the Code Civil, was the concept of the "quasi-contract."
The term covered situations in which a debt was recognized
where no formal contract existed. The quasi-contract was

created by the nature of the relations between the two parties. Léon Bourgeois adopted this legal definition to describe the social relations of *solidarité*.[18] Moral *solidarité* had to be instituted, through state action if necessary, because it was just, because it was in everyone's self-interest, and because debts cannot remain outstanding without jeopardizing all contracts.

Another feature of *solidarité* that made it attractive to bourgeois reformers was its claim to be a synthesis of "egotistic" liberalism and *"etatist"* collectivism, superseding both. In an early speech, Bourgeois stressed that *solidarisme* was equally opposed to collectivism, which "limited the free development of human will and action,"[19] and economic liberalism, which reduced humanity to "a moral servitude, making the individual struggle for existence the goal and law of society."[20] This search for an alternative to both orthodox liberalism and socialism expressed a strongly felt need within the republican elite.[21] Most readers of *Solidarité* pamphlets and most members of the various reform-minded organizations to which Léon Bourgeois spoke, already shared the *solidariste* antipathy to Marxism.[22] They were less likely to accept a critique of liberalism. In Bourgeois' view, economic liberalism was an incomplete theory of society. It only described a portion of reality, that of economic competition. It accepted the preeminence of "natural laws." Liberalism failed to see the social reality beyond the marketplace. Bourgeois underscored the importance of other "rational and moral" demands which transcended the constraints of the "natural laws" of exchange.[23]

Still another important source of the persuasiveness and wide appeal of *solidarisme* was its consideration of several established republican concepts and concerns.[24] One problem which Bourgeois identified was the tension between the principle of individual liberty and that of social justice, which created social conflict. In his view, republicans had to eliminate this tension. They had to end their political immobility in face of this issue. "Thus is imposed on the most faithful sons of the French Revolution the quest for a social law, a social relation in which liberty might be reconciled with justice."[25] Furthermore, Bourgois regarded social conflict as a contradiction of republican beliefs and as a potential threat to the stability of the Republic. Working-class insecurity and de-

pendence denied the ideal of the citizen, the independent
individual which was at the center of republican thought.

This view justified the demands for social reforms favoring
the working class, and at the same time justified opposition to
those demands. The autonomy of the individual could only be
established by property ownership. All republicans accepted
property as the basis of independence and liberty. Property
had a moral as well as a legal and economic character. This
belief supported the defense of private property against any
interference by the state. It also legitimated a critique of
modern capitalist labor relations that made workers' access to
property increasingly difficult. Continuing industrialization
seemed to confound the republican virtues of citizenship, and
particularly to erode any hope of egalitarian relationships.
Some republicans refused to accept the propertyless and
dependent condition of workers as permanent. *Solidarisme*
claimed to offer a peaceful strategy through which workers
would become free and independent citizens. Bourgeois'
ambition was to provide a theory that would eliminate
illegtimate inequalities and genuinely democratize society:
"Democracy is not only a form of government. It is a form of
organizing the entire society."[26]

Finally, Bourgeois' *solidarisme* not only incorporated central tenets and tensions of republicanism, but it linked them to
the more popular ideas of the new sciences, biology and
sociology. Sociology and biology provided striking metaphors
for *solidarisme*, with their shift from mechanical to organic
models. The sciences also offered a standard of objectivity
against which social and political action could be compared. A
rationalist faith in the scientific method as the best means to
remedy social problems had a dominant place in Bourgeois'
scheme. In the 1897 edition of *Solidarité*, he stated, "Natural
social laws are only the manifestation, on a higher level, of the
physical, biological, and psychic laws according to which living
and thinking beings develop."[27]

In many respects Bourgeois' approach to the "social
question" paralleled the analysis of society then being developed by Emile Durkheim. Durkheim, like Bourgeois,
viewed society as a concrete reality that could be dissected and
analyzed. In the opening pages of his monumental 1897 study
of suicide, Durkheim stated, "Sociological methodology, as we
practice it, rests wholly on the basic principle that social facts

must be studied as things, that is, as realities external to the individual."[28] For Durkheim, a major function of the social scientist was to observe, explain, and ultimately alleviate social problems; Durkheim, like Bourgeois, assigned political reformers the same role. Durkheim had contributed significantly to a new view of human relations which placed society at the center of experience. For Durkheim, sociology had proven "that above the individual there is society, and that it is a system of active forces."[29] Bourgeois, influenced less directly by Durkheim than by the general intellectual atmosphere of the period, also gave new prominence to society as a powerful force and standard. Bourgeois, too, called for a new study of society. "A fundamental tendency of our times is the consideration of society, of the collectivity, which increasingly replaces that of individuals, as a special object of study, sociology. From every direction there has been a reaction against individualism."[30] The concept of "society" was critical to Bourgeois the politician. If socialists could employ the category of "class" against the liberals, the reformers now had at their disposal the scientific category of "society" to use against both theories of individualism and of class.

The very term *solidarité* adopts the language Durkheim used in *De la Division du travail social*, published in 1893. There he argued that social interdependence was the necessary and inevitable result of the division of social labor. As the division of labor grew more complex, interdependence became more pervasive and vital for individual and social survival. In Durkheim's view, this increasing specialization and interdependence created full organic social *solidarité*. Such organic *solidarité*, the result of a very advanced division of labor, allowed a rational ordering of society in which individual talents flourish in conformity with collective needs.[31] The relationship between social development and interdependence was a leitmotif of Bourgeois' *solidarisme*. Rather than having any direct influence on one another, it seems likely that both sociology and *solidarisme* were responding to what was perceived as the threat of increasing social dislocation. They incorporated similar premises about the relation between individuals and society, an issue with which the intellectual and political circles of both Durkheim and Bourgeois were deeply concerned.

Bourgeois observed that the new ideal of *solidarité* had

been "disseminated by sociology."[32] Durkheim always viewed his science as one which could provide practical prescriptions for social improvement.[33] While significant parallels existed between *solidarisme* and Durkheimean sociology, of course important differences remained. Durkheim's purpose was to create a new science equipped with a unique methodology and object of study. Bourgeois was a politician proposing a legitimating theory for a specific party and program. Yet Célestin Bouglé, an influential colleague of Durkheim and an expert on German sociological methods,[34] became a prolific advocate of Bourgeois' theory. Bouglé claimed that *solidarisme* had explained to sociology its political obligations.[35] The ease with which Bouglé moved between academic and republican circles reveals the close connections between the academic and governing elites of the Third Republic.

Sociology was only one of the sources from which Léon Bourgeois drew his organic view of society. New developments in biology also served as a model for social interdependence. Concepts of organic unity that had a central place in biology were borrowed to serve an important role in *solidarisme*. Bourgeois frequently identified the study of human society with the analysis of the biological world. "It is biology, once again, which through its study of organism will give to the science of society the elements of its synthesis, and the means to establish its proof."[36] Bourgeois even attempted to enlist evolutionary biology in a refutation of Social Darwinism, which also claimed biology as the basis for its political theories. Bourgeois accepted that individual survival required conflict, but he insisted that "natural" struggle coexisted with a "natural" tendency to cooperation among individuals. Such associations, he argued, were the very condition of individual survival.[37]

Pasteur's theory of microbiology provided "proof" of this vital need for cooperation. The great medical discovery of contagion through microorganisms had revealed the social dimension of disease.[38] For Léon Bourgeois the germ theory demonstrated that only through cooperation could social health be protected. "Pasteur has proven that each one of us could become the seat of death for other living beings and that as a result it is our duty to destroy these fatal germs to assure our own lives and guarantee the lives of others."[39] Bourgeois understood this dictum both literally and metaphorically. He did not recognize any distinction between the problems of tuberculosis and those of workers' poverty in old age. They were both social illnesses to be diagnosed and cured through collective effort. The reform politician was to be a social physician.[40]

Solidarisme contained several elaborate attempts to link social and political theory with more rigorous concepts in law, republicanism, the new social sciences, and the natural sciences. This extensive theorizing only partially masked Bourgeois' uncertainty about how to implement this new system. As a rationalist and republican he identified education[41] as the principle means of introducing his theory. Education was crucial, since *solidarisme* sought citizens' free acceptance of moral duties and the emergence of a general social interest. The stress on education revealed the hope that *solidarisme* might be instituted by logical persuasion. Significantly, one of the few specifically *solidariste* organizations established was the Societé de l'Éducation Sociale. During its short existence from 1900 to 1908, it aimed to disseminate the philosophy of *solidarisme* to educators and reformers. At its first congress, Bourgeois declared, "The social problem is, in the last analysis, a problem of education."[42]

Although moral change and education might hasten the end of conflict, Bourgeois acknowledged that concrete reforms were necessary to improve the condition of the working class. The central *solidariste* proposal was the progressive income tax. It seemed an obvious method to adjust the inequitable distribution of benefits and hardships that had occurred under the conditions of natural *solidarité*. It would also be a means to increase state revenue that might then finance other reforms. The tax, Bourgeois would argue during his ministry, would impose an obligation on those who profited from the collective social effort and would restore, to those whom society owed a debt, at least a portion of this wealth.[43] Léon Bourgeois' brief Radical government of 1895–1896 was dominated and destroyed by the proposal to introduce this progressive income tax.

The new revenue was intended to provide funds for social insurance,[44] the *soldaristes'* second major reform. Bourgeois emphasized the republican belief that the workers' greatest problem was their constant exposure to risks and resultant economic precariousness. Insurance would eliminate destitution. Society had to provide greater stability for the working class; insecurity had to be replaced with *prévoyance*, a guaranteed minimum existence.[45] For several years, Bourgeois vacillated about the method to implement the insurance programs. He originally hoped that private, state-subsidized mutual aid societies could create a national insurance network.[46] However, after 1900 he became a supporter of compulsory state social insurance programs.

> Don't we see all around us the growth of anger and hope? Don't we sense that it is indispensable to create a more generous conception of what the State of tomorrow ought to be? Don't we believe that the present idea of the state is too narrow, and that it must be made more flexible and enlarged, in order to accommodate new elements.[47]

Bourgeois had faulted liberals for assuming that equitable exchanges of goods and services would occur naturally, automatically. Without moral regulation, these exchanges profited only a few, while most suffered. In the end, society, which liberals claimed to defend, was itself weakened. It was threatened by those who had justified grievances and saw no possibility of peaceful redress. *Solidariste* reforms were not intended to remove economic distinctions. Economic equality, Bourgeois was certain, was both "undesirable and impossible."[48] Although Bourgeois rarely discussed class, the application of *solidarisme* was understood to mean the improvement of working-class conditions. In Bourgeois' view, *solidariste* insurance programs aimed to mitigate the impact of the labor market and business cycles on the lives of workers and their families. Protection was feasible in this way against the consequence of particular types of hazards, such as work place accidents, insufficient funds for old age, illness, and even unemployment.

Solidaristes were among the most important champions of social insurance. They advanced the view that workers had a right to some minimal protection, and that society an obligation to provide it. Such legislation "must exclude all inequality of a social nature between contracting parties; it must also, as far as possible, support each individual's effort with collective force, and guarantee everyone against the risks of collective life."[49] Given the *solidariste* vision, the new security would enable workers to function fully in the marketplace as independent individuals and to engage in equitable exchanges. This new context would permit liberal aspirations to be achieved. *Solidarisme* would establish, "the conditions in which individuals, all individuals, will develop most fully, will attain the maximum extension of all their energies and faculties, will possess true liberty."[50] In this ideal society of equal opportunities, the ultimate aim remained the acquisition of personal property. Social obligations having been fulfilled, liberty and property could now be fully enjoyed.[51] Bourgeois hoped to strengthen the concept of individualism by appending to it a view of social interdependence. *Solidarisme* was presented as a means to overcome the contradiction between personal liberties and social justice.

Solidarisme, because of its continuity with the liberal tradition, its close ties to republican ideology and politics, and its abstract, often vague, rhetoric was very well received as a social theory. Bourgeois proudly proclaimed, "All beliefs, all philosophical opinions can easily accept the idea of *solidarité*."[52] Yet this adaptability often eroded any consistent *solidariste* theory or program. A sympathetic observer of *solidarisme* and reform noted, "In its present imprecise form the *solidariste* school provides the most accurate reflection of the tendencies . . . and also the hesitations of parliamentarians toward the colossal task of labor regulation."[53] The term *solidarité* was often used to mean no more than a vague desire to establish class collaboration. "Today it is the word *solidarisme* that is repeated with the greatest success regardless of the diverse concepts it includes."[54] Bourgeois' arch political rival, Jules Méline, who staunchly opposed social reform legislation, spoke often of *solidarité* based "on individual initiative."[55]

Nonetheless, the impact of *solidarisme* was more than a rhetorical flourish at a banquet table. The elaboration of the theory in the late 1890s, as part of an ever-widening debate on social reform, increased the interest of important sectors of the political and academic elites. A key event in this process of dissemination was the Congrès International de l'Education Sociale. The congress was an official event of the 1900 Paris Exposition. The reformist government of Waldeck-Rousseau had entrusted the organization of the congress to the *solidariste* Société de l'Education Sociale. Participants and audience constituted an honor roll of republican academics—the historian Charles Seignobos, the experts on pedagogy, Ferdinand and Henri Buisson, the sociologist Emile Durkheim, and the economist Charles Gide. Also in attendance was the head of the national *mutualité* movement, Charles Mabilleau, and the reform trade unionist, Auguste Keufer.[56] As president of the congress, Bourgeois presented the major address, an exposition of *solidarisme*.[57]

Given the importance which *solidarisme* placed on education, it is hardly surprising that academics responded with great enthusiasm to Bourgeois' theory. The influence of *solidarisme* pervaded the expanding body of republican educators, whatever their position in the educational heirarchy.[58] This group in particular avidly consumed the numerous printings of the *Solidarité* pamphlet. By 1912 it had appeared in seven editions.[59] From the *institutrice* of the rural grammar school, to the *lycée* professor, graduate of the Ecole Normale Supérieure, to the holder of a Sorbonne chair, republican educators were all crucial constituents for *solidarisme*. They brought together Radical politics, Freemasonry, a desire for social peace, and a concern for the working class.

By the first years of the twentieth century, *solidarisme* had become *the* theory of social reform in France. Important groups within the republican elite believed that *solidarisme* might well resolve the "social question." It was especially attractive, since it incorporated older French traditions in social thought. *Solidarisme* also endorsed new policies of social reform. Léon Bourgeois sought to create a philosophical basis for a more active policy on reform. Yet *solidarisme* also endorsed many of the fundamental liberal concepts that could justify opposition to such reforms. Nonetheless, until the First World War, *solidarisme* remained the dominant legitimation of social reform, and its program continued to be the principal one of all reformers.[60] The contradictions of *solidarisme* were the contradictions that affected the entire reform effort in France.

Closely identified with the *solidaristes* were theorists who formulated more vigorous policies of state intervention and more systematic legislative programs. While these interventionists, as they were called, considered themselves part of the broad *solidariste* movement,[61] they differed significantly in training, concerns, and strategies from the reformers of Léon Bourgeois' circle. The interventionists gave little attention to the abstract philosophy of *solidarisme*. Unlike the *solidaristes* who were more directly involved in Radical politics, the interventionists were professional economists. They emphasized a pragmatic approach to social problems, focusing on specific issues and equally concrete solutions. Their support of state intervention was a practical strategy, rather than a philosophical position. The interventionists were persuaded that reform could only succeed when enforced by law. They were trained to measure and analyze economic conditions and to propose feasible solutions. Paul Pic, an important member of the circle, succinctly described their method, as well as what they considered the central issue:

> The problem of the working class is a wage which is insufficient to both support a family and save for the future. This causes the precarious condition of the worker. The remedy is social economy, a science of observation applied to practical realities and possible ameliorations, rather than metaphysical speculations.[62]

Pic also enthusiastically endorsed the larger aim of bourgeois social reform "to create a lasting harmony between capital and labor through measures necessary for the maintenance of equality between the two."[63] Like all reformers of the period, the interventionists espoused the goal of social peace.

The interventionists had neither a formal organization nor a comprehensive theory. Their principal activity was empirical research. They published a large number of monographs and articles, describing specific working-class conditions, and the merits and limitations of proposed legislation. Functioning as experts on reform policies, the interventionists contributed new rigor and persuasiveness to the reformist cause. Their positions as professors of political economy in law faculties created a loose network of reformist academics.[64] Beginning in the 1870s, the institutional status of economics was being steadily upgraded. The creation of more advanced degrees in political economy required more professors throughout the national university system. With this new demand for personnel, some positions went to economists unsympathetic to the then-dominant orthodox liberalism.[65] A prestigious appointment to the Paris law faculty was awareded to Paul Cauwès in 1878. From this prominent post Cauwès led the attack on classical liberalism and campaigned vigorously for protectionism in the 1880s and 1890s.[66] He established the *Revue de*

l'économie politique[67] in 1886 to promote the protectionist
program. Although Cauwès himself was not active in the later
reformist circle,[68] his journal welcomed the contributions and
the editorial collaboration of key interventionist reformers.
Charles Gide[69] and Raoul Jay[70] became editors of the influential *Revue*. Cauwès' appointment to the Paris faculty and
the need for more economists made it possible for other
interventionists to secure academic posts in the provinces and
the capital: Maurice Bourguin at Lille, Charles Gide and
Charles Rist at Montpellier, Paul Pic at Lyons, and eventually
Bourgin, Gide, and Jay at the Paris faculty.

The interventionist economists, like the *solidaristes* and the
young sociologists, participated in the reexamination of
classical liberalism at the end of the nineteenth century. They
asserted that liberalism failed to account for all aspects of
social and economic reality. It offered only an abstract theory
of market relations. Without a method to investigate society,
liberalism was powerless to direct much-needed improvements. Suspicious of global theories, the interventionists'
critique of liberalism was embedded in specific research
projects and reform proposals. Through systematic observation and the analysis of well-defined problems, efficacious
reform policies could be constructed. As one interventionist
stated, "Facts are more powerful than theories."[71] The interventionists viewed the success of reform as dependent on a
legislating, activist state. The debate between interventionists
and liberals focused on the issue of granting new powers to the
state required by specific legislation.

The interventionists proposed the expansion of state
power as an unavoidable response to the new intensity of class
conflict. Only state-enforced reforms, they argued, could
terminate or reduce the dangerously high level of conflict. Pic
observed,

In effect, we are witnessing in industry today an intense triple
struggle which endangers the social order. There exists the
international struggle among industrialists, the intestine conflict between industrialists of the same nation, and the class
struggle. . . . This evil exists, the conflict is manifest. . . .
The legislature in the interest of social peace must concern itself
with bringing it to an end through explicitly interventionist
legislation.[72]

Competition, the generator of liberal progress, was frequently viewed by the interventionists as a threat to social peace. They forecast catastrophe and crisis if a reform policy was not adopted.

The interventionists' greatest strength was the evidence which they collected to support their particular proposals. For example, their call for compulsory state old age pensions followed a minute examination of the inadequacies of traditional private methods to improve working-class conditions. Paul Pic in his *Traité élémentaire de législation industrielle* documented the necessarily high membership fees of the *mutualités*, which inevitably excluded the vast majority of workers.[73] In another case, criticism of economic competition was supported by careful data on strikes, profit margins, and international trade. Economists like François Simiand and Charles Rist were developing a new area of study, correlating wages, prices, strikes, and profits, which provided important data for the political debate.[74]

The strength of their empirical research was also a handicap, however. In their dispute with classic liberalism, interventionists refused to recognize the resilience and pervasiveness of their opponents' ideology. They assumed that a theory that, in their view, no longer corresponded with the facts would automatically be abandoned. The interventionists had little understanding of the profound attachment to liberalism among significant sectors of the bourgeoisie. They tended to ignore the political strength of those myriad *petits propriétaires* whose economic survival and world view depended on the maintenance of liberal attitudes toward property. They also failed to consider the deep commitment that large industrialists had to the principle of nonintervention, particularly when applied to their own factories. By not acknowledging these realities, the interventionists weakened their ability to promote reforms.

The interventionists were not alone in disregarding the vitality of French liberalism. Its collapse was hailed or decried by the Parisian academic and political elite at least after 1900. Socially minded Catholics shared with *solidaristes* and interventionists a critical attitude toward liberalism. Paul Deschanel, a liberal republican, published a collection of speeches on the "social question" in 1898. Despite the liberal content of the volume, Deschanel entitled a key section, "Neither with

Collectivism nor Catholic Socialism nor the Laissez-Faire School."[75] In 1900, the new Minister of Commerce, Alexandre Millerand, confidently proclaimed, "State intervention is no longer debated, except by a few isolated theoreticians."[76] In 1914, a professor of philosophy declared, "The politics of intervention and social legislation have triumphed over the doctrine of laissez faire."[77]

This general opinion that orthodox liberalism was dead or dying appears now to have been a singularly mistaken view. Unquestionably, a more critical attitude toward it did exist immediately prior to the First World War. Some of those critics occupied influential positions, such as the interventionists at the Paris faculty of law or the *solidaristes* in the Chamber of Deputies. A generalized dissatisfaction was expressed about certain liberal tenets, particularly individualism. Yet none of these developments indicated the demise of liberalism. Throughout the period, liberal journals prospered and retained their prestige. The influence of *Le Temps* or *L'Economiste français*, for example, never diminished. Liberal economists, led by Paul Leroy-Beaulieu, continued to hold important posts at the Parisian *grandes écoles*, especially the Ecole Libre des Sciences Politiques and the Ecole Polytechnique.[78] Paul Beauregard of Le Havre and Edouard Aynard of Lyons were only two spokesmen for an articulate liberal group in the Chamber. Furthermore, public figures' political endorsement of protectionism or negative comments about laissez faire did not necessarily mean their support for state intervention in social issues or labor relations. One historian of the period has convincingly argued that "The capitalists and heads of French industry wanted both liberty of contracts and protection for their enterprises."[79] The prestige of liberal theory may have suffered an eclipse in the early years of the twentieth century in some intellectual circles, but liberalism itself was intact and thriving.

Liberalism flourished in the form of the ardently defended linked concepts of individualism and *liberté de travail*, the ideal unregulated labor market. The real battle faced by the interventionists was how to reformulate these concepts and disarm the economic and social interests that defended them. Any legislative proposal which introduced even a minimum of regulation swiftly encountered the powerful and well-directed opposition of employers speaking through deputies, their professional associations, and the semi-official Chambers of

Commerce. Factory regulation was denounced as an assault on the freedom (*liberté*) of adult workers. When asked what employers wanted, M. Resseguier, who had waged a bitter struggle against the workers of his Carmaux glass factory in the 1890s responded, "only one thing, *liberté de travail*."[80] As an autonomous individual, the worker, specifically the adult male, had the "right" to work where he "chose." The corollary of such "liberties" was the employers' complete independence to offer those wages and conditions that would be most profitable. The individual worker was then "free" to reject or accept that offer. Acceptance was viewed as an implicit contractual agreement, the unwritten but powerful *contrat de travail*. The employers rested their demands for an unregulated labor market and their full control over the workplace upon the prerogatives of ownership. The proprietor should organize and administer his property as his interests dictated. *Liberté de travail* was a defense of the employers' unlimited authority within the workplace and over the work force. *Liberté de travail* became a rallying point for broad opposition to labor legislation, a defense of *all* property rights. Discussing the 1900 proposal on obligatory conciliation and arbitration in labor disputes, the owner of a very large St.-Etienne silk trimmings factory (two thousand workers) stated, "I say that the principle itself is bad, because it attacks *liberté de travail*. What everyone will tell you in this region is leave us alone to arrange things between the interested parties, between employers and workers, without outside interference of any sort, and things will work out very well."[81]

The interventionists elaborated two criticisms of *liberté de travail*, which had already been implied in the *solidariste* literature. First, they claimed that *liberté de travail* was an illusion. The individual worker as a proletarian could never have equality with the employer in the labor market. "When he [the worker] negotiates with the employer, he has no resources, since he exchanges his services in order to live."[82] The obvious remedy to this situation was the intervention of the state, which would provide workers with indispensable security, introducing more equality into their relations with the employer. The second interventionist argument promoted the principle of workers' associations as the means to create greater equity in the labor market. For interventionists, strong unions and the right to strike became concomitants of

authentic *liberté de travail*.[83] Although most employers refused
to accept the legitimacy of unions, the legal right of association
had existed since 1884. Radical republicans regarded the right
to organize as a necessary element of citizens' freedoms. The
right of association came to be viewed by some reformists
within the republican elite as a new source of security for
workers. The interventionists, after observing English and
German developments, concluded that well-organized, responsible, and affluent unions could give workers a degree of
security parallel to that derived from property ownership.
Interventionists sought the most effective legislation to promote such unionism and to convince the bourgeoisie that
liberté de travail would thus be better guarded. As we shall see,
they did not succeed.

Despite its apparent unorthodoxy, the interventionist
aproach to reform was circumscribed. Legal reforms could not
and were not intended to alter fundamental social relations.
The interventionists constantly reiterated that social reform
was a means to *preserve* the social order and benefit the entire
society through the improvement of economic and social
conditions. They, like other reformers, regarded the liberals as
narrow individualists whose pursuit of immediate self-interest
would eventually destroy liberty and property, which the interventionists claimed to defend more effectively.

The interventionists vigorously denied the charge that they
were socialists in "academic gowns," but they also refused to
adopt an antisocialist position. The interventionists admitted
the merits of certain aspects of the socialist analysis and
accepted socialist politicians as necessary allies in a reform
coalition. The Marxist theory of revolution and the abolition
of private property, however, remained anathema. Even the
most *étatist* of the interventionists, Maurice Bourguin, categorically stated, "Collectivism is powerless to create anything."[84] Yet he conceded that an avowedly nonrevolutionary
socialism might become "the party of the most radical
innovators, . . . the most advanced representatives of popular
demands. It must restrict itself to adapting to the new needs of
the market and the competitive system. The socialist party must
become a reform party."[85] The more moderate interventionists
acknowledged that their specific program was similar to
"practical" socialist proposals. The interventionists differed
from the socialists in their claim that the implementation of

these necessary reforms would be accomplished "without upsetting the social order, through the cooperation of the state and private initiative."[86]

Regardless of this commitment to existing social relations,[87] the interventionist program was viewed suspiciously by most moderate republican politicians, abhorred by the majority of industrialists, and denounced by small property owners. Even the conciliatory president of the Paris association of construction firms, who sat on the official Conseil Supérieur de Travail, felt as early as 1901 that there was "too much regulation, and reforms were going too fast."[88] Any modification of accepted practices and views in regard to labor relations, property rights, and employer authority could not be tolerated by important strata of the bourgeoisie. Social reforms, while leaving fundamental structures intact, did alter established practices. If the interventionists were clearly not revolutionaries, they were dedicated reformers.

Furthermore, the interventionists conceived of their labor reforms as a necessary aspect of a modernizing French society. They identified themselves with a more efficient, productive France better able to compete with Germany, Great Britain, and the United States, whose social and economic developments the interventionists had carefully measured. They assumed that this "new" France was developing naturally; reforms would simply accelerate a transition already in process. The proposed labor legislation was presented as an appropriate mechanism to ease the introduction of "large-scale capitalist production and democracy."[89] The reformers regarded legislation as a stimulus for continued economic development, as well as a source of greater worker security.

The modernization argument countered the claim that reform, and particularly factory regulation, would ruin French industrialists. The interventionists maintained that legislation, such as the institution of the ten-hour day, would encourage greater efficiency and increase productivity.[90] At the end of a major study on the effects of the eleven-hour-day reform in the textile mills of the Nord, Bourguin stated,

The law . . . by its compulsory nature acts as a catalyst to progress, requiring the employers to improve the organization of labor, to increase the speed of the work, to adopt the latest

mechanical improvements in order to maintain the productivity
of the eleven-hour day at the level of the twelve-hour day.[91]

On another issue, Paul Pic argued that old age pensions would
permit the employer, "to rejuvenate his personnel without
neglecting his humanitarian duty, and to gain an increased
output by eliminating the unproductive workers."[92] Other
interventionists suggested even more far-reaching consequences that might result from legislative reforms. Raoul Jay,
reviewing the technical advances which might be stimulated by
new regulations, speculated that once productivity increased,
profits and wages would rise. Higher profits would permit
employers to accept unions; higher wages would induce
unions to seek contracts, not revolution. Well-paid workers
with leisure time would then constitute a new and important
consumer market. Jay substantiated these speculations by
pointing to conditions in the United States.[93]

The argument of economic rationality was also used by the
interventionists to demonstrate that existing economic conditions logically required the reform of labor relations.
Charles Rist's important 1907 article, "La Progression des
grèves en France et sa valeur symptomatique,"[94] was based on
this approach. Rist correlated fluctuations in rates of strikes
with the export indices of major European nations. He
assumed that the balance of trade reflected the level of
industrial production, therefore permitting him to analyze the
correspondence between workers' discontent and industrial
cycles. Rist concluded that a "relation existed between strike
movements and fluctuation in industrial activity."[95] The
frequency of strikes increased as the economic situation
improved. Rist stated that the principal demand of strikers was
wage increases. Workers resorted to strikes in order to gain a
share of the profits in a generally favorable economic situation.[96]

There were however, some instances where the positive
correlation between strikes and economic upswing did not
occur. The first was the British case. During a period of
expanding exports, 1897 to 1900, the number of strikes
remained stable or even declined. Rist explained this anomaly
as the "result of the different procedures used in England . . .
to adjust the wage rate to new industrial situations."[97] The

"civilized" English method of conciliation boards enabled workers to receive wage increases when the economic conditions warranted them, without recourse to strikes. The second distortion of the correlation between strikes and economic expansion was less beneficial. When workers were motivated to strike for goals other than their immediate interests—wages—the correlation did not hold.[98] This was not merely a problem for the economist, but a disaster for the working class, in Rist's view. In these cases, strikes were often called at times when economic conditions made it impossible for the employer to grant any concessions, exacerbating animosity and frustration on both sides. These "ideological" strikes explained why the French statistics conformed less closely to the "normal" pattern than the German ones. Rist suggested that the revolutionary fervor of syndicalist workers in the C.G.T. was in reality undermining the position of the French labor movement. The article supported the conclusion that class conflict was counter to the workers' interests and a sign of economic immaturity.

This study was a paradigm of the interventionists' approach to the "social question." Statistical economic data had scientifically proven that certain social phenomena—strikes—were inevitable and therefore legitimate. Rist, together with his fellow interventionists, insisted that objective, measurable economic conditions caused social problems. However, his statistical compilation and empirical evidence presented more than just the "facts." The scientific data validated a particular form of labor relations, fundamental cooperation on the basis of shared interests between workers and management, as the only "normal" one. The interventionists suggested that solutions to the "social question" would be easier to discern and more likely to succeed once specific economic causes were identified. Reforms based on empirical observation would then be compatible with existing economic conditions and would, in effect, aid the economy to operate more efficiently. Reform politicians did use Rist's research as evidence when presenting parliamentary proposals for conciliaton and arbitration boards.[99] Such reforms need not interfere with the functioning of capitalism; on the contrary, they would provide greater security for the employer as well as the worker.

However, the prestige of the scientific method and the strength of empirical observations alone were insufficient to support the reform argument. Interventionists had to enlist other justifications. Action by the state was a legitimate aspect of its obligation to preserve order and advance the general social interest. Since the interventionists were also active republicans, they insisted that only state legislation could establish genuine social justice. They also appealed to the traditional concept of the state as the protector of the weak and feeble,[100] a category which they applied to those in precarious economic situations. All these arguments in favor of intervention concluded that the state had a duty to impose on its citizens certain obligations that would improve either their own condition or those of the less fortunate. This intervention would benefit the entire society. The benefit of the entire society was often equated with the "national interest." Reforms would preserve the social order, which was indistinguishable from the nation itself. This was a reassertion of one of the oldest justification for social reform. As early as the 1840s regulation of working conditions had been presented as a necessary measure to maintain the nation's most important economic and military resource, the people. By the turn of the century, interventionists were calling the debilitated physical conditions of workers, the result of factory labor and squalid housing, "a grave threat to national interests."[101] In 1911 an interventionist deputy argued,

> Public authorities cannot be disinterested in the issue of workers' conditions. Against particular interests, which contradict the judicious use of human labor, they must oppose the national interest. They must see that the principal wealth of the nation, its population, is not squandered. There is no particular freedom which takes precedence over this right of the state.[102]

This patriotic justification appeared logical and irrefutable. Although a national outlook was present even in the interventionists' most scientific studies and was unquestionably sincerely believed, their increasing reliance on vague, general appeals to "national interest" reflected the limited success of their more pragmatic arguments. Partly influenced by the general reemergence of nationalism prior to World War I and partly adjusting to the obstacles which reform legislation encountered, many interventionists placed greater emphasis on "national interest" as a justification for social reform. One interventionist proclaimed in 1906, "Today, patriotism and social reform seem to me to be two inseparable terms."[103]

Unable to convince their bourgeois audience of the necessity for reform with economic evidence, the interventionists attempted to defend their position with patriotic sentiment. Paradoxically, this made it easier to present the counter-argument that social reforms were themselves a grave danger to the "national interest."[104]

Interventionists performed the crucial task of publicizing and defending major reform proposals. They also provided expert advice to reform politicians in the years 1900–1914. They endorsed the *solidariste* insurance program and added that only obligatory legislation could create meaningful security for the workers. Unlike the *solidaristes*, the interventionists were willing to examine conditions within the workplace and to propose state intervention directly in the relations between labor and capital. They were major proponents of factory regulation, in particular the legal limitation of the working day. Perhaps most significantly, the interventionists recognized trade unions as the most important potential reform institution. They supported a variety of proposals intended to stimulate reformist unionism and regulate labor relations.

Their success in presenting the reformist position was based on the persuasiveness of their empirical studies, their detailed explications of specific proposals, and their strategic positions within intellectual, academic, and republican circles. The interventionists had an important institutional base in the Paris and provincial law faculties. This interventionist network was in turn embedded in a larger, more amorphous reformist circle which, like almost every aspect of French public life, was dominated by Parisian organizations and residents. Within this general reformist milieu there existed an array of contradictory positions that ranged from conservative Catholic followers of Frédéric Le Play to independent socialists. Members of this circle shared a consensus that a social problem existed and that something must be done about it. The public which the interventionists addressed was often this heterogeneous reformist circle.

The reformers' principal means of communication were the various journals concerned with the "social question." The *Revue de l'économie politique*, edited by Cauwès, remained the most important forum for the interventionists. It addressed the members of the legal profession, the academic community, and the Parisian political world. Although the journal presented the full range of reformist views, it served an invaluable function in the dissemination and elaboration of the interventionist position. Pic regarded it as "particularly the organ of the eclectic [interventionist] or *solidariste* school."[105]

The 1899 editorial board, which included Cauwès, Jay, and Gide, accepted frequent contributions from Paul Pic and Charles Rist. Gide regularly reviewed the economic situation in a monthly column, and until 1908 Rist was responsible for a similar column on labor. After 1908 this column was written by Charles Picquenard, who also edited the official bulletin of the Ministry of Labor. The sociologist and *solidariste* Célestin Bouglé and younger reformist scholars such as Durkheim's protégé, Maurice Halbwachs, and the labor historian, Edouard Dolléans, also wrote for the *Revue de l'économie politique*. Among the journal's international collaborators figured the leaders of the German historical school of economics, Lujo Brentano and Gustav Schmoller. However, the review was not a "party" organ. Its regular political commentator, Edmond Villey, maintained a consistent anti-interventionist position. The liberal economist, Emile Levasseur, was also numbered among the journal's frequent contributors. His concern for the "social question" and his massive study of the French working class made him a recognized expert on reform issues, despite his orthodox liberalism. The very fact that the *Revue* did not congeal into an exclusively interventionist journal indicated that the looser consensus of the larger reform circle always had precedence over any one of the more consistent views contained within it.

A somewhat similar although more narrowly focused journal was established in Lyons by Paul Pic in 1900, *La Revue des questions pratiques de législation ouvrière et d'économie sociale*. Close relations existed between this important provincial publication and the older, more prestigious Parisian journal. In fact the patrons of the *Questions pratiques* included almost the entire editorial board of the *Revue de l'économie politique*. Pic's purpose was to explain the significance and implications of major national reform proposals, to create regional support for these reforms, and to examine specific social and economic problems of the Lyons area. The editors of the *Questions pratiques* were closely involved in local party politics. The original cofounder of the journal, Justin Godart, like Pic a

Lyonnais lawyer and professor of economics, became a Radical deputy in 1906 and served on the Chamber's Committee on Labor, the crucial committee in the progress of any reform bill.[106] Another editor, Emile Bender, later joined Godart in the Chamber and in the Radical Party. Pic himself, although never holding an elected office, provided the Radical Party with expert advice on social issues. He also participated in the regional and national leadership of the party.[107]

The *Questions pratiques* disseminated the perspective of the interventionist group to a Lyonnais audience. Pic's aim was very concrete: to influence legislative decisions by creating a reform-minded readership and by supporting the reformers among the Radicals. He concluded a laudatory review of Raoul Jay's *La Protection légale des travailleurs* with this plea:

> We who have also struggled for several years for this same cause and who have created this journal for its defense can only offer our sincere wish that so eloquent a voice might be heard and that our Parliament might proceed with the task already begun.[108]

This objective had special importance in the Lyons area, one of the more dynamic, industrialized regions of France. Lyonnais endorsement for social reform could be influential in the Chamber of Deputies. By 1906, both on the municipal level and among the national representatives from Lyons, this endorsement was achieved. Pic's journal and lecture program both reflected and encouraged this trend.[109]

The prominence of the "social question" is strikingly illustrated by the easy access which the interventionist reformers had to the pages of the influential *Revue politique et parlementaire*. The editorial policy of this review corresponded to the views of moderate republicans throughout the prewar period. In the 1890s, the journal was considered the "doctrinal organ of the *progressistes*."[110] It spoke for and to the well-educated, affluent bourgeois, who were politically active and who regarded regulatory state social reforms with great suspicion. Nonetheless the *Revue politique et parlementaire* and its audience recognized the tremendous importance of the reform issue. They desperately wanted to devise a strategy which would assure social peace. Marcel Fournier, the journal's anti-interventionist editor, opened its columns to the most advanced advocates of state intervention. It was in an article appearing in the *Revue politique et parlementaire* that one interventionist proclaimed, "Workers' insurance against old age will be obligatory or it will not be."[111] The journalistic debates between the interventionists and their critics indicated both the underlying unanimity among bourgeois politicians and intellectuals about the urgency of the "social question," and the diversity of their strategies to reduce social conflict. Articles by Jay, Gide, Bourguin, and Arthur Fontaine all appeared in the *Revue politique et parlementaire*, while its editorials denounced the legislation that the articles proposed.[112]

Journals and monographs were the interventionists' major means of influencing the educated public and republican politicians. Other institutions and organizations also served to amplify the debate on the "social question." As some progress was made in Parliament, the administrative apparatus needed to interpret and enforce the new legislation expanded. Official posts were slowly becoming available to reformers, even to interventionists. Arthur Fontaine, a graduate of the Ecole Polytechnique, joined the Office of Labor when it was first established in 1891 in the Ministry of Commerce. In 1899, during the reformist government of Waldeck-Rousseau, Fontaine was promoted to the directorship of the Labor Office. Under his guidance the Labor Office provided French reformers with statistical data on working-class conditions without which they could never have presented their case.[113] As the respected Director of this bureau, Fontaine's own support for legislative reforms carried special significance. His position ensured that the Labor Office would welcome reformers to its staff.[114] Also in 1899, Georges Paulet, professor of labor legislation at the Ecole des Hautes Etudes des Sciences Politiques, was appointed to head the Office of Assistance and Social Insurance in the Ministry of Commerce. This bureau, like Fontaine's, lobbied for the reform effort. The activities and prestige of these administrative divisions were considerably enlarged in 1906 with the creation of the Ministry of Labor.

Reformers, particularly interventionists, were increasingly called upon to serve the administrative apparatus of labor legislation.[115] These appointments certainly enhanced the prestige and careers of individual reformers and perhaps, because of that, conferred greater acceptability on reform proposals themselves. The fact that these men were invited to occupy official or semi-official positions reflected changing government attitudes. Yet this new entrée into officialdom produced relatively few tangible advances in reform legislation. Rather, the appointments were the consequences of legislation already secured through long and bitter political conflict.

More important, perhaps, than the direct influence that academic reformers had on legislation was their indirect influence on parliamentarians. Academics and political reformers often established contact in semi-official organizations examining public policy. One such organization in which French interventionists and reformers played a prominent role was the Association Internationale pour la Protection Légale des Travailleurs. The Association, established in 1900 during the festive atmosphere of the Paris exposition, encouraged a European debate on social reform. The first meeting was held in Paris at the Musée Social. Similar congresses had taken place before, but disagreement between interventionists and non-interventionists had made the establishment of any permanent body impossible. The Association formed in Paris accepted the premise of state intervention to aid workers. Its members were academics, politicians, industrialists, labor inspectors, and reform trade unionists.[116] The organization's initial objectives were modest, to establish communications between the various national labor offices and to prepare annual congresses.[117] The following year, the Association had more ambitious plans, "to develop in each nation protective labor legislation, to try to create unified labor laws in Europe."[118] The second objective aimed to disarm a major criticism of all reform proposals. Liberals and industrialists in every European parliament had insisted that reforms would so increase production costs that export industries would no longer be competitive.[119]

Although the Association did facilitate official discussions on international labor treaties limiting night work for women[120] and the use of lethal white phosphorous in match production, it could claim few other tangible achievements before the war. Certainly, uniform Europe-wide labor legislation had not progressed greatly before 1914. However, it did serve as an important meeting place for like-minded reformers from industrialized nations.[121] After the First World War, these contacts would be revived and the Association Internationale pour la Protection Légale des Travailleurs would be absorbed into the International Labor Office of the League of Nations. The first administrative chief at the I.L.O. was a man well prepared for the position, Arthur Fontaine.

Fontaine and other French reformers were extremely active in the prewar Association. The 1900 inaugural congress was presided over by the senior French interventionist Paul Cauwès who stressed the irreversible European trend toward increasing labor legislation.[122] In 1901, the French section of the Association was officially formed. The goals of the section were "to win public opinion to the cause of regulatory legislation and . . . to influence that legislation."[123] Joining Cauwès on the steering committee were Raoul Jay, Paul Pic, Arthur Fontaine, two members of the Musée Social, two reform trade union leaders, and, significantly, the editor of the socialist journal *Mouvement socialist*, Hubert Lagardelle.[124] In the ensuing years, almost every noted French reform politician, administrator, academic, and union leader held a position in the French section of the Association. They ranged from conservative Catholics, like the Count de Mun, to leaders of the Socialist party, like Edouard Vaillant.[125] In 1908 the eclectic reform politician Alexandre Millerand succeeded Cauwès as president. This impressive collaboration of individuals failed, however, to produce any concrete accomplishments. Like other formal and informal groups of the French reform circle, the Association only succeeded in bringing together a number of prominent individuals and reinforcing their agreement on the need to reduce class conflict.

The Musée Social, which had furnished the first meeting place for the Association and whose members participated in the international organization, also served a similar function. Unlike the Association, however, the Musée did not promote any specific approach to social reform. In effect, the Musée Social marked the limits of the large, amorphous reformist circle. The Musée's purposes were primarily educational. It published the results of various sponsored research projects in its *Circulaire*. No particular position was endorsed, but the *Circulaire* encouraged further scholarly investigation. The Musée also organized innumerable lecture series and conferences on the major questions of social reform. Legislative proposals, the cooperative movement, *mutualités*, and union organizations were all debated. In addition, the Musée established an important collection of documents, newspapers, journals, and pamphlets on social problems and labor issues. Although the Musée was ostensibly open to all who supported social reform, its leadership remained wary of state intervention.

The Musée was officially inaugurated in March 1895. It was handsomely endowed by the Count de Chambrun, who was active in its administration until his death in 1899.[126] During the inaugural ceremony, the Count unambiguously indicated his preference for traditional private self-help concepts of reform.[127] The Musée occupied a frontier between opponents and supporters of legislative reform. Jules Siegfried, executive director of the Musée, had little sympathy for interventionist reforms. As a leading member of the moderate republican group in the Chamber, Siegfried concurred entirely with that group's opposition to obligatory social legislation.[128] The administrative staff, which supervised most of the important research, publication, and library work done by the Musée, was largely made up of a group of outstanding statisticians in the Le Playist, paternalist Catholic tradition. Emile Cheysson and Martin Saint-Léon, leading members of this group, also questioned the advantages of legislative reforms.

Perhaps because of this underlying conservatism, the Musée had no hesitation in inviting the entire panoply of French reformers as well as antireformers to its functions. At the inaugural ceremony, the Radical reformist Deputy Gustave Mesureur shared the platform with the rigidly liberal Edouard Aynard. In 1900, an executive body, the Grand Conseil was formed. Its members included inveterate liberal opponents of legislative reform such as deputies Paul Beauregard and Aynard, committed interventionists like Fontaine and Paulet, and liberal economists such as Paul Leroy-Beaulieu.[129] The honorary presidents at the inaugural session of the Grand Conseil were the moderate republican Alexandre Ribot and Léon Bourgeois, the *solidariste* leader.

Although the participation of these men was largely ceremonial (the real direction of the Musée remaining with Siegfried and the administrative staff), their attendance revealed crucial characteristics about the Musée and the reformist circle in general.[130] Supporters of totally contradictory strategies for the resolution of the "social question" had no difficulty in associating with one another. Their shared commitment to establish social peace and class collaboration was much stronger than any disagreements they had on the means to reach that goal.[131] The politically active sector of the bourgeoisie, the entire academic elite, enlightened professionals and many large industrialists were united by their fear of social conflict. At the same time the eclecticism of the Musée Social underscored the enormous difficulty of developing any agreement within the bourgeoisie as to how the "social question" should be resolved. At least two conflicting views on the nature of security in French society coexisted. The reformers were convinced that the extension of greater material security to the working class, by legislation if necessary, would buttress social stability. Their opponents feared that social legislation would disrupt the very order that had provided security for the bourgeoisie.

CHAPTER 3

Reform Politics of the 1890s: Republicans in Conflict

The struggle for reform legislation occurred on two levels. Reformers had to consolidate parliamentary majorities which would enact legislative proposals and generally monitor the implementation of laws. Such a majority required an agreement among republican politicians that the improvement of working-class conditions was an issue of first priority, worthy of state intervention and state expenditures. The success of this political struggle necessitated the adoption of new perspectives about the state and the working class. The second level on which the battle for reform took place was the lengthy debates about the content of specific legislation and the apparatus of implementation. This chapter and the next will analyze broad political realignments which were both a cause and a consequence of the efforts to create a reform majority. Later chapters will examine the struggle surrounding the passage of major laws.

Beginning in the early 1890s, bourgeois theorists of reform had with increasing confidence identified legislation and state policy as the means to resolve the "social question." The growth and militancy of syndicalist and socialist organizations transformed the realities of working-class insecurity into a national issue that politicians could not ignore. The "social question" had indisputably become a political question. The economic downturn of the 1880s had shaken some republicans' faith in liberal orthodoxy. Supporters of reform came to accept the legislature as the only authority which could impose and enforce national standards on conditions affecting all French workers and employers. Following the elections of 1893, a wide spectrum of deputies began to propose new social and economic agendas for the republican state. The parliamentary debates of the 1890s were a victory, of sorts, for the reformers. The politicizing of the "social question" was a first step toward recognizing the reformist proposition that the state had a responsibility to ameliorate working-class conditions.

Throughout the decade, the policy of legislated reform became associated with the Radicals,[1] a contradictory, often ill-defined group of politicians. In part, this identification was created by the ideologues of social reform. Léon Bourgeois consciously fashioned *solidarisme* as a theory to legitimate both social legislation and Radical republicanism.[2] Several of the interventionist economists, Paul Pic for example, assumed that only the Radicals could pursue an advanced program of social reform. Other republican academics, such as Célestin Bouglé and Ferdinand Buisson, also urged the Radicals to pursue a reformist program.[3] The emergence of the socialists as competitors on their left further stimulated the Radicals' interest in reform. Most important, Radical deputies, as well as their constituents, were attracted to the social reform issue.

Radicals, more than any other group, had an immediate political interest in reducing class conflict. The exacerbation of class antagonisms jeopardized the Radical claim to represent no particular interest, but the will of all genuine republican citizens, "all sons of the Revolution." The Radicals' republicanism required that they repudiate the inevitability of irreparable class conflict. They feared that the organizing of the working class and continuing class polarization might seriously undermine their ideology. A threat to republican beliefs might become a danger to the stability of the recently established regime. The effort to replace class conflict with social peace initially seemed to justify legislation to improve working-class life, especially insurance programs to increase economic security. The Radical leaders were convinced that republicanism mandated a social policy of "equal opportunities." They intended to demonstrate that the political categories of justice and equality could be given a social dimension. Such a program seemed to promise several important political rewards to Radicals in the 1890s. The regime would be securely anchored in a more harmonious society. The republican state would achieve new stature as the successful arbitrator between labor and capital. Radical leaders could enhance their prestige. Finally, a left republican electoral coalition, embracing both small property owners and industrial workers, would constitute a powerful political force. The coalition of *"le peuple,"* which Jacobin tradition glorified, would then be revived. These objectives convinced the Radical leadership of the need to champion legislation as a means to social peace.

Two Radical groups were outspoken in their support for the reform effort. The left Radicals,[4] whose outlook was most consistently articulated by Camille Pelletan, asserted their commitment to social reform, working-class rights and anti-reactionary alliances with socialists. They also insisted on their condemnation of Marxist collectivism. Joining the left Radicals in their concern for reform, but significantly less enthusiastic about alliances with the working class, were the *solidaristes*, those who supported Léon Bourgeois and his vision of class harmony. The ability of the two groups to influence other Radicals in the Chamber fluctuated. Throughout the 1890s the Radicals were an extremely open group whose members were not permanently tied to a clear program. Political allegiances among republicans were never definitively fixed.[5] Nonetheless, left Radicals and *solidaristes*, who constituted the most reliable elements of Radicalism, were convinced that social legislation must become the Radicals' policy. It would contribute to the creation of a stronger party and a more stable Republic.

Collaborating with left and *solidariste* Radicals was an even more amorphous group of politicians who occupied the shifting territory between the Radicals and socialists. The boundaries and membership of this group would become more clearly defined in the next decade. Already in the 1890s, its most prominent members, deputies like Alexandre Millerand, were establishing their political influence. While never able to muster the numbers which the Radicals and later the Socialists would have, the independents provided critical leadership in general debates and, even more important, in the committees, bureaus, and ministries that actually formulated and implemented the reform legislation.

The new attention given to the "social question" reflected a heightened fear of revolution.[6] Across the political spectrum in the 1890s, bourgeois politicians called for social peace. The issue was more than political, it had become fashionable. As the moderate republican leader Paul Deschanel noted, "There is no need to define the social question, because everyone agrees on the problem."[7] While there may have been consensus on the problem, there was none about the solution. In 1897, a *Figaro* reporter satirically described the general anxiety about the "social question" and the absence of a strategy to eliminate it.

> There is an indescribable cacophony of good intentions. Passionately felt plans and remedies are offered by the good ladies. Religions, whose role was to preach charity, now accommodate themselves to justice. . . . Professors at the Collège de France now admit certain limits to laissez-faire. Catholic millionaires feel guilty about their millions. Jacobins recognize that civil equality may not be the only thing. Industrialists don't see anything wrong with the eight-hour day. *And above all everyone unanimously declares that something must be done.*[8]

Within this array of conflicting responses, the Radicals moved steadily toward a programmatic policy of legislated reform.

But the Radicals' emphasis on legislation brought them into conflict with moderate republicans. These new conservatives resisted the intervention of the state in the labor market and labor relations. Throughout the 1890s the different republican strategies to establish social peace sharpened the political tensions between moderates and Radicals.

In the half decade between 1890 and 1895, union membership tripled.[9] While this rate of increase was not sustained in the latter part of the decade and while unionists remained a small minority of the working class, employers were astonished and alarmed by this rapid growth. The numerical expansion was accompanied by organizational development with the creation of the Fédération Nationale des Bourses du Travail de France in 1892 and the Confédération Général du Travail (C.G.T.) in 1895. Moderate republicans shared large employers' apprehensions about this union growth. This concern verged on panic as moderate republicans attempted to respond to increasing strike activity, socialist electoral gains, and anarchist bombings. They quickly moved to defend the social order. Under these pressures a new conservative party seemed about to emerge. The moderate republican leadership accepted the support of Catholic conservatives who had recently abandoned their royalism to "rally" to the Republic.[10] Discarding the politics of the 1880s, which had been based on republican concentration against royalism and reaction, moderates now relied on Catholic support and excluded the Radicals from government. The solidly bourgeois *Revue politique et parlementaire* applauded this explicitly conservative stance.[11]

The editorial board of the *Revue* helped to organize the Grand Cercle Républicain, which intended to provide the leadership for a nascent conservative party in the "defense of liberty." The meetings and banquets of the Grand Cercle brought together prominent moderate republicans who had begun to adopt the label *progressiste*.[12] They and the Grand Cercle were supported by economic interest groups such as the Comité National Républicain du Commerce et de l'Industrie. This group had been formally organized in 1897 to ensure the continuation of Méline's protectionist tariffs.[13] The socialist press without hesitation labeled the Grand Cercle as conservative and reactionary.[14] Its membership included republicans with strong business ties: Senator Waldeck-Rousseau, Deputies Deschanel, Barthou, Poincaré, Siegfried, Audiffred, and, most important, Méline. It was through the Grand Cercle Républicain that Eugène Motte, the Roubaix textile magnate, established important national political contacts who supported his campaign for the Chamber in 1898. The social conscience of the Grand Cercle was represented by the affiliation of sociologist Robert Pinot, then a member of the Musée Social, and the liberal economist and chronicler of working-class conditions, Emile Levasseur.[15] These men and their politics dominated the 1890s. With one exception, they formed the governments that first confronted the organized activism of the working class in the Third Republic. Their attitude toward social reform and their conception of social peace continued to have enormous influence long after the apparent political demise of the Grand Cercle Républicain.

Intense antisocialism and the repression of working-class agitation headed the conservative coalition's "social policy." On May 1, 1893, the Dupuy government closed the Paris Bourse du Travail for alleged revolutionary activity. Two months later troops occupied the Bourse for failure to register as required by the law of 1884. It remained closed for two years. The 1895 special laws to facilitate the apprehension of anarchist terrorists, *les lois scélérates*, were used to harass all working-class organizations and restrict the socialist press. These repressive measures were not, however, the sole feature of the conservative coalition's "social program." The politicians who frequented the Grand Cercle Républicain recognized the limits and dangers of a policy exclusively based on force. They were anxious, in fact, to discuss certain reforms, but only those which would in no way infringe on employers' and property owners' prerogatives. The conservatives were eager for social peace, but the republican state must remain outside the factory and could make no financial demands on the bourgeoisie. In their view, social peace could not be established by disrupting what seemed to be the foundations of bourgeois society, private property. The state might encourage certain organizations which would assist workers, but direct intervention was anathema.[16] At all costs, the principle of *liberté de travail* must be protected.

A flurry of administrative activity took place during the early years of the decade. Both the Chamber and the administration created new institutions which, it was hoped, would elaborate an appropriate reform policy. While government policies were controlled largely by conservative republicans, it was the left Radicals, *solidaristes*, and independent socialists who staffed the committees and offices of the embryonic labor bureaucracy. In 1890 the Chamber agreed to form a permanent Committee on Labor. This Committee was to examine proposals, report on them to the general sessions, and work for their passage. The establishment of the Committee on Labor indicated the growing volume of proposed legislation and increased the possibility of its actual passage. The *solidariste* Radical Paul Guieyesse was appointed president of the Committee. A graduate of the Ecole Polytechnique, Guieyesse first entered the Chamber in 1889 after narrowly defeating a conservative aristocrat. He represented an urban constituency from the generally more rural and more conservative Brittany. He was a key figure in the formulation, passage, and implementation of reform legislation until his death in 1914.[17] In 1893 Léon Bourgeois proposed that a second committee on social reform be established. The Committee on Labor would continue to examine proposals concerned with the relations between labor and capital. The new committee would concentrate on pensions, insurance, and cooperative societies.[18] Bourgeois' suggestion was unanimously adopted, and he became the first president of the Committee on Social Insurance (Commission d'Assurance et de Prévoyance Sociale).

In July 1891, the Labor Office was organized in the Ministry of Commerce. Significantly, one motive in the creation of the Labor Office was to counter the socialist proposal that a Ministry of Labor be created.[19] Conservatives hoped to avoid the creation of a strong voice within the administration which would speak for labor. Although one of its functions was to contain the impact of labor on the administration, the Labor Office nonetheless developed into an extremely important institution supporting social reform legislation. Much of this had to do with the commitment to reform of Arthur Fontaine, the young polytechnician, who served on the staff of the Office from its inception and eventually became its director.[20] Just as important, the Chamber had charged the Office with the collection of data on the conditions of workers' lives and labor, and on the impact of social legislation. This vital function provided empirical evidence that strengthened reformers' arguments for legislation.

The Chamber had specifically entrusted the Labor Office with the task of supplying information to yet another newly created administrative body, the Conseil Supérieur du Travail. The function of the Conseil was "to inform the government of feasible reforms and to study, with the help ... of the Labor Office, the increasingly numerous projects for reform."[21] Much like the Labor Office, the Conseil was intended as both a response to increasing pressure for social legislation and an obstacle to more radical demands. Unlike the Labor Office, however, the Conseil continued to retard the passage of labor legislation rather than promote it. Through the 1890s the fifty members of the Conseil were appointed by the Minister of Commerce. They were drawn from four constituencies—parliamentarians, employers, administrators, and workers. These apppointments, weighted heavily toward bourgeois representatives, were often accepted as simply another honorific title, and little was accomplished by the Conseil.[22] Most telling was the appointment of two deputies, Léon Say and Jules Siegfried. One an ardent liberal, the other a staunch moderate, both had opposed the creation of the Conseil on which they now sat.

This administrative apparatus was intended to aid the Chamber in the formulation of reform laws which, like the apparatus itself, would not threaten established labor practices. Many of the major laws enacted after the turn of the century were first proposed during the 1890s, albeit in often significantly weaker forms. Moderate republicans hoped to dominate and restrain the social reform effort. In a November 1894 speech attacking collectivism, Paul Deschanel claimed that moderate republicans were the only political group genuinely interested in the worker's plight. "In what other epoch of our history has the government demonstrated so much sympathy and devotion to the workers."[23] Deschanel included in his list of achievements: the health and safety regulation of 1893, the 1894 law requiring compensation to miners injured in accidents, Siegfried's proposal for subsidized workers' housing (passed 1894), a new statute governing mutual aid societies (passed 1898), and the industrial workers' accident insurance, voted by the Chamber and being considered by the Senate (passed 1898).[24] Deschanel could also have mentioned the major social reform of the previous legislature, the 1892 regulation of the working day for women and children. This roll call of social legislation of the 1890s appears as impressive evidence of the importance given to the "social question." When examined more closely, however, these laws reveal cautious efforts to encourage some improvement in workers' conditions without significantly limiting the employers' powers or increasing that of the state.

The 1892 limitation of the working day for women and children, and the 1893 regulation of workers' health and safety did mark an intrusion of the state into industrial relations. Defense of "national" interest and the family led many moderates and conservative Catholics to support these measures, much to the chagrin of their more orthodox liberal colleagues. Yet the new health and safety standards did not apply to nonmechanized workshops, where a significant number of workers were employed. Furthermore, the small number of factory inspectors made enforcement of the law haphazard at best. The regulation of the working day for women and children also suffered because of inadequate inspection. As late as 1903, there were only 110 factory inspectors to monitor eleven regions, and most were concentrated in the Paris area.[25] In addition, the Méline ministry of 1896–1898 permitted the abrogation, in practice, of the law limiting the working day. Even in formulating this law, the legislators had studiously avoided any consideration of adult male workers. Men were viewed as free independent citizens, and the length of their working day remained governed in practice by *liberté de travail*.[26] It became impossible to enforce laws that only applied to a portion of the labor force.

Legislation to compensate for workplace accidents was first enacted in 1894 to protect miners. Although only partial, it was a reform victory. It had been a legislative breakthrough, but it would be exceedingly difficult to repeat the miners' success. Unlike most French workers, miners, especially those concentrated in the Nord and Pas-de-Calais, were unionized. Since the early 1890s, they had formed a national federation. It was among the few unions to endorse reformist politics, and remained outside the C.G.T. until 1908. As early as 1885, Emile Basly, union leader and socialist, was elected to the Chamber from the mining districts of the Pas-de-Calais. As a Deputy, Basly led the effort to wrest control of the already existing company funds for accident compensation from the employers. The miners were the only sector of the working class to have such an articulate, organized presence in Parliament. The direct role which the miners' political representatives played in the formulation and passage of the law was never again duplicated in the subsequent struggles for labor legislation.[27] Furthermore, the law was applied to a group of employers who had already demonstrated their economic ability to support an insurance program. Many of the large mining companies had established employer-controlled accident and pension funds, *caisses de secours et de retraites*. The high concentration of capital in the mining industry made support of accident compensation possible for employers, whether the programs were privately controlled or state-organized.[28] Finally, the attention given to periodic fatal mining accidents dramatized for a large bourgeois audience the safety hazards affecting this sector of the working class. Accounts of mine disasters recorded in the press or fictionalized in Zola's popular novel of 1885, *Germinal*, made bourgeois voters more willing to accept the necessity of legislation to aid miners.

In 1898 the law on compensation for work place accidents was extended to include all industrial workers. This law was touted by the moderate press as "the most considerable reform of the legislature."[29] Undoubtedly the law did modify the extreme individualist interpretation of the "labor contract." Under the new legislation, neither workers nor employers were personally liable for industrial accidents. Employers assumed financial compensation for accidents that occurred on their property to their employees. However, much of the enthusiasm for the 1898 legislation among conservatives and liberals resulted from their defeat of the section of the law which would have established obligatory insurance. As we shall see in Chapter 5, the law on accident compensation without compulsory insurance was extremely weak.

A great deal of the moderate republicans' efforts for social reform was devoted to supporting and encouraging mutual aid societies, *sociétés de secours mutuels*. The conservative majority passed a law in 1898 which facilitated the establishment of *mutualités* and provided them with state subsidies. Conservatives and liberals hoped that these self-help societies, under the tutelage of their bourgeois *membres honoraires*, would now flourish. They were looked upon as institutions to train the working class in the bourgeois virtues of thrift and savings. *Le Temps* was convinced that the *mutualités* could halt the spread of "collectivism."

> The *mutualités* are the emancipatory force, the instrument by which the individual grows in independence and dignity. As long as savings develop, in other words private property, the collectivist effort will be in vain. . . . Society will be protected from barbarism.[30]

The 1898 law on *mutualité*, often called *la charte des mutualités*, was regarded as a much more important weapon in the struggle to establish social peace than the accident compensation laws.

However, the *mutualités*, even after 1898, were never able to fulfill the expectations of their political promoters. While the number of organizations and members increased, the *mutualités* were unable to attract a significant following among industrial workers. Nor were they able to provide adequate benefits. In 1898 Arthur Fontaine of the Labor Office pointed out the severe limitations of the *mutualités*.[31] Only half of all societies provided even extremely meager old age pensions.

Benefits averaged 73 francs annually.[32] These conditions were not significantly altered by the law of 1898. Reformers and even some reluctant moderates had to admit that state subsidies to private organizations was not an adequate response to the "social question."[33]

The legislation and the administrative decrees of the 1890s reflected the conservative republicans' efforts to both resolve the "social question" and limit any intervention on the part of the state in the labor market and in labor relations. Orthodox liberals, now forced to debate working conditions in the political arena, insisted that working-class insecurity was not a national problem. On the contrary it was, in their view, a series of unique difficulties occurring periodically between some workers and some employers in particular industries in some regions. It could best be solved by employers whose ability to provide higher wages would improve if they were not hampered by legislation. Or the problems of workers would best be addressed by self-help organizations teaching workers to be diligent, save, shun the cafe, and accumulate property. The *Progressistes*, while occasionally less reluctant to endorse some forms of legislation, refused to examine the wages and hours of French workers which made the goal of security so difficult to attain. The close ties between the *Progressistes* and large industrialists made them particularly strong opponents of legislation regulating factory conditions and labor relations. Social policy of the 1890s was buffeted between a mounting sense of urgency that the "social question" must be resolved, and the liberals' and moderates' horror at the idea of state intervention.

This pattern of conservative politics was briefly interrupted from November 1895 to April 1896 by Léon Bourgeois' ministry, the first all-Radical government of the Third Republic. The objectives and failures of these few months deserve more attention than they usually receive.[34] Of particular significance is both the hostility which Bourgeois aroused among conservative republicans and the popular support that his program gained. The experience of this government also gave new focus to the Radicals' efforts to revive their political fortunes.

Despite Bourgeois' continued hesitancy about the extent of state intervention and even though his ministry had little opportunity to propose much labor legislation, it was regarded by all politicians as the first government "to set forth a program of social and economic reforms as the very essence of its existence."[35] The "social question," the government's attitude toward the working class, and the composition of Bourgeois' parliamentary majority dominated the ministry's brief tenure. Bourgeois was supported by a new alignment of political forces in the Chamber: the Radical groups, a small number of moderate republicans unwilling to accept their colleagues' conciliatory attitude toward the Church, and, for the first time, the small cluster of new socialist deputies. On the local level, the alliance between Radicals and socialists was occasionally quite strong. In 1893 the Radical committees of Roubaix enthusiastically endorsed Jules Guesde's campaign. They called on all "partisans of reform" to support the candidate of the Parti Ouvrier.[36] This new electoral and parliamentary alliance was an incipient reform coalition and would reappear throughout the Third Republic.

The coalition was called on to support more consistent and more energetic social legislation. As a result, many conservatives began to identify Radicalism with socialism, and denounced both as a danger to the established order. Paul Deschanel explained the threat: "But the mirage of socialism is dangerous because of the unrealizable hopes which it creates . . . and because it pushes a large number of Radicals who feel overshadowed to engage in an electoral politics of outbidding the socialists."[37] The *Progressiste* Deputy Etienne Dejean condemned the Radicals' social policy since they had "simply and without exception placed themselves behind collectivism."[38]

The specific issue which set off the vituperative battle among republicans was the proposal of the Bourgeois government to institute a very moderate progressive tax on income. During the six months of the ministry's existence, little else was discussed. The income tax had been a standard Radical electoral promise since Clemenceau's program of 1881. It was *the* central reform proposed in Léon Bourgeois' tracts on *solidarité* first published during his ministry. Furthermore, most politicians, regardless of their affiliations, agreed that the fiscal system required some sort of reorganization.

But both supporters and opponents of the ministry clearly understood that Bourgeois was concerned with other reforms as well and that the battle over the income tax was part of a larger struggle over the direction of the state's social policy. In his inaugural speech Bourgeois placed the fiscal measure in a broader context:

> Economies must be made in the public service budget by simplification. Expenditures for assistance and insurance (*prévoyance*) must be increased. Reform must be directed by three ideas: to create a basic equality at the beginning of the struggle for existence, to reduce the inequality among competitors by lightening the burden of the weakest, and to offer the open hand, (*la main tendue*), to the elderly.[39]

The open hand, *la main tendue*, toward the working class, as opposed to the fist of the previous republican regimes, became Bourgeois's motto. In the first month of his ministry, Bourgeois rescinded the government closing of the Paris Bourse du Travail. This important gesture was taken in response to the request of the Paris municipal council.[40] *Le Temps* was enraged, declaring the opening of the Bourse a revolutionary act. From that moment on *Le Temps* called for a conservative majority to oust the Radicals who, in the editors' view, were merely the dupes of the socialists.[41]

The near hysteria of *Le Temps*, which was echoed in the *Revue politique et parlementaire*,[42] hardly seemed commensurate with Bourgeois' clear commitment to law, order, and social peace. As Premier, he called for

> A government faithful to the traditions of the Republic, resolved to defend its laws ... impartially in the economic conflict between labor and capital, equally protecting individual *liberté de travail* and the collective freedom guaranteed by the law on unionization (*syndicats*), knowing how to maintain order and peace in the streets, but ceaselessly preoccupied with the improvement of the future of the little people and the weak, ... convinced, in a word, that the Republic is an instrument of moral and social progress, the constant means to diminish the inequalities of conditions and to increase *solidarité* among men.[43]

This was hardly the statement of a revolutionary or a pawn of the collectivists. Yet while obviously no socialist, Bourgeois was a *solidariste* reformer. The animosity that his ministry evoked among liberals and moderates suggests that programmatic reform requiring state financing and the political allegiance of socialists was as threatening to powerful elements within the bourgeoisie as revolution.

On the 26th of March, 1896, Bourgeois' Minister of Finance, Paul Doumer, submitted the government proposal for a progressive income tax.[44] Rather than vote on the bill, a motion of confidence was narrowly passed (286 for, 270 against). It stated, "The Chamber has confidence in the Government, and is resolved to replace the personal property tax and the tax on doors and windows with a general tax on income."[45] The government majority of socialists, Radicals, and a few moderates remained intact on an issue of principle. The Chamber committed itself symbolically to reform, but it was unlikely that the actual bill would have found enough votes. Fifty-five departmental councils had already registered provincial opposition to the fiscal reform. Yet for the moment, the reform coalition in the Chamber did not waver.

The Senate, in which opposition to the income tax was overwhelming, took on the task of ousting the Radical government. The Senators risked destroying the imperial adventure in Madagascar and provoking a constitutional crisis in order to force Bourgeois to resign. On the 21st of April the Senate decided "to adjourn the vote on credits for Madagascar until it might have before it a constitutional ministry having the confidence of *both* Chambers."[46] Bourgeois promptly stepped down, citing his overriding concern for the national interest.[47] Undoubtedly, Bourgeois had little inclination to lead a constitutional struggle against the Senate which would have required the political mobilization of the left and the working class.

A major obstacle in the pursuit of social legislation would continue to be the contradictions created by a reform coalition in the Chamber. The closer and potentially more successful the alliance between Radicals and socialists became, the more it compromised both groups. In the mid-1980s Bourgeois had gained the staunch support of the various socialist factions. Jean Jaurès stated, a year after the fall of the Radical ministry, "[It] was the first reform ministry, [which] we supported with a constant faithfulness."[48] Even in 1897 Jaurès was still eager to follow a reformist and parliamentary path in alliance with the Radicals. "We have no need to be rebels in this age and in this country where legality, even when well directed, is revolutionary and in which the parliamentary regime can be a formidable engine of transformation and renovation."[49] While somewhat less willing to endorse the theory of reformism, Paul Lafargue of the Marxist Parti Ouvrier also strongly supported the Bourgeois ministry.[50] This consistent socialist support for the Radical government engendered a storm of conservative and moderate criticism. The reformers were preparing the way for revolution; they were the "Trojan horse of collectivism." Socialists, on the other hand, were uncomfortable about this collaboration with the bourgeoisie and its state, and about the meager results of reform. The efforts to enact social reform legislation constantly foundered on the difficulty of creating a reform alliance and then meeting the subsequent outcry within the bourgeoisie against such an alliance. This dynamic brought down Léon Bourgeois' ministry.

Although Bourgeois resigned with embarrassing speed, the popular support which his reformist ministry had stirred did not disappear so quickly. The Senate's action rekindled the democratic animosity to the upper chamber. The old Jacobin demand for its abolition was revived. Socialists and left Radicals launched a popular campaign against the Senate and for a reform program. Parisians were urged to attend a rally on April 25 at Tivoli to protest this new attempt at a "reactionary coup." Banner headlines in the socialist press proclaimed "Constitutional Crisis! Down with the Senate!"[51] According to the socialist *La Petite République*, ten thousand gathered. Most were workers, although *fonctionnaires* and small shopkeepers attended as well. The socialist speakers, led by Jaurès, criticized Bourgeois as a "weak-willed minister who had abandoned the struggle."[52] Camille Pelletan, the leader of the left Radicals, addressed the mass meeting and expressed the same disappointment with Bourgeois. All the orators, with mounting vehemence, denounced the Senate, called for greater social reforms, and promised, "The people will reply to this Opportunist, senatorial corrupt resistance to all progress and reform."[53]

Bourgeois had retreated, but he had not been entirely cowed by his ministerial experience. Throughout the summer of 1896, he and his former ministers defended their program at innumerable banquets and meetings. This activity focused on opposition to the Méline ministry, and heightened as the

1898 elections approached. Bourgeois did reconsider the wisdom of his alliance with the socialists, and he now emphasized his anticollectivism.[54] Nonetheless, he refused to abandon his reformism or to elevate antisocialism to a governing principle. "One cannot govern against an idea, one must govern for an idea, the social ideal."[55] The moderate republicans continued to view Bourgeois' *solidariste* reforms as a serious threat. The *Revue politique et parlementaire* never doubted that the political struggle was between the *Progressistes* led by Méline and the Radicals led by Bourgeois.

This conflict between social reformers and conservative republicans naturally occupied the Chamber during the next ministry of Jules Méline, the quintessential conservative government of the 1890s. Marcel Fournier, editor of the *Revue politique et parlmentaire*, characterized Méline's politics as those of "pacification (*apaisement*), unity, and the reestablishment of executive power and governmental authority."[56] The initial *raison d'être* of Méline's ministry had been the repudiation of Bourgeois' reforms, particularly the income tax.[57] In March 1898, Bourgeois, joined by the independent socialist Alexandre Millerand, interpellated the ministry on its general policies. Bourgeois portrayed the moderates' program as resistant to all legitimate demands of the working class, and therefore inevitably provoking revolution;[58] the Radicals' reform policy, on the other hand, was the only secure guarantee against class war. "The best method to restrain [the masses] is precisely to make reforms, . . . which has nothing in common with collectivist ideas since our aim is to make small private property as universal as possible and to guarantee it against large property and large fortunes."[59]

Méline, on this occasion, took a surprisingly conciliatory stand. He appeared willing to join with the Radicals in a grand republican concentration, if they would only abandon those policies that made them Radicals: the income tax and the electoral alliance with the socialists.[60] The Premier was obviously concerned about the upcoming elections, but Bourgeois refused to be moved by his offer. Fournier of the *Revue politique et parlementaire* was also concerned about the antireformist stance of the ministry, and urged that in addition to the policy of "order," the *Progressistes* "not only talk about progress, but make it . . . by carrying out some of the great reforms which have been studied for over ten years."[61] The hasty enactment in

April 1898 of the accident law and the statute on *mutualité*, both of which had been stymied in the Senate, was the result of this advice. Their passage was intended to serve as an asset in the upcoming elections. Simultaneously, and also in preparation for the elections, the *Revue* intensified its denunciation of the Radicals as harbingers of revolution. "As for M. Bourgeois, he goes all over France grinding out on his barbarous organ the great tune of *solidarité*, while his former accomplices sharpen the knife and prepare the fatal banquet."[62]

Despite all the anxiety and the preparation for the 1898 elections, their outcome did not significantly alter the political composition of the Chamber. The *Progressistes* campaigned on their commitment to defend employers' authority and independence, and their rejection of interventionist reforms. They returned in force to the Chamber. In fact, their unambiguous antisocialism and willingness to favor repression helped the campaigns of several conservatives, notably Eugène Motte in Roubaix, who defeated the Marxist, Jules Guesde.

The republican debate on social reform was never definitely concluded. Most Radicals, like Léon Bourgeois, had been unwilling to pursue a direct confrontation with the opponents of social reform in the spring of 1896. Few republicans, either moderate or Radical, desired any dissension that might encourage an uncontrollably polarized political situation. After 1896, the Radicals increasingly shifted their attack on the *Progressistes* from the "social question" to the more established issue of the Church: Anticlericalism was more likely to divide the ranks of the moderates than were reform policies. It was also an issue that would ally Radicals and socialists without bringing up the difficult problem of private property. This tactic eventually succeeded, and the Radicals triumphed over the conservative republicans.

In this process of political realignment, however, the reform debate, one of the central issues dividing republicans in the 1890s, was displaced. While reformers continued to argue with moderates and liberals about social legislation, the issue of social reform never again assumed the proportions of a potential constitutional crisis. Never again was the governing élite so sharply divided on social policy as it had been in 1896. Not a few Radicals were relieved that this difficult question had been defused. But the increasing activism of the working class would make it impossible to ignore social reform. Politically triumphant, after liquidating the clerical issue the organized Radical Party would again have to confront the "social question" and a militant working class.

CHAPTER 4

Reform Politics, 1900–1910:
The Radicals Triumphant

The Radicals' effort to direct the political struggle for social reform fell into two distinct periods. During the conservative decade of the 1890s the Radical opposition groups challenged the *Progressistes'* social policy. Encountering strong conservative resistance, Léon Bourgeois and other *solidaristes* withdrew from the confrontation. They feared that its repercussions might damage the still fragile republican state and further undermine social peace. During the second phase of social reform politics, from 1900 to 1910, the Radicals were the dominant political group. Their new power was the result of several converging factors. Radical politicians had skillfully manipulated the clerical question, which was amplified by the tensions of the Dreyfus Affair. They had reasserted their commitment to defend the Republic and their continuing concern for social peace at a moment of political instability. In addition, the continuing growth of independent socialist organizations to the Radicals' left opened the possibility for new political alliances. Finally, the temporary disarray of the conservatives postponed the full consolidation of the center and the right. From their newly gained position of political strength the Radicals again attempted to implement a program of social reform. This effort revealed the enormous difficulties surrounding the creation of a reform coalition, since all strata of the bourgeoisie were deeply ambiguous about the "social question" and the working class.

The Radical resurgence was ushered in by the Dreyfus Affair. Méline's dependency on Catholic support had been used by the Radicals to snipe at the ministry and dissuade the more anticlerical moderates from supporting it. The Affair and the activity of the Assumptionist order made the clerical danger seem much more immediate. However, until 1898 parliamentary leaders of Radicalism, such as Bourgeois and Henri Brisson, remained aloof from the Dreyfusard cause.[1] By 1898, however, it had become increasingly difficult to constitute a government that was neutral on the Dreyfus case. The Radicals were sensitive to the extraparliamentary pressure from important intellectuals,[2] the actions of the Ligue des Droits de l'Homme, and individual Radicals, such as Georges Clemenceau and Ferdinand Buisson. Between the summer of 1898 and the spring of 1899 most Radicals began to identify themselves as supporters of the imprisoned Captain.[3] They were to become the principal political beneficiaries of l'Affaire.

The convergence of anticlericalism, which the Radicals had revived, and the Dreyfus Affair, which they had hesitantly entered, gave them sufficient leverage to break the conservative republican majority.[4] A perspicacious group of moderate republicans, led by Waldeck-Rousseau and Raymond Poincaré, agreed that ministerial crises must end. They joined the Dreyfusard camp and supported a ministry of republican defense. Sixty-one former *Progressistes* followed these leaders, especially after Waldeck-Rousseau had accepted the position of Premier in the new government.[5] With the moderates now divided by the Dreyfusard issue, parliamentary power shifted to the 170 Radicals who formed the core of the new majority supporting Waldeck's ministry of republican defense. The allegiance of at least twenty-one socialists further guaranteed the survival of the new government.[6] This motley Dreyfusard coalition was genuinely united on only one issue, anticlericalism. This further reinforced the political weight of the Radicals, the party most able and willing to pursue an anticlerical policy.

The objectives of the Waldeck-Rousseau ministry were the reconciliation of the republican groups, the restoration of political stability, and the protection of the army's prestige.[7] To those ends Waldeck was willing to sacrifice the privileged position of the Catholic Church. The new Premier appointed General de Galliffet as the Minister of War. Waldeck viewed him as the only republican officer who could restore both discipline and prestige to the army. In order to contain the inevitable left-wing objections to the General, who had crushed the Paris Commune, Waldeck-Rousseau appointed the socialist Deputy, Alexandre Millerand, to the Ministry of Commerce. Waldeck-Rousseau, the Opportunist politician and big business lawyer, now led a left-wing government dependent on Radical and socialist support in the Chamber. His government was indirectly accountable to an extraparliamentary sentiment of reform. Millerand himself was anxious to justify his unorthodox and much criticized position within a bourgeois government by producing a successful reform program.

Within a few months of the government's formation, Millerand enthusiastically embarked on a campaign to extend and regularize the administrative apparatus that controlled labor laws and their enforcement. Arthur Fontaine was promoted to Director of the Labor Office; Georges Paulet was appointed to the new Division of Social Insurance whose main function was to implement the 1898 accident law. The same year Millerand reorganized the moribund Conseil Supérieur du Travail by replacing appointed positions with elected ones.[8] Impetuously, the new Minister of Commerce, circumventing the Chamber and the Senate, issued a decree mandating improved labor conditions on government-financed projects.[9] All this activity occurred within less than six months. The following year Millerand successfully maneuvered through Parliament the law on a ten-hour working day, which besides women and children covered at least some adult men.[10] In 1901 the government proposed a bill on old age pensions, and reintroduced the controversial income tax measure.

This apparently activist reform policy[11] evoked considerable discussion in the Chamber. The Radical Deputy Vazeilhes proudly observed that "one question . . . dominates the political situation: It is the social question."[12] Méline and other *Progressistes* were less sanguine about this interest in labor issues. In an 1899 interpellation, Méline reminded the deputies of the challenge of international economic competition and the danger of further undermining France's position.[13] From the other side of the Chamber, Viviani led the parliamentary socialists in praise of Millerand, and the effectiveness of his decrees.[14] Millerand defended his actions in terms that immediately recalled Bourgeois' speeches of 1898. "The best means to attach, to return, if there is any need to do so, the laboring masses to the institutions of the Republic is to show them not only by words but by deeds that the government of the Republic is above all the government of the small and weak."[15]

This concern to "attach" the working class to the Republic was a response to the increased assertiveness of the labor movement after the turn of the century. Levasseur identified 1899 as "the beginning of a new period, or more exactly, an intense phase of working class politics."[16] The labor movement was a key factor in the new political climate of the post-Dreyfusard era. The increased momentum of strikes and the rapid rise in union membership made it a force that could not be ignored. Following several years of stagnation, union strength expanded sharply between 1900 and 1902, from 491,647 members to 614,173.[17] Initially, many workers perceived the Waldeck-Rousseau government as an ally in the new labor offensive.[18] Confident of government sympathy, the miners of Creusot appealed to Waldeck-Rousseau in 1899 to arbitrate their long strike, which he did successfully. However, working-class confidence in the government of republican defense cooled somewhat as troops were used to intervene in the Marseilles dock strikes of 1900. Workers were disappointed when the government failed to enact reforms beyond the partial limitation of the working day. In 1901, the C.G.T. criticized several of Millerand's proposed reforms.

The policies and, perhaps as important, the tone of the Waldeck-Rousseau ministry demonstrated that labor issues had become an important and necessary element of a Radically inclined republican government. Yet the actions of his cabinet also serve to contain the reform impulse. Millerand, for all his activity, could claim only one labor law, the regulation of the working day, a project begun in the previous legislature. His ministerial decrees had little immediate effect. Not surprisingly, most of the government's energies were directed toward ending the Dreyfus Affair and formulating the law on religious associations. But this absorption on the part of Waldeck-Rousseau in the clerical issue was as much by design as by necessity. After his resignation in 1902, he confessed, "We had to make concessions of principle, while all the time endeavoring to avoid their realization. . . . One cannot establish the income tax, nor realize the proposed pension law as it is presently conceived."[19]

This complex strategy of satisfying both the advocates of social reform and the moderate critics of reform legislation became more difficult to pursue in the next legislature. The delicate balance of forces managed by Waldeck-Rousseau had altered perceptibly after the 1902 elections. Radicals who had created a formal party in 1901 capitalized on the general anticlerical and reform sentiment that had been articulated during the Dreyfus Affair[20] and further defined during the Waldeck ministry. The 1902 election resoundingly endorsed the Dreyfusard coalition and the Radical leadership. The number of Radical deputies in the new chamber rose to 233. Although the socialists lost fourteen seats, their parliamentary power increased. The electoral alliance between Radicals and socialists had been crucial for the victory of Radicalism.[21] The Dreyfusard coalition, and particularly the Radicals, promised social reform as a central element of republican defense. In a postelectoral speech at Carmaux, a southern town of worker militancy and republican loyalty, Millerand observed, "Once again the good sense, the devotion of urban and rural workers has given the republican party [i.e. the Dreyfusard coalition] its victory. It would be ingratitude and madness on its part not to recognize this by a more intense preoccupation with social reform."[22] The now-independent Deputy was wrong, however. Paradoxically, this Radical Chamber where the Jaurèsian socialists played a pivotal parliamentary role and which was headed by a ministry of left Radicals, produced practically no labor legislation.

Waldeck-Rousseau, having little sympathy with the new Chamber of 1902, resigned. Emile Combes, a Radical Senator who had headed the Ministry of Education in Léon Bourgeois' cabinet, now formed the new government. The principal commitment of this government was to conclude the clerical issue. The confrontation between the Radicals' mounting anticlericalism and the intransigence of the Church finally led to the separation of Church and state in 1905.[23] To an even greater degree than during Waldeck's ministry, this prevailing conflict relegated social reform to a marginal position. Combes naturally emphasized anticlericalism since it continued to be the one policy on which the Dreyfusard coalition, now more formally organized in the Bloc des Gauches, was unquestionably united. For almost two years France was governed by the Bloc. More than any other prewar government, the Combes ministry conducted itself as the instrument of the parliamentary majority.[24] While socialist participation under Jaurès' leadership remained vital, the strength of the ministry rested on the new Radical party.

By 1900 it was obvious that Radicalism would profit from the post-Dreyfusard political atmosphere. In 1901, the parliamentary Radical leadership was determined to ensure that those profits would be considerable. That June, the Radical Party was officially organized. It declared itself the party of republican defense, anticlericalism, and social reform.[25] It was under this banner that the Radicals swept the 1902 elections and dominated the new Chamber.

The conflict between Léon Bourgeois and the moderate republicans had already identified reform with Radicalism. In 1898 the Comité d'Action pour les Reformes Républicaines, which united Radical deputies like Floquet, Brisson, and Bourgeois with local Radical committees, Masonic lodges, and the provincial Radical press, reasserted its commitment to reform. Its electoral manifesto called for:

> 1. The defense of the Republic . . . against the reactionary and clerical coalition; 2. revision of the constitution to assure the dominance of universal suffrage and the realization of democratic reforms; 3. tax reform . . . specifically the progressive income tax; 4. legislation for insurance and social *solidarité*— old age pensions for urban and agricultural workers; 5. defense of the national savings against speculation.[26]

Further clarifying its position on the social question, the Comité d'Action explained that France's industrial and commercial growth required social peace. The only means to insure social peace was, "to protect the weak and the workers by labor legislation, to regulate the organization of work, to develop union rights, and to establish firmly arbitration and conciliation, as well as insurance laws protecting all workers, not just against accidents, but also against unemployment, sickness, and old age."[27] This program was a considerable advance beyond the original *solidariste* income tax and social insurance.

The same Comité d'Action invited a variety of organizations and individuals to meet in Paris in 1901 to form the Radical Party. Although the formal appeal for a founding congress had originated with parliamentarians, there had also been pressure on the local level for the formation of a permanent organization. One thousand delegates assembled, representing 155 Masonic lodges, 215 journals, 476 local Radical committees, and numerous officeholders.[28] Even before the official founding of the Radical Party, the Masonic lodges and the business interests organized in the Comité Républicain du Commerce et de l'Industrie exerted considerable influence. The Masons' emphasis on education and its secularization had drawn them to the republican reform effort. The Grand Orient lodges had identified with parliamentary Radicalism as early as 1889 when they supported Clemenceau in his opposition to General Boulanger. In 1896 the same lodges endorsed Bourgeois, himself a Mason, and his progressive income tax.[29] Owners of small and medium-sized firms, led by Alfred Mascuraud, a Parisian jewelry manufacturer, had organized the Comité Republicain in 1899. Its aim was to counter the pressure group formed by Méline's big business backers. This anti-Méline position had brought them into contact with Bourgeois' Comité d'Action.[30]

Within the new party it was the parliamentarians who formulated the program on social reform. This leadership included the *solidariste* group, led by Bourgeois, and the left Radicals.[31] Their views shaped the content of the party's social program. Generally, the left Radicals proved more resolute in their support for labor legislation than the rest of the party. They were also considerably more committed to the alliance with socialists and the working class, an alliance that they viewed as an indispensable element of the French revolutionary tradition.[32] Both left and *solidariste* Radicals conceived of social legislation as a crucial policy for the future of the party and the Republic. While the active reformers were a minority, they were, until 1910, an influential one that dominated the Radical leadership.

Camille Pelletan represented the archetype of left Radicalism. Born in Paris in 1846, Pelletan belonged to that generation of republicans who had known the Second Empire, the Commune and the struggle to establish a republican Republic. He began his career as a political journalist, and entered the Chamber in 1881,[33] where he joined Clemenceau in opposition to the Opportunistes. Like other Radicals of that decade, Pelletan's electoral program included support for several important pieces of labor legislation—the right to organize, a legal ten-hour working day, workers' pensions and accident insurance.[34] In 1892 he wrote, "Whatever the workers might do, whatever they might decide, our place is with them. At their side is the honor of the Republic."[35] Conservative opinion was shocked when Combes appointed Pelletan to head the Ministry of the Navy in 1902. Daniel Halévy considered that Pelletan had destroyed the navy.[36] His decrees improving working conditions and establishing an eight-hour day in naval arsenals were regarded in nationalist quarters as a threat to French security. Pelletan's perpetual evocation of the revolutionary tradition exasperated moderate republicans. In 1880, he defended the Commune of 1871 and in 1905 the Russian Revolution of that year.[37] The *Revue politique et parlementaire* dismissed Pelletan as an empty rhetorician of Radicalism.[38]

On the closing day of the 1901 constituent Congress of the Radical Party, it was Camille Pelletan who presented the official declaration. The speech had been composed by both Bourgeois and Pelletan. It opened with a call for the defense of the Republic by "all sons of the Revolution, whatever their divergences."[39] This rhetorical flourish underscored the need for the alliance between Radicals and socialists. Pelletan then enumerated the specific goals of the Radical program. The first of course was anticlericalism. The next was social reform, which, like anticlericalism, required positive "action both bold and daring."[40] Pelletan compared the antidemocratic dangers inherent in large concentrations of capital to those of the clerical menace. Duplicating the *solidariste* proposals of the late 1890s, the Radical Party called for old age pensions and the progressive income tax.[41] These proposals would permit the Radicals to fulfill their larger objective, "to hasten the peaceful evolution by which the worker will possess the product of his own labor, the legitimate remuneration of his work."[42] Pelletan justified this socialist-sounding goal with the principle of individual property. Ownership rights included the inviolable possession of one's person, and therefore one's own labor.[43]

Radicals committed to reform were convinced that workers, in order to exercise genuine control over their person and their labor, had to have better protection from the uncertainty of the labor market. This required both the regulation of working conditions and the increased security of various insurance programs against the hazards of industrial life. Better able to control their "possession," their labor, workers would unite with other small property holders in defense of their common interests. The reformers declared that this revived "union of all republicans will oppose clericalism, the authoritarianism (*césariennisme*) of the employer, and the domination of money. This union of all republicans will support the cause of social justice. This union will be fruitful for the Republic and the nation."[44]

Left Radicals like Pelletan, as well as the *solidaristes*, placed private property at the center of the reform issue. Pelletan affirmed that unlike the "collectivist-socialists," Radicals were "passionately attached to the principle of individual property."[45] It was precisely this commitment which led Radicals to declare their equally strong endorsement of social reform. Pelletan proclaimed at the 1901 Congress, "We will cede nothing to anyone when it is a question of securing old age pensions or, even more important, obstructing large industry from assuming the character of a new feudalism."[46] Reform legislation would eventually create access to new forms of property—insurance funds or the guarantees of collective bargaining. This in turn would extend security throughout society, and would serve the long-range interests of Republican stability. The Radical leadership predicted that a new type of worker would emerge, "a proletariat more educated, more enlightened, more conscious of its rights as well as its duties, more likely to form the solid foundation of democracy."[47]

The Radicals who promoted reform held prestigious positions in the party. Yet their power was never as secure as might be expected. The Radical Party reflected the political interests of the petite bourgeoisie, that amorphous social category which included lower-level civil servants, small property-owning peasants, artisans, shopkeepers, small manufacturers, and provincial professionals. The interests of this petit bourgeois constituency were often local and circumscribed. Such interests could usually be served by routine negotiations among deputies, and between deputies and the administration. Rarely did the petite bourgeoisie as a whole demand major national legislation.

Radical and petit bourgeois ideals of individualism and independence created a party organizational structure in which the particularist interests of local committees dominated.[48] The major objective of the national party was electoral victory,[49] which opened the way to a deputy's seat and services for local supporters. The emphasis on electoral success and the concomitant importance of the deputy gave parliamentarians a preponderant role in the party. On the one hand, this assured the well-established leaders the endorsement and hearty applause of the annual congresses for their national programs. It also gave them a great deal of automony in formulating a broad vision of national priorities. These programs expressed a unifying Radical ideology. At the same time, however, each deputy insisted on his independence. Since their main purpose was to serve local needs, the Radical deputy refused to be bound by party programs and policies.[50] While the constituents welcomed the elaboration of advanced programs, there was never any guarantee that they would be implemented. In his memoirs, Emile Combes complained about the absence of real party organization or program.[51] The prewar Radicals constituted more of an electoral coalition than a modern political party. Yet from 1901 to 1905 the provincial petit bourgeois supporters of Radicalism did not object to the social reform planks in party platforms. On the contrary, in the afterglow of the Dreyfus Affair the ideal of social peace and the transformation of the working class into people more like themselves must have seemed quite attractive.

In 1902 the Radicals had just achieved a major electoral victory and were the key force in French politics. The Combes' government, sustained by the Bloc des Gauches, reiterated the Party program: anticlericalism, "the application of the new law on associations, the income tax, the reduction of military service to two years, the repurchase of the rail system, and workers' pensions."[52] The Jaurèsian socialists and the reform-minded Radicals assumed that the Bloc would proceed from the anticlerical issue, to which the entire left was deeply committed, to the "social question."[53] Yet the Combes' government failed to move beyond the separation of Church and state to a program of labor legislation. The Bloc des Gauches disintegrated under the pressure of the "social question."

In the spring of 1904 several former ministers of the Waldeck-Rousseau cabinet began to attack the government. Alexandre Millerand led a sharp condemnation of the Bloc during an interpellation in March, assailing the government for its failure to enact social reforms.[54] Independents like Millerand were joined by the few moderate republicans within the governing majority who were becoming increasingly uncomfortable with their new allies.[55] These moderate republicans were prompted by a growing fear of socialism. Many of them had always viewed the Bloc as an unfortunate but necessary expedient to resolve the ministerial crises of the Dreyfus Affair. In their opinion this had been accomplished by 1904. The continuing influence of socialists on the government now posed a much greater danger. This view was shared by several deputies within the Radical party,[56] where a new antisocialist sentiment was beginning to spread. Joining these former supporters of the Bloc was a significant body of nationalist, conservative, and moderate republicans who had always condemned the Dreyfusard coalition.

According to Combes, the final blow which destroyed the Bloc des Gauches was the withdrawal of Jaurès and the socialists.[57] Considering the failure to enact concrete labor legislation, Jaurès departure was inevitable. His own prestige was threatened by this apparently fruitless alliance with the Radicals. The general body of socialist opinion, and his own supporters in the Parti Socialiste Français could no longer accept the promise of eventual government reforms. The disheartening experience of the Bloc des Gauches forced Jaurès to accept the creation of a unified Socialist Party and the principle of opposition to all bourgeois governments.[58] The Bloc had avoided the social reform issue in order to preserve its fragile unity; however, it was precisely this policy that contributed to the destruction of the coalition.

The fall of the Combes ministry in January 1905, the withdrawal of the socialists, the end of the Bloc, and the formation of the unified Socialist Party had important repercussions on the Radicals and their social reform program. Whatever its failures, the Bloc had represented the ascendancy of the left Radicals within the party. Its demise soon jeopardized their influence.[59] Ferdinand Buisson, the republican educator and an important member of the reform Radical leadership, feared the consequences of the end of the Bloc des Gauches. "After the republican Bloc was one going to see the crumbling of the Radical bloc itself? Tomorrow, would there be opportunist Radicals and socialist-inclined Radicals?"[60] Pelletan constantly pleaded with his colleagues to maintain their commitment to reformism and to reject rabid antisocialism.[61] Because of these fears and because the left Radicals remained an articulate presence in the party, the hope of reconstituting the alliance with the socialists persisted. Buisson was convinced that this alliance must be revived. "All these controversies do not hinder either Radicalism from particpating in the socialist ideal to the extent that it believes possible, or the various factions of socialism, unified or not, from claiming this common ideal."[62] The myth of the Bloc remained a permanent feature of Radical politics.

The elusive reform alliance with socialists was only one of several difficult issues confronting the Radicals in 1906. That year was a pivotal moment in the development of social reform politics. The election for the Chamber was the first in which the new Socialist Party would present candidates. Radicalism had defeated clericalism; Church and state had been separated. Social reforms were now the first item on the Radical program. At the 1905 Congress, Pelletan promised that, "the next legislature will be a legislature of economic and social reforms."[63]

The May election also opened a period of particularly intense confrontation between workers and the state. The entire national leadership of the C.G.T. espoused revolutionary syndicalism. C.G.T. membership remained only 5 percent of the industrial labor force for most of the years 1906 to 1910, averaging between three hundred and three hundred and fifty thousand unionists. However in 1907 membership leaped to an astounding seven hundred thousand.[64] This suggested that the C.G.T.'s actual support was far more widespread than their reported numbers. Revolutionary syndicalists were also coming to dominate an increasing number of trade unions affiliated with the C.G.T. In 1908 the miners abandoned their tradition of reformist politics and joined the syndicalist-dominated national organization. By 1909 revolutionary syndicalists led new federations of construction and metal workers. The most disconcerting development for the Radicals was the unionization movement among civil servants and their efforts to join the C.G.T. In April 1906, the postal workers defiantly held an illegal strike for almost a month.[65] By 1907 civil servants had organized a new national federation within the C.G.T., strongly influenced by syndicalism. Both the

C.G.T. and the brief Radical government of Ferdinand Sarrien prepared for May Day 1906 as if the revolution had begun. Georges Clemenceau, then Minister of the Interior, ordered that the leaders of the C.G.T. be arrested on April 30 and that Paris be occupied by the army. On the other hand, the reform Radicals argued that now, more than ever, was the time to apply the prophylaxis of reform.

This reformist perspective was shared by other politicians. In preparation for the legislative election, independents who remained outside the new Socialist Party joined with several Radicals who, for various reasons, sought an additional political label. They organized the Comité de la Démocratie Sociale in February 1906. The formal Comité did not survive long after the elections. Probably many of its members viewed the label *démocratie sociale* merely as a useful expedient in the campaign. The very fact, however, that such an affiliation appeared to them to be helpful indicated the significance of reform. The leading force of the Comité was Joseph Paul-Boncour, union lawyer, independent socialist, and former secretary to Waldeck-Rousseau. He presented the new Comité not as a competitor to the Radical Party, but as a potential ally that would reinforce its reformist position.[66] He claimed that the Comité had only one purpose, "to group together the parliamentarians of the two Chambers and the nonparliamentarian adherents of the political organizations—Radicals, Radical-Socialists, or Socialists—in a collective effort that would, as quickly as possible, result in the social reforms demanded by public opinion."[67] Once the election was won, the Comité would "agitate by every legal means to compel Parliament to finally realize social reform."[68]

Paul-Boncour, stressing that reforms posed technical, not political problems,[69] attracted several of the interventionist economists to the Comité. Paul Pic[70] and Maurice Bourguin[71] endorsed the new organization and praised its pragmatic approach. The majority of "social democrats" were politicians who felt that the "social question" must be resolved, and quickly. The roster of participants was impressive. It included almost all the prominent independent socialists, Alexandre Millerand, Aristide Briand, René Viviani, Pierre Colliard, and Georges Renard. The Radical names associated with the Comité were equally well known in reform circles; Ferdinand Buisson, Célestin Bouglé, and Edouard Herriot, the new mayor of Lyons. Most surprising of all, Clemenceau, who had shunned all organizations and who would soon be associated with the defeat of reform, lent his name to the Comité. The brief existence of the Comité de la Démocratie Sociale demonstrated dissatisfaction on the part of some politicians with the inaction of the Radical Party on reform issues. Its rapid disappearance after 1909 indicated how much the political climate had shifted between 1906 and 1909. Endorsement of social reform was no longer a clear electoral asset in 1909.[72] Furthermore, the fate of the Comité de la Démocratie Sociale revealed that the independents lacked the political force and perseverance to galvanize the Radicals or to create a broad reform coalition under their own leadership.

The creation of the Comité in 1906 was only one of many indications that social reform had become *the* political issue of the new legislature. The regrouping of the conservatives, slowly recovering from the Dreyfusard years, the oppositional stance of the Socialist Party, and the increasing activism of the working class, all placed the social reform issue at the center of political debate. Furthermore, these same developments increased the pressures on the newly dominant Radical Party, whose social program would now be tested. Following the impressive victory of 1906, Radicals were the largest group in the Chamber, holding 247 of the 597 seats. The Radicals were constantly challenged to fulfill their social program. From outside the party ranks, Millerand as outgoing president of the Committee on Social Insurance continued his criticism. "The clerical issue is over. The [government] no longer has any excuse not to commit itself fully to the development of the country's grandeur and wealth. . . . The realization of social reforms must occupy the first place among public concerns."[73] Within the party, Pelletan repeatedly insisted that the social program must be passed. He argued that the 1906 victory reflected the electorate's support for an activist social and economic policy. He also implied that the Radicals owed a large debt to the workers who had sustained them during the struggle with the Church. If the new legislature did not enact the income tax, old age pensions, and state purchase of the railroad lines, Pelletan predicted the failure of Radicalism and even more disastrous repercussions.[74] It would be the attitudes of the Radicals, now in control of the Chamber, that largely determined the contours and direction of social policy.

The reform Radical leadership of the party intended to meet this challenge. The Congresses of 1907 and 1908 attempted to clarify the Radical social program. In addition, they sought to define relations with the Socialist Party which also had had significant electoral success in 1906. Finally, Radicals examined their stance toward the alarmingly militant C.G.T. With Pelletan as outgoing president of the Party and Combes as his successor, the reformers had easy access to the Executive Committee and the ad hoc committees that drew up the major points of the program.

Ferdinand Buisson, whose interest in republican reforms now included social and economic issues as well as education, played an important role in the formulation of the Radical reform program in 1907 and 1908. Buisson was a characteristic French reformer. A Protestant born in 1841, he had been the administrative force behind the great republican educational reforms of the 1880s. As Director of Primary Education in the Ministry of Education, it was Buisson who implemented Ferry's republicanization of the educational system. He returned to the university in 1887 and was appointed to the chair in pedagogy at the Sorbonne. In 1902 he began a political career and was elected to the Chamber. His intellectual stature, his long association with the most successful of republican reforms, and his deep involvement in the Dreyfusard movement as president of the Ligue des Droits de l'Homme, gave him a prominent place in the party.

Buisson and younger reformers like Edouard Herriot[75] shaped the 1907 program. Almost every item of the twenty-seven point platform began with the word "reform."[76] Social and economic issues occupied almost a third of the program. These points repeated, perhaps with new fervor, the established Radical hopes for the working class and a just society. Again the principle of private property justified the improvement of working class conditions.[77] *Solidarité* continued to serve as a legitimating concept.[78] The Radicals presented themselves as the party of modernization eager to improve the transporation system, aid commercial expansion, and generally develop the economic wealth of the nation.[79] Significantly, the Radical Party formally declared itself, "hostile to the egotistic concepts of the laissez-faire school, . . . affirming the right of the State to intervene in the relations between capital and labor in order to establish the necessary conditions of justice."[80] Yet, even at this moment of Radical triumph, when the reformers still appeared so powerful in the party, the only legislative commitments made by the Congress were to the long-debated workers' pension and the extension of social assistance.[81] Furthermore, there was no guarantee that Radical deputies would adhere to their own platform.

Buisson clearly recognized the contradictions within the party. He identified the principle of private property as the great obstacle to Radical unity and effectiveness on social reform legislation. Buisson asked if Radicalism could be a doctrine which defended both personal property and the right of the working class to improved conditions. He insisted that it could. Private personal property could coexist with extensive social reforms.[82] Private property did not depend on the perpetual oppression of the workers.[83] Yet he had to admit that Radicals held two opposing views on this issue:

> The debate is between two concepts of democracy. The first dares to guarantee every human being effective liberty, which cannot exist without a minimum of property, *in other words security*, independence, and human dignity. The other [concept], terrified by the sacrifices which such a transformation will cost to a privileged minority, resigns itself to attenuating the evil while perpetuating it.[84]

More than a few Radicals, however, were coming to realize that they might be part of that "privileged minority" threatened by meaningful social reform.

While the 1907 program had stressed general principles, the 1908 report on social reforms addressed more immediate political problems. Concern with unions and strikes dominated the agenda of the Radical Party that year. Paul Pic,[85] interventionist economist, Lyonnais Radical, and member of the party's Rhone *fédération* and Executive Committee, presented the report, prepared in consultation with Buisson. This report represented a last effort to grapple with the syndicalist issue, which was already creating a strong backlash against reform.[86] Pic criticized the "excesses of the Confédération Générale du Travail," but he also clearly distinguished the Radical Party from those "circles . . . hostile to workers' unions."[87] He stressed the Radical Party's commitment to unionism, and declared, "It would be a deplorable policy to destroy the essential instrument of the workers' economic emancipation now in their hands."[88] To counteract the "violent" tendencies within the C.G.T., Pic proposed a legislative program which would encourage the use of collective bargaining, establish permanent arbitration councils, and enact the proposed law to make conciliation and arbitration obligatory.[89] But the report avoided any real discussion of unionization drives among civil servants, the most important labor issue of the moment.[90]

In 1907 and in 1908 the reformist programs were unanimously and enthusiastically endorsed by the party Congresses. The agendas had been set by the reformers and there seemed to be a new intensity in the Radical pledge to social legislation. However, there was no assurance that reform would be implemented. Radical congresses, while theoretically the supreme governing body of the party, were more often occasions to express sentiments without any commitment to action.[91] The leaders' pronouncements coexisted with many deputies' inaction on actual legislation. Unanimous approval for social reform obscured the more profound quandary within the Radical Party and among its constituents about labor issues. As late as 1907, the most numerous supporters of the Radicals, provincial small property owners, still approved the enunciation of an advanced social policy. Yet they remained extremely wary about the consequences of fulfilling it. At the moment when reform seemed politically most possible, after 1906, dissension among Radicals over their social program became more pronounced. For example, Pic's 1908 report criticized the attack on the C.G.T. mounted by Clemenceau and endorsed by a section of the Radicals. The party was also highly critical of revolutionary syndicalism, so that most Radicals were able to view their approval of Clemenceau's actions as consistent with the party program. Buisson regretfully commented, "The same principles are recognized but are understood to require very different applications. . . . The new political direction of Radicalism, Radical opportunism, has at its heart the mass politics of the petite bourgeoisie."[92]

These contradictions destroyed the reform efforts of Radicals when they had to address the intense social and economic conflicts of 1906–1909. These years marked both the ministry of Georges Clemenceau and the highpoint of syndicalist activity. The first government of this fiercely independent politician was formed five months after the great Radical electoral victory of 1906. Major reform legislation seemed inevitable. Even before the elections the Chamber had passed a bill organizing workers' and peasants' pension programs. In October, the new ministry presented itself as a dedicated reform government. One of Clemenceau's first acts was to propose the creation of a Ministry of Labor. The measure passed with amazing speed, and the independent socialist, René Viviani, was appointed to head the new Ministry. All issues affecting labor regulation and social insurance would now be controlled by one administrative unit of cabinet rank.

Viviani's first parliamentary address expressed the government's attitude toward the working class. It was a warning to both conservatives and the left. He boldly stated that the working class was a special social category with unique problems that the government pledged to solve. The creation of the Ministry of Labor, Viviani declared, "marks a new orientation of social policy."[93] He also made clear that neither the Ministry of Labor nor the government would simply endorse labor's activities. The larger purpose of the Ministry would be to direct the working-class movement. "On the painful road on which . . . the workers are advancing toward justice, my task is not to curb them, but to discipline their effort, not to halt them, but to organize their march."[94] Viviani went on to explain why the workers needed the guidance of the new ministry, "[They] have not rid themselves of the belief in a supernatural religion. They have substituted for the old one a new belief in an economic supernaturalism which they ought to hate . . . because it is prejudicial to their future. . . ."[95]

In addition to this ministerial reorganization, Clemenceau vowed to aid the passage of the pension program through the Senate, further reduce the working day, promote collective bargaining, extend accident compensation to agricultural workers, increase the rights of unions, and regulate the statutes governing civil servants.[96] His government declaration corresponded to the Radical Party programs of 1907 and 1908. It also seemed that the Clemenceau ministry would seriously pursue the passage of the progressive income tax.[97] During the first month of the Clemenceau ministry a Radical Deputy offered this political hope and advice to his colleagues: "Be assured, gentlemen, that if the discontented population saw the Parliament in the process of endowing the nation with the workers' pension and the income tax, they would recognize the merits of those whom they have sent to the Chamber. . . . We must pursue . . . with persevering effort the road to social reform."[98]

The expansion of union membership, the strike waves of 1906–1908, and the temporary dominance of the trade union movement by revolutionary syndicalism occurred at a moment of downturn in the generally expanding economy, and most significantly at the beginning of the long-term twentieth-century inflationary trend.[99] This mounting working-class pressure was met by unrelenting opposition on the part of the government, which further exacerbated class conflict. The battle between the Premier and the syndicalists had already begun in 1906. As Minister of the Interior in the Sarrien government, Clemenceau had sent twenty thousand troops to occupy the mining region of the Nord where forty thousand syndicalist-led miners were on strike.[100] During April 1906, the employees of the Post Office also began their strike against the state. During the next month Clemenceau ordered the arrest of the C.G.T. leadership and the military occupation of Paris on May Day, when two hundred thousand workers throughout France were to demand the eight-hour day.

The strike wave continued through 1907, 1908, and 1909. The number of strikes was highest in 1906 and 1909,[101] but even more important were the strikers' demands and their willingness to fight the police and the army. Several strikes became major confrontations between workers and the state, confrontations which Clemenceau encouraged and which the C.G.T. leadership viewed as a possible prelude to a final General Strike. The year 1907 was dominated by the Parisian electricians' strike, the winegrowers' demonstrations in the South, and the mutiny of soldiers sent to the Midi to maintain order. The government considered the unionization demands of the school teachers as particularly ominous, since they had been a pillar of the Republican state. The leaders of the organizing drive among teachers and postal workers were fired in 1907. The strike of Parisian construction workers over wages, conditions, and the enforcement of labor laws in 1908[102] soon escalated into a series of bloody battles. First, two striking workers were killed and ten wounded when the *gendarmerie* intervened to protect nonstriking workers and the

principle of *liberté de travail*. A month later, as the strike
continued and gained wide support among other Paris unions,
the army fired on an angry demonstration of four thousand
people. The casualties included four dead workers, many
wounded among the demonstrators, and sixty-nine injured
soldiers.[103] In response, the government again arrested the
C.G.T. leaders, who were then acquitted by a jury. A second
illegal postal strike occurred in 1909, which the C.G.T.
attempted, but failed, to transform into a General Strike. In
this incident also, strikers and police battled one another.
Paul-Boncour, who then held the position of Viviani's Administrative Assistant in the first Ministry of Labor, acknowledged
the powerlessness of the new Ministry when faced with open
class conflict: "We weren't able to arbitrate all of them and the
violent pace which certain strikes took, when encountering the
strong methods of Clemenceau, led to conflicts where, as at
Draveil [the 1908 construction workers' strike], the blood
ran."[104]

As Minister of the Interior and as Premier, Clemenceau
followed one coherent policy toward the working class. The
same goal justified the creation of the Ministry of Labor and
the use of troops against the syndicalist strikers. The aim was
always social peace. Workers must be dissuaded from revolutionary activity. Repression and reform were different strategies toward the same end. Many of the left Radicals were
genuinely shocked by Clemenceau's methods. They feared the
destruction of the one goal they *all* wanted to achieve, the
pacification of the working class. For the reformers *apaisement*
was intimately linked to other important aims—improvement
of working-class conditions, expansion of political democracy,
and economic development—but social peace remained the
overriding goal.

Solidariste and left Radicals feared that the Premier's
actions would undermine the republican majority which had
emerged from the Dreyfus Affair, shift the political fulcrum to
the right, and thereby limit any further social reform. Yet their
criticisms of Clemenceau remained weak and half-hearted.
Any disavowal of the government would have forced the left
Radicals to join with the Socialists. The old Bloc des Gauches,
once so cherished by men like Buisson and Pelletan, became
less viable in 1907–1909 as the Socialist Party endorsed

antimilitarism and pacifism.[105] Buisson, perhaps attempting to rationalize the ineffectualness of his own group, attributed the declining reform sentiment among Radicals to part of a larger reaction against the antimilitarism expressed by the Socialist extreme left.[106] Provocative statements about planting the tricolor in a dung-heap deeply offended Radicals who were ardently patriotic.[107] The apparent aggressiveness of the Socialists made it impossible for the left Radicals to rely on them in their dispute with Clemenceau. Furthermore, their own antipathy to "anarchism" necessarily made any revival of the Bloc in opposition to Clemenceau extremely difficult.[108]

Isolated from the Socialists, isolated within their own party, the left Radicals did, nonetheless, make two attempts to criticize Clemenceau's policies. The first instance was in May 1907 during the dramatic interpellation of the government for its firing of the leaders of the postal workers' and teachers' unions which had joined the C.G.T.[109] The teaching profession had provided Radicalism with some of its staunchest adherents. Teachers were members of the Masonic lodges, the Ligue des Droits de l'Homme and the Ligue de l'Enseignement from which the reformers had drawn their strength. The organization of civil servants had appealed directly to the Radical Party's Executive Committee for support. The Committee did issue several criticisms of Clemenceau's actions, but each was successively weaker.[110] During the May 1907 interpellation, Jules Steeg led the left Radicals in the difficult maneuver of defending the civil servants without irreparably condemning the government. Addressing Clemenceau, Steeg pleaded, "M. *le Président du conseil* has always been a friend of liberty and he will be one again. . . . We ask our republican friends not to associate themselves with a political panic which has been invented by the conservative press."[111] The following week, Clemenceau replied to his Radical associates that his actions were the only ones capable of creating genuine social reform in the context of social peace. His policy was one,

> which assures public peace through necessary repressions, but which considers mere repression not to be a government policy. In addition, a reform policy which does not base itself on the absolute and rigorous maintenance of public peace would be a

policy that would throw us again into uncertainty, . . . disorder, . . . and civil war.[112]

The reformers had insisted that legislation would create social
harmony. Clemenceau argued that social peace must precede
reform, that his "necessary" repression would provide the
climate for later legislation.

Steeg's motion called for reform of the civil service, but
did not condemn the government. The left Radicals supported
the civil servants' right to organize, but not their right to strike.
This compromise position was defeated (152 for to 309
against), although of all the opposition motions it gained the
largest number of votes.[113] The deputies who voted for it
represented the most loyal members of the old Bloc des
Gauches: left and *solidariste* Radicals, such as Berteaux,
Buisson, Chautemps, Dejeante, Godart, Massé, Pelletan,
Pressensé, Renoult, Steeg; independent socialists, like Colliard,
Millerand, Brousse; the Socialists Allemane, Jaurès, Vaillant,
Zévaès.[114] However, they could no longer produce a majority.
Too many Radicals had deserted the Bloc and even those who
contemplated reviving it were leery about the wisdom of that
strategy in the new political climate. Significantly, despite the
support of the Executive Committee, a motion to criticize
Clemenceau failed by a few votes at the 1907 Radical
Congress.

A similar and perhaps final defeat of reform Radicalism
occurred in 1909. Once again the issue was a civil servants'
strike, this time by the postal workers. The party's Executive
Committee, by a vote of 70 to 47, specifically condemned the
government's policy toward the strike, which had included
firings, arrests, and police action.[115] The Executive Committee
also expressed the deeper concerns of left Radicals that
Clemenceau was undermining the party:

[The party] regrets that by its lack of foresight and its successive
acts, the government of M. Clemenceau has disappointed the
hopes of republican democracy, exacerbated the misunder-
standings between its different factions, and has reduced the
solidarity between the party and the cabinet whose methods are
contrary to the traditions of the party.[116]

This more forceful statement had no greater success than
the criticism of 1907. Clemenceau won the vote of confidence

on the issue of the postal strike by a large margin (365 for, 159 against). The left Radicals, whose control of the party's Executive Committee was loosening, could not influence individual Radical deputies. Even on the national level, left and *solidariste* Radicals were quickly being eclipsed by a new type of Radicalism. Their decline naturally hindered the larger movement for reform, although it was less a cause than a symptom of the difficulties facing social reform in the prewar period. Commenting on the political scene between 1906 and 1909, Paul-Boncour noted: "This agitation [the C.G.T. strikes], by pushing no small number of republicans toward conservatism, was clearly not conducive to the creation of an atmosphere favorable to reforms."[117]

The convergence of several factors had made it impossible for the reformers to challenge Clemenceau's vision of social peace. An effective alliance with the Socialists was not viable because of the Socialists' antimilitarism. Within the Radical party the influence of the left was highly problematic. Most important, the Radical critics of Clemenceau had no real alternative to offer, since they shared his fears about revolutionary syndicalism and his ultimate goal of social peace.

The Radical *solidariste* Célestin Bouglé voiced the help-lessness of reformers when confronted with explicit class conflict, in a series of articles written in 1907 and 1908. "As long as you permit the workers to be represented by anarchists, they will do their anarchist work. And the government will do its task of governing. Violence calls for repression."[118] Clemenceau had no doubt about the justice and necessity of such a policy. The reformers, however, hesitated. Following the battle between troops and construction workers at Draveil, Bouglé wrote of the "anarchists" whom he had earlier denounced: "And in this nostalgia for heroism there is something very noble. One must see in them a reaction against the platitudes, baseness, and verbiage of so much contemporary society."[119] How should Radicals deal with the perplexing phenomenon of revolutionary syndicalism which threatened, and yet was understandable? Bouglé's advice was caution. "The anarchist syndicalists who are antiparliamentarian, antiegalitarian, antipatriotic, and antidemocratic, are still only a general staff without troops. But if we harass them through the courts, as some suggest, then we will soon have made of this general staff an army."[120] Bouglé's cautious and subtle approach, condemnatory but refraining from repression, won few adherents. In the polarized situation of 1906–1909, few politicians were willing to endorse reform as a viable strategy to end class conflict.

Even left Radicals concurred with Clemenceau that revolutionary syndicalism must be eliminated in order to create a trade union movement that would lead to collective contracts and more closely tie workers to the nation.[121] Postal workers and teachers were criticized for their efforts to join the C.G.T. Buisson said of the C.G.T., "It is antiparliamentary; we are parliamentarians. It claims to be neutral, indifferent, and disdainful toward the Republic and the nation; we are attached to the one and the other. The former cannot be separated from the latter."[122]

Clemenceau had accomplished much. He hastened the decline of revolutionary syndicalism. His policies revealed the strength of the more conservative wing of the Radical party and made it clear that a revival of the reformist left majority would be extremely difficult. Clemenceau's interpretation of social peace left the reformers scurrying between criticism and praise. He had clearly identified order as the first priority of government. Since the reformers shared Clemenceau's goal of social peace, their attempts to moderate his methods were handicapped. Reforms were only one of several strategies to defeat revolution.[123] The reformers' uncertainty in the face of Clemenceau's vigorous action exposed their ideological and political weakness.

Reform legislation did not abruptly cease after 1909. The interminable discussions on workers' and peasants' pensions were finally concluded in 1910, when the Senate passed a modified version of the Chamber's earlier bill. The central Radical fiscal reform, the progressive income tax, was voted on one month before the First World War and finally became law in 1916.[124] But these two major reform achievements were only the final enactments of legislation introduced decades earlier under different political circumstances.

After 1909 the Radical Party remained the largest political group in the Chamber and therefore an important power which no government could ignore. Left Radicals continued to make rousing orations at party congresses, with little influence on Radical parliamentarians. The Clemenceau government was followed by the first cabinet of that intrepid independent political entrepreneur, Aristide Briand. This former proponent of the General Strike now followed a policy even more hostile to organized labor than that of his predecessor. With no stake in the government, the Radical leadership engaged in bitter attacks on the new Premier. At the 1910 Congress, Pelletan, seconded by Combes, denounced Briand's famous program of *apaisement* as a fraud.[125] This view was adopted as the official party stance. Nonetheless, many Radicals continued to support and work closely with the new government. When Briand used the army in 1910 to crush the railroad workers' strike, the final blow against the C.G.T. syndicalists, he easily retained the Chamber's confidence.[126] In Lyons, however, Paul Pic inveighed against Briand's "reactionary and repressive policy."[127] The urgency of the left Radicals' opposition seemed to increase as the possibility of their influencing state policy or the votes of most Radical deputies declined.

With the waning of reform sentiment among Radicals, the political viability of reform legislation was damaged. Without concerted Radical support in the Chamber, it was difficult to initiate new reforms or implement those which existed. The possibility of a reform coalition, a productive alliance between Radicals and Socialists during the years 1900 to 1907, had contributed to the militancy of the labor movement. This militancy, in turn, prompted many in the Radical Party to reconsider their support for a reform policy. As the largest party in France after 1907, the changing attitudes of many Radicals represented the rejection by a significant sector of provincial bourgeois and petit bourgeois voters of social reform as a means to achieve social peace.[128]

The eclipse of the *solidariste* and left Radicals did not halt discussion of reform. They had never been the sole promoters of social legislation. They were, however, the key *political* actors in the amorphous reform circle. Although the social reform debate did not immediately end after 1909, it was obvious that the force of the reformers had been dissipated. Open class conflict, a new aggressiveness on the part of large employers and the emergence of a more conservative, nationalist majority in the Chamber limited the persuasiveness of the reformers' principal argument. Military repression, not labor legislation, seemed to have broken revolutionary syndicalism.[129] The meager and often delayed reforms of the first decade of the twentieth century had not succeeded in pacifying the working class. Force appeared much less costly and more effective.

As the prewar period ended, bitterness and frustration pervaded the ranks of the left Radicals. An old and defeated Pelletan addressed the 1913 Congress: "Was it to arrive at this point that we struggled so much? What will become of our party, of the Republic, if we do not arouse ourselves? The year 1906 seemed the triumph of our ideas, not the beginning of a retreat toward the lamentable present situation."[130] The demise of reform Radicalism was indisputable, although its memory would haunt the Radical Party through the interwar period and even into the Fourth Republic.

CHAPTER 5

The Legislation of Social Reform: Insurance

The emergence of a reform coalition, endorsed by key members of the developing Radical Party, was a crucial factor in the history of pre-World War I French social legislation. However, the proposal, endorsement, debate, amendment, enactment, and implementation of reform laws did not simply coincide with the fortunes of *solidariste* and left Radicals. The reform question exposed divisions and alliances among politicians often more profound than party affiliations. The persistence of major debates[1] ensured that specific reform proposals and the reform question in general remained long after some political formations and groups had been replaced by different alignments. In the Chamber of Deputies and the Senate, debates were long, heated, and repetitious. Regardless of how often a fundamental reform principle might be endorsed by either or both chambers, its validity always remained open to further question. Issues of principle were incessantly reintroduced, and each time opponents and supporters eagerly engaged in the revival of oratorical battles. No debate on reform legislation was ever permanently concluded. In 1900 Paul Pic complained that while legislative "results obtained are most respectable, . . . they are not, however, commensurate with the enormous efforts expended."[2]

Once the popularly elected and hence more reformist Chamber of Deputies passed a law, it then had to survive the more orthodox liberalism of the Senate. As late as 1906 one Senator described the upper chamber's criteria for acceptable social reform as, "to be as liberal as possible, to make the minimum regulations, to try not to have any civil servant intervene and not to create more of them, and to permit things to develop slowly toward a state of general repose."[3] Such

99

standards explain, in part, the major revisions which the Senate imposed on reform bills. Furthermore, the different rates of progress of bills in the Chamber or the Senate were often determined by the action (or inaction) of the committees in which the reform projects were first presented. The members of the Commission de Prévoyance et Assurance Social (Committee on Social Insurance) and the Commission du Travail (Committee on Labor) in the Chamber of Deputies often determined the future of a reform and its content. Deputies and senators recognized that social reform merited their serious attention, but agreement on reform in either chamber was difficult, complex, and time-consuming.

The multiple and long-drawn-out arguments that delayed particular bills for years on end were often obscured by the near-unanimous enactment of social legislation on the eve of parliamentary elections. Such overwhelming votes were more an electoral strategy than a new consensus about social policy. The accident compensation law, for example, was hurried through the National Assembly prior to elections in April 1898.[4] Yet its implementation was easily delayed until July 1899. Nor did these staggering majorities reflect the attitudes of the administration or the courts which, in most cases, restricted the application of social legislation. The Marxist leader Jules Guesde bitterly complained, "But I know, and you all know, that these reforms that you claim as having been achieved are still to be realized and that nowhere have any of your decreed prescriptions or laws been introduced in practice."[5]

While these limits on reform legislation did exist, nevertheless the question of social reform—the amelioration of working-class conditions through law—occupied more and more of the parliamentary agenda. During the period 1890–1914 several major laws were enacted and implemented, with varying degrees of effectiveness. As in other industrialized states, three distinct categories of legislative proposals emerged: insurance plans, factory regulation, and projects to improve labor relations. Insurance plans were among the earliest reforms suggested. Legislation on workers' insurance developed from already existing concepts of workers' self-help. Solidariste ideology presented programs of workers' insurance as a general solution to the problem of the precariousness of working-class life. In 1896, while Premier, Léon Bourgeois explained to a suspicious Senate why insurance programs were legitimate forms of state intervention:

> We believe that the Senate has something more to do in society than laisser-faire and laisser-passer. We believe that as long as it intervenes only to aid those who have aided themselves, and as long as it requires an initial effort of individual will, it not only has the right, but a genuine duty to aid those who have helped themselves.[6]

Factory regulation, which already applied to "special" groups of workers, gained greater acceptance after 1900 and began to include adult men, a previously unprotected category. The interventionists, more willing to endorse legislation that directly affected working conditions, actively promoted regulatory statutes limiting the working day and week. The changing attitude toward factory regulation was also influenced by the cumulative impact of the socialist and syndicalist movements for the eight-hour day, the leading demand of the organized working class. The third category of proposed social reform was intended to improve worker-employer relations in the factory. It reflected the concern of such key reformers as Alexandre Millerand to halt the rising rate of strikes, to contain increasing labor militancy, and to end the domination of the labor movement by revolutionary syndicalism.

The essential issue that supporters and critics of reform debated was the social viability and economic efficiency of nineteenth-century labor relations in the new context of universal male suffrage. Reform, as an effort to modify existing conditions of labor, varied in its legislative and practical success. Which proposal was presented, and when, dependend on specific political and social conditions, particularly the parliamentary strength of the reform coalition and the intensity of working-class militancy. Projects which most directly threatened *liberté de travail* encountered the greatest resistance. Reformers, many of whom vacillated in their own commitment to state intervention, often lacked the political and ideological strength to overcome their tenacious liberal opponents. Despite the many limits placed on the legislation and implementation of social reform, the prewar reformers did introduce new attitudes toward the working class, the law, and the relation between state and society.

The merits and disadvantages of social insurance occupied a great deal of the reformers' and parliamentarians' efforts. As early as the 1870s, moderate republicans had presented the argument that the workers' situation would be improved by reducing uncertainty through insurance. They had hoped to increase support for mutual aid societies. The strategy of achieving social pacification by insuring workers against the "inevitable" insecurities of their lives gathered significant support through the 1890s. Insurance endowed the worker with a type of personal property. To the bourgeois, parliamentarian or voter, property was the only acceptable and reliable means to security.[7] *Prévoyance* might become possible even for workers if they possessed a cash reserve no matter how modest.

This *mutalise* tradition and the *solidariste* campaign were strengthened by insurance legislation in other European states. The well-established German social insurance program was constantly introduced into the French debate, either as a model to emulate or as a dangerous precedent to avoid. While the issue of workers' insurance itensified in France in the 1890s, the German health insurance law had been in place since 1883. The Reichstag enacted compulsory accident compensation the next year. Workers' insurance was further enlarged in 1889 with old age pensions.[8] French liberals identified the policy of obligatory insurance with the Prussian imperial state and argued that it was a principle antipathetic to the tradition of French liberty.[9] Interventionists, on the other hand, pointed to social reforms as yet another area in which Germany had advanced far beyond republican France. Some interventionists claimed that social insurance had contributed to the German economic advance.[10]

British legislation on workers' insurance occurred almost simultaneously with the French. The British Liberals led by David Lloyd George and the French Radicals were very aware of one another's social programs. Supporters of accident compensation in both parliaments referred to the progress of the project across the Channel.[11] The British law establishing workers' accident compensation was enacted in 1897, one year before the French. The British system of old age pensions and health insurance, the centerpiece of twentieth-century reformist Liberalism, were instituted in 1908 and 1911.[12] Old age pensions became law in France in 1910. In all major industrial states, workers' insurance dominated the agenda of social legislation.[13] To its supporters it seemed *the* solution to the "social question." It interfered least with the organization of production, and it had the advantage of being based on the bourgeois virtues of savings, security, and individual improvement.

In 1893 the *Progressiste* Deputy Jacques Drake noted that a parliamentary consensus existed on the need to realize "measures necessary to protect workers from the miseries of sickness and old age by the creation of a national insurance and pension fund."[14] The same Deputy also predicted that sharp dissension would surround the practical issue of how to organize such a national insurance program. Drake himself endorsed state support for private pension plans, particularly those already established and funded by employers.[15] Other parliamentarians preferred to expand state subsidies for mutual aid societies. Only a small number of reformers in the 1890s proposed a national compulsory insurance program to which the state would contribute. The interventionist Raoul Jay pointed out that the development and increasing scale of industrial enterprises had made the institution of compulsory workers' insurance essential and urgent.[16] Insecurity was becoming more acute, and private programs could no longer address the problems of the entire working class.

The issue of organizing a workers' insurance program opened a long debate between proponents and critics of state intervention. Could the state obligate workers, employers, and taxpayers to participate in insurance plans? If a state-administered insurance program did exist, against what aspects of workers' precariousness should "security" be provided—accidents, illness, old age, unemployment?[17] If the state did contribute to an insurance plan, what would be the repercussions for its budget? The controversies multiplied. Despite the enactment of legislation, they would remain unresolved before the First World War.

The law on accident compensation was one of the central reforms of the 1890s. As early as 1880, an associate of Gambetta, Martin Nadaud, introduced the first version of a bill on work place accidents. In all its versions, the crux of the law was the principle of *risque professionnelle*: In mechanized or dangerous occupations, employers would automatically compensate workers for accidents, unless proven to be willfully caused by the worker. The question of individual liability would be removed from workplace accidents. Mechanization would be recognized as the cause of an accident and the employer would assume responsibility for the unintended effects of his machines. Reformers insisted that obligatory insurance be added to this principle. Obligatory insurance had originally been proposed in 1883 by Félix Faure, and was finally included in the Chamber bill of 1893.[18] In addition to being required to compensate workers for accidents, the employer would also have to participate in an insurance program guaranteeing his ability to indemnify injured workers.

From 1893 to 1898 this version of the bill went back and forth between the Chamber and the Senate.[19] Until 1898 the Chamber supported both *risque professionnelle* and obligatory insurance. The Senate questioned the legitimacy of *risque professionnelle*, and adamantly rejected obligatory insurance. The brief Radical ministry of Léon Bourgeois pledged to win the Senate's endorsement of the accident proposal. In this, Bourgeois failed: The Senate in 1896 defeated the Chamber's version of the bill once again. Ultimately the more conservative ministry of Méline convinced the Chamber of the need to compromise and accept the Senate's version, which became law in April 1898.

The Senate majority reluctantly accepted the central concept of *risque professionnelle*, a significant departure from established legal principles and a new view of industrial conditions. This acceptance required the defeat of liberal amendments in an 1895 session: Liberal senators proposed to replace automatic compensation with a process of individual judicial decisions. They intended that the law merely condone existing practices rather than change them. Senator Aimé-Etienne Blavier led this liberal opposition to *risque professionnelle*. His argument against this specific reform contained the full repertoire of criticism that met all reform attempts:

> We must not alter the practices of an entire industry from one day to the next. There are *laws* of economic and financial necessity which it would be foolish for Parliament to ignore. . . . If we must think of the workers, we must also think of industry, its forces, and foreign competition. We must think above all of small industry, which will be less able to sustain the great expense of the law.[20]

The *Progressiste* Senator Aleide Poirrier, who had reported the bill out of the Committee on Labor, responded to this liberal criticism. He was seconded by the Minister of Commerce, André LeBon, who delivered a long endorsement of *risque professionnelle* to the Senate in the summer of 1895.[21] These two moderates expressed the views of socially conservative republicans, willing to concede limited reforms that, in their opinion, would ultimately profit both the worker and the industrialist. They shared this attitude with the reformers, but differed as to the extent of needed reforms and the state's role in them. The Radical Senator Louis Ricard argued forcefully and specifically against the liberal effort to retain the status quo. Reform, embodied in the principle of *risque professionnelle*, was vital to social peace. Ricard presented the law as one "of pacification, . . . of conciliation in the relations between employers and workers, . . . a means to ameliorate to a certain degree the relations between capital and labor."[22] The Senate majority, infused with moderate reformism, agreed with Ricard's evaluation. The liberal amendment was defeated by a vote of 169 to 49.[23]

Many senators hoped that the accident compensation reform, with its departure from strict individualism, would be sufficient to appease the working class. By formulating a special law to cover work place accidents, Parliament implied that the individualistic formulas of the Code Civil were not appropriate to factory workers and the labor contract. The tedious and costly process of attempting to win damages from an employer whose personal liability could rarely be proven had long appeared as a blatant injustice to workers. *Risque professionnelle* eliminated individual responsibility and recognized anonymous technological causes for accidents. The employer, although responsible for the compensation of injured workers, could not be charged with personal fault. *Risque professionnelle* suggested that industrial workers were not merely a collection of individuals, but members of a particular class.

Supporters and critics of *risque professionnelle* agreed that it was a major innovation in reform legislation and the beginning of a special body of labor law. Liberals were appalled by this repudiation of individualism, which they regarded as the foundation of law and proper labor relations. Emile Cheysson, a follower of Le Play and administrator of the Musée Social, warned against the law before its passage: "The principle of *risque professionnelle* is already a breach of common law in favor of the workers."[24] From the opposite perspective, Raoul Jay praised *risque professionnelle*: "It established the principle that in addition to wages, which represent the necessary daily subsistence, the employer continues to owe the worker a guarantee of his right to subsist from the day on which an accident lowers his capacity to work."[25] The idea that the employer had obligations to the worker beyond merely the wage set by market forces, shocked liberal opinion. Even more dangerous was the proposal that the state would legally enforce such obligations.

The final passage of the law in 1898 was the result of the moderate republicans' ability to limit its scope and to point out its benefits to employers. Agricultural workers were quickly excluded from coverage.[26] LeBon stressed that *risque professionnelle* met the needs of large industry where technology eliminated the possibility of proving responsibility in case of accidents. The reform would regularize compensation resulting in the reduction of "expenses that might burden an employer."[27] Elaborating this theme in his second speech before the Senate, LeBon contended that the law offered real advantages that the employer had long sought. The industrialist would gain "the exact knowledge of risk to which he is exposed by accidents befalling the workers and . . . the limitation of the responsibility that now weighs on him because . . . of the Code Civil."[28] However, the most persuasive element in the *Progressiste* effort to extract an accident compensation law from the Senate was their wholehearted willingness to join with the liberals to defeat the compulsory insurance section of the Chamber's 1893 bill.

The defeat of obligatory insurance made the 1898 law an official endorsement of already existing big business practices.[29] It also demonstrated the ease with which liberals and moderates abandoned their concern for the small entrepreneur. Several industrywide accident funds had been established in the more paternalist large firms during the 1880s and 1890s. The most famous and successful was created by the association of steel and iron manufacturers, the Comité des Forges, in 1891.[30] The 1898 law altered few of the compensation procedures already operating in the steel industry and in many of the large textile mills of the Nord. Although the large industrialists would have preferred to continue to operate their own company programs entirely unencumbered by state regulations, they had few practical difficulties in adapting to the law of 1898.

The insurance companies had an even more pressing interest in seeing that the state did not require employers to hold accident insurance coverage. All the proposed programs of obligatory insurance would have permitted employers to select their coverage from either internal company programs, mutual aid societies, private insurance companies, or a recently reorganized state fund. The private insurance companies feared that they would be unable to compete with the lower rates of the Caisse Nationale. The actual 1898 law, lacking both obligatory insurance or a special state insurance program, provided windfall profits for many of the large insurance companies. The insurance rates for industrial accidents rose so rapidly after 1898 that the Chamber was forced to introduce a bill the following year to reorganize the Caisse Nationale. The lower premiums of the Caisse would, it was hoped, pressure the private companies to reduce their rates.[31]

Ironically, those employers who suffered most from this situation were the small entrepreneurs in whose name obligatory insurance had been rejected. Those *petits patrons* who refused to pay the exorbitant insurance premiums still faced the possible expense of compensation costs. The reformers argued that it was this rejection of obligatory insurance that burdened small industry. "Obligatory compensation could become a cause of ruin for the small employers. . . . The best means to defend industry against this danger is to appeal to obligatory insurance."[32] As enacted, the 1898 law almost invited employers, particularly small entrepreneurs, to circumvent the reform.

The special circumstances of small industry, its ability or inability to adjust to reform legislation, was an important element in the controversy surrounding not only accident insurance but every reform proposal. Opponents of reform insisted that uniform legislation could not be applied to all sectors of production. In fact they suggested that any type of reform would ruin small industry. In 1899 when the Chamber debated the modification of the accident compensation law, the *Progressiste* Deputy Georges Graux condemned obligatory insurance as a dangerous precedent. He then denounced the existing law for bankrupting the *petit patron*.[33] Although no proposal was made to exempt all of small industry from the accident compensation law, a variety of measures and procedures restricted its full application.

From the workers' perspective the law had many weaknesses. Adopted in the spring of 1898, its implementation was delayed until July 1899. Then several liberal senators attempted to gain a further delay until July 1900.[34] This procrastination reinforced the claim that the law had only been intended as a campaign advertisement. The full text of the law revealed the Parliament's, and particularly the Senate's, unwillingness to enact systematic legislation that would include the entire working class. The general principle of *risque professionnelle* was undercut by the legislators' insistence that it could only be applied to certain types of workers. Accident compensation would be extended to workers in the building trades, factories, quarries, transport, mines, and generally any productive process "that uses a machine moved by a force other than that of a man or an animal."[35] The categories were large and all industrial workers were included, but many French workers remained without the protection of the law. Furthermore, by listing specific categories, the parliamentarians reaffirmed their belief that social reforms were exceptional measures to be applied to "unique" circumstances.

The conviction that social reforms were extraordinary acts to rectify extreme abuses was still widespread within the bourgeoisie. Even moderate reformers shared this view before 1900. One immediate result of the accident compensation law was to reveal the pervasiveness of occupational dangers on a variety of work sites. Almost all workers, whether they worked in the modern, concentrated industries of metallurgy and chemicals, or the traditional crafts of the building trades, were exposed to a shockingly high rate of injury. Under the 1898 law, employers were required to report all industrial accidents to municipal officials.[36] The numbers of recorded industrial accidents in the second half of 1899, following the application of the law, more than quadrupled for the entire nation.[37] In highly industrialized regions the number of reported accidents rose even more steeply. In the first six months of 1899, 4,165 industrial accidents were reported in the Paris region; in the second six months the number was 19,273. In Lille the number climbed from 3,479 during the first half of the year to 15,199 in the second half.[38] The rate of industrial accidents continued to increase, although not as sharply as the first year of the law's application and with some fluctuations, through the entire prewar period.[39] The urgent and widespread need for accident compensation had been irrefutably demonstrated.

The law's commitment to obligatory compensation encouraged much wider reporting of industrial accidents. However, the guaranteed disability pensions were often difficult for workers to obtain. The Chamber's 1893 version of the bill had called for the organization of special arbitration tribunals, similar to those already functioning in Germany. The Senate, however, had rejected this innovation.[40] Presiding Justices of the Peace determined if the accident was indeed covered by the law. They were often unsympathetic, and suspicious of workers' claims. Disputes over awards invariably led to delays. Once they accepted the injury as covered by *risque professionnelle*, the judges could still adjust the compensation level if either the worker or employer was found to have contributed to the accident. Although the intent of the reformers had been to remove industrial accidents from individual litigation, the law failed to accomplish this. Between 1899 and 1906, 79,315 serious industrial accidents were reported, those which caused death or permanent disability. Only 2.7 percent of these did *not* appear before a judge; 62 percent were decided by a justice of the peace and 33.8 percent were further contested before a higher tribunal. Of this last category, a quarter of the cases went on to the court of appeals.[41] The continued reliance on the civil courts as the arbitrator of labor relations placed the worker at a serious disadvantage.

The law itself stipulated that compensation could not exceed the workers' salary. In cases of total, permanent incapacity, the worker received a lifetime annual pension of two-thirds of the yearly salary. Partial permanent incapacity entitled workers to half their salary. In the case of death, the widow or widower received 20 percent of the salary.[42] This frugal compensation scale was further complicated by the difficulty of calculating annual wages. Articles eight and ten of the law attempted to set down the method by which annual salaries could be established for a work force which was rarely employed for twelve consecutive months and in which some workers were still paid in kind.[43] The seasonal and cyclical nature of much employment, as well as the persistence of noncash wages, made intentional and unintentional underpayment of compensation common. One of the most frequent reasons to resort to judicial intervention in accident compensation was the difficulty in establishing the base annual or daily wage.[44]

Most important, since the employer was not compelled to be insured, the possibility always existed that small employers would be unable to idemnify their workers.[45] Senator Ricard, the Radical supporter of the bill, warned his colleagues, "One cannot say to the workers that they have the right to compensation and then leave them to argue at their risk and peril with their employer when the latter is insolvent."[46]

Employers' attitudes to the reform were complex. While all employers rejected the principle of obligatory insurance, not all opposed the implementation of *risque professionnelle*. The existence of industrywide *caisses* in steel and textiles certainly made the acceptance of the law easier for those industrialists. The moderate republican journals, such as the *Revue politique et parlementaire* and the *Revue d'économie politique* which often spoke to, if not for, big business reflected a quiet acceptance of the reform. However, the endorsement of this reform by some employers' organizations, such as the Association des Industriels de France Contre les Accidents du Travail,[47] did not govern the actions of individual employers, small *and* large. Litigants in the court cases disputing the implementation of the law included some of the largest French firms, like the Motte textile company, and some of the most progressive, like Savon Frères of Marseilles.[48] Large industrialists contested the same issues as the *petit patron*—how many days must they pay, what was the salary base, etc. In addition, while large employers were more likely to participate in insurance plans, they often sought to pass the costs on to their workers. In 1902 the Minister of Commerce, Alexandre Millerand, clarified the law to employers: "It had seemed hardly necessary to add, except that the issue was misunderstood by several industrialists and provoked several strikes, that the insurance premium is solely the responsibility of the employer."[49] In the practical implementation of the law, large as well as small employers sought ways to avoid the reform or reduce the costs.

Despite these limitations, critics and defenders of the 1898 law on accident compensation considered it as "one of the most important of the labor code."[50] A breach had been made in the individualistic definitions of labor relations. Subsequent legislation broadened its scope and improved its administration. However, throughout the prewar period, the major handicap of the 1898 law was not removed. Obligatory insurance was never made a part of the accident compensation statute. What many reformers had hoped would be the first component of a general, state-regulated social insurance program became instead a limited law on accident compensation. The opposition to obligatory insurance for accident compensation was part of a larger campaign. The debates on accident insurance were recognized as a prelude to the much larger question of old age pensions. The moderate Senator Poirrier accused the supporters of compulsory accident insurance as seeking "to affirm a method in order to institute old age insurance."[51]

Workers' old age pensions, *la retraite ouvrière*, were one of the central social reforms of the prewar period. Debate began in 1890 and ended in 1910 when Parliament enacted the law. Although annual discussions occurred during the 1890s, it was only after 1898 and the post-Dreyfusard realignment that serious consideration was given to a project on old age pensions. In 1901 the Waldeck-Rousseau ministry proposed a pension plan. In the 1902–1906 Chamber, the Committee on Social Insurance headed by Millerand developed the specifics of the text. Major debates on old age pensions took place in 1901 and 1906. Following the 1906 debate the Chamber enacted the Committee's project, a few weeks before the April elections. It had taken five years to enact a reform that headed the Radical Party's program, which had been endorsed by its congresses, and which had been a campaign promise of most Radical candidates.[52] The five-year effort to pass this Radical reform coincided with Radical domination of the Chamber. Once enacted in the lower house, the Senate examined the law for another four years. The Senate bill of 1910 differed significantly from the Chamber's earlier version. As in the case of the 1898 accident compensation law, the Chamber accepted the Senate bill under the pressure of the upcoming 1910 elections. The more conservative political climate reduced the deputies' willingness to fight for their original, more generous version. The 1910 pension law received nearly unanimous passage in the Chamber of Deputies and the Senate.[53]

Solidaristes, left Radicals, indeed apparently the entire

Radical Party agreed that workers' old age pensions must be instituted. Following the 1902 election and its Radical victory, reformers of the newly organized party, supported by independent socialists, developed a specific plan for the organization of old age pensions. They intended to base their reform on three principles: contributions to a pension fund by workers, employers, and the state; obligatory participation; and the investing of the pension fund (*capitalisation*) so that within thirty years income would offset most of the expenses of the program.[54] The Chamber's 1906 bill on pensions incorporated these three policies.

Since the first debates on a pension program, there had been intense disagreement as to how and by whom old age pensions should be organized. As in all reform legislation, the first controversy was about mandatory participation. The bill presented by Waldeck-Rousseau's government in 1901 assumed that participation in the program would be compulsory. The law on workers' and peasants' pensions clearly established, in theory, the right of the state to compel special groups of citizens to contribute to what the state had determined was their own and the nation's welfare. This concept was bitterly condemned by liberal and moderate politicians. For different reasons, the revolutionary syndicalists also attacked the principle of obligatory insurance.

The reformers' defense of mandatory participation was cogently presented by the *solidariste* Radical, Paul Guieyesse. Minister of Colonies in the earlier Bourgeois government, Guieyesse had been a member of the Chamber's Committee on Social Insurance since 1898. He reported on the pension law in 1901 and 1906. During the final stages of debate, he portrayed the pension program as the ideal method to fulfill the *solidariste* goal. "The Committee [on Social Insurance] recognizes that the present generation must discharge the debts of the previous one. . . . On behalf of the State we will discharge as much as is possible of the social debt that we recognize."[55] The *solidariste* argument alone, however, could never convince bourgeois opinion of the need for obligatory insurance.[56]

Nonetheless, the liberal vision of independent individuals freely entering associations continued to be very persuasive. Emile Levasseur criticized the Chamber's pension law of 1906: "Isn't there a danger that compulsory state insurance will weaken the will to individual foresight (*prévoyance*) among future pensioners and also weaken the desire of employers to create private pension plans in order to retain their personnel?"[57] Similar objections had been raised by the *Progressiste* Deputy Drake, the liberal Lyonnais Deputy Auddifred, and the journalist Edmond Villey.[58] All agreed that the state had no inherent right to compel insurance protection. To counter the Radical project, moderates and liberals claimed that the mutual aid societies, supported by larger state subsidies, could provide adequate pension facilities.

While continuing to be sympathetic to the *mutualité* movement, reformers recognized that the self-help organizations were not equipped to organize a workers' pension program. Even the liberal economist Emile Levasseur had to admit that the *mutualités* could never provide a national system.[59] After 1900, most reformers accepted Raoul Jay's provocative claim that the only possible insurance against old age was obligatory insurance.[60] A compromise was eventually arranged between the defenders of compulsory insurance and the *mutualistes*. The mutual aid societies would participate in the administration of a state program of obligatory insurance. This appeased the *mutualistes*,[61] but not the liberals. The liberal opposition never abated, but merely shifted its attack to other aspects of the pension proposal.

Underlying the issue of compulsory insurance had been the question of what social group or institution would control workers' pensions. Some large employers had created company or industrywide pension programs. The *Progressiste* politicians were especially committed to protecting these workers' pensions.[62] As in the case of the mutual aid societies, liberals and moderates portrayed the employers' private initiative as vastly superior to any compulsory plan. Again, the reformers replied that the employers' efforts were admirable, but could never adequately provide a national pension program. The *caisses patronales* were limited to large enterprises which had the necessary financial resources and an interest in offering services to stabilize the work force. Small and medium-sized firms neither possessed the funds to establish a pension program nor required as permanent a work force. In 1898, Arthur Fontaine estimated that out of a total working population of ten million only six hundred thousand workers participated in employers' pension programs. He concluded that the only "fiscally sound insurance program which would

serve the large and varied population is compulsory insurance
organized by the State."[63]

Undoubtedly, large employers had less cause to oppose
the introduction of compulsory insurance than either their
smaller counterparts or their political defenders. Many were
already accustomed to paying a contribution to a private
pension fund and to the administrative apparatus attached to
such a fund. The 1910 pension law did not dismantle these
existing company plans, but simply modified them.[64] In fact, a
small number of employers even actively campaigned for the
government pension program, claiming that it would improve
worker-employer relations.[65]

The situation for small employers was quite different. In
their case the employers' contribution usually represented a
new expense. In addition to the financial burden, small
entrepreneurs rebelled against what they perceived as an attack
on their central ideology of individualism and personal
liberty.[66] While large employers had less difficulty financially or
ideologically in accepting the new law, they maintained their
solidarity with their smaller fellow businessmen. For the most
part the large industrialists seconded the opposition of the *petit
patron* to the workers' pension.[67] In 1901 the Chamber
authorized a survey of employers' and workers' attitudes
toward old age pensions.[68] Ninety-three of the ninety-four
responding Chambers of Commerce opposed the principle of
obligation.[69] Most employer associations took the same stand.
The important Association des Industriels de France contre les
Accidents du Travail, which had promoted the law on accident
compensation, condemned obligatory pensions as a threat to
"social peace."[70] This unified employer opposition to old age
pensions was modified as conditions altered. By early 1906, for
example, the Chamber of Commerce of Marseilles, where
intense labor conflict on the docks had taken place, reversed its
earlier position and endorsed an obligatory pension program.[71] Such changes in employer attitudes toward state
pension programs remained noteworthy exceptions prior to
the First World War.

Large industry wanted to maintain the employers' unrestricted control of company pension funds. Not only was this
control threatened in the early twentieth century by proposals
for compulsory state insurance, but much more ominously by
workers themselves. The attitudes of various sectors of the

working class toward the pension issue were complex and their diversity constantly confounded parliamentary reformers. Socialists, revolutionary syndicalists, and reform unionists did agree that neither the *mutualités* nor the *caisses patronales* could adequately address the problems of elderly workers. The employers' insurance plans were unacceptable, since their explicit aim was to increase management's control over labor. However, the organized working class had no uniform position on what should replace the limited private pension plans.

Auguste Keufer, Secretary General of the powerful printers' union and the leading reform trade unionist,[72] endorsed the 1906 bill based on obligatory contributions by management, labor, and government. The revolutionary leadership of the C.G.T., on the other hand, remained hostile to the proposed pension plan. In early 1910, as the passage of a pension program became more certain, the syndicalists campaigned against the bill. The C.G.T. had no principled objection to a state pension program. On the contrary, they claimed in a January 1910 issue of *La Voix du peuple*, "Yes, we want pensions. We would have had them long ago if the legislators had been capable of understanding the logical and necessary duty of society toward those who produce. This is possible, and possible honestly."[73] The C.G.T. leadership did object with great vehemence to the investing of the contributions, to the high age of retirement, and, most strongly, to workers' contribution. Workers' pensions, they claimed, were an obligation of the state, not a tax on the working class.[74] The complaints of the C.G.T. expressed the sentiments of at least some workers, who viewed any deduction from their wage as intolerable. In the 1901 Ministry of Commerce survey, the 1,074 responding unions indicated their support for workers' pensions *and* their dissatisfaction with the Chamber's proposal, especially the three-way contribution.[75]

The Socialists were also critical of the reformers' principles of workers' contribution and the investing of the fund. The demand of working-class organizations that there be only one contributor, the state, underscored the distinction between bourgeois reformers and the workers' representatives. Socialists and revolutionary syndicalists insisted that the poverty of elderly workers was due exclusively to capitalist exploitation.

The *solidaristes* and other reformers regarded old age pensions in a very differnt light. The workers' contribution was intended as a form of moral education, inculcating the virtues of individual frugality and responsibility. Workers' contribution, the *solidaristes* claimed, preserved individual dignity and clearly distinguished old age insurance from public assistance. Guieyese in his presentation of the bill in 1906 reiterated that the essence of the law was the triple contribution.[76] Another important consideration for the reformers was the fiscal one. The elimination of the workers' contribution would have vastly increased that of the state. The reformers were already battling liberals and moderates about the cost of reform. To have called for an even larger commitment from the state was unthinkable and politically impossible.

Once it had become clear by early 1906 that the principle of obligatory insurance would be accepted, the debate on workers' pensions focused on its funding. The questions on how to finance the pension plan created a three-sided conflict between the reformers, Socialists, and liberals. Two problems had to be resolved: how would the fund be maintained and what would be the state's responsibility?

The first problem became a choice between the policy of investing pension funds (*capitalisation*) or a policy of distributing the funds (*répartition*) after the initial contributions had been made. The reformers supported *capitalisation*, the Socialists *répartition*, and the liberals disliked both. *Solidaristes* and interventionists viewed the investment plan as the most secure, since in the long run it would establish a self-sustaining fund that could assure annual pensions. In addition, after the transition period the contributions of the state could be steadily decreased, the fund having by then accumulated additional capital.[77] The Socialists stressed the immediate problem of elderly workers who, under the investment plan, could not possibly receive a full pension during their retirement. Some estimates projected that under *capitalisation* the pension program would not be fully operative for another generation. The Socialists proposed that all eligible workers immediately receive their full pension. The state would guarantee present and future funds, assuring an ever-larger state contribution. Reformers attacked this plan not only as fiscally disastrous, but also as inequitable. "It seemed unjust to give workers who had contributed nothing a pension equal to that which a worker will receive fifty years from now who will have contributed for half a century."[78] Socialists viewed workers' old age pensions as a partial restitution of unpaid labor; bourgeois reformers regarded it as a compulsory savings program. The investment (*capitalisation*) policy became part of the Chamber's 1906 bill.

Many liberals and moderates also were critical of the reformers' investment plan. Their fear was the impact that the large capital reserve accumulated by the state through *capitalisation* would have on the financial markets.[79] *Rentiers* were anxious that this new capital source would drive down interest rates, endangering the foundation of Third Republic finances and bourgeois stability, government bonds, and their guaranteed return. This fear, while exaggerated, expressed the belief that social reform directly threatened the material bases of bourgeois security. Liberals and moderates, however, could offer no alternative. To call for the abandonment of state pensions was no longer politically possible after the Radical victory of 1902. The moderates reluctantly accepted the reformers' investment plan, which at least placed limits on the state's expenditures.[80]

The second problem of financing the pension fund was the magnitude of the state's responsibility. The text submitted by the Chamber's Committee on Social Insurance in 1901 was revised several times because of fiscal considerations. In 1901, the Ministers of Commerce and Finance, Alexandre Millerand and Joseph Caillaux, had requested that two million agricultural workers be excluded from the law, to reduce its cost. Millerand and Caillaux also proposed that the state no longer be obliged to directly contribute to the fund, but only to guarantee its 3 percent interest rate. Finally, they suggested a drastic reduction of almost one-third in the annual pension itself.[81] Millerand hoped that such cost-containment efforts would make the proposed law more acceptable to the Chamber and the Senate. Caillaux explained that "the state of our finances will not permit the encumbering of the budget with a crushing burden."[82] These major concessions to "fiscal responsibility," however did not lead to the passage of the proposed pension law in 1901.

The 1906 bill stipulated that the state would contribute the necessary funds to insure that each annual pension equaled

360 francs in those cases where the worker/employer contributions fell below this sum. Millerand, then president of the
Committee on Social Insurance, and Guieyesse, the Committee's reporter on the bill, had the difficult task of securing
the Chamber's endorsement for this expansion of state responsibility. In 1906, Millerand, no longer a cabinet member,
seemed to have become much less cautious about state
expenses than he had been in 1901. These two reformers had to
block both the accusations of fiscal irresponsibility, voiced by
liberals and moderates,[83] and the Socialists' demands for a
higher annual pension.

On January 30, 1906, Millerand and Guieyesse replied to
Jaurès' and Vaillant's call for higher pensions. Workers had
repeatedly stated that 360 francs a year was not an adequate
pension. The reformers stated that the fiscal issue could not
presently be resolved. Any amendment increasing the annual
pension rate would jeopardize the passage of the entire bill.
Millerand pointed out that the state had no choice but to
support the lowest possible pension. He did agree, however,
"that the enactment of the pension law must be followed by a
fiscal reform which will not only secure new resources, but
which will also distribute their burden more equitably."[84]
From the perspective of parliamentary strategy, Millerand was
undoubtedly correct to avoid entangling the pension law with
the tax reform issue. A month later, Millerand defended the
Committee's bill against the attacks of the moderates led by
Jules Roche. He accused them of introducing financial criticism as a ruse to subvert the principle of obligatory old age
pensions.[85] To counter the cries of fiscal irresponsibility, he
and Guieyesse offered the hope that the pension program
would eventually reduce the state's contribution to public
assistance and in the long run eliminate that expense.

The reformers' guaranteed minimum pension rate, as well
as *capitalisation* and triple contributions, were ultimately passed
in 1906 by a Chamber anxious finally to present the voters with
a completed reform law.[86] Key to its passage was the Socialists'
willingness to compromise in order to secure obligatory old
age pensions. In the final vote even the orthodox Marxist Jules
Guesde endorsed the reformers' plan. As one Socialist Deputy
put it, the Socialist Party would maintain the theory of
workers' exemption and *répartition*, while accepting the triple
contribution and *capitalisation*.[87]

After passage in the Chamber, the reformers' three principles of obligatory insurance, triple contribution, and *capitalisation* had to be defended before the Senate. This legislative battle coincided with the Clemenceau and Briand cabinets, years when the reformers were losing their political leverage.[88] To gain a Senate bill that incorporated their principles, they had to agree to concessions. During all of 1908 the Senate Committee reviewed the legitimacy of mandatory insurance. Under much political pressure from the government, the Radical group in the Chamber[89] and extraparliamentary reformers, the Senate finally accepted the principle of obligatory participation.

The senators then turned their attention to the financial issue. The Chamber's final version had called for a guaranteed annual pension of 360 francs to begin at age 60. According to the calculations of the Senate's Committee, this would require an average expenditure by the state of at least 425 million francs. Hearing this, most senators immediately called for the abandonment of compulsory insurance. The Clemenceau government and its supporters in the Senate remained adamant. Obligation must be incorporated into the law. However, since the government was also concerned about the reported amount of the state's participation, the government actively encouraged the Senate to lower the cost of the pension program.[90] The Senate bill of 1910 included major cost reductions from the Chamber's 1906 version. Small farmers and sharecroppers were excluded from compulsory participation. The age of retirement was raised to 65. Most important, the guaranteed minimum pension of 360 francs was eliminated.[91] In its place the state would contribute a uniform 60 francs annually to each pension.[92] The Senate passed this bill on March 22, 1910, by a vote of 266 to 3. The majority of the Chamber, hoping to enact the pension law before the April election, and not necessarily displeased with the cost-containing changes, accepted the Senate bill. The Socialists denounced the bill, but having no alternative they too voted for this truncated reform. Nine days after the Senate's vote, the Chamber passed the workers' and peasants' pension law, 560 for and 4 against.

Many deputies and senators had acceded to the pension law because the political climate of the period 1902–1910 seemed to demand some sign from the Parliament that it was committed to social reform. Workers' pensions had been a Radial electoral promise for almost a decade. After 1905 it headed the Radical Party's program. For a large body of parliamentarians not entirely convinced of the social or political efficacy of reform, the pension plan came to be viewed as the least dangerous and most easily abridged reform. The Radical and independent reformers regarded the law on workers' and peasants' pensions as a significant and long-awaited victory despite the limitations imposed by the Senate. They defended the law as a patriotic act which would benefit the national economy, and, most important, secure social peace.

At the conclusion of the Chamber's debate and vote in the spring of 1906, Millerand made a major speech which the Chamber ordered, by acclamation, to be posted throughout France. He began by noting the material benefits that reform legislation had encouraged in Great Britain and Germany.[93] France too would experience economic improvement as a result of the pension reform.

> What expense better merits the title of "productive" than that which by definition aims to increase the value of the pro-ducer?
> Because we are ardently devoted to the grandeur of our nation, we passionately desire to do everything possible to increase constantly the material, intellectual, and moral worth of her children.[94]

The speech ended on the dominant theme of reform politics, the need for social peace. "You now have to complete the realization of the social program of the Republic. In that lies the internal peace of the nation, its prosperity, and its grandeur. Only in this way can you hope to spare it the troubles and the convulsions that we must do everything to avoid."[95]

The reformers' arguments and pleas seemed to have succeeded in convincing their colleagues that it had become essential to pass a major reform law. They had not, however, adequately demonstrated that the pension law must be one of substance. By 1914 it was obvious that the reformers had enacted pension legislation, but that France still lacked an all-encompassing, compulsory national workers' and peasants' pension plan. The Senate had already reduced the extent of coverage and the amount of state contribution in the final version of the law. At least a portion of the working class viewed the 1910 law as another tax, rather than an improvement in their future living contributions. Pensions that many workers would never live to collect exerted little attraction. Socialists, led by Guesde, denounced the law because of its high retirement age as 'pensions for the dead'.[96] The low annual pension, which furthermore no longer had a guaranteed minimum, offered little incentive for participation. The Senate had also substituted for the Chambers' contribution rate of 2 percent of the annual wage, a flat fee, which especially burdened lower-paid workers.[97] Finally, the investment policy (*capitalisation*) meant that most older workers would never receive a full pension even if they did survive to 65.

All contemporary commentators on the law's implementation stressed the hostility of at least some workers to this reform.[98] This opposition undermined the effectiveness of the law. According to the 1910 law, the worker had to initiate participation in the plan by requesting a pension card from a local official and then presenting it to the employer. Joseph Paul-Boncour, Minister of Labor in the extremely brief Radical government of Ernest Monis (March–June 1911), organized the administration of the new law. In his memoirs, Paul-Boncour described his attempts to forcefully implement the law.[99] His failure to gain workers' confidence was due largely to the real limitation of the law, which could not be explained away. Employers, aided by the courts, used the workers' opposition to this limited pension program as a means to dismantle the principle of obligatory insurance. In a series of decrees issued between December 1911 and June 1912, the Cour de Cassation determined that in those cases where a worker did not present the employer with a pension card, the employer was no longer obliged to contribute to the fund.[100] The reformers had retained their central principle of obligatory contribution by major concessions to parliamentary liberals and moderates. These concessions, in turn, infuriated the working class and led, in practice, to the negation of the obligation to participate.

The judicial decisions did not halt the pension program, but it now became essentially a voluntary one. Concern with pensions continued; while Léon Bourgeois was Minister of

Labor in 1912 an important reform of the law was passed. These changes addressed at least some of the workers' complaints. The retirement age was lowered to 60, and the state's contribution to each annual pension was increased to 100 francs.[101] Nonetheless, these improvements did not alter the irreparable damage done to the compulsory pension program by the Cour de Cassation. Paul-Boncour later claimed that the pension law was ignored prior to the First World War. Of the Ministers of Labor who followed him, including Léon Bourgeois, Paul-Boncour said that "without totally abandoning the application of the law, they seemed more inclined to let the passage of time accustom the population to it."[102] In 1912, there were 12 million wage or salary workers eligible for compulsory old age insurance; only 6,997,971 had applied for pension cards.[103]

Perhaps more than any other reform, the *retraite ouvrière et paysanne* revealed the strength of both supporters and opponents of social reform. After much delay, reformers convinced the majority of deputies in 1906 and the majority of senators in 1910 that a compulsory pension program was a *political* necessity. Conversely, the opponents of state intervention were able to limit the cost and therefore the benefits of the law. Its compulsory principle was circumvented in practice. The long legislative history of the pension program also indicates the lack of communication between parliamentary reformers and the working class. The reformers' willingness to abandon those aspects of the law which many workers considered vital led to the repudiation of the law by a large sector of its intended beneficiaries. This repudiation was adroitly used by employers and moderate and liberal politicians to justify their own opposition. Yet the 1910 law was not altogether a defeat for social reform. The acceptance, even if only in principle, of compulsory insurance was a major advance. Although compulsory state pension programs continued to be suspect in the prewar era, the ideological and legal legitimacy of social insurance had been established. The actual implementation of state social security in the 1920s and more thoroughly after 1945 was aided by the limited successes of the period before World War I.

CHAPTER 6

The Legislation of Social Reform: Regulation

The acceptance by 1910 of workers' obligatory old age insurance, even if accepted only in theory, was made easier since old age pensions had not required the state to intrude directly into the relations between workers and employers. Compulsory old age pensions did not interfere with factory conditions or *liberté de travail*. Some moderates indeed hoped that social insurance would fulfill all demands for change. But after 1900, under the pressure of increasing working-class activisim, social reformers argued that insurance programs alone would not create social peace. Concerned with the growing influence of revolutionary syndicalism and Marxist socialism in the labor movement, many reformers called for more vigorous legislation. Reform policies directly addressing the conditions of workers seemed necessary to counter the appeal of revolutionary strikes and class conflict.

Between 1900 and 1910 two major statutes, one regulating the length of the working day and the second regulating the workweek, were enacted. The debates on these regulatory measures were even more bitter than those surrounding the insurance proposals. Although factory regulation made few demands on the state budget other than administration and inspection, it did place legal limits on the relation between worker and employer. Many entrepreneurs regarded factory regulation as a challenge to *liberté de travail*. The President of the Paris Chamber of Commerce, an important employer in the building trades, unequivocally stated, "Freedom is the first principle. Industry must be absolutely free; that is the basis of modern society."[1] Like all property owners, the employer viewed himself, and was viewed, as *maître chez lui*. To limit the working day and week by law implicitly challenged this authority.

Except for the Socialists and syndicalists, no one dared or wanted to attack the premises of *liberté de travail*. Reformers who called for the regulation of factory work attempted to reconcile the employers' claims to full authority in the work place with the need to protect his workers. Reformers resorted to pragmatic arguments, sustained by references to national interest and social peace. This approach, which aimed to avoid confrontation with employers, characterized the efforts of Waldeck-Rousseau's government of republican defense.

Alexandre Millerand, the controversial Minister of Commerce and independent socialist, was the key architect of these reforms. One strategy to avoid prolonged debate was to remove social policy from the political arena, to substitute administrative decree for legislation. In August 1899, Millerand promulgated regulations on the workweek, hours per day, and salaries of workers in industries contracting with the state.[2] But the impact of such decrees was inevitably limited.[3] Administrative action could not substitute for parliamentary decision on an issue of such national scope as the regulation of workers' hours.

The length of the working day was a major preoccupation of reformers in the late nineteenth and early twentieth centuries. It was an issue which directly affected the actual productive process. Since 1890 the Second Socialist International had been able to mobilize hundreds of thousands of workers to call for the revolutionary eight-hour day. Shorter hours were also an issue in local strikes. The reduction of hours followed wages and hiring/firing practices as the most frequently expressed grievance in strike activity during the period 1899–1913.[4] Within this context of working-class activism, the Waldeck-Rousseau government proposed parliamentary legislation to limit the working day in 1899.

The length of the factory workers' day had already been a concern of the state before the 1890s. Like their British counterparts,[5] French politicians in the 1840s had applied limits to employers' demands. The first post-Revolutionary social legislation, enacted during the July Monarchy in 1841, regulated the hours of child labor in factories. The law had limited the working day of children between eight and eleven years of age to eight hours; twelve- to sixteen-year-olds could work no more than twelve hours. However, the law did little to lessen the actual exploitation of children. Inspectors were unpaid and recruited from retired manufacturers. While the 1841 law did recognize the principle that regulation without inspection was pointless, the system of inspection created by the law was entirely inadequate. Thirty-three years later, in 1874, the monarchist Assembly of the Third Republic extended the 1841 law. All children except those working in family workshops were covered, and, most important, inspection procedures were improved. Funds were authorized to pay inspectors; the position was becoming a profession. But even at this date, there were only fifteen inspectors to monitor all of French industry. The politicians still continued to insist that the only category of workers whom they would or should protect were children.

This early protective legislation was frequently justified on the grounds of national interest and the special status of child labor. During the first half of the nineteenth century, there was much evidence that industrial workers were being physically destroyed by factory work. In 1837, the ten most industrialized departments of France reported that almost 90 percent of conscripts had to be rejected because of infirmities or deformities.[6] The respected *Courrier français* had noted in 1840, "It is the necessity and duty of society to see that the generation of children who will one day become a large part of the nation's population are not crushed almost at birth."[7] Nearly sixty years later similar justifications were again employed to legitimate an 1892 law on the factory working day.

In the 1880s in the now republican-dominated Chamber a new bill had been introduced that included the regulation of the working day of adult women. This proposed departure had then been debated for ten years. In 1892 a law on the working day was finally enacted that limited children of thirteen to sixteen years of age to a ten-hour working day, and adolescents from sixteen to eighteen *and*, for the first time, women above the age of eighteen to an eleven-hour working day.

Paul Pic praised the new protection of women for demographic, national, and moral reasons.

If women who worked to excess would only injure themselves, it might be permissible to argue that the legislator should not intervene; but this is not the case. The woman injures the child she might produce. Without regulation of female labor, society will soon be menaced by a bastardization of the race.[8]

Such natalist concerns were added to a long tradition of state guardianship for minors. Women as well as children, since they were not considered fully independent individuals, in some circumstances required special protection by the state. Defending the 1892 law, the moderate republican Paul Deschanel explained, "The State has tutelary powers over persons because of their weaknesses or for humanitarian reasons. . . . The law owes at least as much protection to women, who, having neither political rights nor ordinarily unions to protect them, are in a situation analogous to minors."[9]

In 1899 Millerand introduced legislation to reduce the working day to ten hours. This proposal differed from the existing laws in two respects: It included children, women and at least some adult men,[10] and it introduced new justifications for this break with tradition. The state's right to protect male workers dominated much of the controversy surrounding the proposal. Liberals had already denounced the 1892 legislation because the regulation of women's hours would lead to proposals for regulating the working day of adult men. They had been correct. By 1899, some employers joined the liberal politicians in their defense of *liberté de travail*. Deputy Aynard of Lyons reiterated that liberals were entirely opposed to the "regulation of the working day of free persons."[11] More pragmatically, social commentators like Emile Levasseur claimed that factory regulation would "hamper the organization of production, and might reduce output."[12]

Many who supported the ten-hour regulation did so less from a commitment to extend the scope of reform than to correct the enormous difficulties created by the 1892 statute. Dissatisfaction with the existing regulation of child and female labor was almost universal. Socialists called for better enforcement and the eventual replacement of the 1892 law with a legally imposed eight-hour day. Liberals denounced all government intervention. An article in *Le Temps* of October 7, 1895, castigated the 1892 regulation:

> Everyone agrees in wanting more physical and moral well-being for the world of labor, but this will not occur by rigid regulation

and leveling. Rather what is needed is rigorous respect for the rights of the individual and the encouragement of initiatives which will serve the cause of labor most efficaciously.[13]

Large employers were less concerned with the ideological implications of the law than with the inefficiency and disorder they claimed it introduced into the workplace. Particularly in the textile industry, which employed men, women and children, industrialists argued that the work process made it impossible to have different schedules for three categories of workers. Problems in the textile industry were felt throughout the entire economy, since 35 percent of all industrial establishments and 27 percent of all workers in 1898 were engaged in textile and allied production.[14] The *progressiste Revue politique et parlementaire* explained, "These laws . . . fail to recognize the uniformity of mechanized work, which in some factories has as its inevitable consequence the unification of the workers' hours."[15] To escape the regulation, some textile owners instituted double shifts, which often increased the working day to thirteen hours.[16] A few employers reduced the hours of male workers, as well as their wages. In 1894, owners of Tourcoing spinning factories went so far as to call for legislation creating a uniform ten-hour working day.[17]

Responding to employers' complaints, the Conseil d'Etat ruled as early as 1893 that small workshops in the food-processing industry, which also employed significant numbers of women and children, were exempt from the law.[18] In November 1893, Senator Maxime Lecomte, a Radical from the industrial Nord, submitted a bill unifying the hours of all workers covered under the legislation. All women and children would work a maximum of eleven hours, increasing the children's workday by one hour.[19] A majority of the Chamber rejected this regressive rationalization of the law. More reform-minded Radicals countered with a bill stipulating a unified ten-hour day for all industrial workers, including adult men. The problems surrounding the 1892 law, with its special categories of workers, led a growing number of deputies to conclude that regulation must cover adult men as well as "minors." In 1896 the Radical Deputy Gustave Dron from Lille reported another ten-hour law out of the Chamber's Committee on Labor. As in 1893, it failed to come to a vote. That year the new Méline ministry implicitly endorsed the

Senate's "reform" and instructed factory inspectors only to enforce an eleven-hour day. Even such limited protection received only partial compliance. In 1897 the Labor Office estimated that the working day exceeded eleven hours in 27 percent of all industries in the Nord.[20] In an 1899 report, the Chamber's Committee on Labor concluded, "At present the law of November 1892 is applied to the detriment of the workers . . . or it remains violated with impunity."[21] Many Radicals and reformers felt that the basic provisions of the law had been abrogated.[22] Meanwhile the *Revue politique et parlementaire*, in the same article that explained the technological necessity for a unified working day in a particular factory, also insisted that any attempt to create a nationally uniform working day was impossible: "It has been proven in practice that the reduction of the working day might produce very positive effects in certain industries, and yet might have the most deplorable consequences in other settings. . . . To attempt to reduce the working day for the entire labor force in all industries is to dream of an unrealizable concept."[23]

The lax enforcement and the problems created by the 1892 law could not continue in the political environment following the Dreyfusard victory. When Millerand became Minister of Commerce in June 1899, French law recognized four different legal working days: the ten-hour day for children, the eleven-hour day for adolescents and adult women, the twelve-hour day for adult men, and an unregulated day for all adult men outside of mechanized production and for those women and children who worked in nonmechanized family workshops. Enforcement of this already complex system was made more difficult by the inadequacy of state inspection. Although their number had been increased to 103, factory inspectors could not enforce these intricate regulations in the one hundred and sixty thousand enterprises for which they were responsible.[24] In reality, the actual length of the working day varied considerably in different regions and occupations. At the turn of the century many factories averaged eleven- or twelve-hour days. In smaller enterprises, and especially in retail establishments, workers' hours matched those that had appalled reformers in the 1840s.[25] Into this confusion and abuse Millerand intended to introduce reform and order.

Millerand, in the fall of 1899, began to work out a compromise between the Senate's eleven-hour bill of 1893 and the Chamber's insistence on ten hours. Rather than immediately impose a ten-hour working day in industries that employed men, women, and children (33% of all industrial establishments[26]), Millerand proposed to reduce the working day over a six-year period from eleven to ten hours. The strongly reformist Chamber Committee on Labor, led by its independent socialist president, Pierre Colliard, called for a shorter transition period of four years. In 1900 the working day of industries with a mixed work force would be eleven hours, in 1902 ten and a half hours, and in 1904 ten hours. Most important, for the first time since 1848 a regulatory statute applied to some adult men. Millerand, explaining the government bill to the Chamber in November 1899, stressed the needs of both employers and workers. "If the unification of the length of work seems indispensable, there is another thing that seems no less indispensable: . . . the ten-hour day with an appropriate delay to enable industrialists to apply it with least injuries possible for themselves or the workers, who must not suffer a reduction of salary."[27]

Defending the ten-hour bill during legislative debates and after its enactment, Millerand and reform deputies stressed its egalitarian function. Under the protection of this law, male workers would be able to function as citizens as well as producers.[28] Regulatory legislation would establish greater equality between worker and employer. The 1899 report of the Chamber's committee on Labor contended that the existing unregulated "labor contract" was an arrangement between "the strong and the weak in which the law must intervene."[29] Labor legislation was, in their opinion, an act required by both humanity and justice. This new view of regulatory legislation as establishing greater equality among citizens distinguished the 1899 debate from earlier arguments based solely on humanitarian and national interests.

Of course the older justifications were not neglected. The protection of workers was also a moral and social necessity as well as a sound republican measure. The Christian Democrats like Abbé Lemire, a committed defender of protective legislation, explained to the Chamber in late 1899 that the ten-hour law would preserve the working-class family.[30] Paul Pic justified state intervention as necessary for the good of future generations. Workers, even adult men, required protection against their own self-exploitation and against the capitalists.[31]

He claimed as well that this protection would stimulate economic growth. Ignoring the significant opposition of employers to the reform, Pic insisted that employers desired the reduction of the working day, but could only accomplish this with the aid of the state. The practices of a small number of unscrupulous industrialists forced all factory owners to have long hours. The legalization of a ten-hour maximum would permit the progressive majority of employers to prevail.[32]

Maurice Bourguin, the interventionist economist on the Lille law faculty, brought together several major arguments supporting the ten-hour working day. He empasized the economic advantages for industrialists: a healthier, more vigorous work force; the end of the confusion created by the 1892 law; the regularization of the industrial market; and the restriction of overproduction.[33] Writing during the first phase of the law, the eleven-hour day of 1900 and 1902, he compared productivity rates before and after implementation. Bourguin concluded that in the long run the new law would not reduce output. On the contrary, the improvement of capital goods and higher hourly productivity per worker stimulated by the reform would soon place output above pre-1900 levels.[34] "The intervention of the State would make up for the deficiencies caused by individual inertia."[35] Regulatory legislation would force industrialists to improve the organization of production. Similar arguments were reiterated several years later by the Lyonnais economist and Radical Deputy, Justin Godart. Under the regimen of shorter hours, employers would have a work force "more disciplined, less inclined to absenteeism and quitting."[36] Godart also predicted that the regulation of the working day would provide the necessary stimulus to modernize the French economy. "Our industry, in order to prosper, must abandon the routine of long hours, and demand from the workers the maximum effort in the least amount of time, placing at their disposal the most advanced plant."[37] Substantiated with statistical evidence and stressing the employers' advantages, arguments such as these aided the passage of the 1900 bill through Parliament.[38] They did not, however, eliminate all opposition to regulatory legislation, nor were they able to block the modifications of the ten-hour law when it was applied.

The views of the large industrialists were divided. They certainly wanted the complicated 1892 statute replaced, but they feared the new regulation of adult male labor. Bourguin observed that large employers were often less explicit in their hostility to state intervention than the theorists of laissez-faire. However, he also noted that industrialists had to fulfill two occasionally contradictory needs: the immediate need to increase productivity and profits and the long-term need to maintain the labor force.[39] In the interventionist view, regulatory measures would make the fulfillment of the second goal possible. Edmond Villey's column in the *Revue de l'économie politique* reflected the ambivalences of the large employers. He praised the ten-hour law for bringing uniformity to the regulations and permitting French industry to reduce the working day of adult men to eleven hours. Villey expressed concern, however, about the economic ramifications of a further reduction to ten hours. More generally he viewed the 1900 limitation of the working day as "one of the most serious laws, since it has extended the police power of the state into the labor contract of free adult workers."[40] Even among those industrialists willing to consider the possible economic benefits of the ten-hour law, the principle of *liberté de travail* remained sacrosanct.

The law, despite many unions' endorsements,[41] did not automatically improve conditions for workers.[42] Millerand had hoped that the staggered implementation of the ten-hour day would allow employers to prepare for the shortened working day and maintain wage levels. On the contrary, the factory inspector for the Nord complained that industrialists refused to make any plans for a ten-hour day and "counted on an amendment of the law which would maintain [the eleven-hour] status quo."[43] Many employers in the textile industry were intent on turning the new reform to their advantage; textile workers responded with strikes to maintain their old pay scale. Strikes occurred in the spinning, weaving, and tulle-making trades.[44] Soon after the law was passed, five thousand workers were on strike in Cherbourg, Tourcoing, Reims, and Paris, defending their wages against reduction.[45] In Lille, a cotton weaver's strike lasted seven weeks. The workers were finally forced to compromise.[46] In addition to wage reductions, threatened and real, workers also faced the danger of firings. Factory inspectors reported that many small and medium-sized industrialists dismissed, or threatened to dismiss, women workers and those under eighteen.[47] In 1900 the main obstacle to implementing the law was this employer policy of firing women and child workers.[48] By creating a labor force exclusively of adult men, they hoped to escape all state regulation.

Compounding the individual actions of employers, the law was further weakened by the courts, the administration, and its own language. A little more than a year after the law was passed, on November 30, 1901, the Cour de Cassation defined mixed establishments, where the law was applicable, as those in which men, women, and children worked in the same room.[49] Although this narrow interpretation severely restricted the application of the law, the Minister of Commerce, Millerand, made no attempt to oppose the judicial decision. Either because of the restrictive interpretation or lax inspection, many small and rural industries avoided regulation entirely.[50] Furthermore, since the original law only applied to adult men in mixed workshops, however that might be defined, a large group of male workers still remained unprotected. In 1899 approximately 47 percent of all industrial establishments had an exclusively male labor force.[51] According to the factory inspectors, large industry, other than textiles, was relatively unaffected by the law in 1900 since an eleven-hour day was already the norm.[52] In smaller establishments and in textiles where even the eleven-hour day would have had significant impact, the law permitted exemptions. This reform, like all others, admitted exemptions when regulation was a "hardship." Inevitably such "hardships" occurred in those work places that traditionally had working days exceeding eleven hours. The vast majority of exemptions were given to textile mill owners and garment manufacturers.[53]

The ten-hour law continued to be the object of controversy between workers and employers and among politicians well after 1900. Strikes accompanied the implementation of the ten-and-a-half-hour and ten-hour stages of the law. In 1904, twenty-five thousand workers in the Nord were on strike demanding the maintenance of their wages despite reduced hours. Strikes also occurred in Normandy and Reims in the same year.[54] Strikes attempting to protect workers from the employers' interpretation of the ten-hour law were an important factor in the doubling of the strike rate in 1904.[55] In 1902 and again in 1903, the powerful Comité de l'Union des

Syndicats Patronaux de l'Industrie Textile protested against the ten-hour law, reminding parliament of the dangers of foreign competition.[56] Their alternative to the ten-hour day was to institute a sixty-hour week. On the eve of the final introduction of the ten-hour day in 1904, Senators Waddington and Lecomte proposed the "limitation" of the work week to sixty hours. The employer could then determine the assignment of those hours throughout the week. Senator Méline offered an amendment calling for a ten-hour day to which employers could add two hours "clean-up time."[57] Such motions to negate the intent of the reform received a sympathetic hearing in the Senate, but were not seriously debated in the Chamber.

The opposition in the Chamber was more inclined to suggest modification than abrogation of the law. During a 1902 debate on a government bill to improve the enforcement of the ten-hour law, the Radical Deputy Gustave Lhopiteau summarized the attitudes of many small and medium-sized entrepreneurs. He claimed to have no quarrel with the principle of the law, but rather with the fact that Parliament was imposing one universal regulation on an extremely diverse economic structure. Although Lhopiteau's main concern was to secure an exemption for the construction industry, he spoke for many others as well.

> One soon noticed that if the law of March 30, 1900, was acceptable for certain industrialists, it was absolutely injurious to others. . . . It is this system of a too absolute uniformity which we have now adopted in the area of labor regulation, a uniformity which excludes the indispensable flexibility required in this area. What suits large industry certainly cannot suit the building contractors and small artisans.[58]

Lhopiteau would accept state intervention, but only if that intervention recognized the various needs of different economic sectors.[59] Other deputies seconded Lhopiteau's position. Those to his right called for the elimination of the 1900 law. Fellow Radicals such as Chauvin merely proposed the extension of the list of exempted industrialists.[60]

Although no amendment to the ten-hour law resulted from these debates, these attitudes, particularly when expressed by Radicals, affected the manner in which the administration enforced the law. Millerand, replying to Chauvin and Lhopiteau, regretfully noted that all social reforms suffered from such problems. "The law of 1900 has shared the fate common to all labor legislation. As they offend certain interests, as they interfere with certain habits, it is inevitable that they will arouse objections."[61]

All regulatory legislation and social reforms were limited, circumvented, and delayed by objections similar to those raised by Deputy Lhopiteau in 1902. Yet reform legislation was never entirely abandoned, since politicians and the broad labor movement continued to exert pressures for its enactment. Labor legislation steadily expanded through the prewar period. With all its problems, the ten-hour legislation of 1900 mandated a shorter working day for an increasing number of French workers. In 1912, while Léon Bourgeois held the position of Minister of Labor in the very moderate Poincaré government, the ten-hour day was extended to *all* adult workers. Once again the reform politicians had to argue the importance of establishing a unitary working day in all sectors of the economy.[62] Like Millerand, Bourgeois acknowledged the power of the industrialists united in their opposition to this new intrusion of the state. Responding to these critics of state intervention, Bourgeois insisted that "The general interest prevails over the particular, and particular interests must bow before a consideration of the general interest. General consensus will occur, peace will be established on the basis of the accomplished reform."[63] In 1912 industrialists remained as unconvinced as they had been in the 1890s that intervention and reform led to social peace. From their perspective, social legislation intensified divisions between worker and employer, among workers, and among employers. The improvement of working-class conditions was occurring without the interference of the state, they claimed. "Why rush it then with unnecessary and poorly prepared legislation?"[64]

The reformers' inability to convince "particular interests" to accept a "general" social interest also weakened legislation regulating the workweek. The collapse of a reform coalition around this issue, the *repos hebdomadaire*, is particularly revealing. The enactment of a six-day workweek, with Sunday as an obligatory day of rest, was the first social reform of the newly elected Radical-dominated Chamber of Deputies in July 1906. Few social reforms received such broad support. Both the Catholic Bishops and the Confédération Générale du Travail endorsed it, as well as socialists and reform politicians. Together with the eight-hour day, which had little possibility of passage, the *repos hebdomadaire* was the only reform for which the C.G.T. actively campaigned. Yet the parliamentary reformers failed to deliver a six-day law that could be enforced, revealing their inability to meet even the most minimal demands of the working class.

In the early decades of the Third Republic, anticlericalism blocked any discussion of a law on the six-day week. The Catholics inevitably introduced the question of the official recognition of Sunday as the day of rest. In fact, in 1880 the newly republicanized Parliament abrogated an 1814 statute which had made Sunday work illegal. This action was an anticlerical gesture, since from the 1830s on this Napoleonic law had not been enforced.[65] Beginning in the 1880s, Catholics sought to reintroduce some type of legislation which would designate Sunday as an official day of rest. During the Méline ministry, the monarchist Deputy from the Vendée, Armand-Charles Baudry d'Asson, had requested the expediting of such a law, whose text relied heavily on religious justification.[66] The republican majority refused to endorse what they viewed as a blatantly clerical political maneuver. Of course, during the liquidation of the Dreyfus Affair and the process of separating Church and state, the Sunday day of rest issue had little opportunity to be heard. However, in the aftermath of the Combes ministry and during the reevaluation of militant anticlericalism by Radicals and reformers, the proposal to legalize Sunday as a day of rest began to seem more acceptable.

The law on *repos hebdomadaire* proceeded through the Chamber and Senate with great rapidity considering the usual delays which most reform legislation encountered. In the early Senate debates the classical liberal objection to any state intervention had been quickly dismissed. Senator Labiche, then president of the Committee on Labor, enumerated the advantages of the proposed law: "I am not a socialist in any way, but precisely because I am not a socialist I do believe that it is necessary to satisfy the largest number of legitimate aspirations. . . . It is humane and prudent to support popular demands such as the one for the Sunday day of rest because they are legitimate, moderate, and perfectly equitable."[67] During the final 1906 Senate debates an unlikely coalition of Catholics and left Radicals emerged to block an amendment that would have permitted the day of rest to vary or be spread over two days.[68] Catholics wanted to elevate the importance of Sunday. Reformers wanted to guarantee workers one full day of rest. In 1906 moderate republicans and the mass of recently elected Radicals also viewed the *repos hebdomadaire* as an ideal piece of legislation. Workers had expressed their support; Catholic public opinion favored the reform and much of large industry and manufacturing had long operated on a six-day week.[69] The majority of the new 1906 Chamber elected on a reformist platform was eager to pass a reform bill that seemed to create little controversy.

But even such a wide range of support could not adequately protect a uniform social reform law. As in the case of the ten-hour day, opponents were able to check the impact of social legislation by arguing the futility of uniform legislation. In his address to the Senate in 1906, Gaston Doumergue, Minister of Commerce for the Radical Sarrien government, already hinted at the potential difficulties which the *repos hebdomadaire* law might raise: "The Parliament must adopt a firm text, *but* one to which practice and experience will later be able to add necessary modifications."[70] The Chamber and the Senate were particularly concerned with the impact of a six day week on small shopkeepers. While the virtues of a Sunday day of rest were rarely attacked, numerous senators and deputies called for major exemptions (*dérogations*) to the law.[71]

The law which was passed unanimously in July 1906 contained more articles explaining the exemptions than describing the regulation itself. Article III listed ten types of establishments where the day of rest did not have to be Sunday.[72] In most cases these were retail enterprises directly serving the public, such as restaurants and cafés. Workers would have either half-days or an alternate day off, or they would work in shifts. The acceptance of shifts was most likely to undermine the principle of the six-day week. Many of the workers in these categories, waiters,[73] cooks, certain salespeople, were the most underpaid and least organized, and worked the longest hours. Even more damaging was Article II, which permitted any employer to apply to the prefect for an exemption from the Sunday day of rest. Exemptions would be granted if proof was given that a Sunday closing would be "prejudicial to the public or interfere with the normal functioning of the establishment."[74] The prefect in consultation with the local Chamber of Commerce would determine if the request met these criteria. Within three months of the law's passage the Paris Police Prefect alone had received 2,515 requests for exemptions.[75] Neither the prefect nor the Chamber of Commerce could be considered entirely neutral in this issue. The encouragement of exemptions from the Sunday rest made inspection and enforcement almost impossible, as the law was weighed down by a tangle of special cases.

This very generous policy of exemptions[76] created considerable dissatisfaction within and outside the Parliament. The Paris unions were determined to make the law effective. The Bourse du Travail appointed a special interunion committee which organized a variety of demonstrations supporting the law. The syndicalists, committed to direct action, picketed those stores which remained open on Sunday in defiance of the law. The Paris Prefect of Police, claiming "that disorder cannot be used in the service of the law,"[77] protected the illegally open stores from the pickets. In January 1907, the C.G.T. organized a large demonstration in support of the law, which the Chamber was then in the process of reviewing. The *repos hebdomadaire* was unique among most social reforms of the period in that it responded to a clearly articulated demand of organized labor. Paradoxically it was just such working-class support, and particularly the militant support of the C.G.T., that made the law suspect to many bourgeois and petit bourgeois critics in the rapidly changing political atmosphere of 1907–1908.

Social Catholics hoping to elaborate a practical reform program had been greatly disappointed by the final version of the law and were even more concerned that it might be undermined in practice. Since 1905 the Paris diocese had been organizing consumer groups to boycott stores that did business on Sunday.[78] After the passage of the *repos hebdomadaire*, Monsignor Armette, a Parisian prelate, urged Catholics to support the new law vigorously. "If for the first time in thirty-five years the Republic has given Catholics a law which coincides in principle with our doctrine, it would be very awkward for us to begin to sulk about it."[79] There were constant efforts to mobilize Catholic consumer boycotts in support of the law.

The combined forces of parliamentary reformers, syndicalists, Socialists, and Social Catholics were not politically powerful enough to counter the demands for increasing exemptions voiced by small commerce and most stridently by Parisian retailers. Among the petite bourgeoisie and their representatives there was a clear consensus that the existing mechanisms for exemptions were not enough. Georges Berry, who had originally entered the Chamber in 1896 as a Catholic *Raillé* and by 1906 used the label Nationalist, led the attack against the *repos hebdomadaire*. Requesting a general modification of the uniform Sunday closing, Berry warned the Chamber, "I will soon find that majority which has never failed when I have proposed measures in favor of small commerce and small industry."[80] Deputy Berry knew that the Radical Party could not and would not ignore the demands of the petite bourgeoisie. This assessment was confirmed when the Radical Deputy Adolphe-Eugène Maujan supported Berry's motion for modification of the *repos hebdomadaire*. Defending this position, Maujan addressed the Socialist deputies, "I know your claim, gentlemen, that the Radical Party is about to betray the working class. We do not accept this conclusion. In order to preserve small commerce from ruin and the worker from unemployement, . . . we will conduct a truly democratic and republican policy."[81] The Catholic Deputy Lerolle, who hoped to preserve the existing law, recognized that once again particular interests had come into conflict with a national reform. "But the question is not whether we are concerned with commerce; the question is whether the interests of commerce require that we sacrifice the law we have just passed."[82] Finally Viviani, the new Minister of Labor in Clemenceau's government, warned that a modification of the law would exacerbate the already tense relations between classes. "What will we say to the workers when they claim that every time a law punishes them it is respected and that when a law benefits them there is always someone who wants to destroy it?"[83]

In the fall of 1906 the reform majority was still intact and Berry's motion for modification was returned to the Committee on Labor. In the spring of 1907, sentiments had changed under the unrelenting pressure of small commerce and new fears about working-class militancy. Viviani's arguments no longer carried as much weight as they had four months earlier.[84] In March 1907 the Chamber voted a blanket exemption from the Sunday closing for all commercial enterprises. In 1908 the Conseil d'Etat and the Cour de Cassation handed down a ruling calling for a narrow interpretation of the law. The high courts questioned the reform's legality and thought it might violate *liberté de travail*. Two years after its passage the law on the six-day week served primarily to confirm the established practice of Sunday closings in large industry and manufacturing. Commercial and retail workers who were most abused continued to work long irregular shifts almost entirely unaffected by the reform.

The unsuccessful history of the most popular of all reform laws, the *repos hebdomadaire*, highlights the serious obstacles facing every reform effort. Any legislation which endangered or was perceived to threaten the immediate interests of any group of employers was unlikely to survive intact in Parliament. Despite these severe limitations, social reformers, supported directly or indirectly by the working class, did achieve in the period 1899 to 1914 the legal regulation of the working day and week, as well as legislation on work place accidents and old age pensions. However, legislative success never guaranteed forceful implementation for any reform. The parliamentarians themselves often made narrow interpretations of the law possible by including major exemptions in the text. Courts, prefects, and employers then further modified the original intentions of the reformers.

In the pre-World War I decades, reform politicians concentrated on legislation that would provide individual workers with greater security and better working conditions. Reformers within the Radical Party hoped to create loyal citizens and active republicans. While insurance and factory regulations had the highest priority for reformers, the issue of strikes and unions became an important political question, especially after 1900. Strikes were increasing in number and becoming more militant.[85] Union membership, particularly in the syndicalist-dominated C.G.T., was expanding. As these activities of the working class came to dominate the political arena between 1905 and 1910, Radical reformers were caught in a dilemma. Eager to aid workers as part of the larger goal toward social peace, they hesitated to support independent working-class activities and organizations that might encourage rather than reduce class conflict.

Reformers responded in two ways when confronted with unions and strikes. Republican politicians had long accepted unions as an essential working-class institution, but one whose aim was to promote material improvement and social pacification. This view had been a major motive behind the legalization of unions in 1884. Many republicans saw unions as institutions of employer-employee conciliation. The Radical Party's position on unions was stated in a 1904 document: "It is in professional associations—powerful, conscious and organized—that the working class must find the means to obtain peacefully the improvement of the labor contract and working conditions. The union organization is the instrument of their emancipation."[86] Even at the height of the conflict between Clemenceau and the C.G.T., the Radical Premier retained some of this attitude toward unions. His refusal to outlaw the national union organization reflected, in part, an effort to preserve the institution which might some day be purged of revolutionaries.

Coexisting with the reformers' great expectations for unionism was a deep uneasiness about them and about strikes. Reformers accepted the legality and necessity of strikes as the workers' ultimate defense. However, in the context of a labor movement dominated by revolutionary syndicalism, increasing strike activity went beyond the protection of workers' immediate interests. The repeated, violent confrontations between the state and the C.G.T. from 1906 to 1910 were occasions of open class conflict. Avoidance of such conflict had been the reformers principal intellectual and political goal. The social polarization of the Clemenceau period and immediately after his ministry presented the reformers with a difficult situation. Their analyses of society claimed that such polarizations could be avoided by judicious reform, but reform became increasingly difficult to enact in the atmosphere of tense class hostilities. The *solidaristes* viewed strikes as an "unnatural" event between two groups who failed to recognize their interdependency. Léon Bourgeois as Minister of Labor in 1912 stated, "The strike is an internal war, a war between two forces equally in need of one another, whose interests are united (*solidaires*) and which justice alone can and must reconcile."[87] All reformers agreed that social peace would mean the end of most strikes.

The reformers then had several objectives in regard to unions and strikes. They introduced bills to encourage and strengthen unions. They promoted reform unionism as an alternative to revolutionary syndicalism. They sought through legislation to regularize the relations between employers and workers. Most important, they developed legislative proposals to reduce the need for strikes. Opposing the proposals of several deputies of the center and right, who had suggested the abolition of the right to unionize and strike, the reformers developed legislation to strengthen unions *and* to reduce strikes. This program did not become law, but the debate around these issues indicated that some politicians were ready to call on the state to regulate what had been considered one of the most private of social relations, the labor contract.

The principal political actor in this effort to reform existing labor relations was the indefatigable Alexandre Millerand. In 1903 he declared, "The overriding motive of my action is the pressing necessity to organize workers. By such organization the working class becomes conscious of its power and also of its responsibilities; [it learns] to cope with realities and to regulate its action and its development."[88] Millerand also insisted that his proposals would encourage economic growth and were, in fact, required by it. He was very concerned with the disruption of production and the ensuing economic problems caused by strikes. Strikes jeopardized national development, Millerand argued, and such economic dislocation was ultimately detrimental to the working class itself. Workers lost their pay, employers their legitimate profits, and the state its tax revenue.[89] The working-class standard of living was tightly bound to national economic development. The long-term material advancement of the working class would be furthered if strikes could be regulated.

Millerand's effort to reorganize labor relations was influenced by several political and ideological considerations. The traditional republican social policy of Waldeck-Rousseau strongly affected Millerand during his tenure as Minister of Commerce, 1899–1902.[90] Waldeck maintained that through organization the working class would eventually become indistinguishable from the solid republican stratum of small property owners and artisans. As late as 1899 Waldeck confidently predicted that once the unions "were allowed to receive and invest capital, they would become the agents of the future solution: the accession of the salaried class to individual property and commerce."[91] Waldeck saw the unions as having two functions: strikes and "regulating, disciplining the workers."[92] If the state encouraged the second role, strikes would become less frequent and less violent.[93]

The views of moderate republicanism that Waldeck continued to promote in 1900 found a sympathetic hearing among more advanced reformers. The interventionist economists were strong backers of Millerand's projects, which carried the imprint of Waldeck-Rousseau. Although they emphasized the active role of the state and insisted that the working class was a permanent reality, the interventionists concurred with Waldeck-Rousseau's hope of reducing strikes and enlarging the mediating function of unions. Paul Pic, a great admirer of Millerand, praised his efforts to establish permanent, state-sponsored boards where labor and management could meet. This administrative decree of 1900, creating regional Conseil du Travail would "accustom employers and workers to meet with one another periodically in courteous discussions, removed from all hierarchial relations, in a setting where their immediate, personal interests do not directly conflict."[94] This view echoed the *solidariste* concept of the unity and mutual interdependence between workers and employers.[95] Charles Rist's widely read 1907 article lent empirical support to the claim that under the proper conditions unions could play a "positive" role in labor relations.[96] Strikes were treated by economists and sociologists such as Rist and Bouglé as logical, measurable phenomena which could be explained causally and therefore controlled. The interventionist economists also stressed the economic functions of reform unionism and collective bargaining, which corresponded to technical and organizational changes in large industry. Raoul Jay defended state-organized collective bargaining on the grounds that "its essential purpose is to regulate competition among workers, as among employers."[97] Finally, Millerand placed his entire labor relations program within the democratic tradition. Worker representation would introduce democracy into the last bastion of authoritarianism, the factory. "Even within the factory one can give, in measured stages, workers the right to speak on those questions that concern them and it is only through this method that one can peacefully resolve the difficulties which rise against us."[98]

During the ministry of republican defense, Waldeck-Rousseau and Millerand formulated two decrees concerning trade unions. Urged by the Premier, Millerand conferred several semi-official functions on unions, to bring them into collaboration with employers in government-created institutions. In the summer of 1899, unions were given the right to elect twenty-two members to the Conseil Supérieur du Travail, where, together with employers' representatives and government appointees, they would deliberate on legislative proposals.[99] A year later Millerand established regional Conseil du Travail by ministerial decree. They were to revive the nearly defunct procedures of voluntary conciliation and arbitration established by the law of 1892. Millerand's decree stated that the Conseil would have four functions: "to inform the public authorities of the actual and necessary conditions of labor, to facilitate collective contracts, to furnish competent mediators in cases of dispute, and to evaluate the effects of protective legislation."[100] Unions and local employers' associations were to elect members to these boards. Millerand frankly admitted that his objective was "to fortify the action of the unions and encourage collective bargaining."[101] The new Minister of Commerce and the Premier hoped to fashion administrative policies which would link the unions to semi-official state institutions.[102]

The unions, while retaining their suspicions of the state, responded more readily to these decrees than did the employers.[103] Large industrialists adamantly opposed Millerand's decrees conferring recognition on trade unions. They claimed that the decree on regional Conseil du Travail was illegal since it contradicted other existing statutes. A major concern of employers was that union membership would increase if unions were given access to institutions with any influence. A key architect of employer opposition to the Millerand-Waldeck decrees was Robert Pinot, a young sociologist. Pinot's activities in the anti-Millerand campaign were rewarded by an appointment to head the Comité des Forges.[104] In the political forum of the Chamber, the newly elected *Progressiste* Deputy from Lille, Paul-Henri Rogez, voiced the fears of the large textile and mining industrialists. They had no objection to institutions that emphasized the common interests of workers and employers.[105] They were, however, deeply concerned with the special status accorded to unions in Millerand's decrees. In Rogez's view this represented a dangerous departure from French law and the existing practice of labor relations. Questioning the Minister of Commerce, Rogez asked,

> Are you very certain . . . that your article V, which tends to make unions obligatory, will contribute to the development of unionism? Don't you fear that by weakening their voluntary character as associations to which one affiliates freely, you will diminish their spirit of discipline and their authority?[106]

Rogez queried Millerand on the decree establishing the Conseils du Travail, "What have you done to liberty and to individual rights?"[107]

Employers' fears were greatly exaggerated, but the new functions given unions in these decrees did convey an aura of semi-official status. This might have suggested that unionized workers would have a greater impact on labor relations and working conditions than the unorganized. Millerand and other reformers specifically intended that this increased prestige would attract a larger number of workers to unions and thereby moderate the demands and tactics of French unionism. The reformers agreed with the syndicalists that the trade union was the central institution of the working class. The reformers, however, hoped to associate unions more closely with the state and ultimately with employers.[108] Through this method revolutionary syndicalism might be eliminated. But liberals, moderates, and in fact the parliamentary majority, although certainly no less hostile to revolutionary syndicalism, rejected these assumptions and viewed any official encouragement of unionism as an infringement of individual liberty. Millerand's ministerial decrees, lacking widespread employer support, having only partial worker cooperation, and encountering political criticism, did not significantly alter traditional labor relations.

Much more ambitious as an effort to transform labor relations were two complementary bills associated with Millerand, one on the legal status of unions and the second on compulsory conciliation and arbitration. Both were first introduced as government projects in 1899 and 1900. As an independent Deputy, Millerand reintroduced them in 1902 and

1906. The recurring discussion on these proposals fluctuated with the frequency of syndicalist activism. Parliament had to come to some decision about the role of unions in the Third Republic. Millerand and a few other reformers proposed that social peace could be protected by encouraging the very thing that seemed to threaten it—the organization of the working class. They insisted that unions could become institutions of class reconciliation rather than instruments of class struggle. Much more than the decrees, both bills called for a fundamental transformation of the aims and structures of French unionism. Deeply impressed with British and German economic development, Millerand was convinced that stable, peaceful labor relations were a major cause of greater productivity and international competitiveness, a belief rejected by economists like Rist. Millerand introduced a far-reaching legislative plan in which the state would encourage reformist unionism that in turn would stimulate economic modernization.

The first bill on the status of trade unions was intended to extend to the unions rights which had been prohibited under the law of 1884. The most important was the legal category of *personalité civile*. An organization possessing this designation had the same rights and responsibilities as a private citizen. With the status of *personalité civile*, unions would be permitted to sign binding contracts, acquire and invest capital, and participate fully in judicial cases.[109] The first two attributes of *personalité civile* were clearly aimed at facilitating the emergence of larger, better-financed union organizations. Several commentators on labor relations claimed that the well-endowed treasuries of the British and German trade unions were a major reason for their greater moderation. As one conservative sociologist noted,

> Doesn't it seem probable that the possession of this capital will give the unions greater wisdom in their conduct? To the extent that the French unions increase their strength and include a greater number of workers, we will see them resolutely entering that path which has been followed by the English trade unions. . . . We are concerned with only one issue: to make the unions reasonable and peaceful.[110]

This view merged with the older republican hope that unions would aid workers to escape from the proletariat by becoming property owners. Bourgeois opinion continued to advance this solution to the "social question" even at the turn of the century. Millerand, when he first presented the bill to the Chamber, explained that one aim of the project "was to aid the creation of union-operated commercial societies."[111]

The proposal to extend the status of *pesonalité civile* to unions received a moderately favorable response among large employers. Several saw it as an opportunity to directly attack revolutionary syndicalism. In a 1910 report addressed to the Valence and Drome Chamber of Commerce, one member, M. Ulysse Roux, revived the discussion of reforming the union statutes. In addition to endorsing the extension of *personalité civile* to the union,[112] Roux proposed further changes. "Any person who had lost his voting rights should be barred from all participation in a union. . . . This would in effect protect the unions against those elements who have nothing left to lose and very often dream of creating sterile agitations."[113] The original proposal had not singled out revolutionary syndicalism, hoping instead that it would simply be submerged by the growth of reform unionism. The employers did not find this sufficient. In order to gain the employers' endorsement of the project, reformers would have been forced to transform the bill into a more direct weapon against revolutionary syndicalism.

Unionists and their supporters reacted strongly to the implications of Millerand's proposal. The reform socialist, Georges Renard, while crediting Millerand with sympathy for the working class, noted that many supporters of *personalité civile* for unions had different purposes. "Others hope to divert union activities into a commercial *embourgeoisement*. They want to extend union rights not out of sympathy to the movement, but out of fear of it."[114] Most socialists and syndicalists were primarily disturbed by the consequences of legal responsibility that the status of *personalité civile* would confer on unions. This designation permitted individuals or organizations to be brought to court for failure to fulfill obligations, contracts, and other legal agreements. Union leaders and the Socialist Party viewed this new "right" as a means to curtail strike activity. A union with *personalité civile* could be sued by employers for a variety of reasons during a strike. When the proposal was reintroduced by Millerand in 1906, the issue of legal responsibility was a prominent theme in the Socialist critique. Vaillant spoke for all the major Socialist leaders when he rejected Millerand's proposal. He claimed that it would introduce in France the same antiunion methods that had created a crisis in the British labor movement five years earlier.[115] The danger of lawsuits might also induce union leaders to increase their control over members in order to avoid the risk of legal action being brought against the union. Rather than *personalité civile*, the Socialists asked simply that unions have the unlimited right to organize. The opposition to Millerand's proposal voiced by working-class organizations seriously undermined many deputies' belief that the extension of *personalité civile* would actually moderate union activity. Neither in 1899 nor in 1906 did the project come to a vote; it was simply returned to the Chamber's Committee on Labor.[116]

Millerand's second project was an even more far-reaching effort to regulate unions and contain strike activity. First introduced in 1900, this proposal elaborated a complex method of compulsory conciliation and arbitration. As the wave of strikes in the first decade of the twentieth century continued, more and more reformers came to view collective bargaining as an important instrument of labor stability. Several also saw it as a necessary complement to greater industrial concentration.[117] Furthermore, there was a tradition among republican, and particularly Radical politicians, of serving as conciliators when requested by workers' organizations. This informal policy had existed since the 1880s and was followed in several dramatic instances in the 1890s—the Carmaux glassworkers' strike and an 1899 strike of workers at Creusot. These interventions of the politicians were not always successful. They did underscore, however, a strong republican and Radical commitment to improving understanding between workers and employers through the process of conciliation and arbitration. By the 1890s many left Radicals went so far as to call for obligatory arbitration.[118]

In 1892 Parliament had formalized this procedure by enacting a system of voluntary requests for mediation. Throughout the 1890s the merits and especially the deficiencies of this voluntary system were debated. By 1900 it seemed clear that the law of 1892 was inadequate. Of 3,370 strikes which had occurred between 1893 and 1899, requests for arbitration had been made in only 773 cases.[119] As the strike rate increased, employers called for the limitation of industrial conflict, although they remained uncertain how this might best be done. The more reformist unions, which had frequently requested state arbitration under the 1892 law, were also interested in promoting greater and more binding use of mediation.

Political figures, ranging from the Social Catholic Count de Mun, to the moderate Deputy LeBon, to the Radical *solidariste* Mesureur, to the Socialist leader Jaurès, all proposed amendments to the 1892 law during the 1890s. As was so often the case with social reform legislation, while a general consensus existed on the need to alleviate a particular problem, there was little agreement among the various political groups on what should be done. An article in the *Revue politique et parlementaire* of 1896 described the variety of disagreements in this debate. "If everyone is agreed on the essential question, dispute continues over whether conciliation and arbitration must be obligatory or voluntary. In the world of labor, workers and employers seem to have little confidence in an obligatory measure. Journalists and politicians are divided."[120] In this context Millerand in November 1900 proposed a system of compulsory conciliation and arbitration.

As Minister of Commerce and again in 1902 and 1906, he called for a major reappraisal of worker–employer relations, the function of unions, the role of the state in labor relations, and the use of strikes in large industry. His aim was to substitute regulation and order for what he viewed as a situation of socially destructive conflict which handicapped French production. "The strike is war. We will sacrifice neither the rights nor the interests of the belligerants, but we will protect the general and superior interest of society."[121] Pierre Colliard, independent socialist and member of the Committee on Labor, succinctly stated the aim of the project on which he reported in 1904. "We want to make strikes less frequent and not as long. We believe we have a method: the establishment of permanent relations between the two parties, and obligatory arbitration."[122]

To achieve this goal Millerand submitted an elaborate structure of worker representation in permanent institutions of worker–employer negotiations. In all factories with more than fifty employees, the workers would elect delegates from their own ranks. The delegates, two for every group of fifty workers, would constitute a factory council, *conseil d'usine*, which would regularly meet with the owner or administrator of the factory. These meetings would resolve labor–management disputes. In those cases where the two parties could not agree, they would each select conciliators. If the conciliators could not mediate the issue within six days, the workers were free to take a strike vote. A minimum of one-third of the entire labor force in the factory had to participate in the strike vote. The decision of the majority voting would be binding on all workers. Either the entire work force remained on the job or they went on strike. If a strike was called, another vote under the same rules would be taken once a week. As soon as the strike commenced, obligatory arbitration would also go into effect. The regional Conseil du Travail, established by Millerand's decree of 1900, would arbitrate and its decision would be binding for one year.[123]

This ambitious proposal created an uproar among parliamentarians, reformers, employers, and workers. Millerand aimed to transform labor relations through the organization of semi-official workplace representatives. He viewed the factory councils as training grounds for French workers. They would learn to have "regular, habitual, and normal relations with management likely to lead to considered and purposeful decisions."[124]

Millerand had no doubt that his proposal served the interests of workers, industrialists, and the nation.[125] However, Millerand did recognize certain obstacles limiting the implementation of his conciliation and arbitration system. From its inception Millerand had always assumed that the proposal could only be applied to large industry. The reform accepted the profound structural differences between large industry and small manufacturing and commerce. The exclusion of all factories of less than fifty workers placed most work sites outside the law. Millerand was primarily concerned about the negative effects of strikes in the most concentrated and industrialized sectors of the economy. "It is in large industry, because of the use of mechanization and the interdependency of the different tasks, that one often sees the strike of a minority of workers create unemployment for the entire work force."[126]

Millerand and his few supporters, assuming that the large industrialists would agree with his argument, underestimated the deep commitment of all employers to maintaining their own authority within their factories. When parliamentary liberals denounced the compulsory character of the proposal, Millerand bowed to this criticism. Not only would the law apply exclusively to large industry, but also only in those instances where the *employer* had specifically accepted the system of conciliation and arbitration in a formal collective contract. Paul Pic complained that with this concession, "It is the contract, not the law which binds the employer. Arbitration remains contractual and not obligatory."[127]

Largely ignored in 1900 and 1902, the proposal for "compulsory" conciliation and arbitration received greater attention in 1906. Millerand stressed that the need for this legislation was even more urgent. "Quite a while has passed since the ministry of Waldeck-Rousseau took the initiative. The frequency and gravity of labor disputes have demonstrated for some time now the impossibility of the state remaining disinterested in the economic civil war that is the strike."[128] The Chamber's Committee on Labor during the 1906 legislature was chaired by Millerand himself. Pierre Colliard, who had collaborated with Millerand on the ten-hour law of 1900, was its vice president. Not surprisingly, Millerand's proposal received an extensive hearing before the Committee. Colliard's report, submitted a year and a half after Millerand had reintroduced the proposal, endorsed the project. Like Millerand, Colliard stressed that a major objective of the law was the reduction of strike frequency. They had multiplied alarmingly; between 1899 and 1906 the incidence of strikes had increased by 83 percent and the number of strikers by 143 percent.[129] To lend greater weight to the urgency of this problem Colliard placed Charles Rist's 1907 article on strikes in the parliamentary record. He praised the article and its author, "one of the economists who knows the contemporary workers' movement the best."[130] Rist had identified the cause of increasing strike activity as a response to improving economic conditions. Just as important, he had also suggested a way to control this disruptive, if nonetheless legitimate, action of the workers—conciliation and arbitration.[131] After reviewing conciliation and arbitration systems in other nations, and the record of the French 1892 law, Colliard concluded that "The state must intervene to prevent strikes and to facilitate the resolution of differences."[132]

Nonetheless, Millerand's bill made little progress in the Chamber. It seemed too threatening to established practices and too long-term a solution for the immediate crisis. Millerand did receive the support of several parliamentary and academic reformers.[133] Yet even this support was only partial. In theory, they agreed that conciliation and arbitration should replace strikes. They concurred with Millerand that a better organized work force would be more stable and "reasonable." They too viewed collective bargaining as a necessary feature of modern industry. However, few reformers dared to deny the principle of *liberté de travail*. Even Millerand, whose entire proposal contradicted the tenets of *liberté de travail*, never explicitly criticized it. His concession on mandatory arbitration and conciliation indicated a hopeless effort to combine *liberté de travail* with collective bargaining. The Radical reformers like Buisson proposed half-way measures such as conciliation and arbitration systems only in those large firms contracting with the state. Paul Pic, usually an uncritical admirer of Millerand, considered his proposal on conciliation and arbritration too advanced for France. Pic contended that the success of such a law required preexistence of powerful and disciplined unions. Millerand believed that the law itself would create such workers' organizations. Pic considered the Millerand proposal utopian for the actual conditions of French labor relations.[134] With such weak support among the reformers, the numerous opponents of the proposal had little difficulty in preventing a general discussion of the project in the Chamber. All parliamentary majorities from 1900 to 1907 viewed obligatory conciliation and arbitration as much too dangerous an experiment. Although it was reexamined at moments of intense labor strife, the project never left the Committee on Labor.

Although parliamentary debate was limited, the proposal on conciliation and arbitration aroused considerable controversy outside the Chamber. In 1900 the *progressiste* journal, the *Revue politique et parlementaire* denounced Millerand as an apostle of collectivism whose program of state intervention would destroy the French economy.[135] Another article appeared a year later elaborating the industrialists' objections to Millerand's proposals.[136] The parliamentary and extraparliamentary opposition joined forces in 1901 when Senator Méline solicited petitions from Chambers of Commerce, employers' associations, and the *progressiste* Association de l'Industrie et de l'Agriculture français condemning the project.[137] The debate was of sufficient interest that a former *Figaro* journalist, Jules Huret, conducted a series of interviews among those who would be directly affected by the proposal. Huret's investigation, published as a book in 1901, revealed the range of attitudes among large industrialists toward the Millerand proposal and toward social reform in general.

The reaction of the large employers was almost uniformly hostile to the proposed system of conciliation and arbitration. Many employers' organizations had been active in Méline's petition campaign. However, this opposition was not without its nuances. Most employers granted that more communication between them and their workers would be welcome, but the Millerand *conseils d'usine* conferred possible power on the workers' representatives. This was unacceptable to employers. Huret observed, "The large employer, like the small, intends to remain *maître chez lui* and will not accept any interference between him and his workers."[138]

This attitude sometimes varied, but only slightly. M. Devillette, the president of the association of masonry firms of the Seine region, conceded that permanent workers' committees might be quite beneficial in some industries such as mining, but not in all industries. And certainly not in his own construction business. "One regulates too much and too quickly."[139] Like many of the more enlightened employers, M. Devillette, a member of the national Conseil Supérieur du Travail, recognized the need for reforms. But the legislation had to adjust to the peculiarities and special needs of different industries. Nationally uniform labor legislation was impossible, in his view. M. Devillette's opposition to worker's representatives in the construction industry was based less on principle, he claimed, than on the seasonal nature of the work and the necessary instability of the labor force. Most employers voiced opposition or reservations about the election of worker delegates. But an administrator at the large Creusot works had nothing but praise for this system. Since Waldeck-Rousseau's arbitration of the 1899 strike, the Schneiders had followed his recommendations and instituted elected workers' committees. The manager interviewed by Huret felt that they were an "excellent innovation which ought to be encouraged."[140]

Although the introduction of democratic procedures into

the factory aroused much controversy, the most negative reception was accorded Millerand's proposal for regulating strikes. Opponents labeled it "the obligatory strike." The employers were correct when they claimed that the binding nature of the strike vote destroyed the principle of *liberté de travail*. The individual worker would no longer be "free" to strike or continue work. The employer would no longer face a collection of separate workers, each governed by personal motives; the employer would be forced to contend with a collective body united, at least temporarily, by their vote. Huret asked a large manufacturer of silk trimmings at St.-Etienne, M. Forest, if he would not accept the method of strike votes in order to eliminate the possibility of frequent strikes led by small groups of workers. M. Forest's unequivocal reply was No; *liberté de travail* must be preserved at all costs.[141] M. Motte, the leading textile manufacturer of Roubaix, deeply involved in *Progressiste* politics, offered a more complex explanation of his opposition to Millerand's attempt to regulate strikes. He viewed Millerand's solicitude for the workers as an encouragement to strike. On a psychological level, reforms bred labor conflict, rather than reduced it. More important, the major demand in most strikes was wage increases. "Extreme" labor legislation made it impossible for employers to raise wages since they were so burdened by the cost of meeting new government regulations.[142] In M. Motte's view all interventionist legislation, and M. Millerand's proposal in particular, were antagonistic to the workers' "true" interests, which would be served best by the unhindered growth of industry.

Among Huret's interviews of a dozen or so industrialists only one employer supported Millerand's conciliation and arbitration proposal wholeheartedly. M. Savon, whose firm loaded and unloaded half the cargo entering the port of Marseilles, employing one thousand dockers, declared himself a complete partisan of the Millerand proposal. M. Savon's analysis of the project coincided entirely with Millerand's own view of its eventual benefits to industry. "It would introduce regulation in the place of disorder and the unknown. . . . I know nothing more harmful to the market and the prosperity of an industry . . . than insecurity."[143] As for the industrialists' fears of "obligatory strikes," M. Savon predicted that the exact opposite would result from the law. The number of strikes would be greatly reduced; those that occurred would be much briefer, and spontaneous strikes led by a small group of "agitators" would be eliminated.[144] M. Savon concluded his interview with a plea to his fellow employers that they recognize the need to adapt to new times and new conditions.

> We must recognize once and for all that the age of the employers' arbitrary rule is over, unfortunately. We must finally become wise and philosophical. A tide threatens to drown us; to try to stop it from advancing is impossible. Let us channel it; let us dam it.[145]

Savon's appeal evoked little response among employers. During the seven years that the conciliation and arbitration proposal was pigeonholed in the Chamber, the employers, with a few exceptions,[146] remained consistent in their opposition. Recognizing that they ought to do more than criticize the proposed reform and genuinely desiring a reduction in the number of strikes, many employers offered alternatives to Millerand's system. The Lyons Chamber of Commerce, after having condemned the Millerand project as a threat to private property and workers' freedom, proposed instead the institution of obligatory conciliation.[147] The nearby St.-Etienne Chamber of Commerce also prepared a similar proposal. The employers' principal alternative to reduce labor conflict was to restrain the right to strike.[148]

This alternative became increasingly attractive as labor agitation intensified, but the Chamber majority, still dominated by Radicals, rejected such an infringement of workers' rights. Although the Radical Party, or rather its leadership, would not directly interfere with the right to strike, the majority of Radical deputies were hardly staunch supporters of Millerand's proposal. This lack of enthusiasm for the conciliation and arbitration reform among Radicals was at least partially influenced by the critical report issued by the Comité Républicain du Commerce et de l'Industrie. This important Radical fund-raising association, comprised of small and medium-sized businessmen, voiced the same complaints about Millerand's proposal as those expressed by the large industrialists. The Comité, too, stressed the need to preserve *liberté de travail*.[149]

Employers and reformers alike desired to reduce the incidence of strikes. Unlike the employers, however, reformers, and particularly Millerand, regarded the expanding strength of responsible unions and the institution of collective bargaining as a means to achieve this end. In 1900 and in 1906 Millerand viewed his proposal as "a manifestation of confidence in organized workers."[150] Few industrialists shared such confidence. Employers continued to view workers as children to be either protected or disciplined.[151] Such views, which supported the immediate interests of employers, made any expansion of unionism appear as a threat to employers' authority. Although variations and exceptions existed among the employers,[152] few industrialists agreed with either M. Savon or Millerand that it had become necessary to institute a new era of labor relations.

The response of workers was more heterogeneous. Among revolutionary syndicalists the antipathy to the project was even stronger than among employers. Supporters of the conciliation and arbitration reform constantly stressed that it would develop union organizations,[153] but they also made clear that the destruction of revolutionary syndicalism was an equally important objective of the project. Millerand's promise of order, regulation, and the end of "anarchy" in labor relations[154] expressed his desire to replace syndicalism with a more reformist and, in his view, more constructive type of workers' organization. The reformers who guaranteed industrialists that the arbitration and conciliation proposal would halt strikes hardly expected the endorsement of the C.G.T. leadership, which viewed strikes as the necessary instrument of revolutionary change. Predictably, the syndicalist Committee for Propagating the General Strike denounced the proposal. "Under its good-natured appearance, this law is one of the most villainous (*scélérates*) that the legislature has ever conceived."[155] The section of the project instituting a binding majority strike vote directly attacked the syndicalist theory of revolutionary activity propagated by a dedicated minority. The national committee of the Bourse du Travail claimed that "The authors of the project want to smother the initiative of that enlightened minority that terrifies the employers. . . . They know that by introducing parliamentary procedure into strike decisions they will kill the legitimate spirit of rebellion which animates these."[156]

The syndicalist hostility to Millerand's proposal was not the only view expressed by members of the working class or their representatives. Several of the larger, more reformist unions, which might have accommodated with little difficulty to Millerand's proposal, did not immediately denounce the project. In 1905, the National Mineworkers Congress in fact called for the establishment of arbitration and conciliation boards.[157] Among the Socialists, opinions were divided. In 1900 Jaurès supported the major principles of the proposed conciliation and arbitration reform—election of workers' delegates, compulsory strike votes, and binding arbitration.[158] After the creation of the unified Socialist Party and the growing militancy of the C.G.T., Jaurès' support for the reform diminished. Guesde rejected the project as serving only the interests of the capitalists. He criticized Millerand for having prostrated himself "at the feet of the employers."

The attitude of less articulate workers is more difficult to gauge. Undoubtedly many members of the C.G.T. shared their leaders' complete opposition. The grandiose promises of labor stability made by the parliamentary reformers must have cast suspicion on the benefits of the reform for workers. However, the record of appeals for arbitration under the voluntary law of 1892 indicated that at least a sector of the working class desired some form of regulation of labor conflict. In a four-year period, from 1893 to 1897, the total number of requests for conciliation remained quite small, 487 requests compared to 2,262 strikes. However, of the 487 appeals for state conciliators 256 were initiated by workers' organizations. The employers had petitioned for conciliators in only nineteen cases.[159]

The absence of strong, uncontested support for the project on conciliation and arbitration within the working class certainly weakened Millerand's position. The employers' adamant refusal to endorse the project further seriously limited the possibility of passage of his proposal. Finally, on this issue at least, Millerand was relatively isolated even among reformers. His project, however, cannot be dismissed as simply an idiosyncratic scheme.

Such a far-ranging plan by so prominent a politician of the period, together with the strong opposition it aroused, reveal both important trends within the social reform movement and the formidable barriers to reform in France prior to the First World War. Millerand, like other reformers, stressed that social peace required the amelioration of workers' conditions. Working-class economic dependency and insecurity must be reduced. Millerand was the most willing to introduce legislation that carried this view directly into the workplace.[160] The security of regulation and order had to govern not only the individual lives of workers, but also their collective experience with employers.[161] To this emphasis on security, regularity, and predictability, Millerand and the interventionists added concerns about economic development. Millerand's proposal on conciliation and arbitration not only promised the employers a reduction of class conflict, but also a more reliable and productive work force. Once workers could be shown that their genuine interests depended on economic growth, then their organizations would contribute to expansion and not to impeding it. This new departure in social reform policy found little support in French society, steeped in republican individualism, the veneration of personal private property, and a strong commitment to *liberté de travail.*

Ironically, despite the complete defeat of Millerand's proposal, the procedures of collective bargaining became more common in French industry immediately prior to the war. As the labor movement became more defensive, and revolutionary syndicalism fell into disarray, individual industrialists became confident enough to negotiate with more conciliatory unions.[162] There was no contradiction in the employers' opposition to Millerand's proposal and their intermittent acceptance of collective bargaining. None of Millerand's concessions had removed the aura of state intervention and legislated obligation from his proposal. If employers succeeded individually in negotiating with their workers, why then should they permit the state to interfere in their factories? After 1911, the efficacy of repression, coupled with the weakness of the C.G.T., made more "stable" labor relations possible for at least some industrialists without any reduction of employer authority.

Regardless of how handicapped the actual laws may seem when compared with the demands of the working class or the reformers' own goals, most industrialists regarded reform legislation as a dangerous threat and an illegitimate state intrusion onto their property. Small entrepreneurs clearly perceived themselves as most threatened by the regulatory legislation. Unquestionably, the limitation of daily working hours and the workweek would disrupt small workshops and small retail concerns whose economic viability depended on long hours of manual labor for low wages. The opposition of the *petit patron* was intensified by the republican ideology which glorified autonomous, individual property owners and by the political reality that small businessmen and shopkeepers formed an important constituency of the Radical Party. The reaction of the petite bourgeoisie to the *repos hebdomadaire* was only the most dramatic instance of this opposition. Unlike large employers, who had more discrete methods of influencing parliamentarians and other means to circumvent labor legislation, the petite bourgeoisie had to present its opposition to reform in the public, political arena. However, the vocal resistance of the petite bourgeoisie need not obscure the less public but persistent reluctance of large industrialists to accept social reform.

Almost unanimously, employers believed that they had the right to remain *maître chez soi*. Some large industrialists finally did accept certain laws, such as accident compensation and pensions, as long as they did not unduly interfere with their established practices. These moves did not indicate that they were becoming more sympathetic to the principle of reform. *Liberté de travail* was vitally important to all employers regardless of the size of their enterprise; it represented concrete and sometimes crucial advantages. Large employers as well as small were committed to preserve the inviolability of their authority. Almost all businessmen believed that the success of their enterprise required the stringent control of their employees. This sentiment, which was tied to more general beliefs in individualism and personal property, limited the reformers' attempt to create a systematic program of social reform.

But although all employers were united in their defense of *liberté de travail*, it did not serve the same function in large and small enterprises. Large industrialists were less economically dependent on the existence of an unprotected and unregulated labor force. These differences in the organization of production in fact served as the strongest argument against reform. Employers and their political allies insisted that no uniform law was feasible. The granting of numerous legislative, administrative, and judicial exceptions to each law indicated that the state itself recognized that no single statute would be acceptable to all sectors of the economy. The different motives of the opponents reinforced one another, making a national policy of social reform difficult to implement.

Conclusion:
The Limits of Social Reform

By the early 1890s, French politicians, administrators, academics, small employers, and industrialists were all anxious to identify the causes of the alarming increase in working-class activism. Relations between workers and employers had been changing under the pressures of spreading industrialization,[1] intensification of the factory system, and the growth of syndicalist trade unions. Politically, the working class was represented in the Chamber of Deputies by socialist parties, steadily more closely affiliated with the Second International. The organized working class had become an inescapable economic and political reality. A group of republican politicians and social scientists suggested that this new militancy reflected the reaction of enfranchised and frustrated workers to their daily conditions of economic precariousness. This, then, was the "social question." According to *solidaristes*, left Radicals, interventionist economists, and independent socialists, it was a problem that could be solved. The causes of economic insecurity could be located and their impact softened, thereby creating social peace. By the turn of the century reformers were cautiously suggesting that the state through legislation could reduce some aspects of working-class instability. The authority of law would bring security through compulsory insurance, improved working conditions through uniform regulation, and class harmony through state-supervised negotiations.

The social reform debate was the consequence of both working-class assertiveness and divisions within the bourgeoisie. In an effort to contain the new militancy of workers, bourgeois politicians and intellectuals developed a variety of often conflicting strategies to reduce or eliminate class conflict within the structure of the republican state. While workers' organizations had originally transformed the realities of working-class life into a political issue, they could not direct its parliamentary resolution. The socialists' ultimate response to workers' poverty was social revolution and the abolition of private property. Even at their most conciliatory, they viewed reform legislation as a partial restitution of exploited labor and insisted that the expense of reform be the responsibility of the employer and the state. Such alternatives obviously received no support from other parties. On the contrary, the goal of the reformers was to block such socialist objectives. The actual formulation of the reform program, the parliamentary struggle to secure its passage, and the administrative effort to implement it depended on the interests, divisions, and alliances within the bourgeoisie.[2] Under these circumstances the "social question" became a key political issue of the Third Republic and one that persistently remained unresolved.

The limits of the reform effort were defined by the bourgeois debate about the nature of social peace and the legitimate role of the state in creating it. All bourgeois interests agreed that *la paix sociale* must be maintained, reinforced, and where broken, restored. Social peace was equated with material security solidly based on some form of property. The bourgeois vision of security was rooted in the accumulation of personal property and the guarantee of its inviolability. Such possessions insured the protection of society and the individual, who would then responsibily exercise his rights as citizen. This central economic, political, and cultural ideal of social harmony based on property insured by the state, was a powerful force binding together all the distinct elements of the bourgeoisie.

Bourgeois reformers, hoping to broaden this ideal, proposed a definition of security to which workers might gain access. The reformers' republicanism, as well as the workers' political activism, demanded that the values of property, material accumulation, liberty, and the individual be tempered by equality and justice. In this context reformers began to propose legislation which would address what was recognized as the workers' central problem, their propertylessness. Laws would create the opportunity to gain some variety of property and some of its social benefits. From the reformers' perspective the achievement of social peace seemed to depend on linking workers more securely to the political and social structures of the Republic. In their view the failure to adopt such a policy would destroy the very security and stability so valued by the bourgeoisie.

These republican reformers feared that continuing class polarization and the organization of the working class might undermine the ideology of egalitarianism and citizenship, thus disrupting the structure of the state. It was essential, in their view, that the Republic retain the loyalty of all "sons of the Revolution." In pursuit of a political base, alliances, and a legitimate ideology that would rally industrial workers to the Republic, the more advanced republican reformers linked legislation to improve working-class conditions with democratic principles. They intended to demonstrate that the political categories of justice and equality could be given a social dimension. Léon Bourgeois' *solidarisme* was an important effort to introduce social and economic concerns into republican politics. The academic reformer Paul Pic explained why it was crucial for republicans to take on these questions.

In our opinion the means to insure the *maximum liberty to the individual* does not in any way reside with the systematic abstention of the state, in the deceptive formula of laissez-faire. It is rather in association, in laws based on *solidarité* that [the individual] will find genuine liberty and the means to safeguard, even in crises, . . . the dignity of the free man and the citizen.[3]

In the 1890s the concerns of the emerging republican elite coincided with and amplified the "social question." This new elite still feared for the security of the Republic, had not gained full control over state bureaucracies, and was uncertain about its relations with the powerful industrial and financial interests, as well as with the recently enfranchised working class. The resolution of the "social question" promised a number of important political gains to members of this elite: The Republic would be anchored in a more harmonious society; the state would achieve new stature as the successful arbitrator between labor and capital; republican leaders would enhance their prestige; a republican electoral coalition, including property owners and the working class, would constitute a powerful political force. These goals encouraged the reformers to pursue legislation as a means to social peace.

The supporters of reform claimed to represent the interests of both the bourgeoisie and the entire nation. They were professional politicians, administrators, and academics. Their careers placed them in institutions that, among their other functions, strengthened national unity. The parliamentary regime and republicanism offered a cohesive national identity for many strata of the bourgeoisie and, in theory, for all classes in France. Republicanism legitimated the pursuit of individual interests, denied the existence of irreparable class divisions and maintained the ideal of national solidarity. The positions of the reformers in the Chamber, the administration, and the university system made them especially uneasy about those claims of workers' organizations which emphasized class antagonism rather than republican unity.

The Radicals, led on the national level by *solidaristes* and left Radicals in the mid-1890s, asserted their commitment to integral republicanism and social reform. Of all the republican factions their legitimacy was most dependent on the ideology of egalitarianism and the citizen. They were the most closely linked to the Jacobin tradition of coalitions between small property owners and urban workers. The Radical leaders, Léon Bourgeois, Camille Pelletan, and Ferdinand Buisson, were convinced that republicanism mandated a social policy of "equal opportunities." Reform would create a more equitable society populated by genuinely republican citizens. At the same time reform would also block the dangerously divisive growth of revolutinary syndicalism and Marxism.

These Radicals were supported in the complex politics of reform by independent politicians, such as Alexandre Millerand, René Viviani, and Joseph Paul-Boncour. Having rejected, or having been rejected by the organized working-class parties, these men aimed to establish their independent political careers through the successful enactment and implementation of national policies of reform. They often adopted a clearer interventionist position than their Radical colleagues and argued more consistently for nationally uniform legislation. They were more willing to present the issues in terms of relations between the bourgeoisie and the working class. Legislation, in their view, had economic as well as political and social benefits. Millerand and other independent deputies insisted that labor reform, economic growth, and national power were all closely related. In their efforts to secure reforms, they presented industrial modernization, class conciliation, and international prestige as the consequences of legislation.[4]

This position was strongly backed by republican academics in the fields of political economy and sociology. In part, the professors were drawn to the reform issue as a continuation of their struggle to republicanize educational institutions. As important in their commitment to reform were the internal developments in the fields of economics and sociology. The theoretical problems of growth, stability, and their interrelation led these academics to conclude that the working class must be convinced to support the political and social institutions of industrial society. As professionals within the administration and the university, state intervention seemed the obvious means to alleviate the economic precariousness of workers which made it so difficult for them to act as responsible citizens.

Solidaristes and left Radicals were keenly aware of the political dangers involved in pursuing a program of social reform. The debate could set off volatile divisions within the larger republican circle and among their most reliable constituents, small property owners. The reform program did come close to creating a permanent rupture between Radicals and moderate republicans in the late 1890s. Léon Bourgeois' proposed progressive income tax galvanized the *Progressistes*, led by Méline and encouraged by Waldeck-Rousseau, to mount a successful opposition to this "expropriation" of property. In this case, as in all others, the Radicals retreated from an irreparable break with the republican critics of reform. The decline of parliamentary Radicalism was reversed during the turn-of-the century Dreyfus Affair. Profiting from the broad republican alliance generated by the Affair, a newly created Radical Party came to dominate the Chamber by 1902. The continuing escalation of class conflict and working-class organizing made the "social question" unavoidable, however. The Radical leaders reiterated their commitment to programmatic social legislation; a fervent call for reforms headed the 1906 party platform.

In the search for ways to fulfill these promises, reformers found themselves in collaboration with the Socialist Party. Just as any fundamental break with moderate republicans was impossible for the reformers, so too was any permanent, productive alliance with the Socialists. The Radicals, independents, and academic reformers all endorsed social legislation as a means to strengthen national political unity. As the Socialist Party emphasized its class nature and as the C.G.T. attacked the republican state as another exploitative boss, it was increasingly difficult for the reformers to maintain their link with these organized sectors of the working class. The Radicals in particular had difficulty in explaining their alliance with a party whose left wing attacked the nation and nationalism. During the 1907 Radical Party Congress a resolution was passed that stressed their distance from the Socialists' antimilitarism and criticism of nationalism: "We ask all citizens . . . to pledge themselves to combat the antipatriotic propaganda which surrounds us. . . . We are a party of reforms, a people's party, but we must also assert that we are a party of Frenchmen."[5] On the other hand, the Socialist Party increasingly questioned an alliance that brought so few benefits to workers.

The reformers were buffeted between their fear of permanently alienating the moderates and possibly encouraging the formation of a powerful conservative party, and their mounting anxiety of being drawn into the alien class perspective of the Socialists. In the end these political contradictions immobilized the reform effort and especially the reform leaders of the Radical Party. The atmosphere of open class conflict from 1906 to 1910 convinced much of the Radical rank and file that organized workers, and not their economic precariousness, were the major threat to the republican state. Radical deputies repudiated their own leaders and their party program to join independents, moderates, liberals, and nationalists in support of repressive action against the most militant organization of workers, the C.G.T.

The reformers were unable to establish a parliamentary coalition which could sustain the passage and implementation of a consistent social policy. The Radical leaders failed to convince members of their own party of the necessity to support their own reform proposals. Nor could the independents transform their ministerial positions into successful lobbies for fundamental reform legislation. Alexandre Millerand, who had the greatest opportunity to use an administrative position as a means of social transformation, was easily blocked. As Minister of Commerce in the Waldeck-Rousseau government, Millerand intended to redesign the unions into institutions of class collaboration.[6] Yet the only permanent accomplishment of his cabinet tenure was the rationalization and extension of the existing laws on the working day. Without question the employers' intransigence played a major role in the defeat of Millerand's reform ambitions. As important, however, was his political isolation as an independent socialist. No permanent political constituency existed to support the independents' reform proposals.

The Radical leadership's inability to hold its most important constituency, small property owners, to its reform platforms undermined efforts for social legislation. Between the victory of the Bloc des Gauches in 1902 and the fall of the Clemenceau government in 1909, Radical voters drifted away from the party's social program. The leaders were stranded with policies that they could not implement. *Petits propriétaires*, small employers, and retailers were divided over the best strategy to pursue in relation to the working class. They responded to programs that satisfied their strong desire for social peace and national unity and that also protected their own particular interests. A segment of urban retailers came to fear that the cost of social legislation and organized working-class demands immediately threatened the viability of their shops. Some of these voters, such as the Parisian *petits commerçants*, abandoned the Radicals and supported the new nationalist politicians.[7] This defection alarmed Radicals and led many to reconsider their endorsement of reform and electoral alliances with the Socialists. In 1906 a Radical Deputy, Antoine de Lannensan,[8] explained the petit bourgeois fear of socialism and the potential danger it held for the Radical Party:

> Unlike the rich bourgeois who can dismiss collectivism and the revolutionaries because he has a thousand ways to avoid them, the small shopkeeper, the small farmer, or the small employer dreads revolutionary threats much more, even the most hollow ones, since they know no means to escape them. As long as the collectivists were content with sonorous phrases, they remained indifferent, as if deaf; now collectivism speaks of acting. *The*

petite bourgeoisie trembles, and they are ready to throw themselves into the arms of whoever will extricate them from this nightmare.[9]

At the other extreme, the small wine-growers of the Midi moved away from the Radical Party precisely because of its inability to pursue a state interventionist program.[10] The winegrowers identified their interests with the reform demand that the state protect its citizens from the insecurity of the market. The *Midi rouge* that had endorsed the position of the most outspoken Radical reformers, such as Camille Pelletan,[11] shifted its electoral allegiance to the Socialist Party. School teachers who had been important supporters of the Radical left were also gravitating toward the Socialists during the crisis over their unionization. Radical politicians were in a contradictory position. They feared losing their petit bourgeois electoral base if they systematically supported social reform. At the same time, failure to pursue reforms energetically alienated those petit bourgeois elements of the Radical electorate who had most enthusiastically endorsed reform and the national reform leadership. By 1909 the mass of the party could no longer be expected to support reform as the means to create social peace. The unreliability of the Radical Party's shifting petit bourgeois constituents placed sharp limits on reform legislation.

Yet within the record of failure, limitations and delay there were important gains for social reform. Under the conditions of sustained working-class pressure at the workplace and in the Chamber, reformers were, at least until 1907, able to convince a sufficient number of their colleagues of the political necessity for social legislation. Universal male suffrage required some acknowledgement of the workers' situation. The laws which were passed—affecting occupational accidents, old age pensions, the length of the working day and week—as well as the expansion of the administrative apparatus to implement and enforce these laws, were real gains. Although legislation had a limited impact on actual working-class conditions, each law reinforced the concept that workers had a right to expect greater security, protection, regularity, and predictability in their workplace and homes. The pre- 1914 reforms established the legitimacy of state intervention in areas that had previously been regarded as private. The state acquired the responsibility to contain working-class insecurity as well as working-class militancy. A consensus began to emerge that the parliamentary regime could not tolerate the totally unrestricted impact of the market economy on enfranchised workers. Each new reform law strengthened the proposition that a national problem of the entire working class existed and could only be mitigated by legislation. Perhaps most important, the reformers linked the bourgeois ideal of security to the political vision of equality, thereby justifying legislative intervention in relations between workers and their employers. However, neither these principles nor the limited parliamentary gains of the reformers secured the goal of social peace.

The reformers—Radicals, independents, and academics—all identified the introduction of greater uniformity and order in workers' daily lives and in labor relations as a primary objective. They viewed this goal as the basis for class harmony and collaboration. As early as 1898, while discussing the accident compensation law, Paul Pic pointed to this larger aim:

> The intention of the legislature of 1898 was to institute a *general* system of protection capable of including *all* industrial accidents *without any distinctions* among large, medium-sized, or small industry.[12]

The reformers sought to convince their political colleagues and articulate groups within the bourgeoisie that the actual imposition of uniform standards on employers and workers was necessary to achieve social peace. This objective was much more difficult to accomplish than the political acknowledgment of working-class voters. In fact, it remained unfulfilled. To accept uniformity of standards would have been an admission that the social question was not only a problem of political stability and national unity, but one of actual class relations that the state could and had to affect.

In failing to gain broad acceptance of this principle, and in sometimes failing to articulate it clearly, the reformers compromised their own social program. Ultimately, neither the Radical Party nor the bourgeois voters accepted the view that social and political stability required a redefinition of economic security to include the working class. While reformers had gained several partial political victories prior to 1909, they were unable to enact and implement systematic policies to protect workers from the fluctuations of the industrial economy.

To some extent the reformers undermined their own position. Although they proposed new methods of national scope to limit social conflict, they nonetheless continued to endorse the basic assumptions espoused by their critics. All bourgeois parties in the reform debate acknowledged social peace as the overriding goal. The continued inviolability of personal property, the material foundation of the republican citizen, was central to that objective. These shared values strengthened those who opposed reform and their campaign to limit, restrict, and postpone social legislation. The critics of reform succeeded in demonstrating that social peace could be established by methods other than programmatic legislation. These critics were further able to claim that labor reform was expensive, controversial and, in fact, a threat to social peace.

Opponents of reform were strengthened by the economic divisions within the bourgeoisie. The different criticisms advanced by large and small employers, and their political representatives reinforced one another. Specific laws and proposals elicited quite different reactions from large and small capitalists. For example, large industry, in most instances, was relatively unconcerned with the legal imposition of the 1906 six-day workweek.[13] Retailers, on the other hand, led the concerted political battle to limit the law. The intense and nearly unanimous opposition of large industrialists to Millerand's proposal reorganizing labor relations in 1901 and again in 1906 swiftly ended discussion of reform in that area. Finally, once the courts had established that the 1910 old age pensions would be voluntary, large industrialists were quite willing to expand their existing programs in conformity with the law. Conversely, this judicial dismantling of obligatory pensions permitted many small entrepreneurs to ignore the program entirely. The cumulative effect of such varied opposition was to stymie and overwhelm the reform effort.[14]

By the turn of the century large industry had become a considerable economic and political force. Following the lead of the iron and steel manufacturers, many industrialists had organized associations to protect their immediate economic interests and to advance their more general social and political goals.[15] The *Progressistes*, while they did not speak exclusively for large industry, certainly expressed many of the industrialists' concerns. In certain regions, such as the economically dynamic Nord, the alliance between *Progressistes* and industrialists was extremely close. Eugène Motte represented the most obvious case of the convergence between industrialists and moderate republicans. Large capital, secure in its economic and political power, tended to express its preferences directly to those politicians and administrators who wrote and implemented the law. Large industry did not hide its opposition to certain reforms, nor did it shun public debates in the Chamber; but its objectives were more effectively achieved by bringing its influence to bear in the less politically charged atmosphere of committee rooms and administrative bureaus.[16]

Faced with the new assertiveness of the working class, industrialists anxiously sought methods to prevent, diminish, or control union and strike activity among their workers. Some employers were interested in improving relations between labor and capital. In many large enterprises, managerial logic encouraged the stabilization of industrial relations and the work force. However, during the entire prewar period large employers, with a few rare exceptions, remained confident that they could accomplish these improvements on their own. Neither the requirements of productive efficiency nor the pressure of the working class were so great as to compel large industrialists to accept state intervention as the only method capable of ensuring labor peace in their factories. They insisted that whatever ameliorations might be necessary the employers would voluntarily institute them, thus keeping their authority intact.[17]

An 1898 article in the *Revue politique et parlementaire* observed, "Only large industry ... with its enormous resources is capable of the correct reforms to ensure the improvement of all workers—the increase of salaries, insurance and mutual aid societies."[18] This program of social reform did not require the intervention of the state. It was the one which large employers might directly administer, reinforcing their control of the workplace. As late as the 1920s, Robert Pinot, still Secretary General of the Comité des Forges, continued to praise the fringe benefit programs provided by large industry as vastly superior to legal reforms. Private programs permitted industrialists to expand or contract benefits in relation to the success of the individual enterprise. "They are not imprisoned in the vise of a uniform and immutable legislative text."[19]

Rarely did the large industrialists deny the importance of reform. When faced with labor legislation, associations of large employers, like the Comité des Forges, pursued two aims: to prevent additional costs and to maintain the employers' authority.[20] In a 1905 debate, M. Louis Guérin, head of the linen cartel and the association of linen manufacturers, expressed the large industrialists' attitude toward labor legislation: "I am not an intransigent noninterventionist. . . . Social peace! We are one with you there, in this area we will accept everything which is acceptable. Only we ask you not to move too quickly."[21] "Acceptable" legislation had to leave the principle of *liberté de travail* intact.

"Acceptable" legislation from the industrialists' perspective also had to recognize the diversity and complexity of French manufacturing and commerce. The critics of legislated reform stressed the overriding necessity of the state's protecting *all* bourgeois interests. These critics insisted that no law could adequately accommodate the myriad differences that characterized employers, workers, and their relations with one another. Economic particularism was presented as a moral virtue to be defended against the impossible demands of an abstract uniformity imposed by the law. During an 1896 debate in the Chamber of Deputies, Hippolyte Boucher, Méline's Minister of Commerce, enunciated this particularist view, which would be repeated during every subsequent debate on social reform. "Each diverse aspect of the problem must be taken one by one and considered separately. If you view commerce in all its various branches as the same . . . you will waste your time and that of your inspectors."[22] Six years later the *Revue politique et parlementaire* criticized another reform project on the same principles. "The defect of these general laws is that they are applied to an entire industry whose operations are so varied."[23] Economic particularism emphasized the distinctions between small and large units of production, the diversity among enterprises in the same industrial sector and the uniqueness of each work site. These conditions were presented as making reform laws unacceptable and impossible to implement.

The most significant victory which the opponents of

reform secured was their ability to include the defense of such economic particularism in the text of every reform. Each law was couched in terms of compromise and qualification. Many laws gave more space to listing and explaining *dérogations* than to outlining new regulations. The administration and the courts amplified these exemptions and established cases of special consideration and delay. The inspection system always remained understaffed and underpaid.[24] The legislative history of every law and reform project involved a retreat from the principles of legal obligation and national uniformity. The law on accident compensation was stripped of obligatory insurance; the old age pension was transformed into a voluntary program; the limitation of the working day and week was burdened by innumerable exemptions;[25] the reform of industrial labor relations never left the Chamber's Committee on Labor. The opponents of reform could not halt the enactment of legislation, but they did impose on the reform laws the severe handicap of accommodation to economic particularism.

Employers, particularly those in large industry, and their political representatives accepted the existence of problems among workers. However, these could not be problems of a class, they argued, since differences of craft, region, and industry were so overwhelming. The solution of workers' insecurity could not be arranged uniformly at the national level. They might, however, be resolved within each enterprise under the auspices of the employers' authority.[26] In some instances this led to the rejection of laws creating uniformity, such as the six-day workweek. In other cases, laws establishing special categories of protected workers, such as the 1892 regulation of the working day for women and children, were condemned.[27] The implementation of all laws encountered the obstacle of economic particularism. The inspection system broke down when faced with the great variety of *petits ateliers* in which a large proportion of French workers were employed.[28] In all cases the aim of industrialists and moderate republican politicians was to ensure the employers' prerogatives over their own labor force. Each enterprise had to be preserved as entirely unique, autonomous, and comprehensible only to its owner. Economic particularism denied the existence of a cohesive working class and defended the diversity of interests within the bourgeoisie. In aiming to protect all employers' interests precisely because they were so varied, economic particularism reinforced the unity of the entire bourgeoisie.

The efforts of large industrialists on behalf of economic particularism and *liberté de travail* coincided with and supported the opposition of small employers. Small manufacturers and retailers formed the core of that elusive but important social category of the Third Republic, the petite bourgeoisie. Like large industrialists, small entrepreneurs were socially defined by the nature of their business activity. However, the ability of the petite bourgeoisie to limit social reform derived from the importance of their political and ideological position within French society. Small employers did organize to protect their economic interests. One example of such organization was the Comité Républicain du Commerce et de l'Industrie. Yet the significance even of this group depended on its affiliation with the Radicals. The Radical Party itself was perhaps the most important organization of the small employer. As we have noted, the changing attitude of the petite bourgeoisie toward reform influenced the party's retreat from its own social program in the years 1906–1910. Nonetheless, Radicalism did not attract or retain all small entrepreneurs. The vociferous Parisian *petits commerçants* had abandoned the Radicals by the turn of the century to support the nationalists.

Regardless of who their deputies were, the small entrepreneurs well understood and successfully deployed their considerable political clout. Georges Renard, a reform socialist, decried the political power of the petite bourgeoisie.

> Small property energetically defends its interests, demanding the protection of the State. . . . They are a political force. *The dominant ideas insist that all small [owners] must be given advantages.* . . . It is also a question of numbers, which play an important role in the elections. . . . The maintenance of the middle classes, even artificially, is viewed as the best method to block the progress of socialism.[29]

The opposition of the small employer to social reform was more complex than that of the large industrialist. On one level, small entrepreneurs simply claimed that they could not afford the expense required to provide the working class with stability and security. Whether these increased costs were direct, such as employers' contributions to workers' pensions, or indirect, in the form of shorter working hours, small manufacturers and retailers charged that the state was attempting to bankrupt them. However, small entrepreneurs actually organized a strong opposition to reforms only after 1905.

Until then many small employers had considered themselves members of a republican coalition in support of social reform. In 1900 the Comité Républicain du Commerce et de l'Industrie reviewed the most far-reaching reform of the period, Millerand's proposal for obligatory conciliation and arbitration. Although this organization of small employers was critical of Millerand's unorthodox scheme, they prefaced their remarks with an endorsement of the reform effort.

> It is appropriate that merchants and manufacturers, who are the most important element of the nation's wealth, should be an example of discipline and respect toward the French government by not rejecting *a priori* a government proposal. On the contrary, we should study it with the firm intention of *reconciling the ideas of individual liberty and social justice.*[30]

But by the time the *repos hebdomadaire* was enacted in 1906, a very different attitude toward reform guided the small entrepreneurs. Retailers were vehement in their denunciation of the compulsory six-day work week. This change was a reaction both to mounting activism of the working class and to the clarification of the social reform program. While the cost of legislated reforms became clearer and less acceptable to the *petit patronat*,[31] their opposition and its strength cannot simply be explained by economic rationality. Equaly pertinent was the concern among small employers that social reform represented a threat to *liberté de travail* and implicitly to the privileges of all property ownership.

This fear permeated the petite bourgeoisie and the bourgeoisie as a whole. The prerogatives of property ownership had to be defended as inviolable. In the case where a property owner was also an employer, the unencumbered use property meant that the employer would have full authority over the labor force. This central principle of the bourgeois social order, *liberté de travail*, required that labor relations continue to function as "private contracts." No "external" agent, neither the state nor a trade union, could interfere with the "individual" exchange between employer and worker. The enforcement of reforms, particularly those regulating working conditions and labor relations, did infringe on *liberté de travail*.

Reform was also feared as a threat to a bourgeois life style based on property. During a remarkable parliamentary interchange in June 1896, the Parisian nationalist deputy, Georges Berry, who represented the small *propriétaires*, voiced this deep concern. A bill had been introduced to extend the regulation of working hours to women and children employed in restaurants and cafés. Deputy Berry rose to denounce the reform:

> If you should arrive in Paris on the evening train and this train is unfortunate enough to get in after 8 P.M., you can forget about eating. Once in your hotel, will you be able to ask for some cold cuts to be brought in? No, you will not. Everything will be closed by 9 P.M., since the delivery boys aged thirteen to eighteen won't be able to work after that hour. These are the absurd consequences to which this law will lead. The same holds true for the small *patisseries*. It will be necessary with your law to dine in Paris as they do in Germany, at 4 or 5 P.M., because if you want an ice you won't be able to have one after 9 P.M.. You will force Paris to change its life style; you jeopardize its very existence.[32]

M. Berry certainly exaggerated the disruption of urban habits, but the daily life of the turn-of-the-century bourgeois did depend on a vast array of subordinate, underpaid workers employed in the commercial and service trades. M. Berry, speaking for Parisian retailers, captured the bourgeois fear that concessions to workers endangered the legitimate and hard-earned privileges of property owners. This sentiment was a powerful source of unity for the bourgeoisie. It provided cultural and ideological reinforcement to the more specific economic considerations of large and small employers.[33]

The views of the small employers were critical in formulating the general opposition to social reform. Small entrepreneurs were no more committed to limiting reform than large industrialists. However, the resistance of the *petit patronat* was weighted with crucial political and ideological implications. The votes of the petite bourgeoisie were key in the elections of the Third Republic. Their support was critical for the Radical Party. Furthermore, this stratum of the bour-geoisie embodied the republican ideals of citizenship and independence derived from personal property. This ideology was an important element in legitimating republicanism. The aim of social reform had been to confer on workers conditions that would parallel property ownership, thus permitting them to function fully as individuals and citizens. When these very reforms were perceived as endangering already established property rights and prerogatives, they could no longer be seriously pursued. The opposition of the small employers brought these contradictions into focus.

Although social reforms were enacted during the prewar period, the laws did not establish uniform labor conditions. Nor did they address the problems of the most vulnerable workers. The state did not in fact impose any major new expense on employers, and *liberté de travail* remained uni-versally respected. Large industrialists succeeded in keeping the state, whose reliability was suspect during episodes such as the Bloc des Gauches, outside the factory gates. Labor conditions and relations did change during the years 1890–1914, but changes resulted from the continuing intensification of the factory system and negotiations between employers and workers.[34] The state remained the enforcer of law and order based on the privileges of property, and not the initiator of an expanded version of security. The severe limitations placed on specific reform laws contributed significantly to weakening the entire reform effort.

Despite continued increases in the number of socialist voters and trade union members, the working class offensive began to recede in the years immediately before the war. The French working class was a divided and far-from-fully-organized political and social force. The majority of workers rejected any formal organizational allegiance. The variety of competing working-class organizations further constrained the effectiveness of the workers' militancy and independence. Under these conditions, the repressive measures of the state against revolutionary syndicalism, which Clemenceau had initiated and which small property owners increasingly en-dorsed, succeeded.[35] The dynamism of working-class assert-iveness was significantly reduced after 1909.

The mounting hositility of the republican state to working-class activism reinforced the industrialists' intransigence on the questions of authority and *liberté de travail*.[36] By 1914 large industry could claim a remarkable political accomplishment. It had resisted the parallel developments of working-class assertiveness and republican social reform, which had seemed so powerful in 1902. Instead employers had reaffirmed their political influence in the administration and the parliament.

The "social question" had emerged as the result of two related but independent developments—the expansion of representative institutions and the growth of industrial capitalism. Universal male suffrage and the factory system placed male workers at the center of politics and the economy. However, their position in these two structures was quite different, if not contradictory. The ideology of parliamentarianism increasingly endorsed the political equality of all citizens. Yet the factory imposed rigid hierarchy and authority in which the workers' autonomy was steadily reduced. This contradiction was particularly acute in pre-World War I France. The asymmetry of the political and economic structures was even more apparent because both parliamentarianism and industrial capitalism came to dominate politics and the economy simultaneously during the first half of the Third Republic. Furthermore, French republicanism, with its egalitarian tradition, played an especially important role in legitimizing the state and supporting national unity. Industrialization, on the other hand, was concentrated regionally. It was associated with older paternalist ideologies, and coexisted with small-scale manufacturing and commerce. In this particular configuration, a working class with an extremely militant minority developed, while a new republican political elite, strongly committed to preserving the regime, was gaining ascendancy.

In the prewar era the resolution of the "social question," an issue generated by industrial capitalism, became linked to the viability of the democratic state. However, systematic labor legislation encountered several serious obstacles in the Third Republic. First, the reformers' own commitment to social peace brought them into agreement with their opponents. Reformers and their critics shared ultimate objectives and the assumption that property, in one form or another, was the indispensable means to individual security and therefore to social stability. Reform politicians always retreated when critics claimed that legislation threatened that stability. Secondly, the opponents of social reform argued from the undeniable reality of a highly diversified economy. Employers' demands for special consideration were supported by the actual difficulties of imposing national uniformity on an economy not yet fully industrialized. Finally, while the diversity within the bourgeoisie strengthened its opposition to reform, the diversity within the working class made it vulnerable to attacks from both employers and the state. The assertiveness of the working class, which had created the political debate on social reform, was not able to withstand the repressive strategy of the government and the new aggressiveness of employers. Selective repression proved a more efficient, less divisive, and less costly method of dealing with working-class militancy and open class conflict.

The resilience of the opposition to social legislation was based on the economic diversity of the bourgeoisie and on its social ideology, which linked individualism, liberty, property, and authority. Ultimately, social peace was equated with the defense of particular interests and of these principles, not with the politicians' efforts to tie the working class more closely to the Republic. The employers were adamant in their opposition to regulation. Eugène Schneider, owner of France's largest metal works, Le Creusot, expressed their intransigent rejection of any modification of labor relations. His condescending condemnation of state intervention in 1897 exemplified the position of all employers throughout the pre-World War I period.

> I never allow a prefect to become involved in strikes. It's the same with any labor regulation, whether of women or children. Useless, restrictive obstacles are placed on those who are supposed to be protected. In the end, employers are discouraged from hiring them. . . . The eight-hour day? Sure I'd like it. . . . But salaries will be reduced or the cost of living will increase. . . . Don't you see the eight-hour day is a foolish obsession [*un dada*]. . . . *The worker should be left alone to work as long as he wishes; that's his choice.*[37]

Economic diversity reinforced the opposition to state intervention and impeded its application. Reforms appeared to threaten the privileges of property owners as much as did class conflict. Social reform proposals were promoted as inescapable state policies to ensure social peace, and, at the same time, were successfully blocked as a threat to social stability.

The development of the reform program in France, and its limitations, while shaped by the specific political and economic structures of the Third Republic, were part of a larger trend. The issue of reform prior to 1914, as well as the obstacles it encountered, were political phenomena of all industrial states.[38] All parliamentary regimes had been significantly strained by the emergence of an organized working class. The efforts at programmatic social reform in this period were one response to the new political reality. However, immediately before the war, the alternate strategy of repression, which was less expensive and less disruptive to the industrial order, gained broader endorsement. Within the bourgeoisie and among political elites, repression appeared to be the best defense against working-class political and economic demands and the best support for social peace. In all industrial parliamentary states incipient reform alliances were no longer able to function by 1914, or had been shattered. The implementation of reform was everywhere constrained, and further enactment of legislation was halted.

The "social question" remains a persistent and recurring issue with ever-greater consequences for regimes where economic and class realities contradict the assumptions of political democracy. From this perspective the French reformers in the prewar decades did make some real advances. They irrefutably identified the "social question" as a central political issue. The problems of insecurity in the labor market and the inequality of labor relations were placed high on the domestic political agenda. Secondly, the limited legislation which was enacted provided a framework for later more far-reaching social policies. Most important, reformers linked the bourgeois ideal of security based on property to the republican vision of equality, in an effort to justify state intervention. This last accomplishment suggests how audacious the pre-World War I reform effort was in France and in other industrial parliamentary states. The proposition that a representative government cannot permit the working class, or any significant sector of the working class, to exist in conditions of material insecurity has never been entirely accepted. Today in the late 20th century we still continue to debate the extent of economic insecurity that the electorate will tolerate.

Notes

INTRODUCTION

1. Henri Hatzfeld, *Du Pauperisme à la sécurité sociale. Essai sur les origines de la securité sociale en France, 1850–1940* (Paris: Armand Colin, 1971), p. 31. All quotations are my translations, unless otherwise indicated.

2. The debate has been especially intense in Great Britain and the United States. Two examples of the literature in this area are James O'Connor, *The Fiscal Crisis of the State* (New York: St. Martin's Press, 1973) and Frances Fox Piven and Richard A. Cloward, *The New Class War: Reagan's Attack on the Welfare State and Its Consequences* (New York: Pantheon, 1982).

3. Jacques Julliard, *Clemenceau, briseur des grèves. L'Affaire Draveil-Villeneuve-St. Georges, 1908*(Paris: Collections Archives, 1965), pp. 57–8. Michael Hanagan, *The Logic of Solidarity: Artisans and Industrial Workers in Three French Towns, 1871–1914* (Urbana, Ill.: University of Illinois Press, 1980), p. 32.

4. Bernard Moss, *The Origins of the French Labor Movement, 1830–1914: The Socialism of Skilled Workers* (Berkeley and Los Angeles: University of California Press, 1976), p. 101.

5. Michelle Perrot, *Les Ouvriers en grève, France, 1871–1890* (Paris: Mouton, 1974), p. 31.

6. Leslie Derfler, *Alexandre Millerand: The Socialist Years* (The Hague: Mouton, 1977), p. 232.

7. Serge Bernstein, *Histoire du parti radical. La Recherche de l'âge d'or, 1919–1926* (Paris: Presses de la Fondation Nationale des Sciences Politiques, 1980). This is one of the most recent and best studies of the Radical party.

8. *Dictionnaire de la Troisième République*, Pierre Pierrard, ed. (Paris: Larousse, 1968), p. 208.

9. Theodore Zeldin, *France, 1848–1945: Politics and Anger* (New York: Oxford University Press, 1973), pp. 334-35, 351.

10. Madeleine Rebérioux, *La République Radicale? 1898–1914* (Paris: Editions du Seuil, 1975), pp. 49-56, 59-65.

11. Ibid., pp. 106–17.

12. J.E.S. Hayward, "Solidarity: The Social History of an Idea in Nineteenth Century France," *International Review of Social History, 4 (1959)*, 261–84; "Solidarist Syndicalism: Durkheim and Duguit," pts. 1 and 2, *Sociology Review* (July and December 1960), 17–33, 185–200; "The Official Social Philosophy of the French Third Republic: Léon Bourgeois and Solidarity," *International Review of Social History*, 6 (1961), 19–48; "Educational Pressure Groups and the Indoctrination of the Radical Ideology of Solidarity, 1895–1914," *International Review of Social History*, 8 (1963), 1-17.

13. Hayward, "The Official Philosophy of the French Third Republic," p. 19.

14. Zeldin, pp. 293–96.

15. Sanford Elwitt, *The Making of the Third Republic: Class and Politics in France, 1868–1884* (Baton Rouge: Louisiana State University Press, 1975).

16. Ibid., p. 150.

17. Ibid., p. x.

18. Ibid., p. 259.

19. Ibid., p. 229.

20. Terry Nicholas Clark, *Prophets and Patrons: The French University and the Emergence of the Social Sciences* (Cambridge, Mass.: Harvard University Press, 1973); Robert J. Smith, *The Ecole Normale Supérieure and the Third Republic* (Albany, N.Y.: State University of New York Press, 1982); Katherine Auspitz, *The Radical Bourgeoisie: The Ligue de l'Enseignement and the Origins of the Third Republic, 1866–1885* (Cambridge, Mass.: Harvard University Press, 1982), George Weisz, *The Emergence of Modern Universities in France, 1863–1914* (Princeton, N.J.: Princeton University Press, 1983).

21. Leo Loubère, *Radicalism in Mediterranean France: Its Rise and Decline, 1848–1914* (Albany, N.Y.: State University of New York Press, 1974); "The French Left-Wing Radicals and Their Views on Trade Unionism, 1870–1898," *International Review of Social History*, 7 (1962), 203–30; "Left-Wing Radicals, Strikes and the Military, 1880–1907, *"French Historical Studies* 3, (1963–1964), 93–105; "Les Radicaux

d'extrême-gauche en France et les raports entre patrons et ouvriers, 1871–1900," *Revue d'histoire économique et social*, 62 (1964), 89–103.

22. Loubère, *Radicalism in Mediterranean France*, pp. 188–90.

23. Ibid., pp. 148–51.

24. Charles W. Pipkin, *Social Politics and Modern Democracy*, 2 vols. (New York: Macmillan, 1931).

25. Perrot, pp. 69–70.

CHAPTER 1

1. Strike Rate in Western Europe, 1899–1913 (1899 = 100)

Strikes	*1899*	*1902*	*1904*	*1906*	*1907*	*1908*	*1910*	*1911*	*1912*	*1913*
France	100	74	119	176	151	129	172	171	139	129
Germany	100	82	145	258	176	105	164	199	195	165
Strikers										
Britain	100	85	41	114	73	162	279	602	893	374
France	100	114	113	279	110	49	163	112	134	118
Germany	100	53	112	286	189	67	153	214	400	250

Source: Peter N. Stearns, *Lives of Labor: Work in a Maturing Industrial Society* (New York: Holmes & Meier, 1975), p. 314.

Strikes in the United States, 1895–1905

	Number of Strikes	*Number of Strikers (1000s)*
1895	1,255	407
1900	1,839	568
1902	3,240	692
1903	3,648	788
1904	2,419	574
1905	2,186	302

Source: Tables D 973 and D 981 in U.S. Department of Commerce, Bureau of the Census, *Historical Statistics of the U.S.: Colonial Times to 1970*, pt. 1 (Washington, D.C.: U.S. Government Printing Office, 1975), p. 179.

Statistics were collected by the Commissioner of Labor only to 1905. No U.S. government agency collected figures for the years 1906–1913.

2. The intensity of French revolutionary syndicalism is successfully captured in Jacques Julliard's analysis of the 1908 construction workers' strike and the violent confrontation with the government at Draveil. Note particularly a workers' description of the events. *Clemenceau, briseur des grèves. L'Affaire de Draveil-Villeneuve-St. Georges* (Paris: Collection Archives, 1965), pp. 197–200 and *passim*. For a further analysis of French workers and revolutionary syndicalism, see Bernard H. Moss, *The Origins of the French Labor Movement, 1830–1914: The Socialism of Skilled Workers* (Berkeley and Los Angeles: University of California Press, 1976) and Michael P. Hanagan, *The Logic of Solidarity: Artisans and Industrial Workers in Three French Towns, 1871–1914* (Urbana, Ill.: University of Illinois Press, 1980).

3. Eric Hobsbawm's essay on "General Labour Unions in Britain, 1889–1914" relates the growth of militant industrial unionism, particularly among dockers to a broad international reorganization of trade unions, labor, and socialist parties following the Great Depression of 1873–1896 in *Labouring Men: Studies in the History of Labor* (New York: Basic Books, 1964), pp. 211–39.

4. Klaus Saul, "Staatsintervention und Arbeitskampf im Wilhelminischen Reich 1904–14," in *Sozialgeschichte Heute: Festschrift für Hans Rosenberg zum 70 Geburtstag*, Hans Ulrich Wehler, ed. (Göttingen: Vandenhoeck & Ruprecht, 1974), pp. 479–94. From 1895 on, this mounting strike activity confronted an Imperial German government which was emphasizing the repressive aspects of its social policy. Kenneth D. Barkin, *The Controversy over German Industrialization, 1890–1902* (Chicago: University of Chicago Press, 1970), pp. 184, 275, and passim.

5. This strike was led by the Western Federation of Miners, which functioned for a few years as the core of the Industrial Workers of the World whose revolutionary syndicalism paralleled that of several French unions. Melvyn Dubofsky, *We Shall Be All: A History of the Industrial Workers of the World* (Chicago: Quadrangle, 1969), pp. 38–56, and *Industrialism and the American Worker, 1865–1920* (Arlington Heights, Ill.: Harlan Davidson, 1975), p. 107 and ch. 1 and 3 for an excellent survey of the period and its historiography.

6. Alexandre Millerand, "Préface," in Jules Huret, *Les Grèves* (Paris: Editions de la Revue Blanche, n.d.), p. 2.

7. The statement was made by Ferdinand Buisson, reform educator and Radical, in *La Politique radicale. Etude sur les doctrines du parti radical et radical-socialiste* (Paris: Girard & Brière, 1908), p. 218. In the same passage, Buisson also cited the earlier, more pointed observation of de Tocqueville; "It is a contradiction that the people

should be both miserable and sovereign." Similar opinions were expressed by the liberal social historian, Emile Levasseur, *Questions ouvrières et industrielles en France sous la Troisième République* (Paris: Arthur Rousseau, 1907), p. 518, and by the more conservative Catholic sociologist, Emile Cheysson, *La Famille, l'association et l'état* (Paris: Musée Social, 1904), p. 4.

8. These views were expressed by an anonymous Roubaix textile manufacturer, quoted in Jules Huret, *Enquête sur la question sociale en Europe* (Paris: Perrin, 1897), p. 89, and a statement by a high-level manager at the Creusot Metal Works in a 1901 interview series by the same reporter, Jules Huret, in *Les Grèves* (Paris: Edition de la Revue Blanche, n.d.), p. 80. In the same interviews, an industrialist sympathetic to worker demands, M. Japy, an elevator manufacturer, declared that "French workers were slow and lazy." Ibid., p. 125. For a more general analysis of this French patronal attitude, see Jean Lambert, *Le Patron: De l'Avènement à la contestation* (Brussels: Bloud Gay, 1969), p. 89 and *passim*.

9. The earlier bourgeois search for order and control is analyzed in Louis Chevalier, *Classes laborieuses et classes dangereuses à Paris pendant la première moitié du 19e siècle* (Paris: Plon, 1958).

10. The most important of these organizations was the Association Internationale pour la Protection Légale des Travailleurs, founded in 1900 at the Paris Exposition. The German reform academics and administrators were strong supporters from the beginning, joined very quickly by the French. The British and the Americans affiliated in 1906. The organization, in the postwar period, became the core of the International Labor Office attached to the League of Nations. See Chapter 2 for a fuller discussion of its origins and functions.

11. H. Stuart Hughes, *Consciousness and Society: The Reorientation of European Social Thought, 1890–1930* (New York: Random House, 1958), pp. 42–51. Hughes' study identifies for us the generation of intellectuals in the immediate pre-World War I decades as crucial innovators in social thought who contributed to the "emerging critical consciousness of the twentieth century," pp. 9–14.

12. Joseph Schumpeter, *History of Economic Analysis*, Elizabeth Boody Schumpeter, ed. (New York: Oxford University Press, 1954), pp. 811–12.

13. Hughes, p. 294.

14. Ibid., pp. 294–95.

15. The German historical school had a direct influence on

Charles Booth, whose monumental study of poverty, *Life and Labour of the People of London* first appeared in 1891. Through Booth, the German sociologists and historical economists also influenced the Webbs and the entire Fabian group. Bentley B. Gilbert. *The Evolution of National Insurance in Great Britain: The Origins of the Welfare State* (London: Michael Joseph, 1966), pp. 45–56. A.M. McBriar, *Fabian Socialists and English Politics, 1884–1918* (Cambridge: Cambridge University Press, 1966), pp. 50–51, 54–55. For the United States, see the broad connections implied in Eric F. Goldman, *Rendezvous with Destiny: History of Modern American Reform* (New York: Knopf, 1952) and Robert Wiebe, *The Search for Order, 1877–1920* (New York: Hill & Wang, 1967).

16. An important French economist and promoter of social reform claimed that all those supporting state intervention in France had been influenced by the German historical school, which viewed the state as the expression of general rather than particular interests. Paul Pic, *Traité élémentaire de législation industrielle. Les Lois ouvrières*, 2nd ed. (Paris: Arthur Rousseau, 1903), pp. 29–33. For specific French economists and sociologists influenced by the German theories, see Chapter 2.

17. It is paradoxical that the German state and German politicians and academics were the most active in the International Association for Labor legislation in the prewar period, while German labor legislation encountered the greatest obstacles. The International Association was largely financed by German government subsidies and its largest membership was the German section. Etienne Bauer, *Rapport présentée au Congrès mondial de l'Association internationale pour la protection légale des travailleurs. Origines, organisations, oeuvre realisée, documents.* (Brussels: 1910).

18. The first two insurance measures included no state contributions, and accident insurance was entirely controlled by the employers. The passage of the old age pension took another five years precisely because a state contribution was included and because the coverage was extended to agricultural workers and servants. Hajo Holborn, *A History of Modern Germany, 1840–1945* (New York: Knopf, 1969), p. 291.

19. Elie Halévy, *Imperialism and the Rise of Labour, 1895–1905*, E. I. Watkin, trans. (New York: Barnes & Noble, 1961), p. 227. Halévy, of course, exaggerated.

20. Quoted in Gaston V. Rimlinger, "Welfare and Economic Development: A Comparative Historical Perspective," *Journal of Economic History* 26 (December 1966), 566.

21. One example of this correspondence between repression and reform was the 1901 Taff-Vale decision in Great Britain. This judicial attempt to destroy British trade unionism took place in the midst of the Conservatives' effort to woo the workers and only five years before the great reform victories of the Liberals. Halévy, pp. 257–73.

22. Holborn, pp. 291–92. Even more important, Bismarck had come to reject the reform element of his own antisocialist policy. By 1889 Bismarck was interested in pursuing an exclusively repressive program. J. Alden Nichols, *Germany after Bismarck: The Caprivi Era, 1890–1894* (Cambridge, Mass.: Harvard University Press, 1958), p. 18.

23. V. R. Berghahn, *Germany and the Approach of War in 1914* (New York: St. Martin's, 1973), p. 3, 11–13, 22–25.

24. The massive Social Democratic Party remained effectively isolated in the Reichstag. The German left Liberals whose social base had some parallels with French Radicals, British Liberals, and American Progressives, remained a small, weak political force, terrified of any contact with the S.P.D.

25. Robert Weibe describes the emergence of a new middle class in the Progressive era which was eager for new political strategies. The components of this class have some interesting similarities with supporters of reform legislation in France. What is particularly noteworthy is the role of professionals, state employees, and academics. *The Search for Order, 1877–1920*, pp. 112–13 and passim.

26. The Liberal government, with Lloyd George as Chancellor of the Exchequer, had presented a budget in 1909 which shifted the tax burden from indirect to direct taxes, expanding the amount of revenue from the already established income tax. The "People's Budget," as it was called, was an effort to extract greater revenues from the wealthy by increasing the fixed proportion of taxes on higher incomes, increasing inheritance taxes, and introducing a tax on undeveloped land and a surtax on all incomes above £5,000. It was this budget that created the confrontation between the Liberals and the House of Lords. Unlike the somewhat parallel constitutional crisis between Léon Bourgeois and the French Senate in 1896, the British reformers won their battle against the upper house and established new state revenues to finance social insurance programs and a policy of military build-up. Elie Halévy. *The Rule of Democracy, 1905–1914*, E. I. Watkin, trans., (1948; reprint. N.Y.: Barnes & Noble, 1961), p. 266, and George Dangerfield, *The Strange Death of Liberal England, 1910–1914* (1935; reprint. N.Y.: Capricorn, 1961), pp. 19–24.

27. Political sensitivity to the working class vote, which had been granted in 1867 and 1884, was already clear in the 1890s when both Conservatives and Liberals were courting workers. In 1894, the two parties agreed to relax the most punitive aspects of the early nineteenth-century Poor Laws. Charles W. Pipkin, *Social Politics and Modern Democracy*, 1 (New York: Macmillan, 1931), p. 372.

28. While there continues to be a debate on the objectives of Progressive reform in the U.S., there is agreement that this period was critical in creating modern twentieth-century government and policies. See George E. Mowry, ed., *The Progressive Era, 1900–1918: Recent Literature and New Ideas*, 2nd ed. (Washington, D.C.: American Historical Association, 1964); James Weinstein, *The Corporate Ideal in the Liberal State, 1900–1918* (Boston: Beacon, 1968), p. 253 and passim.; Gabriel Kolko, *The Triumph of Conservatism: A Reinterpretation of American History, 1900–1966* (New York: Free Press, 1963), pp. 270–80.

29. Kolko, pp. 284–86.

30. Dubofsky, *We Shall Be All,* p. 103.

31. Gilbert, pp. 447, 452.

32. The most important was the 1847 Factory Act, which established a ten-hour day for women and young workers in industry.

33. Sanford Elwitt, *The Making of the Third Republic: Class and Politics in France, 1868–1884* (Baton Rouge: Louisiana State University Press, 1975), pp. 183–97.

34. These laws were passed between 1879 and 1886. Several of the educational reformers, Ferdinand Buisson for one, were active in the campaign for social insurance and labor legislation in the next two decades. Jean-Marie Mayeur, *Les Débuts de la IIIe République, 1871–1898* (Paris: Editions du Seuil, 1973), pp. 11–19, 105–7, and Theodore Zeldin, *France, 1848–1945: Politics and Anger* (New York: Oxford University Press, 1973), pp. 262–63.

35. "La Marseillaise" became the official anthem of the Republic in February 1879, and the 14th of July the national holiday in 1880.

36. The *scrutin d'arrondissement* was reinstituted in 1889 by the Radicals and moderate republicans to block the electoral strategy of General Boulanger. Under the *scrutin d'arrondissement* votes were cast for individual candidates who represented the *arrondissement*, the smallest administrative division. This system replaced the larger electoral district of the department, where votes had been cast for a

programmatic list of candidates. Radical politicians soon became adept at using the *scrutin d'arrondissement* to their advantage and it came to serve as an important institutional base for Radical political power. After 1910 the majority of the Radical Party defended this system against the demands of Socialists and conservatives for electoral reform. Zeldin, pp. 210–13.

37. Pierre Sorlin, *La Société française, 1840–1914*, 1 (Paris: Arthaud, 1969), pp. 40–41.

38. Although the original structural conservatism of the Senate imposed by the monarchists in 1875 had been somewhat reformed in 1884, the Senate still remained socially and economically more conservative than the Chamber. More republicans were senators after 1884, but they were primarily moderate republicans with a strong commitment to classic liberalism in labor relations. For an overview of the functions of the Senate, see Mayeur, pp. 34–35.

39. Elwitt, pp. 146–49 and passim.

40. Tihomir J. Markovitch, "The Dominant Sectors of French Industry," and François Crouzet, "Annual Index of Nineteeth-century French Industrial Production," in *Essays in French Economic History*, Rondo Cameron, ed. (Homewood, Ill.: Irwin, 1970), pp. 226–44, 245–78.

41. A quintal which had sold for 30 francs in 1860 was worth 19.5 francs in 1892. Sorlin, pp. 50–58.

42. Mayeur, pp. 82–83.

43. Sorlin, pp. 54–55.

44. The total rural population was even higher. In 1876, 67.5% of all French men and women lived in the countryside. In 1896, the total rural population had fallen only slightly, to 61%. In 1891, 45.5% of the French population was engaged in agricultural production. Mayeur, p. 73.

45. However, the contrast with Imperial Germany and the United States was much less extreme. In 1900, 35% of the active German population and 38% of the U.S. population were engaged in agriculture. Carlo Cipolla, *The Economic History of World Population* (Baltimire: Penguin, 1962), p. 28.

46. In Germany it constituted only 20% of the gross national income. Furthermore, land tenure and modes of exploitation differed greatly among all the nations. Arno Mayer, *The Persistence of the Old Regime* (New York: Pantheon, 1981), p. 24.

47. Peter Stearns has characterized turn-of-the century France as

"a country with an unusually widespread and efficient domestic manufacturing system, paternalistic factories, and a high dependence on labor control." *Paths to Authority: The Middle Class and the Industrial Labor Force in France, 1820–1848* (Urbana: University of Illinois Press, 1978), p. 107. For a discussion of the resistance to industrialization and the factory system, see Pierre Léon, "Le Moteur de l'industrialisation. L'enterprise industrielle," in *Histoire économique et sociale de la France; L'Avenement de l'ère industrielle, 1789–années 1880*, E. Labrousse et F. Braudel, eds., 3 (Paris: Presses Universitaires Françaises, 1979), p. 519.

48. For the general increase in metallurgy, see Sorlin, p. 163, and for a description of the Nord, see Pierre Léon, "Les nouvelles répartitions," in *Histoire économique et sociale de la France*, 3, pp. 563, 579.

49. Markovitch, p. 243, identifies the overall growth rate during the period 1885 to 1914 as averaging 2% annually, a steady, if unspectacular, rate. This compares favorably to the 1.6% annual growth rate of the period 1875–1894, and to the period 1905–1924, with its 1.3% growth rate.

50. However, this source, François Crouzet, assigns as slower average rate to the last decades of the nineteenth century, 1.46% annually. "Annual Index of Nineteenth-century French Industrial Production," in Cameron, p. 274.

51. Ibid. For a somewhat less dynamic portrait of the French economy, see Richard F. Kuisel, *Capitalism and the State in Modern France: Renovation and Economic Management in the Twentieth Century* (New York: Cambridge University Press, 1981), pp. 26–28.

52. Comparative industrial production 1900–1904:

	COAL (millions of tons)	STEEL (millions of tons)	TEXTILES (millions of spindles)
France	31.8	1.7	5.9
Germany	110.7	7.3	8.5
Great Britain	226.8	4.9	46.4
United States	—	16.4 (1902)	—

Source: For France, Germany, and Great Britain, Michel Branciard, *La Société française et les luttes de classe, 1789–1914*, 1 (Lyon: Chroniques sociales de France, 1967), pp. 165, 216. For U.S., Department of Commerce, Bureau of the Census, *Historical Statistics of the U.S.*, part 2, p. 689.

53. Cited in Henry Vouters, *Le Petit Commerce contre les grands magasins et les cooperatives de consommation* (Paris: Arthur Rousseau, 1910), p. 12.

54. Mayer, pp. 38–39.

55. Vouters, p. 12.

56. Cited in Henry Peiter, "Institutions and Attitudes: The Consolidation of the Business Community in Bourgeois France, 1880–1914," *The Journal of Social History*, 9, No. 4 (1976), 511.

57. Sorlin, p. 185. The long-term increase in real wages, as well as the fluctuations within this trend, was an international phenomenon, explaining in part the general trend of working-class activism and the movements for reform. Shepard B. Clough and Charles Cole, *The Economic History of Europe*, 3rd ed. (Boston: Heath, 1952), p. 667.

58. A twelve-hour day was also the norm in the Creuzot Metal Works. Interview with chief foreman in Huret, *Enquête sur la question sociale en Europe*, p. 16.

59. Branciard, p. 136.

60. Jean Bouvier, *Histoire économique et histoire sociale. Recherches sur le capitalisme contemporain* (Geneva: Droz, 1968), pp. 40–41.

61. Bouvier, p. 49.

62. Joan Scott, *The Glassworkers of Carmaux* (Cambridge, Mass.: Harvard University Press, 1974.)

63. Jolyon Howorth, *Edouard Vaillant. La Création de l'unité socialiste en France* (Paris: Syros, 1982).

64. Claude Willard, *Le Mouvement socialist en France. Les Guesdists, 1893–1905* (Paris: Editions Sociales, 1965), pp. 56, 69, 74, 84–90.

65. Quoted in Moss, p. 101.

66. Peiter, p. 511.

67. The Comité had been originally established in 1864, but was significantly reorganized by Robert Pinot in 1904. Pinot was a sociologist trained in the conservative Le Playist school. For Pinot's views on the social responsibilities of the employer, see his *Comité des forges. Les Oeuvres sociales des industries métallurgiques* (Paris: Armand Colin, 1924), and his biography, André François-Poncet, *La Vie et l'oeuvre de Robert Pinot* (Paris: Armand Colin, 1927), pp. 23, 62.

68. The most thorough work on the Comité, with a long and detailed chapter on its lobbying activity, is Michael Jared Rust,

"Business and Politics in the Third Republic: The *Comité des forges* and the French Steel Industry, 1896–1914," Ph.D. dissertation, Princeton University, 1973.

69. Motte was reelected in 1902, defeating Guesde for a second time. In 1906 he chose not to run, thereby avoiding being swept away in the Radical and Socialist victory in which Guesde regained his seat. The Mottes are a good example of family-owned large industry. In 1901, the family had twelve factories employing 7,000 workers. The group of large industrialists who sat in the Chamber of Deputies also included Eugène Schneider, whose family had always held political office.

70. Herman Lebovics, "Protection against Labor Troubles: The Case of the Méline Tariff," unpublished paper (Stony Brook, N.Y.: xerox typeprint).

71. Frédéric Le Paly (1806–1882) published his empirical study, *Ouvriers européens*, in 1855. His major contribution to the discipline of sociology was to stress monographic research over general theory.

72. This was written in 1904 by an opponent of state intervention and a regular columnist for the *Revue de l'économie politique*, Edouard Villey. "La Desagrégation sociale et la lutte des classes," *Revue de l'économie politique*, 18 (1904), 451.

73. Ibid.

74. Huret, *Enquête sur la question sociale en Europe*, pp. 24–34; A. R. Vidler, *A Century of Social Catholicism, 1820–1920* (London: Society for Promoting Christian Knowledge, 1964), p. 124; Adrien Dansette, *Religious History of France*, 2, John Dingle, trans., (Freiburg: Herder, 1961), p. 114.

75. For example the political and social activities of some Christian Democratic *abées* were condemned in 1901 by a new pope, Leo XII, in an encyclical, *Graves de Communi*. See also John McManners, *Church and State in France, 1870–1914* (New York: Harper & Row, 1972), p. 88.

76. Adeline Daumard, *Les Bourgeois de Paris au 19e siècle* (Paris: Flammarion, 1970), p. 348.

77. Madeleine Rebérioux, *La République radicale? 1898–1914* (Paris: Editions du Seuil, 1975), pp. 220–22.

78. Gustave Flaubert, *Madame Bovary*, 1856.

79. D. R. Watson, "The Nationalist Movement in Paris, 1900–1906," in *The Right in France, 1890–1919. Three Studies*, David Shapiro,

ed. (Carbondale, Ill.: Southern Illinois University Press, 1962), pp. 49–84.

80. As early as 1886, a Ligue Syndicale pour la Défense du Petit Commerce was formed. In 1906, a Paris-based national organization of retailers was established, La Féderation de Détaillantes. Conservative sociologists of the Le Play tradition found readers for their monographs on the *classes moyennes*. Titles included: Victor Brants, *Le Petite Industrie contemporaine* (Paris: Bibliothèque d'economie sociale: 1902), Henry Vouters, *Le Petit Commerce contre les grands magasins et les cooperatives de consommation* (Paris: 1910), Emile Noyer, *Les Sacrifices. Essai d'étude sociale sur la situation de la classe moyenne en France au commencement du XXe siècle* (Paris: Imprimerie de Langy, 1909). Representatives of the French and German petite bourgeoisie met in international congresses in 1905, 1908, and 1911, under the auspices of more powerful bourgeois ideologues of the Institut International pour l'Étude du Probleme des Classes Moyennes.

81. Emile Zola, *L'Assomoir*, L. Tancock, trans., 1876, p. 379. The novel also opens with a precise inventory of the lack of property. "Their trunk stood in the corner wide open, with nothing in it except an old hat of his, right at the bottom, under some shirts and dirty socks, while hanging over the backs of the chairs around the room were a shawl with holes in it, a mud-stained pair of trousers, in fact the last remaining garments the old clothes dealer wouldn't take. In the middle of the mantlepiece, between two odd zinc candlesticks, was a bundle of rose-pink pawn tickets" p. 23.

82. Pierre Sorlin, *Waldeck-Rousseau* (Paris: Armand Colin, 1966), pp. 272–73.

83. René Waldeck-Rousseau, *Action républicaine et sociale* (Paris: Charpentier, 1903), p. 194. For further discussion of the success and limits of the *mutualité* movement, see Zeldin, pp. 296–301. This has a very useful description of the mutual aid societies, although it does overstate the identification between *solidaristes* and *mutualists*.

84. Alexandre Millerand, *Le Socialisme réformiste français* (Paris: Société Nouvelle de Librairie et d'Édition, 1903), p. 117.

CHAPTER 2

1. Paul Pic, professor of labor legislation at Lyons and a consistent interventionist, identified *solidarisme* as a component of the general interventionist trend. *Traité élémentaire de législation industrielle.*

Les Lois ouvrières. 2nd ed (Paris: Arthur Rousseau, 1903), p. 48. The interrelation of *solidaristes* and interventionists was also confirmed by a liberal critic of both schools: Emile Levasseur, *Questions ouvrières et industrielles en France sous la Troisième République* (Paris: Arthur Rousseau, 1907), pp. 230–1. The development of the reform politics of such academics as Ferdinand Buisson and Célestin Bouglé demonstrated the ease with which the transition from *solidarisme* to state intervention could be made.

2. For the strength of liberal ideology and its hold on state policy in the pre-World War I decades, see the opening chapter of Richard F. Kuisel's important study, *Capitalism and the State in Modern France: Renovation and Economic Management in the Twentieth Century* (New York: Cambridge University Press, 1981), especially pp. 3–15.

3. Levasseur, p. 432.

4. Pic, p. 5.

5. Immediately after the experience of the all-Radical cabinet, Bourgeois was slightly less prominent. He refused to form a government when asked in 1899 and 1902. In 1905 he was elected to the more sedate Senate. He continued, nevertheless, to hold ministerial posts in several governments. His importance in the politics of the Third Republic was undiminished. His central role in the formation of the Radical Party will be discussed in Chapter 4. Beginning in 1899, Bourgeois' commitment to the arbitration of disputes drew him to international diplomacy. He was the French representative to the Hague Peace Conference before World War I and a leading French advocate of the League of Nations after the war. Maurice Hamburger, *Léon Bourgeois. La Politique radicale-socialiste, la doctrine de la solidarité, l'arbitrage internationale et la Société des Nations* (Paris: Marcel Rivière, 1932), pp. 15–21, and *Dictionnaire de biographies français*, 6 (Paris: Librairie Letouzey et Aine, 1954), pp. 1475–76.

6. Ernest Lavisse, "Préface," in Léon Bourgeois, *La Politique de la prévoyance sociale. La Doctrine et la méthode*, 1 (Paris: Charpentier, 1914), p. ix.

7. Ecole des Hautes Études Sociales, *Essai d'une philosophie de la solidarité. Conférences et discussion. Présidées par MM Léon Bourgeois et Alfred Croiset* (Paris: Felix Alcan, 1902), p. 2.

8. Ibid.

9. Ibid., p. 194.

10. Bourgeois, *La Politique de la prévoyance sociale. L'Action 2*, p. 73.

11. J. E. S. Hayward, "The Official Social Philosophy of the French Third Republic: Léon Bourgeois and Solidarism," *International Review of Social History* (1961), 27.

12. Léon Bourgeois, *Solidarité*, 2nd ed. (Paris: Armand Colin, 1897), p. 136.

13. Ibid., p. 101.

14. Ibid., p. 138.

15. "Nothing is more detestable than the incitement to internal war, be it class conflict, or racial or religious strife . . . among the children of the same nation." Léon Bourgeois, *Solidarité, augmentée de pleusieurs appendices,* 3rd ed. (Paris: Armand Colin, 1902), p. 245.

16. Bourgeois, *Solidarité*, 3rd ed., p. 177.

17. Célestin Bouglé, *Syndicalisme et démocratie. Impressions et réflexions* (Paris: Rideur, 1908), pp. 113–14.

18. Bourgeois, *Solidarité*, 2nd ed., p. 133. Bourgeois was often criticized for introducing this legalistic formula. Even fellow reform advocates like Charles Gide and Charles Rist reviewed the quasi-contract as an "artifice, . . . a justification, . . . a concession to individual liberalism." *History of Economic Doctrines from the Time of the Physiocrats to the Present Day*, R. Richards, trans., 2nd ed. (Boston: Heath, 1947), p. 555.

19. Bourgeois, *La Politique de la prévoyance sociale*, 1, p. 5.

20. Ibid.

21. Gide and Rist, p. 549. Bouglé also noted the antisocialist thrust of *solidarisme* when he wrote, in the *Dépêche de Toulouse*, "It is above all the *solidariste* perspective that has the ability to exasperate our revolutionary intellectuals. They became enraged at the least suggestion that concessions might be possible, that the democratic spirit would be capable, perhaps, of convincing the privileged to make concessions, that it would be capable of involving the disinherited in compromise." *Syndicalisme et démocratie*, p. 100.

22. Not everyone was convinced that *solidarisme* was genuinely opposed to socialism. Liberals viewed Bourgeois' theory as the first step to socialism. Emile Levasseur, reviewing social doctrines in 1907, suggested, "It might also happen that the theory of *solidarité*, rather than containing socialism, will serve, in practice, as the bridge upon which it will advance little by little." Levasseur, p. 582.

23. Bourgeois, *La Politique de la prévoyance sociale*. 1, p. 123.

24. The theme of association and the effort to legitimate state intervention, so important in Léon Bourgeois' theory, had been equally important in the work of the republican philosopher Charles Renouvier during the 1870s and the analyses of Alfred Fouillée in the 1880s. These men, like Bourgeois in the 1890s, hoped to eliminate the potential threat to society and to the republican state posed by a propertyless class. See issues of Renouvier's journal *La Critique philosophique* (1872–1889), and Fouillée, *La Science sociale contemporaine* (Paris: Hachette, 1880). See also John A. Scott, *Republican Ideas and the Liberal Tradition in France. 1870–1914* (New York: Octagon, 1966), pp. 59–69.

25. Bourgeois, *Solidarité*, 3rd ed., p. 237.

26. Bourgeois, cited in Ferdinand Buisson, *La Politique radicale. Etude sur les doctrines du parti radical et radical-socialist* (Paris: Girard et Brière, 1908), p. 221.

27. Bourgeois, *Solidarité*, 2nd ed., p. 27. This reduction of society to a natural phenomenon governed by natural laws constantly plagued Bourgeois as a politician who sought to reform society. There was a tension between naturalistic determinism and social change in the concept of *solidarité*. Bourgeois had to modify this determinism. Science, rather than revealing permanent laws, provided the means to alter social reality. "As the discovery of the laws of the physical world has permitted the transformation of material life, the discovery of the laws of the moral and social world must permit the transformation of social life itself," p. 29.

28. Emile Durkheim, *Suicide. A Study in Sociology*, John A. Spaulding and George Simpson, trans. (New York: Free Press, 1951), pp. 37–38.

29. Emile Durkheim, *The Elementary Forms of the Religious Life*, Joseph Ward Swain, trans. (New York: Free Press, 1965), p. 495.

30. Bourgeois in Ecole des Hautes Etudes Sociales, p. ix.

31. Emile Durkheim, *De la Division du travail social. Etude sur l'organisation des sociétés supérieures* (Paris: 1893), p. ix.

32. Ecole des Hautes Etudes Sociales, p. 13, and "Revue de la division du travail social par Emile Durkheim," *Revue politique et parlementaire*, 4 (1895), 544 (hereafter cited as *RPP*).

33. Durkheim, *De la Division du travail social*, p. vii. Durkheim devoted the last chapter of the study on suicide to "Practical Consequences." His specific nostrums had less direct effect on Bourgeois than on other turn-of-the-century reformers, such as

Joseph Paul-Boncour, but the point here is Durkheim's sensitivity to the need for social reform. *Suicide*, pp. 361–92.

34. Terry Nicholas Clark, *Prophets and Patrons: The French University and the Emergence of the Social Sciences* (Cambridge, Mass.: Harvard University Press, 1973), p. 180.

35. Célestin Bouglé, *Le Solidarisme* (Paris: Girard et Brière, 1907), p. 117.

36. Bourgeois, *Solidarité*, 2nd ed., p. 53.

37. Ibid., pp. 61–62.

38. Louis Pasteur (1822–1895) definitively refuted the theory of spontaneous generation with his experiments in fermentation. Pasteur's germ theory gave irrefutable empirical evidence to earlier hypotheses of contagion through microorganisms—bacteria. Pasteur applied his theoretical discoveries to agricultural and industrial problems. The production of wine, beer, and vinegar were aided by his work on fermentation. The germ theory led to the control of diseases affecting silkworms and cattle. Pasteur began his work during the Second Empire in the universities of Dijon, Strasbourg, and Lille. From 1857 to 1867, he taught at the Ecole Normale Supérieur in Paris, an institution increasingly staffed by academics sympathetic to reform and some version of republicanism. In 1868 he moved to a post at the Sorbonne which he held until 1889. The Third Republic viewed him as their leading scientist, and rewarded Pasteur's contributions with the establishment of a state-funded research institution in 1888, the Pasteur Institute, which he headed until his death.

39. Bourgeois, *La Politique de la prévoyance sociale*. 1, p. 57.

40. Ibid., p. 39.

41. Bourgeois specifically endorsed the extension of the re-publican program of free access to lay education to secondary and higher institutions of learning. Ecole des Hautes Etudes Sociales, pp. 84–86, and *La Politique de la prévoyance sociale*, 2 pp. 5–6.

42. Bourgeois, *Solidarité*, 3rd ed., p. 182.

43. "The general income tax is a means to correct those inequalities [of the tax system] and to distribute more honestly the burden of taxes." Bourgeois' ministerial address, cited in Maurice Lasserre, "Impôt général sur le revenu," *RPP*, 6 (1895), 409.

44. Bourgeois, *Solidarité*, 3rd ed., pp. 200–2.

45. Ecole des Hautes Études Sociales, pp. 86–87.

46. Echoing the traditional republican view, Bourgeois praised the mutual aid societies as "one of the most efficacious means to justify and peacefully transform the entirety of social relations." Bourgeois, *La Politique de la prévoyance sociale*. 1, p. 148.

47. Ibid., p. 181.

48. Ecole des Hautes Études Sociales, pp. 86–87.

49. Bourgeois, *Solidarité*, 3rd ed., p. 187.

50. Ecole des Hautes Études Sociales, p. 34.

51. Ibid., p. 45.

52. Ibid., p. xv.

53. Pic, p. 48.

54. Levasseur, pp. 430–31.

55. Félix Roussel "Chronique de la politique intérieure," *RPP*, 14 (1897), 467.

56. Scott, p. 181, and J. E. S. Hayward, "Educational Pressure Groups and the Indoctrination of the Radical Ideology of Solidarism, 1895–1914," *International Review of Social History* 8 (1963), 8.

57. Bourgeois, *Solidarité*, 3rd ed., pp. 159–251. The issues at the first congress were pursued in two subsequent conferences held at the Ecole des Hautes Études Sociales. Buisson and Gide were again present. Other participants at the conferences held significant administrative or academic positions: the dean of the Faculty of Letters, University of Paris; two professors from the prestigious Lycée Louis le Grand; an instructor (*maître de conférence*) from the Ecole Normale Supérieure; and the director of the Ecole Normale d'Instituteurs de Seine. Ecole des Hautes Études Sociales, pp. i–iv. Important journals were impressed by these *solidariste* gatherings, and favorable articles appeared: Charles Brunot, "Solidarité et charité," *RPP*, 28 (1901), 524–52; Edouard Serre, "Les Questions ouvrières à l'Exposition de 1900," *Grande Revue*, 14 (Sept., 1900), 332–55, 620–53. However, the next congress was not held until 1908, at Bordeaux.

58. "The greatest enthusiasm was shown for the new doctrine, especially in the universities and among the teachers in the 100,000 schools." Gide and Rist, p. 551.

59. The eleventh and final edition was published in 1926, the year after Bourgeois' death. Each edition was expanded with new speeches.

60. Hayward has said, "Solidarism . . . played a major part in galvanizing and rallying protagonists of state intervention and voluntary associations, uniting them in the task of building by a series of piecemeal reforms inspired by a simple principle of a multiplicity of imperative needs what has come to be known as the welfare state." "The Official Social Philosophy of the French Third Republic," 19. This assessment, while correct in its general thrust, perhaps overstates *solidarisme's* influence and makes too close a link between *solidarisme* and the welfare state.

61. Gaëton Pirou, *Les Doctrines économiques en France depuis 1870* (Paris: Armand Colin, 1926), p. 166. For example, the interventionist Paul Pic placed Bourgeois' famous statement, "We are all born indebted to each other," on the title page of his *Traité élémentaire de législation industrielle*.

62. Pic, pp. 981–82.

63. Ibid., p. 21.

64. Levasseur, p. 377. Levasseur mentioned Professors Bourguin and especially Jay as well as state functionaries like Fontaine and Paulet.

65. Joseph Schumpeter has claimed that the newly victorious republicans actively sought to appoint nonliberals to the new provincial chairs. *History of Economic Analysis*, p. 842, and Levasseur, pp. 364–65.

66. For Cauwès' arguments during the protectionist debate, see Eugene O. Golob, *The Méline Tariff: French Agriculture and Nationalist Economic Policy* (New York: Columbia University Press, 1944), pp. 132–145.

67. Levasseur called the *Revue de l'économie politique* the "principal organ of the Paris law faculty professors," p. 371.

68. Unlike Great Britain, where Joseph Chamberlain elaborated a causal relation between protectionism and social reform, the two programs were only tenuously connected in France. Improvement of working-class conditions as a result of economic expansion under the protection of high tariffs was only one theme in the protectionist argument. See Herman Lebovics "Protection against Labor Troubles: The Case of the Méline Tariff," unpublished paper (Stony Brook, N.Y.: xerox typeprint). On the other hand, two prominent supporters of social reform, Paul Pic of Lyons and Charles Rist, were free traders. Rist even stated that the underlying cause for the workers' agitation was "tariff policies which make the cost of living more expensive, reduce . . . real wages without being able to create a

compensating industrial expansion." "Chronique ouvrière," *Revue de l'économie politique*, 19 (1905), 844. (Hereafter cites as *REP*). Reformers did, however, point to tariffs as a precedent for state intervention in the economy. Raoul Jay, an interventionist economist, argued that workers had a right to the same protection the state afforded industrialists. "Les Lois ouvrières," *Questions pratiques de législation ouvrière et d'économie sociale*, 7 (1906), 298–99 (hereafter cited as *QP*).

69. In addition to his support for insurance and protective legislation, Gide continued to promote consumer cooperatives. He believed that the steady growth of consumer coops would peacefully eliminate the capitalist employer and the struggle between labor and capital. Gide viewed reform legislation as a temporary palliative; the alternative he offered was the traditional one of cooperative societies. Charles Gide, *Consumers' Collective Societies*, the staff of the Cooperative Reference Library, trans. (New York: Knopf, 1922), p. 234 and passim.

70. Jay's commitment to social reform was apparently influenced by Christian democracy. He contributed to the most radical social Catholic publication, Marc Sangier's *Eveil démocratique*. Yet whatever the personal significance of his religious convictions, all his public writing remained secular and "scientific," even those in Sangier's journal. Raoul Jay, *La Protection légale des travailleurs. Premiers Eléments de la législation ouvrière*, 2nd ed. (Paris: Librairie de la Société du Recueil J. B. Sirey, 1910), p. 162, and "Protection douanière et protection ouvrière," *L'Eveil démocratique*, 6 June 1909.

71. Pic, p. 48.

72. Ibid., pp. 8–9.

73. Ibid.

74. Charles Rist, "La Progression des grèves en France et sa valeur symptomatique," *RPP*, 21 (1907), 161–93, and François Simiand, *La Salaire des ouvriers des mines de charbon en France* (Paris: E. Cornély et Cie., 1907).

75. Paul Deschanel, *La Question sociale*, 4th ed. (Paris: Calmann Levy, 1898), p. 126.

76. Millerand, "Préface," in Jules Huret, *Les Grèves* (Paris: Edition de la Revue Blanche, n.d.), p. 3.

77. Gaston Richard, *La Question sociale et le mouvement philosophique du 19ᵉ siècle* (Paris: Armand Colin, 1914), p. 43.

78. Pirou, pp. 104–17, and Kuisel, pp. 3–5.

79. Adéline Daumard, "L'Etat libéral et le libéralisme économique," in *Histoire économique et social de la France. L'Avènement de l'ère industrielle, 1789–années 1880*, F. Braudel and E. Labrousse, eds., 3 (Paris: Presses Universitaires Françaises, 1976), p. 149.

80. Huret, *Les Grèves*, p. 19.

81. Interview with owner of MM.Forest Frères of St.-Etienne, Huret, *Les Grèves*, p. 40. For further discussion of these interviews, see Chapter 6.

82. Pic, pp. 512–13.

83. Ibid., p. 211.

84. Maurice Bourguin, "Socialisme," *RPP*, 28 (1901), 521.

85. Ibid., p. 522.

86. Pic, p. 10.

87. The liberal Levasseur admitted, "Interventionism does not want to suppress liberty, nor change the fundamental basis of work and property; it wants to introduce more justice with greater equality in the relations between classes, especially in those between workers and employers." Levasseur then completed his observation stating that interventionism was not required to bring about these changes which were already occurring, p. 373.

88. Interview with M. Devillette in Huret, *Les Grèves*, p. 28.

89. Maurice Bourguin, "La Nouvelle Réglementation de la journée de travail. . . ." *REP*, 15 (1901), 236.

90. Pic, p. 613.

91. Bourguin, "La Nouvelle Réglementation de la journée de travail," p. 339.

92. Paul Pic, *Les Assurances sociales en France et à l'étranger* (Paris: Felix Alcan, 1913), p. 177.

93. Raoul Jay, *La Protection légale des travailleurs*, p. 362. Like other French reformers who observed conditions outside France, Jay tended to be selective. U.S. workers did, on the average, enjoy a higher standard of living than their French counterparts, and skilled craft unions of the A.F.L. did negotiate successfully with employers. However, Jay ignored other realities of U.S. labor relations in 1910. He mentioned neither the adamant refusal of most employers to

recognize any organization of the mass of unskilled workers, nor the bitter violence of many strikes in this era, nor the significant influence which revolutionary syndicalism, as espoused by the Industrial Workers of the World, had on American workers.

94. Charles Rist, *REP*, 21 (1907), 161–93.

95. Ibid., p. 168.

96. Ibid., p. 185.

97. Ibid., p. 173.

98. Ibid., p. 183.

99. See below, Chapter 5. Rist's direct involvement in social policy planning increased with time. In 1924 he participated in the formulation of the social and economic program of the Cartel des Gauches. David Arthur Rogers, "The Campaign for the French National Economic Council," Ph.D. dissertation. University of Wisconsin, 1957, p. 169.

100. Pic, "Législation ouvrière," *QP*, 1 (1900), 2.

101. Jay, "Les Lois ouvrières," p. 248.

102. Collège Libre des Science Sociales. Etudes Économiques et Sociales, *L'Oeuvre sociale de la Troisième République. Leçons professées au Collège libre des sciences sociales pendant l'année 1911 par MM. Godart, Astier, Groussier, Breton, F. Buisson, et al.* (Paris: Girard et Brière, 1912), p. 14. The Deputy was the Radical Justin Godart of Lyons.

103. Jay, "Les Lois ouvrières," p. 248.

104. The political development of one reformer who was close to the interventionists indicates the shifting relation between reformism and nationalism. Alexandre Millerand's political career began with a socialist commitment to reform, and then evolved to a more pragmatic reformism in the period 1900–1902. By 1908–1910 he had completely identified reforms with the national interest and saw reforms as *following* from national prosperity. Eventually, during the war and after, this nationalist priority led Millerand to oppose workers' demands and to justify the use of the army against strikes. For the prewar evolution, see his speech during a 1908 banquet commemorating the Second Republic, cited in "Chronique législative et politique," *QP*, 9 (1908), 153.

105. Pic, *Traité élémentaire*, p. 38.

106. Godart, while still coeditor of the *Questions pratiques*, had begun his political career in the Municipal Council of Lyons, which

was headed in 1905 by the Radical mayor Edouard Herriot. The relation between Godart and Herriot continued after both men had moved on to national politics. In the 1924 Radical government led by Herriot, the *Cartel des Gauches*, Godart held the position of Minister of Labor and Health. He also played a role in the formulaton of the National Economic Council. For the postwar history, see Rogers, "The Campaign for the French National Economic Council," pp. 1–4 and passim.

107. See below, Chapter 4.

108. Pic, "Bibliographie," *QP*, 5 (1904), 176.

109. In 1903 Pic established the Office Social, which presented lecture series to both the enlightened bourgeoisie and workers' organizations. After 1905, the reformist Radical mayor of Lyons, Edouard Herriot, frequently officiated at the programs. Although the content of these lectures tended to support the interventionist position, the structure of the Office closely paralleled that of the Parisian Musée Social.

110. Pierre Sorlin, *Waldeck-Rousseau* (Paris: Armand Colin, 1966), p. 547. The journal had been established in 1894 by Marcel Fournier, and immediately engaged with great enthusiasm in Méline's protectionist campaign.

111. Raoul Jay, "L'Assurance ouvrière et les caisse nationale des retraites pour la viellesse," *RPP*, 4 (1895), 84.

112. Raoul Jay, "L'Assistance obligatoire contre le chômage dans le Canton de St.-Gall," *RPP*, 1 (1894), 267–77; Maurice Bourguin, "La valeur dans le système collectivist," *RPP*, 28 (1910), 18–60, 335–52, 478–522. For Arthur Fontaine's regular column on labor, see especially *RPP*, 19 (1899), 145–49.

113. Michelle Perrot in her study on strikes has commented on the importance of the data gathered by the Labor Office. "The Labor Office and the Ministry of Labor played an essential role in the development of empirical sociology." *Les Ouvriers en grève. France, 1871–1890* (Paris: Mouton, 1974), p. 19.

114. Perrot has stated that the staff of the Labor Office included, "permanently or intermittently, most of those who were concerned with the world of labor." Ibid.

115. In 1901 the Chamber of Deputies approved the compilation of a Labor Code. Millerand, then Minister of Commerce, appointed Jay, Bourguin, Fontaine, and Paulet to prepare the text. The Code remained incomplete, however, as late as 1914. "Code du

travail," *QP* 6 (1905), 59, 125; and Renard, *Le Parlement et la législation du travail*, pp. 25–26. In 1906 François Simiand, the economic historian, was appointed librarian in the newly formed Ministry of Labor. In 1912 Paul Pic joined the Advisory Committee on Disputes in the Ministry of Labor.

116. Pic, *Traité élémentaire*, p. 103.

117. Ibid., p. 105.

118. Justin Godart, "La Protection légale des travailleurs," *QP* 2 (1901), 318.

119. Célestin Bouglé, *Syndicalisme et démocratie*, p. 162.

120. In September 1906, fourteen European nations signed a convention in Berne outlawing night work for women. Jay, pp. 210–11.

121. In 1901, delegates to the Basel conference represented eight nations: Germany, Austria, Belgium, France, Hungary, Italy, the Netherlands, and Switzerland. Seven years later at Lucerne, eighteen countries were represented. The original eight had been joined by Denmark, Spain, the United States, Great Britain, Japan, Luxembourg, Norway, Russia, the Vatican, and Sweden. Godart, "La Protection légale des travailleurs," p. 318, and "La 5e Assemblée générale de l'Association internationale pour la protection légale des travailleurs," *QP* 9 (1908), 323.

122. "So general a legislative movement has profound economic and social causes. To explain this as a tendency toward what is derogatorily called state socialism, or to believe that it is simply a matter of imitation . . . is to be content with superficial and valueless explanations." "Discours de M. Cauwès," *QP* 1 (1900), 343.

123. "Chronique," *QP* 2 (1901), 95.

124. Ibid.

125. The politicians also included the democratic Christian, Abbé Lemire. The leaders of the printers' union, Auguste Keufer, and of the precision toolmakers' union, Edmond Briat, also participated in the Association. Pic, "Commission internationale de Bâle. Industrie insalubre et travail du nuit des femmes," *QP*, 5 (1904), 44, and "La 5e Assemblée générale de l'Association internationale pour la protection légale des travailleurs," *QP* 5 (1904), 323.

126. The Chambruns were an old aristocratic landowning family, but their fortune derived from their fine crystal and glass factory, the Baccarat firm.

127. "If there do exist some limited and restricted areas in which state intervention is necessary, the state must respect the action of individuals and of associations, and encourage them rather than impede or attempt to supplant them. The great current of public opinion that supports this position . . . must be endorsed and fortified now more than ever." Musée Social, *Inauguration, 25 mars 1895* (Paris: 1895), p. ii.

128. Siegfried had himself proposed a classical piece of moderate republican legislation, a bill to provide state aid to private organizations involved in constructing inexpensive workers' housing, *habitations à bon marché*. The bill was enacted November 1894.

129. Musée Social, *Procès verbaux du Grand Conseil*, N⁰.1, Séance de constitution, 6 July 1900.

130. See Sanford Elwitt, "Social Reform and Social Order in Late Nineteenth-Century France: The Musée Social and Its Friends," *French Historical Studies*, 11 (Spring 1980), 431–51, for an important analysis of the conservative thrust of reformist ideology.

131. Marcel Fournier, editor of the *RPP*, lauded the establishment of the Musée. "At the same time that certain demagogues, more politicians than philosphers . . . try to introduce dangerous illusions among the popular masses, . . . it is a comfort to witness the emergence of these generous initiatives which seek to educate the people." "Musée social," *RPP* 2 (1895), 321–22.

CHAPTER 3

1. The official name of the party, formed in 1901, was the Radical-Republican and Radical-Socialist Party. To avoid confusion I have referred to it throughout as simply the Radical Party and those associated with the party as Radicals.

2. Two interventionist economists sympathetic to Bourgeois observed, "The *solidaristes* are more of a political party than a doctrinal school and their best work has been done in association with the Radical Party." Charles Gide and Charles Rist, *History of Economic Doctrines from the Time of the Physiocrats to the Present Day*, R. Richards, trans., 2nd ed. (Boston: Heath, 1947), p. 558.

3. See throughout Célestin Bouglé, *Syndicalisme et démocratie. Impression et réflexions* (Paris: Rideur, 1908), Paul Pic's Lyonnais journal, *Questions pratique de législation ouvrière et d'économie sociale,*

1900–14, and Ferdinand Buisson, *La Politique radicale* (Paris: Girard et Briere, 1908).

4. The limits of left radicalism have been suggested by Pierre Sorlin in his study of *Waldeck-Rousseau* (Paris: Armand Colin, 1966), p. 356. Leo Loubère has provided a fuller analysis of the left Radicals' sympathy for the working class, and its fading after 1901, in "Left-Wing Radicals, Strikes and the Military, 1880–1903," *French Historical Studies*, 3 (1963–1964), pp. 93–105, and "The French Left-Wing Radicals: Their Views on Trade Unionism, 1870–1898," *International Review of Social History*, 7 (1962), pp. 203–30. Loubère has also explained the regional and sociological base of the Radical party's left wing in his study of *Radicalism in Mediterranean France. Its Rise and Decline, 1848–1914* (Albany, N.Y.: State University of New York Press, 1974), pp. 182–86, 188–194. We shall return to this regional support for left Radicalism as one reason for its inability to pursue a national reformist program.

5. See Jacques Kayser, *Les Grandes Batailles du radicalisme des origines aux portes du pouvoir, 1820–1901* (Paris: Rivière, 1962), p. 40, passim.

6. Sorlin, p. 358.

7. Paul Deschanel, *La Question sociale*, 4th ed. (Paris: Calmann Levy, 1898), p. 181.

8. Jules Huret, *Enquête sur la question sociale en Europe* (Paris : Perrin, 1897), p. 9. Emphasis added.

9. Jean Bron, *Histoire du Mouvement ouvrier français. La contestation du capitalisme par les travailleurs organisés, 1884–1950*, 2 (Paris: Editions Ouvrières, 1970), p. 77.

10. Jacques Chastenet, *Histoire de la Troisième République. La République triomphante, 1893–1906* (Paris: Hachette, 1955), p. 59.

11. Félix Roussel, "La Vie politique et parlementaire en France," *Revue politique et parlementaire*, 1 (1894), 99. (Hereafter cited as *RPP*.)

12. The term *progressiste* had been coined by Paul Deschanel.

13. This group should not be confused with the small business organization of the Comité Républicain du Commerce et de l'Industrie formed in 1899.

14. A. Veber, "Quelque Propos," *La Petite République*, 19 September 1897.

15. Marcel Fournier, "Notre Oeuvre et notre but," *RPP* 11 (1897), 1–2; "Grand Cercle républicain," *RPP* 16 (1898), 22–23.

16. One analyst of the origins of French social security legislation has labeled this conservative period one of "subsidized liberty." Henri Hatzfeld, *Du Pauperisme à la Sécurité sociale. Essai sur les origines de la Sécurité sociale en France, 1850–1940* (Paris: Armand Colin, 1971), p. 58.

17. After 1898, Guieyesse was vice president of the Committee on Social Insurance. He reported on the pension proposal to the Chamber in 1904 and was a key actor in its passage. See Chapter 5.

18. Léon Bourgeois, *La Politique de la prévoyance sociale. La Doctrine et la méthode*, 1 (Paris: Charpentier, 1914), p. 197.

19. Paul Pic, *Traité élémentaire de législation industrielle. Les Lois ouvrières,* 2nd ed. (Paris: Arthur Rousseau, 1903), pp. 117–22.

20. For Fontaine's importance among the reformers, see Chapter 2.

21. Pic, p. 113.

22. In 1899 Alexandre Millerand, Minister of Commerce in Waldeck-Rousseau's government of republican defense, reorganized the Conseil. Millerand decreed that only a third of the now sixty-six members would be appointed. Another third would be elected by employers' organizations and the final third by workers' unions. Even this bold innovation was unable to vitalize the Conseil.

23. Paul Deschanel, "Discours, Chambre des députés, 20 novembre 1894," in *Question sociale*, p. 75.

24. Ibid., pp. 75–79.

25. Regular state inspection had been established in 1874, accompanying a law regulating child labor. Pic, pp. 583–84.

26. An 1848 law did exist that limited the working day of adult men to twelve hours. It was ignored. See below, Chapter 6.

27. See Hatzfeld, p. 230.

28. An article in the *Revue politique et parlementaire* noted that in 1894, ninety-seven mines employed 126,000 workers. Of this number, 13,874 had received company accident compensation, an indication of the enormous risks involved and the employers' interest in compensating at least some of the injured. Arthur Fonsalme,

"Revue des questions ouvrières et de prévoyance," *RPP* 16 (1898), 153.

29. Fonsalme, "Revue des questions ouvrières," p. 157.

30. *Le Temps*, 23 July 1893.

31. Arthur Fontaine. "Revue des questions ouvrières et de prévoyance," *RPP* 18 (1898), p. 197.

32. "Les Lois sur les mutualités," *RPP* 13 (1897), p. 87.

33. Paul Pic, *Les Assurances sociales en France et à l'étranger* (Paris: Félix Alcan, 1913), p. 105. See also Theodore Zeldin, *France, 1848–1945: Politics and Anger* (New York: Oxford University Press, 1979), pp. 290–301. Zeldin gives a good survey of mutualism, although he overstates the *solidaristes'* commitment to the voluntary societies.

34. See Edward Whiting Fox, *History in Geographic Perspective: The Other France* (New York: Norton, 1973), pp. 143–44. This is a provocative and illuminating discussion of the significance of Léon Bourgeois' ministry.

35. Arthur J. Minnich, Jr., "The Third Force in France, 1870–1896," in *Modern France: Problems of the Third and Fourth Republics*, Edward M. Earle, ed., (1951; reprint. New York: Russell & Russell, 1964), p. 118.

36. Cited in Alexandre Zévaès, *Notes et souvenirs d'un militant* (Paris: Marcel Rivière, 1913), pp. 157–58.

37. Paul Deschanel, "Discours, Les Conditions de travail," in *Question sociale*, pp. 176–77.

38. Etienne Dejean, "Le Nouveau Classement des partis," *RPP* 10 (1896), 282.

39. Cited in Marcel Marion, *Histoire financière de la France depuis 1715. La Troisième République jusqu'à la guerre, 1876–1914*, 6 (Paris: Arthur Rousseau, 1931), p. 185.

40. The municipal council of Paris was controlled by an alliance of socialists and Radicals. By 1900 this Parisian left-wing coalition of "le peuple" had been replaced by a nationalist right-wing majority. For the significance of this change, see D.R. Watson, "The Nationalist Movement in Paris, 1900–1906," in *The Right in France, 1890–1919: Three Studies*, David Shapiro, ed. (Carbondale, Ill.: Southern Illinois University Press, 1962), pp. 49–84.

41. *Le Temps*, 6–14 November 1895.

42. In the regular column of the *Revue politique et parlementairee,*

Félix Roussel denounced the Radicals: "The Radical Party is obviously destined to be absorbed by the socialists. . . . They colaborate in a revolution which they are powerless to direct or control." (1896), 747–49.

43. Quoted in Maurice Hamburger, *Léon Bourgeois. La Politique radical-socialiste, la doctrine de la solidarité, l'arbitrage internationale et la Société des Nations* (Paris: Marcel Rivière, 1932), p. 98.

44. The tax would apply to annual incomes over 2,500 francs. The rate was to increase from one to 5%, and all incomes over 50,000 francs would be taxed at 5%, hardly a measure of expropriation. Chastenet, p. 87.

45. Assemblée Nationale, *Annales, Chambre des députés. Débats*, session ordinaire, 26 March 1896, pp. 822–23. (Hereafter cited as Assemblée Nationale, *C.D. Débats, s.o.*).

46. Cited in Hamburger, p. 195. Emphasis added.

47. Ibid., p. 197.

48. Jules Huret, p. iv.

49. Ibid., p. xi.

50. Paul Lafargue, "Le Parti socialist et le Ministère Bourgeois," *La Petite République*, 20 February 1896 and 2 March 1896.

51. *La Petite République*, 24 April 1896.

52. "Paris contre le Sénat. Le Meeting du Tivoli. Le Reveil du peuple," *La Petite République*, 26 April 1896.

53. Ibid.

54. Jean Bourdeau, "Revue du mouvement socialist," *RPP*, 10 (1896), 17 3. The following year the same journalist wrote, "The apostle of *solidarité* has convinced himself how much the warm applause of the revolutionaries discredited him." "Revue du mouvement socialist," *RPP* 12 (189 7), 136.

55. June 1896 speech at *fête cooperative*, in Bourgeois 1, p. 119.

56. Marcel Fournier, "L'organisation du parti progressiste," *RPP* 14 (1897), 236.

57. Robert Kaplan, "France 1893–1898: The Fear of Revolution among the Bourgeoisie," Ph.D. dissertation Cornell University, 1971, p. 24.

58. Assemblée Nationale, *C.D. Débats, s.o.*, 12 March 1898 , p. 1522.

59. Ibid., p. 1526.

60. Ibid., p. 1522.

61. Fournier, p. 236.

62. "Revue du mouvement socialist," *RPP* 15 (1898), 397.

CHAPTER 4

1. The Méline ministry, which still retained a slim majority in the new legislature of 1898, lost that support by its refusal to discuss the decision of the court martial. The subsequent Radical ministry of Brisson fell for the same reason. Jacques Kayser, *Les Grandes Batailles du radicalisme des origines aux portes du pouvoir, 1820–1901* (Paris: Marcel Riviere, 1962), p. 275.

2. Joseph Paul–Boncour, *Entre Deux Guerres. Souvenirs sur la Troisième République. Les Luttes républicaines, 1877–1918*, 1 (Paris: Plon, 1945), pp. 125–126.

3. Ferdinand Buisson, president of the Ligue des Droits de l'Homme, praised this identification as "an act of moral courage," but he noted that it was also one "of the highest political wisdom." *La Politique radicale. Etude sur les doctrines du parti radical et radical-socialist* (Paris: Girard et Brière, 1908), p. 81.

4. In 1900 Marcel Fournier sadly conceded that the Dreyfus Affair had destroyed the Grand Cercle Républicain and the hope of an organized conservative party. "Notre Oeuvre de cinq annés," *Revue politique et parlementaire,* 24 (1900), 25. (Hereafter cited as *RPP*.)

5. Bourgeois had refused to form another ministry, and suggested Waldeck-Rousseau as the best choice.

6. Emile Combes, *Mon Mininstère. Memoires, 1902–1905*. Maurice Sorre, ed. (Paris: Plon, 1956), p. xii .

7. Paul-Boncour, 1, p. 92.

8. Charles François, "Un Ministère du travail," *Questions pratiques de législation ouvrière et d'économie sociale,* (1901), 7. (Hereafter cited as *QP.*) See below, Chapter 6.

9. Paul Pic, *Traité élémentaire de législation industrielle. Les Lois ouvrières*, 2nd ed. (Paris: Arthur Rousseau, 1903), p. 681.

10. For a full analysis of this crucial law, see Chapter 5.

11. In the 1903 edition of Waldeck–Rousseau's speeches, the anonymous introduction (probably written by Paul–Boncour) repeatedly underscored the former Premier's wish "to take up with urgency the task of economic and social progress." René Waldeck–Rousseau, *Action républicaine et sociale* (Paris: Charpentier, 1903), p. ii. Seven years after the Waldeck–Rousseau ministry, Buisson, then a Radical Deputy, continued to praise Waldeck's reforms. *La Politique radicale*, pp. 86 –91.

12. Assemblée Nationale, *Annales, Chambre des députés. Débats*, session extraordinaire, 6 November 1900, p. 9. (Hereafter cited as Assemblée Nationale, *C.D. Débats*, s.e.).

13. "The country must fix its attention on external matters in order to present a united, reconciled nation, not one rent and divided against itself." Assemblée Nationale, *C.D. Débats*, s.e., 16 November 1899, p. 44.

14. Ibid., 14 November 1899, p. 24.

15. Ibid., 23 November 1899, p. 119.

16. Emile Levasseur, *Questions ouvrières et industrielles en France sous la Troisième République* (Paris: Arthur Rousseau, 1907), p. 917.

17. Jean Bron, *Histoire du Movement ouvrier français. La Contestation du capitalisme par les travailleurs organisés, 1884–1950*, 2 (Paris: Editions Ouvrières, 1970), p. 80.

18. Pierre Sorlin, *Waldeck–Rousseau* (Paris: Armand Colin, 1966), p. 471.

19. Evaluating his ministry, Waldeck–Rousseau's biographer, Sorlin, has said, "His action in the social area lacked vigor and originality. One can count to his credit a certain understanding of the worker's agitation and a long period of stability. Only the 'republican defense' gives real originality to the longest ministry of the Third Republic" (p. 485). See also Combes, p. xiii.

20. Roger Henry Soltau, *French Political Thought in the Nineteenth Century* (1931: reprint; New York: Russell & Russell, 1959), p. 350.

21. The *Revue politique et parlementaire* observed prior to the elections, "The most advanced groups, seeing the progress of socialist ideas in the industrialized centers, believed that the interest of democracy was to maintain contact with their followers and to include in their programs certain rather vague concessions to the workers." "Les Classes dirigeantes," *RPP* 27 (1901), 25.

22. Alexandre Millerand, *Le Socialisme réformist français* (Paris: Société Nouvelle de Librairie et d'Edition, 1903), p. 48.

23. For a discussion of the anticlericalism of the governments of Waldeck–Rousseau and Combes, and the essential continuity between the two, see Malcolm O. Partin, *Waldeck–Rousseau, Combes, and the Church. The Politics of Anticlericalism, 1899–1905* (Durham, N.C.: Duke University Press, 1969).

24. The views of that majority were expressed through the twenty-six-member Délégation des Gauches. Although only five socialists participated in this informal but powerful body, Jaurès became its driving force. In his *Mémoires* Combes explained, "The Délégation des Gauches was the essential mechanism of my political system" (p. 228). See also Harvey Goldberg, *The Life of Jean Jaurès* (Madison, Wisc.: University of Wisconsin Press, 1968), pp. 293–301.

25. "Revue du mouvement socialist," *RPP*, 29 (1901) , 393.

26. "Manifeste du Comité de l'action pour des républicaines," cited in Buisson, pp. 286–287. The Comité, first organized in 1895, included 70 local Radical committee, 53 Masonic lodges, and 62 republican journals.

27. Ibid., pp. 284–285.

28 . Tony Revillon, *Camille Pelletan, 1846–1915. Quarante-Cinq Années de lutte pour la République* (Paris: Marcel Rivière, 1930), p. 148, and Jean Bourdeau, "Revue du mouvement socialist," *RPP* 29 (1901), 393. Bourdeau gave the number of delegates as 700 to 800.

29. J.E.S. Hayward, "Educational Pressure Groups and the Indoctrination of the Radical Ideology of Solidarism, 1895–1914," *International Review of Social History,* 8 (1963), 4–5.

30. Originally these employers had been interested in modifying Méline's protectionist policy so that they too might benefit. Priding themselves on their integral republicanism, these local businessmen hoped to promote responsible republican governments, based on an alliance between Radicals and a section of moderate republicans. Their Comité Républicain was a major source of funds for the Radical committees in 1900 and then for the Radical Party in the 1902 and 1906 elections. Daniel Bardonnet, *Evolution de la structure du parti radical* (Paris: Editions Montchrestien, 1960), pp. 251–254.

31. The titular leader of this left Radical group, Georges Clemenceau, insisting on his individual liberty refused to participate formally in the new party.

32. This left wing of the party led by Combes, Monis, Masse, Steeg, Pelletan, and Bertaux, linked its sympathy for the working

class to the most instransigent anticlericalism. Jacques Julliard, *Clemenceau, briseur de grèves. L'Affaire de Draveil Villeneuve-St. Georges, 1908*, (Paris: Collections Archives, 1965), p. 57.

33. During this first campaign, when multiple candidacies were still possible, Pelletan ran both in a popular Paris *arrondissement*, the Tenth, and in the semi-rural, southern wine-growing region of Aix. Successful in both races, he chose to represent Aix rather than Paris. He remained the deputy from Aix for thirty years. In 1910 he entered the Senate for this southern department. Pelletan's left radicalism and working-class sympathies coincided with the political development of winegrowers in southern France. Leo Loubère, *Radicalism in Mediterranean France. Its Rise and Decline, 1848–1914.* (Albany, N.Y.: State University of New York Press, 1974), pp. 166, 178–79 and passim.

34. Revillon, pp. 45–47.

35. This appeared in Clemenceau's newspaper *La Justice* following the unsuccessful efforts of Clemenceau, Millerand, and Pelletan to arbitrate the glassblowers' strike at Carmaux. Cited in Revillon, p. 110.

36. Daniel Halévy, *La République des Comités. Essai d'histoire contemporaine, 1895–1934* (Paris: Grasset, 1934), p. 61.

37. Camille Pelletan, *La Semaine de mai* (Paris: Dreyfous, 1880) and *Discours sur la Revolution en Russie* (Paris: Sociéte des Amis du Peuple Russe et des Peuples Annexés, 1905).

38. "Pelletan's eloquence accommodates itself marvelously to interminable phrases which, when he considers social reality and wants to express his observations, take on a natural incoherence." "Portraits politiques: Camille Pelletan," *RPP*, 24 (1900), 641.

39. Déclaration du Parti Radical, quoted in Albert Milhaud, *Histoire du radicalisme* (Paris: Sociétés d'Éditions Française et Internationales, 1951), p. 267.

40. Ibid.

41. Ibid., p. 268. This was a more attenuated list than the program described by the *Comité de l'action pour les Réformes Républicaines* in 1898.

42. Ibid.

43. Ibid. In addition to drafting the declaration with Pelletan, Bourgeois himself repeated the same theme at the Congress. "Individual property seems to us to be the necessary guarantee of liberty, dignity, human activity. . . . We believe that it is better de-

fended . . . by the social reforms which we want to realize." Cited in
Maurice Hamburger, *Léon Bourgeois. La Politique radicale-socialiste, la
doctrine de la solidarité, l'arbitrage internationale et la Société des nations*
(Paris: Marcel Rivière, 1932), p. 98.

44. Quoted in Milhaud, p. 270.

45. Ibid., p. 268.

46. Ibid.

47. Buisson, p. 252. Emphasis added.

48. Bardonnet, pp. 56–57.

49. Revillon, p. 148.

50. Bardonnet, p. 135.

51. Combes, p. 10.

52. Quoted in Revillon, pp. 156–57.

53. Since at least 1902, anticlericalism has been criticized as a
Radical ploy to avoid the social question. While much of the Radical
Party may have deserved this criticism, it should not be forgotten that
the anticlerical tradition was shared by socialists, reformist, and
revolutionary union leaders, and much of the working class. These
anticlericals had assumed that the newly triumphant Radicals would
destroy the Church's privileges *and* enact labor legislation. See also
John McManners, *Church and State in France, 1870–1914* (New York:
Harper & Row, 1972), pp. 142–43.

54. The Combes' government retained the Chamber's confidence by a margin of only ten votes following Millerand's interpellation. R.A. Winnacker, "The Délégation des Gauches: A
Successful Attempt at Managing a Parliamentary Coalition," *The
Journal of Modern History*, 9, no. 4 (December 1937), 466. Combes was
convinced that Millerand headed a conspiracy to topple his ministry
because Millerand had been excluded from a ministerial position.
Combes, p. 150. Whether Millerand was motivated by opportunism
or principle, the Combes' government could not deny that
Millerand's ties to the Bloc des Gauches had already been loosened
when Jaurès' Parti Socialist Français had expelled him in January
1904.

55. They were led by Paul Doumer who had significantly shifted
his political affiliations since his dramatic role as Léon Bourgeois'
Minister of Finance in 1896. He had accepted Méline's appointment
to the Governor-Generalship of Indo-China, where he served from

1897 to 1902. When he returned to the Chamber in 1902 his relations were less than cordial with his former Radical colleagues.

56. Winnacker, p. 465.

57. Combes recognized that the end of the Bloc was certain as soon as the Amsterdam congress of the Second International, which met in August 1904, condemned socialist participation in bourgeois governments. Jaurès did not officially withdraw from the Delegation des Gauches until after the fall of the Combes cabinet and at the moment that the unified French Socialist Party was officially formed in April 1905. Combes, p. 226; Goldberg, pp. 339–40.

58. Goldberg, pp. 329–38.

59. Tony Revillon, a young member of the left Radical group, admitted their reliance on socialist support. "The Radical-Socialists deprived of socialist cooperation would often in the future be reduced to powerlessness" (p. 176).

60. Buisson, p. 113.

61. In 1906, as president of the Radical Party, he addressed an audience in Lille: "And if it occurs that our allies, the collectivists, unjustly attack us, as has already happened, let us defend our ideas and our doctrines. We can never defend them better than by action. There can be no more decisive reply to their reproaches than the reforms which we must accomplish." Cited in Revillon, p. 184.

62. Buisson, p. 233.

63. Quoted in Revillon, p. 181.

64. Bron, pp. 119–20.

65. Judith Wishnia, "French Fonctionnaires: The Development of Class Consciousness and Unionization, 1884–1926," Ph.D. dissertation, State University of N.Y. at Stony Brook, 1977, pp. 50–52 and passim. This is a very useful study of these developments.

66. Reprint of Paul-Boncour interview in *Progrès de Lyon*, no. 10, February 1906, in "Chronique politique," *QP* 7 (1906), 85.

67. Ibid.

68. Ibid.

69. Ibid.

70. Pic's Lyonnais organization, l'Office Social, formally joined the Comité and his journal, *Les Questions Pratiques*, devoted con-

siderable space to the activities of the Comité. "Chronique politique," *QP* 7 (1906), 85.

71. Gaëtan Pirou, *Les Doctrines économiques en France depuis 1870* (Paris: Armand Colin, 1925), p. 167.

72. J.E.S. Hayward, "Solidarist Syndicalists: Durkheim and Duguit, Part II," *Sociological Review* (December, 1960), p. 198.

73. "Discours, Réunion electoral, XIIᵉ arrondissement Paris," 23 February 1906, reprinted in "L'Oeuvre de la legislation prochaine," *QP*, 7 (1906), 97–98. Millerand then enumerated seven legislative proposals which he felt were of the greatest urgency: workers' old age pensions, the extension of the ten-hour working day to all workers, the six-day week, the improvement of unions' legal status (*personalité civile*), the organization of regional labor boards, the extension of agricultural insurance to reduce rural migration, and the establishment of obligatory conciliation and arbitration, pp. 98–99. Several of these will be analyzed in later chapters.

74. "Discours," 1906 Congrès Radical, cited in Buisson, pp. 331–33.

75. Edouard Herriot began his long political career as the Radical mayor of the important industrial center in Lyons. Herriot pledged to be a reforming municipal official. He started an urban renewal program, increased public assistance funds, and improved relations between the municipal government and local unions. He was supported by Paul Pic and the group of Lyonnais Radicals in the Chamber. His municipal activity won him early recognition within the Radical Party. Herriot's career ended in 1954 after he had served several times as Premier. He was among the most important leaders of the Radical party in the interwar years, Michel Soulié, *La Vie politique d'Edouard Herriot* (Paris: Armand Colin, 1962), pp. 35–38, 43, and Sabine Jessner, "Edouard Herriot in Lyons: Some Aspects of His Role as Mayor," in *From the Ancien Régime to the Popular Front: Essays in the History of Modern France in Honor of Shepard B. Clough*, Charles K. Warner, ed. (New York: Columbia University Press, 1969), p. 152. For a discussion of Herriot's key role in the Radical Party see Serge Bernstein, *Histoire du parti radical. La Recherche de l'âge d'or, 1919-1926* (Paris: Presses de la Fondation Nationale des Sciences Politiques, 1980).

76. Senatorial and legislative elections, the ministerial bureaus, the judiciary, the status of civil servants, education, and the fiscal system all were to be reformed. "Programme du parti radical," no. 1-12, cited in Buisson, pp. 129–94.

77. Ibid., no. 14, p. 206.

78. Ibid., no. 17, p. 207.

79. Ibid., no. 22, p. 209.

80. Ibid., no. 16, p. 207. By 1907 Léon Bourgeois had explicitly called for state intervention. See his 1907 discourse before the Lyons Alliance pour l'Hygiène in *La Politique de la prévoyance sociale. La Doctrine et la méthode*, 1 (Paris: Charpentier, 1914), p. 39.

81. "Programme du parti radical," no. 17, in Buisson, p. 207. By linking these two policies of insurance and assistance, the party ignored the reformers' hope that insurance would eliminate assistance.

82. Buisson, p. 227.

83. Ibid., p. 226.

84. Ibid., p. 236. Emphasis added.

85. Especially after Herriot's 1905 election as mayor and his coeditor Godart's election as Lyonnais Deputy in 1906, Pic had become more active in Radical politics.

86. This is not to suggest that after 1908 Radical congresses ignored the social question or the role of the unions. On the contrary, reform planks proliferated. But after 1908 Radical reformism was reduced to a rote exercise, with little political significance.

87. "Rapport sur la politique sociale du parti radical," Congrès de Dijon, October 1908, published in "Chronique politique," *QP* (1908), 345.

88. Ibid.

89. Ibid., p. 346.

90. In a telling footnote, he admitted that divisive questions like that were best not discussed. Ibid., footnote 1.

91. Bardonnet, p. 73.

92. Buisson, p. 109.

93. Assemblée Nationale, *C.D. Débats*, s.e., 8 November 1906, p. 61.

94. Ibid., p. 62. In his history of the Ministry of Labor, Jean-André Tournerie has suggested that a very immediate concern motivated the creation of the new Ministry. It was intended to aid the moderate reform unionists who had just been defeated at the 1906

C.G.T. Congress at Amiens. *Le Ministère du travail. Origines et premiers développments* (Paris: Cujas, 1971), p. 182.

95. Assemblée Nationale, *C. D. Débats*, s.e., 8 November 1906, p. 62.

96. Tournerie, p. 184, and "Le Nouveau Minister," *QP*, 7 (1906), 382.

97. The new Finance Minister, Joseph Caillaux, submitted a proposal in July 1907 which was warmly endorsed by the president of the Chamber's Committee on Finance, Camille Pelletan. Assemblée Nationale, *Annales, Chambredes députés. Débats*, Session ordinaire, 1 July 1907, p. 871. (Hereafter cited as Assemblée Nationale, *C.D. Débats*, s.o.).

98. Ibid., p. 872.

99. Lévy-Leboyer, "La Croissance économique en France au 19e siècle," *Annales ESC*, 23, no. 4 (1968), 798–99, and Jean Bouvier, *Histoire économique et histoire sociale. Recherches sur le capitalisme contemporain* (Geneva: Droz, 1968), pp. 29, 49.

100. This miner's strike, the first ever to be led by syndicalists, had originally evoked considerable support outside the working class. It was sparked by a mine disaster in which eleven hundred miners had been killed. Clemenceau's first response had been a promise to send no troops. Julliard, p. 22.

101. In 1906 there were 1,319 strikes (76% more than in 1899). There was a slight decline in 1907 to 1,131 strikes (51% more than in 1899); a further decline in 1908 to 969 strikes (29% more); and a rise the following year to 1,060 strikes (41% more). This relatively high rate of strikes continued to 1911. Peter Stearns, *Lives of Labor: Work in a Maturing Industrial Society* (New York: Holmes & Meier, 1975), p. 378.

102. The strike began among quarry workers who demanded a 20 centimes raise in their hourly wage, bringing it to 70 centimes an hour, and the end of piece work. They also demanded the enforcement of the ten-hour day, since their trade, like so many others, had been excluded from protection under the 1900 law. (See Chapter 6) In addition, they called for the application of the 1906 law on the six-day week, which had become a dead letter. Julliard, p. 41.

103. Julliard, pp. 47–53, 90–94.

104. Paul-Boncour, *Entre Deux Guerres*, 1, p. 173.

105. The 1907 Radical program called for electoral alliances with Socialists, but only on condition that those Socialists not

support the antimilitarist position of their own party. Buisson, p. 121.

106. Buisson stated, "What finally determined the retreat of the Radical spirit—in spite of its resistance to anarchism—was the detestable antipatriotic propaganda of Hervé." Buisson, p. 103.

107. Gustave Hervé, the source of such provocation and the main exponent of the Socialists' new militant antiwar, antimilitary position, appalled all Radicals. Buisson, p. 121.

108. Interestingly, the danger of a resurgent Bloc or of *combisme* was very much a concern of moderate republicans and conservatives. They considered the possibility of a new Combes-Jaurès alliance both real and frightening. "Le Combisme renaissant," *Le Temps*, 3 March 1908.

109. Wishnia, pp. 92–96.

110. Ibid., p. 101.

111. Assemblée Nationale, *C.D. Débats*, s.o., 8 May 1907, p. 37.

112. Ibid., 14 May 1907, p. 128.

113. Ibid., pp. 135–36.

114. Ibid., 8 May 1907, p. 143.

115. Wishnia, pp. 147–49 and passim.

116. Quoted in Bardonnet, p. 109.

117. Paul-Boncour, *Entre Deux Guerres*, 1, p. 173.

118. Célestin Bouglé, *Syndicalisme et démocratie. Impressions et réflexions* (Paris: Rideur, 1908), p. 70.

119. Ibid., p. 105.

120. Ibid., p. 203.

121. In 1907 reformers joined with Clemenceau to preserve the C.G.T. organization from the right. Conservatives, moderates, and even a few Radicals intended to smash trade unionism, as well as revolutionary syndicalism. Clemenceau and the reformers were certain that one day the C.G.T. would house an entirely different sort of unionism. It needed to be protected for that future. They also feared that an attack on the C.G.T. as a whole might provoke a confrontation of monumental proportions with the working class. In May 1907 the efforts of the right to dissolve the C.G.T. were repelled.

Buisson praised Clemenceau's "defense of trade unionism." Buisson, pp. 106–7.

122. Quoted in Milhaud, p. 301.

123. Addressing the Chamber on June 11, 1908, Clemenceau summed up his policy, "The Chamber will decide if it is going to condemn or endorse our politics. Is the Chamber with us, for the future social reform to benefit the greatest number, in the struggle against the revolutionaries who want disorder and violence? The Chamber must say if it wants to work with us for a legal order of reforms, against revolution." Cited in Michel Branciard, *La Société française et les luttes des classes, 1789–1914*, 1 (Lyons: Chroniques Sociales de France, 1967), p. 175.

124. Ironically, the purpose of this fiscal reform had little correspondence with Léon Bourgeois' original conception. It represented a political maneuver to divide the fragile left coalition of the 1914 election. The vote for income tax was to dampen Radical criticism of the three-year military service law of 1913. The implementation of the tax was further delayed another two years until the pressure of military expenditures made new revenue sources crucial. Even after the war the low rate of taxation and the numerous loopholes made the progressive income tax only a supplement to the old fiscal system.

125. Quoted in Revillon, p. 185.

126. Two independent reformers, Millerand and Viviani, held ministerial positions in Briand's cabinet, the former as Minister of Public Works, the latter continuing as Minister of Labor. They too accepted Briand's action against the railroad workers' strike.

127. Paul Pic, "Le Grève des Cheminots," *QP* 11 (1910), 289.

128. There is also evidence that in the South the Radical Party's failure to enact its reform program was one of several factors which led the small property-owning winegrowers to abandon the Radicals for the Socialists. The winegrowers of the Midi had been among the most progressive of the Radicals' provincial constituencies. By 1909 many had concluded that the Radicals in government had failed to develop a national program to address their economic difficulties. They were in turn attracted to the more vigorous, programmatic position of the Socialist Party. While many Radical supporters were becoming more cautious about endorsing a reformist program, those most likely to call for this policy were abandoning the party, thus reinforcing the rejection of the social reform strategy and an alliance with the working class. Loubère, pp. 223–28; 232.

129. Bernard Moss has also suggested that the success of Clemenceau's action against the C.G.T. was possible because of the organizational and internal weaknesses of the syndicalists themselves. He has attributed this weakness to the various ambiguities of trade union socialism and the economic context of turn-of-the-century France. *The Origins of the French Labor Movement, 1830–1914: The Socialism of Skilled Workers* (Berkeley and Los Angeles: University of California Press, 1976), p. 151.

130. Quoted in Revillon, p. 191.

CHAPTER 5

1. The law on accident compensation was debated for eighteen years, from 1880 to 1898. The pension law was first introduced in 1890 and enacted in 1910.

2. Paul Pic, "Législation ouvrière," *Questions pratiques de la législation ouvrière et d'économie sociale*, 1 (1900), 12. (Hereafter cited as *QP*.)

3. Senator Charles Prevet. Assemblée Nationale, *Annales, Sénat. Débats*, session ordinaire, 3 April 1906, p. 395. (Hereafter cited as Assemblée Nationale, *Sén. Débats*, s.o.) A moderate republican, Prevet was also an important manufacturer of canned food in France and in the colonies, as well as a mine owner.

4. As the *Revue politique et parlementaire* indicated, the *Progressistes* wanted to present the electorate with a reform law before the 1898 summer elections. "Let it not be forgotten in the Senate that something more is necessary to present to the country. . . . The tangible reality of mature reforms accomplished at an opportune moment is needed." "Chronique de la politique intérieure," *Revue politique et parlementaire*, 14 (1897), 473. (Hereafter cited as *RPP*.) Méline also applied pressure on the Senate to conclude its endless theoretical debate and pass some kind of reform legislation.

5. Assemblée Nationale, *Annales, Chambre des députés. Débats*, session ordinaire, 11 June 1896, p. 250. (Hereafter cited as Assemblée Nationale, *C.D. Débats*, s.o.)

6. 1896 address to Senate, cited in Maurice Hamburger, *Léon Bourgeois. La politique radical-socialiste, la doctrine de la solidarité, l'arbitrage internationale et la Société des Nations* (Paris: Marcel Rivière, 1932), p. 32.

7. Henri Hatzfeld, *Du Pauperisme à la sécurité sociale. Essai sur les origines de la sécurité sociale en France 1850–1940* (Paris: Armand Colin, 1971), p. 27.

8. It is important not to lose sight of the distinction between the German state insurance system and its implementation. See Chapter 1, notes 17 and 18. Soon after 1890, the new Kaiser, William II, abandoned any further extension of social reform legislation as a strategy for social pacification. J. Alden Nichols, *Germany after Bismarck: The Caprivi Era, 1890–1894* (Cambridge, Mass.: Harvard University Press, 1958), pp. 74–77.

9. In an 1897 article, "Accident du travail en Allemagne," the liberal economist Yves Guyot denounced the German law as "a class-biased law that violates the principle of citizens' equality before the law. . . . " *RPP* 13 (1897), 463.

10. Maurice Bellom, "Les Assurances ouvrières en Allemagne," *RPP* 12 (1897), 336–54.

11. Maurice Bellom, "Les Accidents du travail en Angleterre," *RPP* 15 (1898), 560–65.

12. While the British accident compensation law closely followed the German model of compulsory insurance, the insurance laws of the Liberal government contained some important innovations in social reform. The 1908 old age pension was a noncontributory program financed from general revenue. This break with liberal tradition and existing social insurance concepts reflected the enormous political pressure which the Trade Union Congress could bring to bear on the Liberal Party. Their demand for noncontributory pensions was incorporated into the law of 1908. A similar trade union and Socialist Party demand was never even seriously considered in France. The British law did include restrictions which Liberals, still loyal to laissez-faire principles, had been able to introduce. The age of eligibility was quite high, 70, and pensioners had to pass a means test proving that they were among the "deserving poor." Nonetheless the reform was extremely well received by British workers. Bentley B. Gilbert, *The Evolution of National Insurance in Great Britain: The Origins of the Welfare State* (London: Michael Joseph, 1966), p. 159 and passim. It was, in part, the fiscal requirements of the new pension law which sparked the Lloyd George-House of Lords conflict. Victory in that constitutional struggle aided Lloyd George and the Liberals in the enactment of an even more comprehensive reform program, the 1911 National Health Insurance Act. Elaborating on the German model, health insurance would be funded by a triple contribution of state, workers, and employers. The most innovative aspect of the law was coverage

for unemployment in certain selected industries. The British were the first to attempt even limited unemployment insurance, funded by triple contributions. The Liberals' social reform program was, without question, the most ambitious and most effective of any prewar government.

13. Many European states, in addition to Germany, Great Britain, and France enacted some form of social insurance legislation prior to 1914. Belgium had old age pensions in 1900; Austria, accident compensation in 1887. In the United States there was a growing interest among the Progressives in social insurance legislation, but no serious effort was made to introduce legislation on a national level. The specific economic and political development of the United States limited legislation to state laws on workers' accident compensation; the first was passed in New York in 1911. Gaston V. Rimlinger, "Welfare Policy and Economic Development: A Comparative Historical Perspective," *Journal of Economic History*, 26 (December 1966), 567–68.

14. "La Caisse nationale de prévoyance devant le Parlement," *RPP*, 2 (1894), 33.

15. Ibid., p. 39.

16. Raoul Jay, "L'Assurance ouvrière obligatoire," *Revue de l'économie politique*, 13 (1899), 105. (Hereafter cited as *REP*).

17. While insurance for accidents and old age was proposed, most reformers considered unemployment too unpredictable a risk for which to provide security. In 1903 the independent socialist Pierre Colliard, president of the Chamber's Committee on Labor, introduced a bill to establish a Caisse de Chômage in the Ministry of Labor; the bill was never brought up for debate. In 1905, responding to the very high 1904 unemployment rate of 10.2%, the Parliament voted special subsidies to union unemployment funds. It was indicative of the reformers' isolation from the working class, and their continuing attachment to the importance of a "free labor market," that they failed even to consider any programmatic solution to the problem of unemployment, which was a major "insecurity" facing workers. For unemployment statistics, see Peter Stearns, *Lives of Labor: Work in a Maturing Industrial Society* (New York: Holmes & Meier, 1975), pp. 37, 91, 102.

18. In 1890, the Radical Deputy Ricard had reintroduced Faure's bill on accident compensation and obligatory insurance, which the Chamber finally discussed and passed in June 1893. Georges Paulet, "Responsabilité des accidents industriels," *Revue de législation ouvrière et sociale*, no. 1 (1898), 145.

19. Paralleling parliamentary activity, the accident compensation issue attracted wide interest. The political and economic journals ran numerous articles on this question in the early 1890s. Issues of the *Revue politique et parlementaire* for 1894 were filled with articles analyzing social insurance. Maurice Bellom, "La Question des accidents du travail," 1 (1894), 65–78; Jacques Drake, "La Caisse nationale de prévoyance devant le Parlement," 2 (1894), 33–53; Eugêne Rochetin, "Différents Projets de caisse de retraite," 2 (1894), 507–25.

20. Assemblée Nationale, *Sén. Débats*, s.o., 11 June 1895, p. 58.

21. Assemblée Nationale, *Sén. Débats*, s.o., 13 June 1895, pp. 76–78; 4 July 1895, p. 224. Poirrier himself was the owner of large chemical and dye companies.

22. Assemblée Nationale, *Annales, Sénat. Débats*, session extra-ordinaire, 25 November 1895, p. 125. (Hereafter cited as Assemblée Nationale, *Sén. Débats*, s.e.)

23. Ibid., p. 127.

24. "Le Congrès d'accident à Milan et la garantie obligatoire de l'indemnité," *RPP*, 3 (1895), 263.

25. Raoul Jay, *La Protection légale des travailleurs. Premiers Eléments de la législation ouvrière*, 2nd ed. (Paris: Société du Recueil J.B. Sirey, 1910), p. 285.

26. The Senate debated this issue July 4, 1895. The large landowners were led by Senator Edmond Teisserenc de Bort, and supported by Liberals such as Aimé-Etienne Blavier and René Béranger. Assemblée Nationale, *Sén. Débats*, s.o., 4 July 1895, p. 217. In the new legislature of 1898, this blatant inequity was partially overturned and the small group of agricultural workers who worked on mechanized farms were covered by the accident compensation statute. The independent socialist, Léon Mirman, introduced this reform in 1899. Paul Pic, *Les Assurances sociales en France et à l'étranger* (Paris: Felix Alcan, 1913), pp. 64–65. Despite the reform, numerous court cases occurred over the question of coverage for agricultural workers, Ministère du Commerce, de l'Industrie, des Postes et des Télégraphes, Direction de l'Assurance et de la Prévoyance Sociale. *Accidents du travail. Jurisprudence.*, 2 (May 1900), pp. 102–3, 135–36. (Hereafter cited as Ministère du Commerce, *Accidents du travail. Jurisprudence.*)

27. Assemblée Nationale, *Sén. Débats*, s.o., 13 June 1895, p. 76.

28. Ibid., 4 July 1895, p. 224.

29. Boissard, "La Loi du 9 avril 1898," *REP*, 14 (1900), 269. Senator Sebline, explaining why the law could easily be applied to industry, stated, "Large industry in particular will not be unprepared for the law on accidents; it has anticipated it. All the industries of any importance in the country are already insured." Assemblée Nationale, *Sén. Débats*, s.o. 13 June 1895, p. 69.

30. Approximately 100,000 workers were covered by the accident insurance program of the Comité des forges and the Caisse des Industries Textiles. Musée Sociale, *Circulaire,* series A, no. 24 (22 December 1898), 580. Other employer funds included the Auxiliaire de Lyon, Caisse Syndicale de la Maçonnerie, Union des Industriels de Lyon, Caisse Syndicale des Forges de France, Caisse des Chambres Syndicales, Syndicats du Nord, Caisse des Entreprenneurs de Reims. A. Boissard, "La loi du 9 avril 1898. Quelque résultats. . . . *REP* 14 (1900), 269.

31. Boissard, p. 265.

32. Pic, "Accident du travail," *REP*, 12 (1898), 507. Arthur Fontaine, Director of the Labor Office, also criticized the failure to enact obligatory insurance. "In my opinion 'free' insurance will be more costly than obligatory insurance." "Revue des questions ouvrières," *RPP*, 20 (1899), 149. Boissard in his 1900 article in the *Revue de l'économie politique* also made the same point, p. 281. See also Senator Ricard, Assemblée Nationale, *Sén. Débats*, s.e., 3 December 1895, p. 209.

33. Assemblée Nationale, *Annales. Chambre des députés. Documents*, session ordinaire, s.o., 56², 2 May 1899, p. 1518. (Hereafter cited as Assemblée, Nationale, *C.D. Documents*, s.o.).

34. Assemblée Nationale, *Sén. Débats*, s.o., 20 May 1899, pp. 611–12. Proposition of MM. Bonnefille, Ollivier, etc.

35. J.-M. Jeanneney and Marguerite Perrot, *Textes du droit économique et sociale en France, 1789–1957* (Paris: Armand Colin, 1957), p. 580.

36. Prior to the accident compensation law large industrialists had never reported accidents that caused less than the loss of 14 working days. Small and medium-sized shops only reported deaths or extreme injury. In the first six months of reporting, July to December 1899, the highest injury rates were in construction, metallurgy, and machine shops. Ministère du Commerce, de l'Industrie, des Postes et des Télégraphes. Direction de l'Industrie,

Rapports sur l'application pendant l'année 1899 des lois réglèmentant le travail, Rapports des Inspecteurs divisionnaires du travail, Rapports des Ingénieurs en chef des mines (Paris, 1900), p. xiv. (Hereafter cited as Ministère du Commerce, *Rapports sur l'application, pendant l'année 1899 des lois.*)

37. From January to June of 1899, a total of 20,490 accidents were reported; from July to December, 83,708. Ibid., Table 18, p. 569.

38. Ibid.

39. Industrial accidents per 1,000 workers in all professions covered by 1898 law:

1901	1902	1903	1904	1905	1906	1907	1908	1909	1910
63.4	60.6	54.9	52.8	61.3	70.7	80.1	77.9	82.9	87.2

Source: Ministère du Commerce, de l'Industrie, des Postes et des Télégraphes, Direction de l'Assurance et de la Prévoyance Sociale, *Recueil des documents sur les accidents du travail, 9e Rapport sur l'application de la loi du 9 avril 1898, 44* (1910), p. 79. (Hereafter cited as Ministère du Commerce. *Recueil des documents sur les accidents du travail.*)

40. The Senate passed the amendment on civil courts by a vote 169 to 57. Assemblée Nationale, *Sén. Débats*, s.e., 8 November 1895, p. 53.

41. Ministère du Commerce, *Recueil des documents sur les accidents du travail. 2e Statistique des accidents du travail*, 40 (1910), pp. 20–21, 51.

42. Jeanneney and Perrot, p. 281.

43. Ibid.

44. Ministère du Commerce. *Accidents du travail. Jurisprudence*, 4 (February 1901), index.

45. Paul Pic, "Accidents du travail," *REP* 12 (1898), 597.

46. Assemblée Nationale, *Sén. Débats*, s.e., 26 November 1895, p. 145.

47. This group of industrialists had accepted the principle of *risque professionnelle* since 1894. They acknowledged the benefits of certainty and freedom from personal liability which the law offered. Maurice Bellom, "La Question des accidents du travail," p. 72.

48. Ministère du Commerce, *Accidents du travail. Jurisprudence*, 1 (1900), pp. 117–20 (Motte), p. 384 (Savon).

49. Ministère du Commerce, *Recueil des documents sur les accidents du travail*, 1, (1902), p. 107.

50. Emile Levasseur, *Questions ouvrières et industrielles en France sous la Troisième République* (Paris: Arthur Rousseau, 1907), p. 470, and Arthur Fonsalme, "Revue des questions ouvrières et de prévoyance," *RPP* 16 (1898), 156.

51. Assemblée Nationale, *Sén. Débats*, s.o., 10 June 1895, p. 45.

52. Of the 589 deputies elected in 1902, approximately three hundred fifty had expressed support for some form of pension plan. Assemblée Nationale, Chambre des députés, *Programmes et les professions de foi et engagements electoraux des députés* (Annexe au procès-verbal de la séance du 3 juillet 1903, no. 1162), p. 10.

53. The final Senate vote was 280 for, 3 against; the Chamber vote, 504 for, 4 against. "Chronique de mouvement de la législation de France," *QP* 11 (1910), 164.

54. Ferdinand Buisson, *La Politique radicale. Etude sur les doctrines du parti radical et radical-socialist* (Paris: Brière, 1908), p. 253.

55. Assemblée Nationale, *C.D. Débats*, s.o., 8 February 1906, p. 719.

56. Only in 1901 did Léon Bourgeois categorically support obligatory insurance. He continued to stress, however, that the choice of the insurance institution must be left up to the individual. "1901 Discours, Mutualité banquet" in Bourgeois, *La Politique de la prévoyance sociale. La Doctrine et la méthode.* 1 (Paris: Charpentier, 1914), p. 158.

57. Levasseur, p. 514.

58. Edmond Villey, "Chronique législative," *REP*, 15 (1901), 786, 794; Jacques Drake, "Prévoyance sociale," *RPP*, 8 (1896), 517.

59. Levasseur, pp. 796–98.

60. Raoul Jay, "L'Assurance ouvrière et les caisse nationale des retraites pour la viellesse," *RPP* 4 (1895), 84.

61. During the 1906 debate in the Chamber, Millerand then president of the Committee on Social Insurance, reversed the liberals' argument, and suggested that compulsory insurance would "produce as an immediate effect, the revitalization of the concepts of social insurance and develop the *mutualités*." Assemblée Nationale, *C.D. Débats*, s.o., 24 January 1906, p. 205. Again in February, Millerand spoke in the most conciliatory terms about the importance

of the social services performed by the *mutualités*. 1 February 1906, p. 503. After the law was passed, Charles Mabilleau, head of the largest national organization of mutual aid societies, actively aided the Ministry of Labor in promoting the old age pension program.

62. Drake, "Prévoyance sociale," 519.

63. Arthur Fontaine, "Retraites ouvrières," *RPP* 18 (1898), 203.

64. Robert Pinot, *Les Ouevres sociales des industries métallurgiques* (Paris: Armand Colin, 1924), pp. 73–74. Although Pinot regretted that the Comité des Forges had not been permitted to function independently, he noted that the government program had not greatly altered its administration. The 1910 law added a worker's contribution to the one already existing for employers, p. 82.

65. M. Storck, who headed a printing firm with facilities in Lyons and Paris, urged the employers' association of master printers to endorse compulsory old age insurance in 1900. This atypical employer position may have reflected the particular structure of employer-worker relations in a highly skilled and relatively well-unionized trade. M. Storck's commitment to legislative reform also attracted business to his firm. In 1903 Paul Pic transferred the publication of his interventionist journal, *Les Questions pratiques . . .*, to the firm of Storck & Cie. "Rapport présenté au 7e Congrès des Maîtres Imprimeurs de France," *QP* 2 (1901), 18–21.

66. Henri Hatzfeld in his analysis of the development of French social security locates the major opposition to compulsory workers' pensions among the small employers, p. 148.

67. Ibid., p. 141.

68. Millerand, as Minister of Commerce, distributed a questioinnaire to unions, Chambers of Commerce, and employers' and agricultural associations. Of the 7,860 inquiries sent out, 2,380 were returned. Bellom, "La Question des Retraites ouvrières," *RPP* 31 (1902), 119.

69. Questionnaires were sent to 196 Chambers of Commerce; 94 replied. The St.-Etienne Chamber alone accepted the principle of obligation. Ibid., p. 124.

70. Ibid., p. 323.

71. Assemblée Nationale, *C.D. Débats*, s.o., 22 February 1906, p. 1194.

72. By 1905 Keufer was a member of the Musée Sociale and of

the official advisory body to the Parliament, the Conseil Supérieur du Travail.

73. Georges Yvetot, "L'Escroquie des retraites ouvrières. Pour les Retraites, contre la duperie," *Voix du peuple*, 2–9 January 1910. The willingness to accept some type of pension program may have been an indication of the transformation the C.G.T. was already experiencing in 1910.

74. Ibid. The syndicalists argued that the employer's contribution would also be indirectly passed along to workers either through lower wages or higher prices.

75. The questionnaire was sent to 7,664 worker and employer organizations (*syndicaux*); there were 2,286 replies, of which 1,074 were from workers' unions. Bellom, "La Question des retraites ouvrières," pp. 20, 124, 133.

76. Assemblée Nationale, *C.D. Débats*, s.o. 18 January 1906, p. 21.

77. G. Olph-Galliard, "Le Projet de la loi sur les retraites ouvrières," *QP*, 8 (1907), 201–5. The author of this article was closely involved with these questions since he held a position in the insurance section of the Ministry of Labor.

78. A. Chaussé, "La Loi des retraites ouvrières et paysannes," *QP* 11 (1910), 202.

79. Olph-Galliard, p. 205.

80. A few members of the business community even made a virtue of the *capitalisation* plan, hoping the new investments would benefit industry. In early 1906, Millerand reported to the Chamber the opinions of M. Sciama, a member of the Paris Chamber of Commerce: "He estimated that half of these 20 billion francs . . . could be used by national enterprises and industries rather than, as is often the custom with French savings, being invested abroad. In this way, the pension law would insure both the security of the worker and the prosperity of the employer." Assemblée Nationale, *C.D. Débats*, s.o. 22 February 1906, p. 194.

81. "Chronique legislative," *QP* 2 (1901), 122.

82. Ibid., p. 161.

83. As early as 1896, Deputy Drake had claimed that any contribution by the state to a pension program "is impossible without profound and essentially unpractical changes." "Prévoyance sociale," 526.

84. Assemblée Nationale, *C.D. Débats*, s.o., 30 January 1906, p. 405; for Guieyesse's comments, see pp. 399 and 403.

85. Ibid., 22 February 1906, p. 1193.

86. Analyzing the Chamber's bill, which was considered by everyone, except the Socialists and syndicalists, as extremely generous, Pic suggested that many deputies had voted for it because they "counted on the vigilance of the Senate . . . to add to the text important alterations giving it more acceptable proportions." "Chronique législative," *QP* 7 (1906), 83.

87. Assemblée Nationale, *C.D. Débats*, s.o., 18 January 1906, p. 155.

88. "Chronique législative. Les retraites ouvrières au Sénat," *QP* 9 (1908), 126; Buisson, p. 342.

89. "Chronique législative," *QP*, 8 (1907), 322–23. Pressure was also exerted by Clemenceau's Minister of Labor, Viviani. Joseph Paul-Boncour, *Entre Deux Guerres. Souvenirs sur la Troisième République*, 1 (Paris: Plon, 1945), p. 178.

90. Georges Bonnefous, *Histoire politique de la Troisième République. L'Avant-guerre, 1906–1914*, 1 (Paris: Presses Universitaires Françaises, 1956), p. 169.

91. Pic, *Les Assurances sociales*, p. 105.

92. This modification of the state contribution became Article IV of the final law. Jeanneney and Perrot, p. 304.

93. Assemblée Nationale, *C.D. Débats*, s.o., 22 February 1906, p. 1194. Paul-Boncour in his memoirs would reiterate the importance of the German model, p. 208.

94. Assemblée Nationale, *C.D. Débats*, s.o. 22 February 1906, p. 1194.

95. Ibid., p. 1195.

96. In the Chamber and in *L'Humanité*, Jules Guesde had led the bitter denunciation of the 65-year-old age requirement. Bonnefous, p. 172. The Socialists' outrage was hardly inappropriate since the 1901 census had reported that among working men only 2.5% survived beyond 65, and only 2.8% of working women reached that age. Levasseur, p. 277.

97. Nine francs a year were to be deducted from male workers' wages, and six from women's. Article II of pension law. Jeanneney and Perrot, p. 303.

98. "Chronique des questions ouvrières," *REP* 26 (1912), 102; Paul-Boncour, p. 203.

99. Working largely through the mutual aid societies, Paul-Boncour sought to explain to the workers the administration and benefits of the pension law, p. 209.

100. Pic, *Les Assurance sociales*, p. 184. Hatzfeld has commented on this decision: "The interest of the employer obviously was to see that the insubordination of the workers to the law persisted, an insubordination which, we hasten to say, had very different motives [than the employers' opposition]," p. 63.

101. Pic, *Les Assurance sociale*, p. 107.

102. Paul-Boncour, p. 208.

103. Pic, *Les Assurance sociales*, p. 106.

CHAPTER 6

1. Jules Huret, *Enquête sur la question sociale en Europe* (Paris: Perrin, 1897), p. 104.

2. In order to avoid any conflict with Parliament, the decree was promulgated in August during the legislature's adjournment. The decree stipulated that in industries contracting with the state, workers must have a weekly day of rest; the working day would be limited to the "normal number of hours usual for the particular region, profession, and skill"; the salary also would correspond to the generally accepted one in the region for each trade; finally, the number of foreign workers employed would be restricted according to region. Paul Pic, *Traité élémentaire de législation industrielle. Les Lois ouvrières*, 2nd ed. (Paris: Arthur Rousseau, 1903), p. 682.

3. On the one hand the decree was a major departure in its inclusion of wage standards. Millerand was relying on a reform strategy that continues to be used. He took advantage of the state's role as direct or indirect employer, using the double authority of the law and of the employer's prerogative to legitimate regulations. It was intended that new standards in one sector would influence other employers by force of example and by pressure on the labor market. However, even this administrative act was significantly circumscribed. It recognized wage and hour differentials determined by

region, profession, and skill. Local officials, whose cooperation was necessary, were slow to administer and enforce the ministerial decree. By 1901 the Labor Office had published all the various wage and hour lists, but only some of the industrial departments and cities applied the decree: the departments of the Seine, Rhône, Nord, Loire, Gironde, and several large urban industrial centers, including Paris. Pic, p. 686.

4. Peter Stearns calculates that demands to limit the workday accounted for an average of 15.5% of strikes in France in the period 1899–1913. Wage demands dominated the strike movement, being the issue in 63% of all strikes. Rehiring of workers or the firing of foremen and directors motivated 24.3% in the same period. The strikes motivated by demands to limit hours varied considerably according to year and occupation. In 1902, 17.2% of strikes were related to the issue of hours, an increase linked to the imple-mentation of the 1900 law. In 1906, a year of tremendous labor militancy, hour demands occurred in 34% of all strikes. By 1912 and 1913, strikes around the hour issue had dropped to 10.2% and 9.3%, respectively. Occupational variations were equally great. From 1899 to 1913 strikes on the issue of hours comprised 36.1% of all strikes in the paper and printing industry and 25.9% in food processing, but in only 9% of textile workers' strikes, and 6.3% of transport workers' *Lives of Labor: Work in a Maturing Indusrtrial Society* (New York: Holmes & Meier, 1975), pp. 377–79.

5. The path-breaking British reform occurred during the first major crisis of industrial capitalism in the mid-nineteenth century: a ten-hour daily limit was placed on the labor of women and young workers in industry.

6. The exact figure was 8,980 men out of 10,000 recruits. Jean Bruhat, "L'Affirmation du mondse du travail urbain," in *Histoire économique et sociale de la France. L'Avènement de l'ère industrielle, 1789–années 1880*, 3, F. Braudel and E. Labrousse, eds. (Paris: Presses Universitaires Français, 1976), p. 784.

7. *Courrier français*, 21 July 1840, quoted in Bruhat, p. 784.

8. Pic, p. 503.

9. Paul Deschanel, "Les Conditions du travail et le collect-ivisme," *Revue politique et parlementaire*, 10 (1896), 7. (Hereafter cited as *RPP*.)

10. We can ignore an 1848 law limiting the working day to twelve hours for all workers, since it was nowhere enforced. Emile Lavasseur, *Questions ouvrières et industrielles en France sous la Troisième République* (Paris: Arthur Rousseau, 1907), p. 438. This

twelve-hour law of 9 September 1848 had replaced an even more radical limitation of the working day which had been enacted during the revolutionary month of March 1848. The earlier statute had reduced the working day to eleven hours in the provinces and ten hours in Paris. Raoul Jay, *La Proection légale des travailleurs: Premiers Eléments de la législation ouvrière*, 2nd ed. (Paris: Société du Recueil J.-B. Sirey, 1910), p. 111.

11. Quoted in Raoul Jay, "La Protection des travailleurs, est-elle nécessaire?" *Revue de l'économie politique*, 16 (1902) 147. (Hereafter cited as *REP*.)

12. Levasseur, p. 447.

13. "Le Droit du travail," *Le Temps*, 7 October 1895.

14. Ministère du Commerce, de l'Industrie, des Postes et des Télégraphes. Direction de l'Industrie, *Rapports sur l'application pendant l'année 1899 des lois réglèmentant le travail, Rapports des Inspecteurs divisionnaires du travail, Rapports des Ingénieurs en chef des mines* (Paris, 1900) p. xiv. (Hereafter cited as Ministère du Commerce, *Rapports sur l'application pendant l'année 1899 des lois*.)

15. Léon Milhaud, "Réforme de la loi de 1892," *RPP* 12 (1897), 356.

16. Ibid., 365. In 1892, near St.-Etienne, women braiders went out on strike against the double shift system and in support of the protective legislation. Michael P. Hanagan, *The Logic of Solidarity: Artisans and Industrial Workers in Three French Towns, 1871–1914* (Urbana, Ill.: University of Illinois Press, 1980), p. 66.

17. Pic, p. 545.

18. Jay, pp. 78–79.

19. Ibid., p. 117.

20. Maurice Bourguin, "La Loi de 1900 et les industries textiles de Nord," *REP*, 15 (1901), 253–54. The industries surveyed employed 20% of the labor force of the department.

21. Assemblée Nationale, *Annales, Chambre des députés. Documents*, session extraordinaire, 11 December 1899, p. 342. (Hereafter cited as Assemblée Nationale *C.D. Documents*, s.e.).

22. Ibid., p. 118.

23. "Réforme de la loi de 1892," pp. 367–68.

24. "Les Questions ouvrières," *RPP*, 9 (1896), 420. As late as 1909, after Millerand's further improvement of the inspection

system, there were still only 110 inspectors. Jay, p. 236. All reports of regional inspectors echoed that of M. Despaux of the Tours area. He called for "an expanded budget and staff, a reduction of paper work," and in general greater support from the Ministry. Ministère du Commerce, *Rapports sur l'application pendant l'année 1899 des lois*, p. 97.

25. Female workers in the needle trades were often the most abused. As late as 1905 a labor inspector reported Parisian seamstresses spending as many as 28 hours at a stretch in the workshop with only a two-hour interruption for meals. Cited in Jean Bron, *Histoire du mouvement ouvrier français. La Contestation du capitalisme par les travailleurs organisés, 1884–1950*, 2 (Paris: Les Editions Ouvrières, 1970), p. 42.

26. Ministère du Commerce, *Rapports sur l'application pendant l'année 1899 des lois*, pp. 548–49.

27. Assemblée Nationale, *Annales, Chambre des députés. Débats*, session extraordinaire, 23 November 1899, p. 119. (Hereafter cited as Assemblée Nationale, *C.D. Débats*, s.e.)

28. Alexandre Millerand, *Le Socialisme réformist français* (Paris: Société Nouvelle de Librairie et d'Edition, 1903), p. 9.

29. Assemblée Nationale, *C.D. Documents*, s.e., 11 December 1899, p. 341.

30. Assemblée Nationale, *C.D. Débats,* s.e., 21 December 1899, p. 598.

31. Pic, p. 511.

32. Ibid., p. 101.

33. Bourguin, p. 242.

34. Ibid., p. 338. The factory inspectors' reports for 1900 indicated that the reduction of one hour did not affect productivity. Ministère du Commerce, de l'Industrie, des Postes et des Télégraphes. Direction de l'Industrie, *Rapports sur l'application pendant l'anée 1900 des lois réglèmentant le travail, Rapports des Inspecteurs divisionnaires du travail, Rapports des Ingénieurs en chef des mines* (Paris, 1901) p. xlvi. (Hereafter cited as Ministère du Commerce, *Rapports sur l'application pendant l'année 1900 des lois.*)

35. Bourguin, p. 338.

36. Collège Libre des Sciences Sociales, *L'Oeuvre sociale de la Troisième République* (Paris: M. Girard et E. Brière, 1912), p. 12.

37. Justin Godart, "Le Loi de 10 heures," *Questions pratiques de législation ouvrière et d'économie sociale*, 13 (1912), 187. (Hereafter cited as *Q.P.*) The official *Bulletin* of the Labor Office went to great lengths to demonstrate that average productivity had not declined when the working day was reduced by one hour. "Chronique législative," *QP* 3 (1902), 219.

38. Millerand greatly accelerated the passage of the ten-hour law by promising that if the new statute was not enacted by January 1, 1900, he would then apply the 1892 law rigorously. Bourguin, p. 240.

39. Ibid., p. 242.

40. Edmond Villey, "Chronique législative. Journée de travail," *REP* 14 (1900), p. 109.

41. Bourguin, p. 340.

42. The content of the new law had also been criticized by several Socialist deputies since it would increase the working day of children from ten to eleven hours. In place of Millerand's bill they had called for the enforcement of the 1892 law and the eventual implementation of a general eight-hour day. Vaillant speech, Assemblée Nationale, *C.D. Débats*, s.e., 20 December 1899, pp. 586–90.

43. Ministère du Commerce, *Rapports sur l'application pendant l'année 1900 des lois*, p. 180.

44. Levasseur, p. 443.

45. Ibid., note 5, p. 443.

46. Bourguin, p. 263.

47. Ministère du Commerce, *Rapports sur l'application pendant l'année 1900 des lois*, pp. xliv–xlv.

48. Ibid., p. cxxiii.

49. Jay, p. 129.

50. Ministère du Commerce *Rapports sur l'application pendant l'année 1900 des lois*, p. xliii.

51. Ministère du Commerce, *Rapports sur l'application pendant l'année 1899 des lois*, pp. 548–49.

52. Ministère du Commerce, *Rapports sur l'application pendant l'année 1900 des lois*, p. xiii, 6.

53. Ibid., pp. 508–9, 518–19.

54. Charles Rist, "Chronique ouvrière," *REP* 18 (1904), 588.

55. Charles Rist, "Chronique ouvrière," *REP* 19 (1905), 844.

56. Raoul Jay, *La Limitation légale de la journée du travail en France. Rapport présenté a l'Association internationale pour la protection légale des travailleurs* (Paris: Felix Alcan, 1906), pp. 68–69.

57. "Chronique législative" *QP* 5 (1904), 133.

58. Assemblée Nationale, *C.D. Débats*, s.e., 21 November 1902, p. 446.

59. Ibid., p. 448.

60. Ibid., p. 449.

61. Ibid., p. 457.

62. This was despite the fact that 73% of French industry already worked on a ten-hour day schedule in 1910. Bourgeois' speech in the Chamber, 29 February 1912, in *La Politique de la prévoyance sociale. La Doctrine et la méthode*, 1 (Paris: Charpentier, 1914), p. 231.

63. Ibid., p. 212.

64. Edmond Villey, "Chronique législative," *REP* 26 (191), 230.

65. Levasseur, p. 448.

66. Assemblée Nationale, *Annales, Chambre des députés. Débats*, session ordinaire, 17 March 1896, p. 659. (Hereafter cited as Assemblée Nationale, *C.D. Débats*, s.o.).

67. Assemblée Nationale, *Annales, Sénat. Débats*, session ordinaire, 25 May 1905, pp. 1125–1126. (Hereafter cited as Assemblée Nationale, *Sén. Débats*, s.o.).

68. Assemblée Nationale, *Sén. Débats*, s.o., 3 April 1906, p. 397.

69. In 1900, the president of the Lyons Chamber of Commerce had spoken in support of the *repos dominical*. He stated that in the Lyonnais region manufacturers generally observed Sunday closing. *QP* 1 (1900), 138.

70. Assemblée Nationale, *Sén. Débats*, s.o., 3 April 1906, p. 397.

71. Senator Poirrier, the reporter of the bill, insisted that small shopkeepers be permitted greater flexibility in instituting a weekly

day of rest. Assemblée Nationale, *Sén. Débats,* s.o., 25 May 1905, p. 1120.

72. The ten categories of businesses exempted from obligatory Sunday closing were: food processing, hotels and restaurants, tobacconists and florists, hospitals and pharmacies, bath houses, newspapers, places of entertainment, bookstores and ticket offices, electrical power plants and water supply stations, transportation, and any industry whose product would deteriorate rapidly during an interruption of work. J.-M. Jeanneney and Marguerite Perrot, *Textes du droit économique et social français, 1789–1957* (Paris: Armand Colin, 1957), p. 296.

73. In the 1890s a waiter in a café worked from 8:30 A.M. to midnight and earned only tips. Bron, p. 42.

74. Jeanneney and Perrot, p. 296.

75. Henri Rollet, *L'Action sociale des Catholiques en France, 1871–1914,* (Bruges: Descelée de Bouwer, 1958), p. 353.

76. The law not only allowed exemptions, but made certain that they would multiply. Immediately before the law was passed Senator Georges le Chevalier commented on Article II. He predicted, "In order to avoid the competition of those businesses remaining open, those that are closed will seek uniformity. This uniformity will be established, because everyone will ask to avail themselves of the exceptions provided by Article II." Assemblée Nationale, *Sén. Débats,* s.o., 3 April 1906, p. 402.

77. Quoted in Levasseur, p. 450.

78. Rollet, p. 331.

79. Quoted in Rollet, p. 338.

80. Assemblée Nationale, *C.D. Débats,* s.e., 20 November 1906, p. 264.

81. Ibid., pp. 280–81. The left Radicals disassociated themselves from Maujan and claimed that he did not speak for the Party, which, avoiding a difficult political issue, had taken no official stand on the modification.

82. Quoted in Rollet, p. 352.

83. Assemblée Nationale, *C.D. Débats,* s.e., 20 November 1906, pp. 264–65.

84. Assemblée Nationale, *C.D. Débats,* s.o., 23 march 1907, pp. 984–86.

85. Rate of Strikes and Strikers in France, 1899–1913 (1899=100)

	1900	1901	1902	1903	1904	1905	1906
Strikes	108	71	74	78	119	106	176
Strikers	123	94	114	64	113	122	279

	1907	1908	1909	1910	1911	1912	1913
Strikes	151	129	141	172	171	139	129
Strikers	110	49	101	163	112	134	118

Source: Peter Stearns, *Lives of Labor*, p. 314. Michelle Perrot identifies the period 1898–1906 as the years of most intense strike activity prior to the First World War. The longer-term trend, according to Perrot, was an increase of 1,667% in the number of strikes between the years 1866 and 1911, and a 925% increase in the number of strikers. *Les Ouvriers en grève. France, 1871–1890*, 1 (Paris: Mouton, 1974) pp. 49, 62.

86. Quoted in Ferdinand Buisson, La Politique radicale. *Etude sur les doctrines du parti radical et radical-socialist* (Paris: Girard et Briere, 1908), p. 315.

87. Bourgeois, 1, p. 208.

88. Alexandre Millerand, *Le Socialisme réformist français* (Paris: Société Nouvelle de Librairie et d'Edition, 1903), p. 51. See also the (extremely sympathetic) biography of Millerand by Raoul Persil, *Alexandre Millerand, 1859–1943* (Paris: Société d'Éditions Françaises et Internationales, 1949), p. 8.

89. Persil, p. 9.

90. Pierre Sorlin, *Waldeck-Rousseau* (Paris: Armand Colin, 1966), p. 480.

91. Quoted in Levassaur, p. 480.

92. Speech to Chamber, 19 January 1900, quoted in Sorlin, p. 474.

93. Waldeck-Rousseau and other reformers of labor relations and organizations seemed to ignore the extent of state encouragement that this would entail. Union development had been the result of strike activity. If this primary arena of unionization were to be reduced, an entirely new structure and ideology of unionism would have to be created. The reformers were hardly in a position to offer support for such massive changes, nor were unionists or

employers at all receptive to such changes. On the relation of strikes and unionization, see Harvey Mitchell and Peter N. Stearns, *The European Labor Movement, the Working Classes, and the Origins of Social Democracy, 1890–1914* (Itasca, Ill.: Peacock, 1971), p. 163.

94. Pic, p. 138.

95. See Bourgeois' speech to the Conférence Internationale du Chômage, September 1910, in Bourgeois, p. 314.

96. See Chapter 1.

97. Raoul Jay, "Le Contrat collectif du travail," *REP* (1907), 576.

98. Assemblée Nationale, *C.D. Débats*, s.o., 6 June 1907, p. 353.

99. The conferring on unions of such a quasi-official function was not well received by all deputies. A few months after the decree, a bill was introduced that would have granted *all* workers the right to participate in elections of representatives to the Conseil Supérier du Travail, thus denying any special function to unions. While the bill was easily defeated, it did demonstrate opposition to Millerand's strategy, whose aim was to provide workers with greater participation in the state through the unions. Such unions, it was hoped, under the influence of their ever-increasing association with the state and employers' organizations, would come to recognize that the workers' interests coincided with the general "national interest."

100. Persil, pp. 25–26.

101. Quoted in Pic, p. 138. By 1903, however, Conseils du Travail had only been established in five highly industrialized cities: Paris, Lyons, Marseilles, Lille, and Douai, p. 138.

102. Sorlin, p. 475.

103. This was the case in the September 1900 and January 1901 elections for the five Paris Conseils du travail. "Chronique législative," *QP* 2 (1901), 329, and Alfred-Léon Gerault-Richard, "L'Oeuvre de Millerand," *La Petite Républicaine socialiste*, 12 September 1900.

104. André François-Poncet, *La Vie et l'oeuvre de Robert Pinot* (Paris: Armand Colin, 1927), p. 138.

105. Assemblée Nationale, *C.D. Débats*, s.e., 22 November 1900, p. 349.

106. Ibid.

107. Ibid., p. 350.

108. Ibid., p. 351.

109. Pic, p. 280.

110. Léon de Seilhac, "Revue des questions ouvrières et de prévoyance," *RPP* 23 (1900), 124–27. De Seilhac was an important member of the Musée Social.

111. Assemblée Nationale, *C.D. Documents*, s.e., 14 November 1899, p. 125.

112. Ulysse Roux, "Rapport présenté à la Chambre de Commerce de Valence et Drome," *QP* 11 (1910), 260.

113. Ibid., p. 258.

114. Georges Renard, *Le Parlement et la législation du travail* (Paris: Librairie de la Démocratie, 1913), p. 71. Even the reform unionist Auguste Keufer was suspicious of the implications of *personalité civile*. Edouard Dolléans and Gérard Dhove, *Histoire du travail en France. Mouvement ouvrier et législation sociale. Des Origines à 1919* (Paris: Domat Montchrestien, 1953), p. 381.

115. Vaillant was referring to the Taff-Vale decision of 1901, in which the British House of Lords determined that a union was corporately liable for any injuries or damages caused by its members. Assemblée Nationale, *C.D. Débats*, s.e., 3 November 1906, pp. 204-5.

116. The status of *personalité civile* was extended to unions in 1920 during Millerand's brief tenure as head of the cabinet.

117. See: Levasseur, p. 481; Célestin Bouglé, *Le Syndicalisme et la démocratie. Impressions et réflexions* (Paris: Rideur, 1908), p . 112; Jay, "Le Contrat collectif du travail," p. 660; Henri Chambon, "Le Projet de loi sur le contrat du travail," *QP* 9 (1908) , 174.

118. Leo Loubère, "Les Radicaux d'extrême-gauche en France et les rapports entre patrons et ouvriers, 1871–1900," *Revue d'histoire économique et sociale*, 62 (1964), 98.

119. Assemblée Nationale, *Annales, Chambre des députés, Annexes*, Session ordinaire, 12 June 1906, p. 465. (Hereafter cited as Assemblée Nationale, *C.D. Annexes*, s.o.).

120. André Spire, "Conciliation et arbitrage. Facultatifs ou obligatoires?" *RPP*, 9 (1896), 341.

121. Millerand, p. 119.

122. Quoted in Dolléans and Dhove, p. 373.

123. For a detailed description of Millerand's project, see Assemblée Nationale, *C.D. Annexes*, s.o., 12 June 1906, p. 467.

124. Millerand, p. 12.

125. Ibid.

126. Assemblée Nationale, *C.D. Annexes*, s.o., 12 June 1906, p. 467.

127. "Conciliation et arbitrage," *QP* 10 (1909), 131. Pic also observed that the law would affect only 1.3 % of the industrial establishments that employed about one million workers.

128. Assemblée Nationale, *C.D. Annexes*, s.o., June 1906, p. 465.

129. Assemblée Nationale, *C.D. Documents*, s.e., 27 December 1907, p. 473.

130. Ibid., p. 474.

131. Ibid., pp. 474-475.

132. Ibid., p. 476.

133. See 1911 lecture by M. Grossier for one of the strongest endorsements of Millerand's position. Collége Libre des Sciences Sociales, *L'Oeuvre sociale de las Troisième République. Leçons professées au Collège libre des Sciences sociales pendant l'annee 1911 par MM. Godart, Astier, Groussier, Brenton, F. Buisson, et al.* (Paris: Girard et Brière, 1912), pp. 69–91.

134. Pic, p. 977.

135. Jean Bordeau, "Revue du mouvement social," *RPP* 26 (1900), 402.

136. D'Eichthal, "Le Projet de loi sur l'arbitrage et la grève obligatoire," *RPP* 27 (1901), 511–26.

137. Jules Huret, *Les Grèves* (Paris: Edition de la Revue Blanche, n.d.), p. 156.

138. Ibid., p. 141. See also Peter Sterns, "Against the Strike Threat: Employer Policy toward Labor Agitation in France, 1900–1914," *Journal of Modern History* 40, No. 4 (1968), p. 479.

139. Huret, *Les Grèves*, p. 128.

140. Ibid., p. 82.

141. Ibid., p. 42.

142. Ibid., p. 113.

143. Ibid., p. 56.

144. Ibid., p. 60.

145. Ibid., p. 63.

146. M. Savon's unusual position is perhaps partly explained by the nature of his business, which placed him at the center of intense labor conflict at the turn of the century, the Marseilles docks. Furthermore, the head of a cargo-handling firm certainly had less ability to hold out during a long strike than a steel manufacturer.

147. Huret, *Les Grève,* p. 74.

148. An attempt to restrict the right to strike had been made in the Senate in the 1890s. See in particular Las Casses' address to the Société Industrielle du Nord, "La Liberté de travail et les projets Millerand," *Réforme Sociale,* series 5, no. 1 (1901), 820–837.

149. Huret, *Les Grèves,* pp. 170–99.

150. Assemblée Nationale, *C.D. Annexes,* s.o. , 12 June 1906, p. 467.

151. Interview with manager at Creusot. Huret *Les Grèves,* p. 80 , and Peter Stearns, *Lives of Labor,* p. 175.

152. Certain employers' views did change over time. The association of textile manufacturers, which had condemned the proposal in 1901, gave it conditional endorsement in 1903. Although critical of elected delegates, the Amiens Chamber of Commerce broke ranks and partially supported the proposal in early 1907. Assemblée Nationale, *C.D. Documents,* s.e., 27 December 1907 , p . 483.

153. Ibid., p. 482.

154. Millerand's preface to Huret, *Les Grèves,* pp. 7–8.

155. Quoted in Assemblée Nationale, *C.D. Documents,* s.e., 27 December 1907, p. 482. See also Briand's speech of 1901, when Briand was still an important advocate of the syndicalist General Strike. Huret, *Les Grèves,* pp. 157–163.

156. Quoted in Félicien Challaye, *Syndicalisme révolutionnaire et syndicalisme réformist* (Paris: Felix Alcan, 1909), p. 19.

157. Assemblée Nationale, *C.D. Documents,* s.e., 27 December 1907, p. 482.

158. Jaurès, "Une Programme," *La Petite Républicaine Socialiste,* 10 October 1900; Jaurès, "Aux Pieds du patronat," *La Petite Républicaine socialiste,* 20 December 1900; Jaurès cited in Huret, *Les Grèves,* p. 149.

159. Of the remaining requests, twelve were drawn up by workers and employers together, and 200 by departmental judges. Assemblée Nationale, *C.D. Documents*, s.o., 24 May 1899, p. 1603.

160. Bouglé, pp. 114–15. Michelle Perrot has identified Millerand's project on conciliation and arbitration and his general labor policies as one element of a much larger set of forces transforming nineteenth-century liberal attitudes toward state policies and labor relations. Perrot, p. 69.

161. Bouglé, pp. 113–14.

162. Stearns, "Against the Strike Threat," pp. 498–500.

CONCLUSION

1. The period 1895 to 1913 was one of significant increases in profits and wages. However, wages lagged behind profits and were further offset by the beginning of a secular inflationary trend in 1907–1908 that intensified workers' struggles. Jean Bouvier, *Histoire économique et histoire sociale. Recherches sur le capitalisme contemporain* (Geneva: Droz, 1968), p. 27.

2. Henri Hatzfeld in his study of the origins of social security, while recognizing the importance of the working-class presence, argues, "It is very difficult to attribute those laws that prefigure social security [i.e., the 1910 pension program] to working-class pressure." *Du Paupérisme à la sécurité sociale. Essai sur les origines de la sécurité sociale en France, 1850–1940* (Paris: Armand Colin, 1971), p. 31.

3. Paul Pic, "A Propos des retraites ouvrières," *Questions pratiques de législation ouvrière et d'économie sociale*, 6 (1905), 324. (Hereafter cited as *QP*.)

4. The independents' early argument, which stressed national strength and economic growth as the result of social legislation, prepared the way for a later position in which social reform became an easily ignored subsidiary of national and economic priorities. Already in 1907 Millerand asserted to the Lyons chapter of the Comité Républicain du Commerce et de l'Industrie, "A nation cannot make social reforms if it is not *first* prosperous and rich. . . . *First* the state must do everything it can to maintain and increase economic advantages. . . . This social policy can be summed up by the words 'peace,' 'labor,' and 'unity.'" Quoted in Raoul

Persil, *Alexandre Millerand, 1859–1943* (Paris: Société d'Éditions françaises et Internationales, 1949), p. 61. (Emphasis added.) With some further adjustments this position came to support state intervention against strikes that threatened "national security." This view enabled both Millerand and Viviani to accept Briand's repression of the railroad workers' strike in 1910. For a further discussion of Millerand's position and its essential consistency, see Leslie Derfler, *Alexandre Millerand: The Socialist Years.* (The Hague: Mouton, 1977), pp. 232–, 262–6 and *passim.*

5. Quoted in Madeleine Rebérioux, *La République radicale? 1898–1914* (Paris: Editions du Seuil, 1975), p. 115. All Radicals were extremely concerned about being tainted with the anarchism of the C.G.T. or the antipatriotism of Hervé's faction in the Socialist Party.

6. Impressed with Millerand's goal, the journalist Jules Huret commented on his efforts in 1901. "Until now nothing has been attempted in France to establish regular relations between workers and employers by legislation . . . except the regulation of the working day. . . . Never have [regular] relations been so urgent. Never has the need for collective contracts, arrived at freely between the various forces, been so keenly felt. . . . The collective contract [would be] a work of education and social organization, . . . the guarantee of social progress through reason, . . . the application of the scientific method, the accomplishment of an ordered progress made necessary by the transformation of the economy," Jules Huret, *Les Grèves* (Paris: Editions de la Revue Blanche, n.d.), p. 255. See also Derfler, pp. 178–89.

7. D.R. Watson, "The Nationalist Movement in Paris, 1900–1906," in *The Right in France, 1890–1919: Three Studies*, David Shapiro, ed. (Carbondale, Ill.: Southern Illinois University Press, 1962), pp. 62–70.

8. Antoine de Lanessan exemplified the majority of Radical deputies who drifted to the center of the political spectrum and who by 1909 constituted a weighty opposition to reform. Lanessan received a medical degree and was active in Parisian Radical politics in the late 1870s. He was elected to the municipal council in 1879 and founded the important Radical journal, *Le Reveil*, in 1882. He entered the Chamber in 1881 and in 1891 was appointed Governor General of Indochina. He served as Waldeck-Rousseau's Minister of the Navy and was reelected to the Chamber in 1902. He was active in that group of dissident Radical deputies who opposed the alliance of Radicals and Socialists in the Bloc des Gauches. In 1904 he became editor of the moderate republican journal *Le Siècle*.

9. July 1906, *Le Siècle*, quoted in Ferdinand Buisson, *La Politique Radicale. Etude sur les doctrines du parti radical et radical-socialist* (Paris: Girard et Brière, 1908), p. 112.

10. Leo Loubère, *Radicalism in Mediterranean France: Its Rise and Decline, 1848–1914* (Albany, N.Y.: State University of New York Press, 1974), p. 232.

11. Pelletan represented Aix from 1881 to 1910. Loubère, pp. 163, 186.

12. Paul Pic, *Les Assurances sociales en France et à l'étranger* (Paris: Felix Alcan, 191), p. 139.

13. In some cases large industry was concerned with the six-day week, but their strategy was to influence the administrative implementation of the law. The Comité des Forges, presenting its case directly before the parliamentary committee preparing the text of the law, received an exemption from the obligatory Sunday rest for all *usines à feu continu*, in other words all blast furnaces. Michael Jared Rust, "Business and Politics in the Third Republic: The *Comité des forges* and the French Steel Industry, 1896–1914," Ph.D. dissertation, Princeton University, 1973, p. 230.

14. For a different analysis, see Hatzfeld.

15. Particularly after its reorganization in 1890 and the appointment of Robert Pinot as secretary general in 1904, the Comité des Forges set the tone and the pace for the stance of large industry toward the state, especially in the area of labor legislation. André François-Poncet, *La Vie et l'oeuvre de Robert Pinot* (Paris: Armand Colin, 1927), pp. 96–100, 138.

16. Michael J. Rust attributes the association's flexibility on labor legislation to its "participation in such an intimate way in the preparation of the legislation and regulation which would affect the steel indsutry," p. 230.

17. Jean Lambert, *Le Patron: De l'Avènement à la contestation* (Brussels: Bloud & Gay, 1969), pp. 135–137.

18. "Aristote et la programme sociale de la Troisième République," *Revue politique et parlementaire*, 18 (1898), 186. (Hereafter cited as *RPP*.)

19. Robert Pinot, *Les Oeuvres sociales des industries métallurgiques* (Paris: Armand Colin, 1924), p. 220.

20. Rust, p. 229.

21. Louis Guérin, "Discours," *Fédération des industriels et commerçants français* (11 novembre 1905), pp. 117–121. Emphasis added.

22. The specific issue was the extension of the regulated working day to women and children in commercial enterprises. France. Assemblée nationale. *Annales. Chambre des députés. Débats*, session ordinaire, 22 juin 1896, p. 362. (Hereafter cited as Assemblée nationale, *C.D. Débats*, s.o.)

23. "Revue des questions ouvrières et de prévoyance," *RPP*, 31 (1902), 608. The project under question called for an eight hour day for miners. The authors were arguing for the exemption of the less profitable southern coal fields from the proposed reform.

24. The labor inspector reports always ended with a plea for increased budget allocations to expand the staff and increase salaries. France. Ministère du Commerce, de l'Industrie, des Postes et de Télégraphes. Direction de l'Industrie. *Rapports sur l'application pendant l'année 1899 des lois réglèmentant le travail, Rapports des inspecteurs divisionnaires du travail, Rapports des Ingénieurs en chef des mines.* (Paris: 1900), p. xciv. (Hereafter cited as Ministère du Commerce, *Rapports sur l'application pendant l'année 1899 des lois.*)

25. Paul Pic complained that the 1900 statute on the working day had "much too numerous a list of exceptions." *Traité élémentaire de la législation industrielle. Les Lois ouvrières*, 2nd ed. (Paris: Arthur Rousseau, 1903), pp. 596–597.

26. This position was repeatedly expressed in the interviews collected by Huret, *Les Grèves*, pp. 24–30, 40–41, 53, 90.

27. Léon Milhaud, "La Reforme de la loi de 1892," *RPP*, 12 (1897), 346.

28. See inspectors' report, Ministère du Commerce, *Rapports sur l'application pendant l'année 1899 des lois* (Paris: 1900), pp. xv–xvi.

29. Georges Renard *Le Parlement et la législation du travail* (Paris: Librairie de "La Démocratie," 1913), p. 120. Emphasis added.

30. "Manant rapport," Comité Républicain du Commerce et de l'Industrie. Cited in Huret, *Les Grèves*, p. 172. Emphasis added.

31. Parliamentary debates on the old age pension and progressive income tax presented irrefutable evidence of the reluctance on the part of small and large employers to finance social reform. Many regarded any transfer of their profits and income as the violation of property rights.

32. Assemblée nationale. *C.D. Débats*, s.o., 22 juin 1896, p. 360. The parliamentarians' ambivalence on social reform is exempli-

fied by the votes on Berry's amendment. All businesses which prepared and sold food directly to the public were to be exempt from the regulation of female and child labor. This amendment passed 318 to 245, but was then further amended in order to regulate the hours of children. This second amendment also passed 268 to 257. Ibid., p. 365.

33. M. Berry's criticism of reform is especially rich in that it captures more than one bourgeois attitude toward work and leisure. The deputy was defending both the propertied, affluent bourgeois (a wealthy, provincial manufacturer, for example) who had the leisure and resources to travel, stay in hotels and dine, and the *petit commerçant* whose business provided the amenities and luxuries for the bourgeoisie. While these two bourgeois strata are socially and economically distinct, they share a similar commitment to property and perhaps more important, a dependence on cheap labor. For the bourgeois as consumer, cheap labor created the rewards of affluence. For the petit bourgeois retailer, cheap labor insured a profit and a livelihood. In one case property guarantees leisure and pleasure (*aisance*); in the other property guarantees profit. Berry intended to protect both.

34. For an analysis of the introduction of collective bargaining in labor relations under the aegis of the employers' initiative in the period 1910–1914, see Peter N. Stearns, "Against the Strike Threat: Employer Policy toward Labor Agitation in France, 1900–1914," *Journal of Modern History* (December 1968), pp. 474–500.

35. Bernard H. Moss, *The Origins of the French Labor Movement 1830–1914. The Socialism of Skilled Workers* (Berkeley: University of California Press, 1976), p. 151 and *passim.*

36. Henry Peiter, "Institutions and Attitudes: The Consolidation of the Business Community in Bourgeois France, 1880–1914," *Journal of Social History* (Summer 1976), p. 513.

37. Jules Huret, *Enquête sur la question sociale en Europe* (Paris: Perrin & Cie., 1897), p. 21. Emphasis added.

38. Michelle Perrot links developments in pre-war France to other parliamentary industrial states. "These efforts, these reflections which were parallel rather than convergent illustrate the social transformation that the capitalist states had begun on the eve of the First World War. Among the most perceptive and realistic groups within those societies, the necessary to break with an out of date liberalism and to organize labor appeared indisputable." p. 717.

Index

By the same Author

IN A PROVINCE

VENTURE TO THE INTERIOR

THE AUTHOR

VENTURE
TO THE INTERIOR

By

Laurens van der Post

1952

THE HOGARTH PRESS

LONDON

PUBLISHED BY

The Hogarth Press Ltd

LONDON

★

Clarke, Irwin & Co. Ltd

TORONTO

FIRST PUBLISHED: JANUARY 1952
SECOND IMPRESSION: JANUARY 1952
THIRD IMPRESSION: JANUARY 1952
FOURTH IMPRESSION: FEBRUARY 1952
FIFTH IMPRESSION: APRIL 1952
SIXTH IMPRESSION: JUNE 1952
PRINTED IN GREAT BRITAIN
ALL RIGHTS RESERVED

For
INGARET GIFFARD
in order to defeat the latest
of many separations

*I owe a great deal to Frances Cornford,
Robert Chapman and my wife, Ingaret
Giffard, for helping to prepare the manu-
script of this book for publication*

CONTENTS

*

MAPS

Preface

ON the morning of May 10, 1949, I sat, full of resentment, at Air Terminal House in London. With me were about twenty other persons, waiting for a bus to take us to the aerodrome at Heath Row. I was painfully aware that once again my life was not proceeding according to my conscious plan. My bitterness, although it may not have been excusable, was certainly understandable. Ever since as a soldier I left England in 1940, I had been longing and planning to get back, but hitherto the over-all pattern of my life had shown very little regard either for my planning or my longing. I was not to see England again between 1940 and 1945.

My own war had taken me further and further away from England to increasingly unexpected and remote places, with the prospects of leave at home growing correspondingly less and less. It had led me, with the most meticulous timing and with an air of predetermined finality, from behind the enemy lines in Abyssinia, from the Western desert, Syria and the Transjordan frontier, through the jungles of the Dutch East Indies, to several years of incarceration in Japanese prisoner-of-war camps. Then, in August 1945, when the wars of most other soldiers were coming to an end, mine rediscovered itself and found in the nationalist resurgence in Java and Sumatra justification for continuing my own private and personal part well into 1947.

Except for one tantalizing fortnight in October 1945, when Lord Mountbatten sent me to London to report to the Prime Minister and the War Cabinet, I did not see England from 1940 until the August of 1947.

I had come back eagerly then. My prisoner-of-war conscience was at last at rest. I felt that I had tried to put the sum of the whole above the sum of my own individual part of life, for as long as had been useful or necessary; and perhaps from my own selfish point of view, for even longer than was reasonable or wise.

I had done freely without any kind of outside compulsion all that I could to redeem those grim, inarticulate years in prison. For the first time since I had walked into a Japanese trap, nearly five years before, in Java in the valley of Lebaksembada—which as its Sundanese name nicely implies was "so well made"—I seemed rid of a certain sense of humiliation. For during those long, seasonless and tranced Indonesian years, I had been dogged by the thought of my friends and countrymen going out daily to battle, while I withered behind prison walls.

I had promised myself then that if I survived, which at that moment seemed most unlikely, I would never again return to a life of nothing but private profit and personal gain. I would try never again to say "NO" to life in its full, complete sense, no matter in how humble or perplexed a guise it presented itself.

From where I was in the midst of it, the war seemed essentially a product of profound negation; the fearful problem child of "NO" parents; of so many generations of such a planned, closely-argued, well-reasoned and determined no-ness, that just saying "NO" to living in its deep, instinctive aspects had become the dreary unconscious routine. By this wilful, persistent no-ness we had turned one half of life, potentially a rich and powerful ally, into the active and embittered enemy of the other. . . .

One afternoon in 1949 a letter summoned me to an annexe of Whitehall. I was told that in Nyasaland—I always thought of it as the old British Central Africa—there were two tracts of country about which London could not obtain any information it really wanted. One was a huge, rugged mountain mass in the extreme south of the Protectorate; the other a large plateau abruptly and precipitously set from eight to nine thousand feet above the lakes and plains of the extreme north of the territory. Neither, of course, was completely unknown. Both had been partially explored; casually looked at by all kinds of people in the past. Enthusiastic botanists, odd prospectors and hunters, the more enterprising district commissioners, forestry officers and other government officials had all been to these two areas from time to time. They had even been put on the map with a confident air of detailed precision. But now the knowledge that was being gained from flying over them by aeroplane suggested more and more that the maps were misleading, if not spurious, and in any case woefully inadequate.

When all this miscellaneous information was put together here in London it did not amount to much, and was not the sort of knowledge that could be put to any specific use.

Something more definite and up-to-date about these two areas was wanted. And so they asked me if I would go and have a closer look at them on foot, and come back and tell them what they really looked like, not in the days of Livingstone and Tippo Sahib but in this desperate year 1949. And if I was prepared to go, would I go at once, please?

The matter was urgent. Production of food in the world, and particularly in the Empire and Britain, was beginning to fail, in a sort of geometric retrogression, to keep up with increases of population. Moreover, as our troubles with the Argentine so clearly showed, anything that could help to make Britain independent of alien sources of food should be done, and done as quickly as possible. There was a chance that these areas might help.

Put in this way, I hope it is clear from what I have already said that whatever my own wishes, convenience and determination in the matter, I could not have refused to go without doing violence to conscious convictions.

And yet for me, who may well have to face this decision again, the questions inherent in this paradox are not so easily answered. One of the most striking features of the desperate age in which we live is its genius for finding good reasons for doing bad things. We, who are its children, can never be altogether free of this characteristic. Consciously or unconsciously, we live not only our own individual life but, whether we like it or not, also the life of our time. We are our own dark horses. All day long we avow motives and purposes that are oddly at variance with the things that we do. For example, we have talked more about reason—we have, on the face of it, loved, honoured and obeyed reason more in the last century and a half than at any other epoch, and yet cumulatively and collectively, in the grand total of all our individual lives, we have produced more unreason, bigger and fiercer wars, than any other age in history.

The theme needs no elaboration. I can only say that it has become almost axiomatic with me to look for a person's overriding motive, his wider purpose, his deepest plan, in his achieved results rather than in the eloquent avowals that he makes to himself and to others. The outer trend confirms the inner pattern. We all obviously have motives and forces inside ourselves of which we are stupendously unaware: I believe that it is the strongest motive, irrespective of our degree of awareness of it, which produces results.

I am not suggesting that outside influences, the world of demonstrable fact and circumstance, have no bearing on the matter, but that is a point of view which has been so long in favour and enjoys the patronage of such powerful and distinguished intellects, that it can well be left to take care of itself. What needs our understanding and friendship at this restricted moment in time is this other side of life, so brutally locked out of our awareness that it can only draw attention to itself indirectly, humbly and secretly in the joylessness of the results around us. In this nightfall of the spirit, I have only to look over my shoulder to see this other side of life coming up over the horizon of our consciousness, like a dark Homeric hull sailing before winds blowing from the uttermost limits of time.

Plainly, conscious conviction was not the only thing concerned in my case. I could not have spent one half of my life leaving Africa for Europe and the other half returning from Europe to Africa, if it were no more than that.

I would tend to put it down rather to an unresolved conflict between two fundamental elements in my make-up; conscious and unconscious, male and female, masculine and feminine; the continuation of my father and the presence of my mother in me. On one side, under the heading "AFRICA", I would group unconscious, female, feminine, mother; and under "EUROPE" on the other: conscious, male, masculine, father.

PART I

THE JOURNEY IN TIME

"We carry with us the wonders
we seek without us: there is all
Africa and her prodigies in us."

SIR THOMAS BROWNE

Chapter One

AFRICA is my mother's country. I do not know exactly how long my mother's family has lived in Africa; but I do know that Africa was about and within her from the beginning, as it was for me. Her mother, my grandmother, was cradled, if not actually born, in an ox-wagon driving in the thirties of the last century steadfastly deeper into the unknown interior of Southern Africa. The ox-wagon was part of the small and ill-fated Liebenberg Trek. My mother's grandfather was its leader. This little caravan consisting of no more than seven or eight wagons, this small group of people numbering no more than forty or fifty souls, had moved in the far forefront of a vast exodus. They formed part of the great Trek of Dutch farmers from British rule at the Cape.

They had crossed the Karroo safely; hauled their wagons laboriously through the boulder-strewn drifts of the Orange River; crossed the wide, melancholy plains of the Free State and forded the deep, yellow Vaal River. They had gone safely across the highveld of the Transvaal, which was plundered bare and still smoked after the raids of Zulu and Matabele, and were moving into the Bushveld, somewhere near where the town of Louis Trichardt stands to-day, when they in their turn were attacked. We shall never know precisely what happened.

My grandmother was little more than a baby; she could just run about and speak. All that is known about the attack is what was gathered afterwards from the incoherent account in broken Afrikaans given by the half-caste maid, who looked after my grandmother and her baby sister.

According to the maid, the wagons, after a long and exhausting trek, had come to rest the night before on the banks of a fairly big stream. During the night the two little children were very restless and had kept their parents awake with their crying. As a result, the maid was ordered just before dawn to dress the children and take them out of earshot of the wagons. One gets a clear impression from this order of how little the sleeping lager suspected what fate had in store for it. The maid had collected the children and had taken them down to the stream, as she had some washing to do.

She had not been there many minutes when the quiet—that lovely musical, rhythmical quiet of the Bushveld at dawn—was broken with the war-cries and yells of the attacking Kaffirs. She must have walked through a gap in the encircling *impi*[1] just before it drew its horns tight around the sleeping wagons. She snatched the two little girls and, with one under each arm, ran ducking along the side of the stream until she came to a wide, shallow waterfall. The stream fell, as I myself have so often seen them do in Africa, over a wide, overhanging ledge of stone. Behind the water there was a dry hollow, and shelter. The nurse dodged in behind this curtain of water and sat there fearfully all day with her terrified, uncomprehending charges. Late that night she crept out. She found the wagons burnt out and the battered, disfigured bodies of all who had been in them strewn far around.

Somehow, sheltering behind the waterfall by day and going out to forage when it became dark, she kept herself and the children alive. Nearly a week later they were picked up by a party of horsemen, who were wisely patrolling the disturbed country ahead of a much bigger trek following in the Liebenberg tracks.

I have no intention of writing a family history, but this

[1] "Impi" is the Zulu or Sindabile for an army or regiment. This force usually attacked in a formation shaped like a crescent moon: thin and light at the tips of the horns; deep and solid in the centre. The task of the horns was to spread out and surround the enemy; that of the centre constantly to reinforce its extreme flanks.

4

much appeared necessary because it shows, as nothing else can show, how much Africa is my mother's country. Her mother told her the story repeatedly from as early as she could remember; I heard it similarly from her. I heard it over and over again from my aunts, each telling it with their own slight, colourful variations; but, alas, I never heard it from my grandmother, because she died before I was born. I heard it, however, from my grandfather who lived to be nearly a hundred.

And he, too, whatever his ancestral origin, was essentially a part of that same Africa. He also, as a young boy, was involved in the great trek to the north; at the age of fourteen and a half he was carrying a man's rifle on his shoulder and was captured by the redoubtable Sir Harry Smith at the battle of Boomplaas in 1848. He fought in the Kaffir and Basuto wars and helped to clear the Free State hills of their last marauding bushmen.

His own farm was called Boesmansfontein, the fountain of bushman. And what a farm it was! I remember, as a child, sitting with him on a hill one Sunday morning, and his pointing out to me how his land stretched as far as we could see in every direction. He had twelve miles of river running through it; a river with a name that suggests an individual and special history of its own: the Knapsack River. His land had long ranges of hills down the centre of it; wide, flower-covered vleis; plains thick with sheep, wild horses, cattle and flickering springbuck.

We were told with an air of implied, delightful and flattering secrecy by my mother that he had bought it all from the Griquas for a couple of barrels of Cape Brandy— red lavender the Griquas called it—and two dozen frock coats and top hats.

My grandfather's house was filled with the strangest, most colourful collection of warm-hearted human relics and harmless scoundrels from the Free State's great and vanishing past. When they became too much for his generous but circumspect spirit, they fled to my mother, whom they had known ever since she was born. In defiance of the cold convention already being thrust on the country by self-conscious patriots from the Cape, who had never risked life and limb in war or trek, they never used the formal "mistress" or even the slightly warmer "Nonna" of the Cape Malays, but insisted on calling her, as her family always did, "The Little Lamb".

There were two little bushmen, for instance, whom my grandfather had brought back with him from the Commando which went to clean up the bands of Jacob Jaer and Pieter Windvoel, the last of the bushmen marauders in the Free State. They were tiny little men, extremely highly strung and at the age of sixty still unashamedly terrified of the dark. But they had a fascinating fund of stories that were religion to them, about animals, insects and worms, about spiders, praying mantises and the moon.

There were also the last lingering strains of the Hottentots, with skins like newly strung telephone wires and haunted Nylotic faces. They too told us endless stories about animals, about wolves, jackals, hares and tortoises, about elephants, birds and baboons, but also about beings half-animal, half-human, and stories of witchcraft and magic under the moon.

Again there were serious, rather business-like Basutos who, under my grandfather's firm hand, carried the real responsibility of working his vast lands. And there were disreputable old Griquas, who knew intuitively that no matter how drunk they became or how often they were jailed for petty theft, they were certain of forgiveness and a sure sustenance, because of my grandfather's conscience. And they knew that they were loved by my mother and her entire family.

There was in particular one old Griqua, Jan Kok, too old for either virtue or sin. He was so old that his age was popularly estimated at anything between one hundred and one hundred and twenty years. But no one, least of all he himself, knew for sure. He was a nephew of Adam Kok, the greatest of the Griqua kings, who had in his day concluded treaties with the British Government. He would sit all day long sunning himself in the kitchen courtyard and often he would tell me, in a blurred voice, the strangest things about Africa. He told me, for instance, that one part of the Griqua people—the other part, of course, was European— had come from the far northern Interior of Africa, from the other side of mountains which shook and rumbled, sending fire and smoke into the sky.

When his dim old eyes were troubled, he would frequently sing to himself a hymn learnt nearly a hundred years before from the great missionary Dr. Philip, who is hated by so many of my countrymen to this day as though he were still alive. It began: "Lord, how does thy light fall towards the sea," and as he sang I used to think, "Poor old Jan, he has never seen the sea and never will."

After supper in the evenings, all that was human in and about my grandfather's home gathered in the dining-room to listen to him reading from THE BOOK. At those moments there could be seen by the lamplight, lifted attentively to catch some terrible words from the Old Testament, a wrinkled old face of almost every race and colour that had contributed to the history of the country. I have never forgotten the eyes of those Bushmen and Hottentots, on those evenings forty years ago. Those dark eyes that were solemn and glowing with the first light of the world's history; warm and content with the secret of man's earliest days. Some of those races have since vanished for good, and those places that once knew them so well are now only occupied, as though by ghosts, by people of our own colour. And so I could continue for a long time but these fragments must suffice to suggest how it was at the beginning.

One final word about my mother. At the age of seventy she suddenly distressed her children, grandchildren and her vast circle of friends and acquaintances by refusing, in the most resolute and absolute fashion, to live peacefully, quietly and comfortably in civilized surroundings. Instead, she installed herself, with a European maid, on one of her largest farms which had deteriorated under hired management. It proved too lonely and rough a life for the maid, who soon left. My mother, however, continued for some years alone with her Basuto servants, until the property was completely rehabilitated and once more pleasing to her fastidious eye. Her children then hoped that she would have had enough, and tried to persuade her to come and live in comfort, where they could see and visit her regularly. But she refused, for she had only ended the first stage of another life.

She moved on to an even more remote and backward farm. In due course that too was restored to the semblance of a well-cared-for establishment and my mother promptly gave it to a son who had just come back from the war in Italy. Then, before the old argument could again be raised by her children, she went even further away.

Many years ago my father had bought a vast tract of land on the edge of the Kalahari desert. For fifty years no one had made any effort to develop it, and those broad acres were left there, lying parched and unwanted in the desert sun. There my mother went at the age of eighty. The only people who seemed willing to accompany her were displaced persons; there was a German geologist who had been interned during the war; a delicate Bavarian missionary, whom she made her secretary; and an Italian carpenter and mason, an ex-prisoner of war, who became her foreman.

A hundred miles from the nearest village, they pitched their tents and started looking for water, without which no permanent settlement was possible. At first they hired from private contractors the machines to drill for the water. The German geologist's knowledge of his science and my

8

mother's intuitive assessment between them determined where the drilling should take place. The first contractor drilled down to 150 feet, struck iron stone—or so he said—and refused to continue.

There was a terrible scene out there in the desert between the determined old lady who refused to change the site of the contractor's task, for she was convinced that water was there, and the cynical technician whose profits, if any, decreased the deeper he drilled. In the end the contractor departed.

A second contractor, drilling a few feet away from the first hole, after going down 147 feet, lost all his tackle in the shaft and moved away in disgust. A third contractor, drilling still in the same narrow area, found after 153 feet that he had sunk his shaft at an angle, and could not continue. He too went, bitter and deeply out-of-pocket. By this time no new contractor could be tempted to try his fortune at this notorious site. There was nothing for it but for my mother to buy her own drilling machine. The aged geologist was apprenticed for some months to one of the few remaining unestranged drilling contractors in the area, in order to acquire this new craft; then drilling was resumed in earnest.

Nearly three years had gone by out there in the Kalahari desert, with the burning suns of its summer, and the searing, cold winds of its winter. One of the worst droughts in memory, bringing great storms of dust and sand, broke over them. But the party continued confidently.

Every morning at six my mother rang a hand-bell and handed her employees steaming bowls of coffee that she had made herself. "Men are like that," she says, "they are like children who will get out of bed for food if for nothing else."

Having thus enticed them out of bed, she set them drilling. At 157 feet, only four feet deeper than the deepest shaft sunk by a contractor, they struck water.

"It was most dramatic," my mother said. "I was watching the machine at that moment quite by chance"—of course, her eyes never left it—"when suddenly I saw it lurch slightly. All the slack in the rope of the drill disappeared. The bore was through the stone and in a deep vein of water. It came gushing up the shaft."

So sure had she been all along that water would be found, that the pumps were there waiting; they had been waiting for three years ready to go up the moment that water was found.

There my mother is to this day, a slim, lovely, upright, gracious old lady, whose skin looks as if it has never known anything but a European sun. She is still active, vigorous, young in spirit and convinced that she will live to be a hundred and twenty. She builds, plants trees and orchards, and grows corn in a desert where neither corn nor grass grew before.

We, her children, have all been bitterly reproached by close friends and well-meaning relations for letting her live in this way. Frankly I have not even the excuse that the others have, for they have done their best to dissuade her, whereas I have actively and whole-heartedly encouraged her. She seems to me happier now than she has ever been, in spite of the difficulties, anxieties and extreme discomforts of this new way of life.

It has often occurred to me that the heavy burden of bearing and rearing children—and my mother reared thirteen—has, in a sense, been irrelevant to the deepest and most vital purpose of her life. I have never been able to believe that a woman's task in life is limited to her children. I can quite well conceive that in my mother, as with more and more women of our own day, there is an urge to creativeness which lies underneath and deeper, above and beyond the begetting of children. These women have a contract with life itself, which is not discharged by the mere procreation of their species. Men recognize and try to honour this contract in themselves as a matter of course. Their contribution to life vibrates with their passionate rebellion against the narrowly conceived idea that would restrict their role to that of protectors and feeders of women and children. They do not acknowledge and respect the same thing so readily in women. Perhaps until they do the world will not see the full creative relationship that life intends there should be between men and women.

As far as my mother is concerned, I was moved and re-assured by this development so late in her life. For me her story is a source of unfailing confidence in the future. After many years in which the need to create must have been consciously forgotten, overlaid by a thousand anxieties of birth and death, war and peace, when it should, by all the dictates of reason, have vanished for good, then suddenly as an old lady my mother was able to turn round and find the same urge close beside her, throwing, in the gathering darkness round her feet, the clear, familiar light she had known as a child. For this it is that mother has done and I would like it to be told as a memorial of her. After sixty uninter-rupted years as a wife and a mother she turned confidently to the authentic and original vision of her life, and was at once enabled to pursue the dream of her African girlhood.

Chapter Two

HOW different was my father's background and beginning. Again, I promise not to go into a detailed history of my family; I will keep only to a few selected facts, which may possibly help to define this most difficult and intangible dimension of my African journey.

My father was born in Holland; he was of Europe as even my mother could never be of Africa. For, far back, something of Europe must have gone into the making of my mother's family, but there were no known un-European elements even in my father's remotest beginnings. He was the eldest member of a family which had its roots deep in the life and, to a not undistinguished extent, in the history of the country. One ancestor, for instance, as far back as 1572, had played a noble role when Leyden was desperately besieged by the forces of the grim Duke of Alva. Since then representatives of the family have kept on appearing and reappearing at all kinds of dramatic moments in the history of the Netherlands; here on a battlefield; there following the House of Orange to exile in Britain; now at Quatre-Bras refusing a royal command to withdraw, because of a half-shot-away arm, with a "God, sire, damnation to the thought while I have the other"; then leading an expedition to the Indies; and so on. No one action perhaps important enough to justify inclusion in text-books, but more than enough to bring a warm glow into the cold archives and legends of the family.

Unfortunately, I knew my father's parents only from their portraits. One of the major disadvantages of being a thirteenth child is that one appears on the family stage when so much that is old, interesting and traditional in its trappings has either changed irrevocably for the worse, or disappeared for good. So many of the principal actors have by then spoken their piece, and gone home. Both my grandparents were dead by the time I was born, but my grandmother in her pictures looks a most lovely, slim, elegant woman, with fearless, warm, inexhaustible eyes.

She was not Dutch, but came of a French family distinguished for its devotion to music and the arts. According to my mother, my grandmother herself sang beautifully, and her voice was greatly favoured at the Court of Holland, where, judging by the notes in her music books, she sang on many intimate occasions. I myself have fingered her music books, carefully and lovingly preserved, and, as a child, tried to play from the yellowing score that she had transcribed in her clear, fastidious hand.

About her husband, my grandfather, there had always seemed to me to be a conspiracy of silence in the family. People would talk about my grandmother with a warm, infectious enthusiasm as if the recollection of her gave them joy. But at the mention of my grandfather they became either completely silent or very evasive. I have not to this day heard the true story.

It appears that some disgrace, some shattering financial disaster was connected with him. I do not know what it was, but, very far back, very near the conscious beginning, I seem to remember my father saying to someone: "It was not his fault really, it would not have happened if he had not guaranteed the debts of his greatest friend."

But I know that just over half-way through the last century my father's family suddenly uprooted itself, and disappeared from Holland for good. Just about a century ago my grandfather, profoundly embittered, dropping a title and half the name of the family on the way, arrived suddenly with his wife and three children in South Africa. So foreign was Africa to them, so outside their experience and imagination, so unforeseen, that, when a husky negro at Capetown came wading out to their boat to carry them ashore my grandmother is reported to have cried out with dismay: "Oh, Bill, please do not surrender the children to the devil."

The burden of this unforeseen and precipitate migration fell heavily on my father. Looking back on it, and making full allowance for the fact that I was not there, I think he was extremely gallant about it; and I feel that his life would have been easier if there had been people with him who could have appreciated this and told him how brave he was being.

He resolutely put behind him all that there had been of promise and expectation in Europe, and at an early age started to be the main support of his family.

His only asset was his European background, with its culture and education. He went into the remote interior, and hired himself out as a teacher to the children of the Trekker Boers. They, like my South African countrymen to this day, had a respect and hunger for education that must be experienced to be fully believed.

His first employment as a teacher brought him his keep and a pound a month. He asked for his first payment to be made in silver, not only because it had to be carefully distributed to his family, but also because, like that, it would seem much more. For a time he taught children of all ages and sizes, from far and near in the Southern Free State. Amongst these was my mother, a sturdy little girl of seven, who, day after day, solemnly and somewhat hypnotized, stared at him out of large grey eyes which were nearly hidden under a thick crown of rich brown hair.

All this time he was teaching himself the law of the New Republic; and in due course he qualified as a barrister. In time he had the largest legal practice in the Free State. He threw himself with great determination into the work and life around him, driven I suspect far more by will than by instinctive enthusiasm. He took part in everything outside his profession; in farming, mining and building railways; in opening-up new country; and in politics. At one time he was well in the running for the presidency of the Free State. He would have got it, I think, if the people had not found something foreign in him.

Hollanders—cheese-heads as they are disdainfully called to this day in South Africa—were not popular in the Republic. Anyway, my father never became President, but at the outbreak of the Boer War he was chairman of the Executive Council of the Old Free State Parliament. For two years he was out on Commando. My mother's only brother was killed at his side. On one occasion he slipped through the advancing British lines, and went far back into the hills of the Southern Free State in a vain effort to rally the discouraged burghers, who were flocking home in their hundreds. For months, abandoned by everyone except a kinsman of my mother, he slept out in bushveld and on hilltops, with enemy fires by night and enemy patrols by day round him, separating him from his own armed forces, rather as I did for some years, in this last war, with Italians in Abyssinia, and Japanese in Java. About eight months before the end, while Commandant of Barberton, he was caught by General French. He was the second prisoner-of-war in my family; I was the third.

When Vereniging came, my father refused to take the oath of allegiance, and consequently was refused permission by the British authorities to return to the Free State. For the first time in his life he felt consciously and profoundly bitter. He was a generous, chivalrous and essentially a fair person. Not just the defeat of the Republic, but the actual fact that there could have been such a war, was a profound shock to him. He was present at that fatal meeting between Lord Milner and Kruger in Bloemfontein in 1899. He was one of the few people there who knew English and Englishmen well; he admired them, and had a host of English friends. But he came back from that meeting with a clear conviction that no matter what concessions were made, Milner would have his war.

For four years he refused to alter his decision not to become a British subject. He and his family were confined to Stellenbosch in the Cape. In those four years he wrote two novels about South Africa's itinerant past. He wrote them partly in Dutch and partly in Afrikaans, which was still an unrecognized, unwritten, apologetically spoken language. Then came Campbell-Bannerman's great gesture. My father's bitterness left him. He discovered then in his heart not only forgiveness, but also a living, constructive appreciation of something magnanimous. He packed up at once, returned to the Free State, and worked heart and soul for the Union that came in 1910.

It has always been to me one of the more frightening ironies of Afrikaner life that people like my father, who with Smuts and Botha had actually fought and suffered in the war, could forgive and begin anew, whereas others, alive to-day, who were never in the heart of that conflict, can still find it so hard to forgive an injury that was not even done to them. And how can there ever be any real beginning without forgiveness?

I noticed something similar in my own experience when I met War Crimes officers, who had neither suffered internment under the Japanese nor even fought against them. They were more revengeful and bitter about our treatment and our suffering in prison than we were ourselves.

I have so often noticed that the suffering which is most difficult, if not impossible, to forgive is unreal, imagined suffering. There is no power on earth like imagination, and the worst, most obstinate grievances are imagined ones. Let us recognize that there are people and nations who create, with a submerged deliberation, a sense of suffering and of grievance, which enable them to evade those aspects of reality that do not minister to their self-importance, personal pride or convenience. These imagined ills enable them to avoid the proper burden that life lays on all of us.

Persons who have really suffered at the hands of others do not find it difficult to forgive, nor even to understand the people who caused their suffering. They do not find it difficult to forgive because out of suffering and sorrow truly endured comes an instinctive sense of privilege. Recognition of the creative truth comes in a flash: forgiveness for others, as for ourselves, for we too know not what we do.

This perpetuation of so-called "historic" and class grievances is an evil, dishonest and unreal thing. It is something which cannot be described adequately in the customary economic, political and historical clichés. The language that seems far more appropriate is the language of a pathologist describing cancer, the language of a psychologist describing a deep-seated complex and obsessional neurosis. For what is Nazism, or present-day Malanism in this Southern Africa of my youth, but the destruction of the whole by an unnatural proliferation of the cells of a part, or a wilful autonomous system that would twist the whole being to a partial need?

I have gone into this aspect at some length because no one to-day can let his mind dwell on the Africa which is moving darkly and secretly to fulfilment, without becoming aware of this diabolic absence of good.

It is even more relevant to the immediate story that my father himself could never understand or reconcile himself to this fundamental South African irony. And when finally it reared its head again obstinately and fanatically in the significant Hertzog-Botha and Smuts breach, he withdrew altogether from politics, from public affairs and even from his own profession, and retired to his many thousands of acres of land.

It is in this short period that I have my clearest recollection of him. It is a portrait of someone finally recognizing himself as alien to the life and country about him; of someone whose nerves were frayed almost to breaking-point by

17

the world about him. Everything in his town house and in the numerous farms where he stayed from time to time, suggested then an instinctive rejection of Africa, and a reaffirmation of Europe.

The walls were covered with old Dutch oil paintings; the carpets and furniture were Dutch, and the long corridor of the large house in town was laid out with cool, black and gold tiles, specially imported from Holland.

Even the food we ate was curiously un-African. Once a month a large case containing cheeses like full moons, preserved fish, tinned hams, Chinese ginger in Delft jars and rare delicacies came to us from a merchant in Holland, who knew my father's numerous brood by name, and from time to time included some tasty surprise for one or another of them.

To our horses on the farms, to the cattle and the pet cows, to the sheep, dogs, cats and numerous tame animals of all kinds which he allowed to wander freely round the houses and, in the early mornings, even in the bedrooms of the children, he gave the most resounding names taken from the history of the Netherlands. I had two pet lambs who answered to the names of Hoorn and Egmont, and who were permitted to make spirited overtures to me while still in bed. There were two superb, prancing golden stallions, specially imported from Gelderland, they glorying in the names of Gouda and Treslong, the Lords of Holland who led the Beggars of the Sea against Philip's Spanish galleons. These stallions his eldest sons and one daughter mounted and fell from with gallant and desperate regularity.

His library, where he spent much of the day, was filled with a most comprehensive and unusual collection of European literature, in five languages. In the centre of his desk always stood a mortar and pestle made from the muzzle of a gun captured from the Spaniards by his favourite ancestor. At one side was a large cabinet filled, appropriately, with a remarkable selection of rare and ancient European coins;

the currency of his spirit was obviously not there, then and of that moment.

In those last years, a tremendous warmth, tenderness and love went out from him to everything round about him, as if to balance the growing estrangement with the outside world. In retrospect there seems to me to have been a deep, vale-dictory quality about it; an inarticulate foreknowledge that his day was drawing to a close. But into all his relationships of those years and into the life about him he seemed to pour an unfailing stream of kindliness, of generosity and love. It excluded nothing; the trees, the flowers in the large garden, the servants and employees, the contractors and shop-keepers, the animals, the dogs, the pet monkeys, the tame lynxes and jackals and birds; all shared in it. Early every morning he was out in the garden, and would himself call his daughters with a flower freshly picked for each and his sons with a peach, pear, fig or bunch of grapes. No man, beast or animal called on him in vain for help. He wore his heart on his sleeve. The lame dogs from miles around flocked about him. A little one-legged African wagtail came regu-larly into his study in the mornings to be fed. His children, when they speak of him as he was at this period, betray the quality of the man in the warm animation that breaks into their voices.

But I know he was profoundly unhappy. I remember one night being snatched out of bed and being made to hold him round his knees and plead with him not to go out and kill someone. I do not know precisely what was the trouble, but he stood there shaking with rage, his sword in his hand. He would sit for hours playing melancholy tunes to himself on an ancient concertina, or humming to himself his old Commando hymn: "Rough storms may rage, around me all is night. But God my God will not forsake me."

How could one, at the age of seven, have known what it was all about? How could one have known that it was not possible to understand and return, as it should have been returned, this tremendous outpouring of tenderness and affection in that place, at that time and in those circumstances; that love is

> "*The unfamiliar name*
> *Behind the hands that wove*
> *The intolerable shirt of flame,*
> *Which human power cannot remove.*"

Finally, how could any of us, who had not shared his beginnings, have known that, night and day, his blood murmured its own sense of his exile like a far sea in his ears. He died in 1914 within a few days of the outbreak of war. When it happened it seemed to me as if the walls of a warm, brightly lit room, in which I had been sitting, had suddenly collapsed, allowing the night from beyond the farthest range of stars to come rushing in.

The doctors said he died of double pneumonia. I know he died of exile.

There was not a part of my being to which that knowledge did not penetrate in the years that followed, and with it a growing realization that somehow my life must find a way out between my father's exile and my mother's home. It was as if far back at its source, long before birth, life had divided into two deep streams flowing on parallel courses that could not meet this side of infinity. It presupposed, in its ultimate meaning, this among other journeys.

PART II

THE JOURNEY THROUGH SPACE

"Notre vie est un voyage
Dans l'Hiver et dans la Nuit,
Nous cherchons notre passage
Dans le Ciel ou rien ne luit."

OLD SWISS SONG

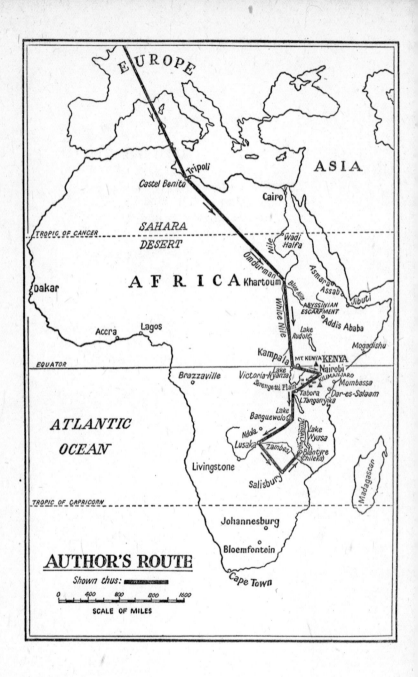

EUROPE

ASIA

Tripoli

Castel Benito

Cairo

TROPIC OF CANCER

SAHARA

DESERT

Nile

Wadi
Halfa

Omdurman

Asmara
Assab

Dakar

AFRICA

Khartoum

Blue Nile

Jibuti

ABYSSINIAN
ESCARPMENT

White Nile

Addis Ababa

Accra

Lagos

Lake
Rudolf

Mogadishu

Kampala

MT. KENYA

KENYA

EQUATOR

Brazzaville

Victoria-Nyanza

Lake

Nairobi

KILIMANJARO

Serengetti Plain

Mombassa

Tabora

Dar-es-Salaam

ATLANTIC

L.Tanganyika

Banguewelo

Lake

OCEAN

Ndda

Lusaka

Zambesi

Lake
Nyasa

NYASALAND

Blantyre
(Chileka)

Livingstone

Salisbury

Madagascar

TROPIC OF CAPRICORN

Johannesburg

Bloemfontein

AUTHOR'S ROUTE

Cape Town

Shown thus:

0   400   800   1200   1600

SCALE OF MILES

Chapter Three

I AM by now aware that I have talked almost exclusively about the mental load I was taking with me on my journey. I have said nothing, though it is traditional on these occasions, about what I had packed in my suitcases. The truth is that the journey might well have proved incomprehensible without some account of the state of mind and feelings that I brought to it, whereas the load in my suitcases was light and of little interest.

I do not know how the average traveller to the more remote parts of Africa equips himself nowadays for the journey. He used to do fantastic things before the war, and probably still does. I have always bought as little and made as few arrangements in advance as possible.

For instance, I had not ordered special boots, shoes or leggings. Nor was I tempted to buy any Stanley-Livingstone headgear, green and white pagodas (topees with sun-flaps lined with red flannel) having for years suspected the designers of these things of being bald persons determined to promote baldness in others. The tropical sun is kinder to European heads than they perhaps deserve, and I myself do not find it necessary to wear anything more in Africa than I would for the midsummer sun of Europe.

I had no pre-conceived theory about the kind of rifle I should take with me. I knew all about the famous pre-war controversy over rifles: the merits and demerits of the .22, the light high-velocity sporting make, the .375 magnum express, the Paradox, and the heavy elephant gun. I did not waste a thought as to whether one or a combination of two or more of these would best serve my particular purpose. I ordered no special supplies of food, ammunition or medicine. I felt as if I already had inside me all the medicine that I could ever need, as a result of the absurd and ever-growing number of injections inflicted on air travellers.

It has always been a source of wonder to me what the trader, be he Jew, Greek, Indian or lonely Scot, can produce from behind the counter of his galvanized-iron store, even in the most out-of-the-way parts of Africa. I have an immense respect too for the experience and opinions in these matters of the men on the spot. In a continent as vast as Africa the needs of an individual vary enormously according to locality and I have found that it pays well to shop, prepare, organize and seek advice as near as possible to the starting-point of my journey.

So all I did was to add to my store of khaki clothing, to choose some books for the journey, because they can be difficult to find in Africa, and to lay in a small supply of sealing-wax. I was doubtful whether I could get sealing-wax at my destination and I could not risk being without it as I needed it for making secure the samples I hoped to collect on my journey. But all in all, I was taking so little that my friends, with their warm and affectionate concern for what is individual and eccentric, quickly created a legend among themselves. Would one believe it, they said, that I had gone off again to Central Africa with a stick of scarlet sealing-wax in one hand and a copy of George Meredith's *Modern Love* in the other?

Broadly speaking, it was in this mood and in this manner that the journey began for me. On May 10 at noon precisely our plane took off from Heath Row aerodrome. It is a measure of the newness which still infects air travel that, although once in the air it completes a journey between two points with the utmost dispatch, at the same time it condemns travellers to dreary hours of waiting and preparation on the ground; to tiresome formalities with Customs, Exchange and Immigration controls at all kinds of places, and finally to cumbersome and ponderous journeys by road to and from aerodromes. It took us two hours, after leaving Victoria, to get into the air. But once in the air, no one could have had any complaints over the speed at which we travelled.

I do not know what my twenty companions were thinking as we took off, but once again I was struck by the brutal, impersonal quality of this form of departure. I have never ceased to be touched in some indefinable way by a ship casting off and moving out to sea. There is something symbolic about it to which the hungry, starved rationalism of our twentieth-century mind instantly and inevitably responds. The ship is of the authentic, antique material of the imagination. It must be impossible for a person of average sensitiveness to say good-bye to someone he loves who is going away in a ship, without experiencing, whether he likes it or not, something of the truth of the trite, but none-the-less pointed French proverb *"Partir c'est mourir un peu"*. Even at a railway station, the flutter of a handkerchief, the wave of a hand or a face looking back at one from a window, to some extent redeems the train's impersonal yet hysterical departure. The aeroplane makes none of these concessions. There is no interval between the "being here" and the "going there"; the two conditions are created, as it were, with one stroke of the knife, and one is left with a vague, uncomprehended sense of shock. One feels as if one had been subjected to a lightning amputation.

At one moment we were in England in the spring, and at the next we were above it in seasonless and indeterminate air. We climbed quickly. One familiar landmark after another slid into view with a certain irrevocable ease and then floated out of sight behind us. We had not been up many minutes when I noticed with dismay that we were already coming over the South Downs. It was not until that moment that I realized fully the enormity of the accomplished break.

Only a few days before, on the Saturday and Sunday, I

had walked with a friend through those fields and beside those hedges. It had been my first taste of spring for ten years. I now looked at my diary and saw the drawing I had made that Sunday of a cart-horse grazing in a field, with the long line of the downs behind, a fluff of cloud above, and the spit of a modest, stone-tiled spire topped by a crooked weather vane. And I remembered that while I was sketching, the air was so charged with sunlight, with invisible essences and the steady rhythmical movement of trees, so filled with the scent of flowers and fields in bloom, that the bees appeared not to fly through the air but to swim in it. For there is no spring, as Europe knows it, anywhere in Africa or the tropical east. There is never a comparable process of such complete, utter and uncompromising renewal of every detail of natural life. Well, we might be over that world now, but we were no longer of it.

Some children began to play in the plane. There was a little girl with the old-young face of the European child in Africa. Over her shoulder was slung a leopard-skin bag, and I could tell almost for sure at which shop in Nairobi she had bought it. There was a little boy wearing the colours of a well-known preparatory school in Southern Rhodesia, already a little white master of everything except himself. And there were the parents with the strained, set official faces that one knows from experience will only become warm and smiling, in Africa, with sunset and the sundowner.

The man in front of me was a plumber from Birmingham. He had heard that the mines in Johannesburg were short of plumbers so he had taken a few weeks off, at his own expense, to look at conditions. If he liked it, he would settle in South Africa for good. Despite all the money he made, he did not like post-war Britain; "too cramped", he said, "too many restrictions". I thought to myself: "There he is, the Pilgrim Father, 1949 model, complete with motive."

There was a young surveyor still wearing Varsity flannels

and a brown tweed coat, pleased and thrilled to be on his way to work for the Colonial Survey Department in the neighbourhood of Tabora. There was a business man from Tanganyika; strangely he looked more like a certain general, under whom I had served, than the general did himself.

There was a Director of Agriculture, a nice man with a record of devoted service, but already assuming, with a certain relief one suspected, some of the importance that would automatically descend on him at his destination. There were some other officials returning from leave; an army sister on her way to Eritrea; a missionary and his wife on the way back to Uganda; and two commercial travellers, in the grand manner, dressed just a little too well for the occasion.

The plane itself was being flown by a South African crew. It was a well-known, popular, much-advertised American model, which I personally rather dislike. It is fast and reliable, and technically, I am sure, a very good machine. But it is designed, like so many American aircraft, with only one aim: to hurl through the air, as fast as possible, the maximum number of people. I longed for the slower, more comfortable, British flying-boats with their obstinate, old-fashioned respect for privacy and individual needs.

By the time lunch was served we were high over Paris. The lunch dealt another blow to the memory of Europe. Everything—the meat, the fruit, the salads—was South African, with the sharp, almost metallic tang of the typical Southern African product. The people who served it had an equivalent tang in their voices; as I looked at them I suddenly realized that the world of modern travel is very small. Living in London or Paris, unless one plans carefully, it is difficult to see enough of one's friends. But on the highways and skyways of the world one meets and re-meets the same faces. Even I recognized several of the crew with whom I had travelled before.

I was not surprised, therefore, when the captain of the aircraft, as he came down the plane towards me, looked like someone I had seen before. But I was startled a minute later when he stopped by me and said laughingly, "You don't still think I am a German?"

I recognized him instantly. His name was Jakobus Gerhardus van Waveren. He had been to school with me, was three years my junior and came of an old Free State family. As a pilot he had come to my rescue once during the war in Abyssinia. It is like that with the war. One thinks one has forgotten about it, and then a certain look on the face of a stranger one passes in the street, the sunlight on a broken wall, the distant sound of blasting in the hills, the village butcher shooting a pig in his backyard, the smell of rubber in the rain, a bar of music at nightfall, and there is the war back at once, fresh and alive, deeply embedded in naked senses. The violence with which the memory assails one is always startling. How clearly I remembered this occasion!

Nine years before, Jakobus Gerhardus's plane had flown out of the blue sky one afternoon, circling round our first landing-strip in the Gojjam. He flew a three-engined machine with corrugated wings. At that time the only plane I knew shaped like that was the German Junkers bomber. I remembered being dismayed, thinking "Are we now going to have real Prussian precision bombing on top of everything", and I nearly ordered my men to open fire with all we had. But the plane's apparent friendliness and its determination to land held me back. None the less, we kept it covered until I saw, in that crystal-blue nostalgic light of the Abyssinian mountains, men in South African uniform step out of it. So near had I been to shooting, so overcome was I by the narrowness of my escape, that I had greeted Jakobus Gerhardus ungraciously, saying something like: "How the hell do you expect people not to take you for a German if you fly about in a thing like that?"

28

He had taken it kindly and replied: "Never you mind. Come and see what I've got for you."

From that day onwards, all of us who were with Dan Sandford and Orde Wingate had had an assured source of supply from the air. Our long and precarious supply line depending on camels whose route one could have followed blindfold for hundreds of miles, going only by the stink of dead animals, could at last be closed.

"I hardly thought it could be you," Jakobus Gerhardus now said, "when I saw your name on the passenger list. I thought the Japanese did for you. I read your obituary notices in the papers years ago. Are you going home? What do you think of my new kite?"

I was tremendously pleased to see him, and I enjoyed to the full this moment of being with someone whom I had known when I was young. He had a rich fund of information, about persons whom I had not seen for years. But talking of our past in Africa, when I said "I would rather like to go back there for a bit", he hesitated and then remarked, "I don't think you would, much."

"Why not?" I asked, surprised.

He answered at length. Things had changed a lot. Many of our old friends had gone; many of the older families had moved out. A lot of people had come from the South, from the Cape, "R-rolling bolanders", to take their place. "Paarl, Wellington and Dal Josafat run the show now," he said. "A bunch of fanatics, you know. Politics is a dirty game." Then he hastened to add loyally, "I am sure our Union politics are no worse than other people's. But when you think how we whites quarrel amongst ourselves, with all those blacks about, and the Communists . . ." He paused and then told me that John had become a Communist, had adopted a black baby and was bringing it up in the same nursery with his own white child.

I was deeply interested. John was a school friend. His grandfather had served with my father on the Free State

Council, and accompanied Botha and Smuts on their great mission to Britain. "But why a Communist?" I asked.

"He says that it's the only honest solution to our problems. But God, Communism is going very, very, very far. As for adopting a black son, God, it is going much too far. We can't stand for that. It just can't be done. My God, you know that."

He looked at me, obviously troubled, and added: "And yet you know old John has always been one of the best. I don't understand what's bitten him." He then jumped up suddenly and said: "Come and look at my kite!"

I would have liked to ask more about John but I dared not. I followed him silently into the cockpit.

We were well over France. Grenoble was just coming up under the starboard wing. The air was blue, cool and clear. Suddenly the peak of Mont Blanc, not white but a deep, golden colour, came out of the haze of the horizon. It lifted its head like the muzzle of a great polar bear sniffing the air for news of ice.

"Seldom see it like that!" the pilot shouted in my ear. "It's obviously your lucky day." But it was really his luck and his pleasure, and my irony.

The river Isère, blue and silver, flashed the sun back at us from the ground. Just outside the town of Grenoble, I could see plainly La Ponatière, a house of which I had many happy memories. It stood out formal and flat like an architect's drawing of itself, with the trees of the avenue that runs from the gates up to the house looking more like shrubs in pots than the plane trees they really are.

"Look, the Alps!" he called again. And there they were far to the east, a remote vision of snow, ice and celestial blue, their sharp white peaks gently brushed every now and then by the tip of a long, aluminium wing. A kind of hush, an involuntary silence seemed to spread from them into the plane. At the back, people became quiet, observing an unofficial minute's silence, as it were, for that dead world, that other kingdom of snow. Hard by on a ledge, I could distinctly see a small military cemetery with a large tricolour flying over it. I thought I recognized one of the many sad cemeteries of Resistance dead that there are everywhere in those hills.

And now the golden, the rich, the fertile valleys of France fell away from us, that fruitful sun-drenched earth responding so warmly to the spring and to thousands of years of love, care and civilized attention. A long series of peaks, broken and jagged, too low for snow and too high for human cultivation, tossed us about like a life-boat on a stormy sea. We came out into the still air over Cagnes. A speed-boat was laying across the bay a curve of foam that looked, on that sea so blue and still, more like a smoke-screen across a noon-day sky. A long way behind us a plume of snow sank gently into the afternoon haze.

A steward called us for tea. I had forgotten how well and how much my countrymen eat. The plumber, leaning back over his chair, asked me if everybody ate like that in South Africa.

I said: "Yes, most white people do." And he said: "Crikey!"

Over Corsica, afternoon was turning into evening. The ravines, which were deep, narrow clefts in the flanks of steep mountains, began to fill with purple shadow. The shadows of the peaks themselves lengthened and sped forward eagerly towards the distant sea; one sharp, volcanic cone threw its bar of darkness right across a wide plain which was still gold and gold-green with sunlight. The first golden line of Africa appeared in front of us just as the sun began to sink rapidly towards the horizon. Were it not for that hour and for that light, such a vast quantity of sand would have looked desolate and dull.

The plumber was obviously dismayed and disappointed.
"Is that the actual coast of Africa?" he asked.

"Yes, technically," I said, trying to comfort him. "But you will hardly think so when you come back."

Were it not for the difficulties of speech in these planes, I would have tried to explain that what we were looking at was in the first place Mediterranean; secondly Levantine; thirdly Oriental; and only then, by the blind grace of geography, African. The more one knows of Africa, the less one feels this northern end to be part of it and the more one knows the Mediterranean the more one sees its continuity even on these bleached and sandy shores of Northern Africa. The labyrinthine cord of an ancient culture, from Crete, Cyprus and Troy, from Greece, Carthage and Rome, was not broken even by the Normans, the Turks, the Arabs or the Moors. And as if to illustrate the point, the view began to produce something of Provence, of Italy and the European end of the Mediterranean. Some red-tiled homesteads, with pink and yellow walls, appeared, and silver green orchards, and cypresses, orange groves and vineyards. A tower of yellow stone and a honey-coloured wall held the sunlight for a moment. A flash of coral-pink and barbaric red shot across the Western sky; and then over Tunis it was quite dark.

We landed at Castel Benito in time for dinner. But that same morning, only eight hours before, we had been in Britain and in the spring.

Chapter Four

A T Castel Benito a new crew took over. Jakobus Gerhardus came to say good-bye.

That night the man who looked like my general, the plumber and I dined together in a restaurant built inside an old Italian hangar. The hangar was still pierced and holed in scores of places by the machine-gun bullets and bomb-splinters of the North African campaign. North African Italians served us, smilingly, with a large Mediterranean meal: with minestrone, ravioli, a fritto misto, tomatoes, pimentos, sabaglione and platefuls of large yellow apricots.

Afterwards we paced up and down the tarmac, watching the ground-staff refuel the plane under enormous arc-lights. Two N.C.O.s of the British military administration came and stood outside the hangar and watched also apparently speechless and half-asleep. The plumber suddenly went over to speak to them. Cigarettes came out, a lighter spluttered and broke into flame, and soon the three exiled heads were close together.

The business-man then talked to me about Britain with some bitterness and much concern. He was typical of the best of his kind—and the best is so very good—and his anxiety was typical of the deep and growing concern for the fate of Britain that one encounters everywhere to-day. Whenever what Britain stands for in people's minds is felt to be threatened, in all sorts of unsuspected places, even among people who have no historical, economic or blood ties with Britain, this concern comes alive. I find it most moving. I was to notice it over and over again on my journey, to take heart from it, and to hope that we would be worthy of it. My companion now said nothing unusual.

33

He simply shared the general fear that Britain might be finished, that bad leadership, extravagance, inefficiency and bad workmanship had dealt it a vital blow. Above all he feared, hating himself for the fear, that it had become less honest.

I told him I could not believe that. A people as old as the British could not change their character over-night. There was much confusion, there were tremendous mistakes being made in Britain, but in the right cause. This latest vision of a just society could not be dismissed by argument, but had finally to be worked out in practice. Its worth had to be proved in an honest process of practical trial and error. I myself was stimulated and excited by post-war Britain. It was to me a remarkable proof of the spiritual vitality of the nation, that it could launch this great social experiment at the end of a great war of which it had borne the heaviest burden. Knowing Britain and its history I was sure it would not fail.

I found it very important that at this moment a nation should try to be fair, good and true, and not merely an industrial sausage-machine in the great, mass production manner, however profitable that might be. Southern Africa had already made one uneasy with its atmosphere of medieval privilege, a world of heartless white Barons and black serfs. For how long did he think that would last, I asked him?

I had seen riots in Durban; I had seen in the suburbs of Johannesburg at nightfall terror creeping into the hearts of the European inhabitants. I had seen them bolt, bar, lock and re-lock their houses after dark for fear of what the black people might do to them. Almost everyone I knew in Johannesburg kept a loaded pistol handy. No white woman felt safe alone in a suburban street at night. Fifteen years ago it was not so. The writing, as a young South African had said to me, was up in neon signs all over the continent for people to read, yet people continued to believe that it could last indefinitely. Wherever we looked in the world to-day the whole of life was plunged into this great conflict: social good and private evil on the one hand, and private good and public evil on the other. I was more impressed than I could say, therefore, by this instinct of the British people, which made them give priority, at no matter what material cost to themselves, to a solution of this conflict.

I spoke, I am afraid, with considerable emphasis, for obviously none of us who care about the British way of living can be free of anxiety at this moment. I am sure that my vehemence put him off. I knew intuitively that he would mistrust emphasis just as much as he would avoid it in his own thinking and behaviour; probably the only emphasis he would understand was in moustaches, which was why his own was of a general's and not a subaltern's pattern.

"Well, I don't know, I am sure," he said. "It is all very difficult and perhaps you are right—but what about trying to get another drink before we push off?"

Two hours after landing we took off again. The plane had a new supply of petrol and oil, a new crew; its inside had been cleaned, dusted and sprayed and now smelt strongly of insecticide.

It was by this time very dark. For a while the lights of the town made a pretty pattern on the ground behind us, but they quickly disappeared. Soon there was no concentration of light anywhere below. Here and there the flash of a fire, a suffused glow, came up at us, but the intervals between one glow and the next lengthened rapidly.

When one's eyes had grown accustomed to the night, they became suddenly aware of the fact that down there it was all desert. At first one was surprised, because one had forgotten how hard the Sahara pressed upon the town and the surrounding land. For a long time there was nothing but the desert and the dark. But suddenly a new sort of light appeared, not an electric light but a fire of flame and living warmth. It was unmistakable, and one's imagination and experience immediately surrounded it with camels, black tents and Bedouins. The sight cheered and warmed me. After a while another and then yet another appeared, and then finally it became completely and absolutely dark, and even that faint awareness of the desert beneath us was dimmed.

The new stewards came round, took the last orders, brought out extra blankets, lowered chairs and tilted them as far back as they would go, helping passengers to settle for the night. The plumber drunk some South African beer out of a bottle with a lion on it, which delighted him. The business man had a double whisky and soda. "One for the road if you can call it that," he called out to me, with an engaging smile.

"Better than a stirrup-cup," I said. "I wonder what the equivalent would be for a machine like this?"

"Something for the tank," the plumber said with a wink.

"Why not?" I remarked; "I had an R.A.F. pigman with me in a Japanese jail who used to talk of twelve-cylinder sows."

It all seemed so normal and commonplace, there, at twelve thousand feet in the night over the Sahara. I wondered if it was quite right, and hoped that it was not too provocative.

The main lights were switched off. The curtains were drawn across the windows. Only a few of the tiny reading lamps in the side of the plane still shone their square beams of light, illuminating a magazine page here, the knuckles of a hand there. The aircraft stopped climbing. One could tell it was high by the sting of the air in one's nostrils and its taste upon the palate. The engines found the pitch they wanted and settled down to a steady, rhythmical roar. At last even the reading lamps went out, and it was dark except for one blue light over the pantry door. There we were, each alone in his own segment of the night.

I have flown many times by night. But I have never quite got used to that first moment in the dark when one sits with folded hands, alone, speeding through the air at a pace one cannot feel or adequately imagine. The night looks on steadily, its feet on the earth far below, its head in the stars. It is a solemn moment; sensations you have not felt and thoughts you have not thought since childhood come back to you. You feel yourself then to be really on a journey in the fullest sense of the word; not just a shifting of the body from point to point but a journey that moves through all conceivable dimensions of space and time, and beyond. For a voyage to a destination, wherever it may be, is also a voyage inside oneself; even as a cyclone carries along with it the centre in which it must ultimately come to rest. At these moments I think not only of the places I have been to but also of the distances I have travelled within myself without friend or ship; and of the long way yet to go before I come home within myself and within the journey. And always when the curtains are lifted, the night is without, peering in steadily and constantly, with the light of the stars far beyond.

Round about this moment it became apparent that we were not only flying over the desert but also through desert air. The aircraft began to pitch and toss violently. The stewards came hurriedly to the aid of their passengers. The hostess dashed to the children. Safety-belts were quickly fastened with complete impartiality round both waking and sleeping bodies. Lights flashed on and off. The children were the first to succumb, the older people were next.

The aircraft creaked and groaned like a ship in a gale and, even more alarming to amateur ears, the engines sounded as if they were beginning to beat irregularly, to shut off and cut in again with unexpected power at each new pitch and toss. At times one felt as if one were in a lift dropping down a vast shaft or through an empty hole in the sky. At other moments the machine flew up like a cork on an Atlantic comber or like the head of a startled stallion. A very fine dust began to fill the air. It became extremely hot.

To me, peering through the window, it looked as if we were flying through the smoke of an immense fire. I thought of a night in a thunderstorm over the Arabian desert when I was thrown far out of my seat, and hoped it would not happen again. Every now and then the exhaust pipes under the wings shot out large bright blue flames and showers of sparks. For a brief second I would see the wing trembling like an acetylene-green jelly or having a spasm of its own in thick swirls of dust. Those passengers who were not sick were soon tired from the violent movement.

The worst thing about it was that the plane possessed no recognizable rhythm which one's body could respond to, as in even the worst storm at sea. It was unpredictable; and so it continued all night. Dawn came eight hours later, flying up to meet us, smoking, surly, fuming with dust, high up in the air, while the desert down below was still in the dark. By then, everyone not prostrate was exhausted and possibly, like myself, somewhat frightened.

Just before sunrise, nearing Khartoum, we started to lose height with a sort of hoppity-skippity-hop motion. We were over the Omdurman hills, which always move me, not only because of the welcome variation they bring in the monstrous monotony of the Sahara, but also because history is here so near that one has only to stretch out one's hand to touch it.

They were still in shadow but one peak looked, in that whirling mist, like a yellow rag of sunlight. I tried to point out the sights to the plumber, who of us all seemed least affected by the storm. I told him it was near there that the Lancers, and Mr. Winston Churchill with them, charged the Dervishes.

"What!" he said, "Our Old Winnie!"

"Yes," I said, "Old Winnie!"

"Old Winnie charged the Fuzzy-Wuzzies?" He seemed not to know the story.

"Yes! Against the Fuzzy-Wuzzies!" I answered.

He looked out again, shook his head, smiled, and said: "Good Old Winnie!"

Within a minute we saw the native town of Omdurman. It too was still in the shadows, but in scores of little brown courtyards, by the bare, unadorned mud walls of houses that looked exactly like cardboard boxes turned upside down, on the edges of the tree-less streets, on the swirling sands of the desert itself, by the side of crouched camels, one saw hundreds of figures in what looked like white cotton nightshirts. They were all either prostrate on small square mats or were lifting their hands, then bowing, then lifting their hands again, in prayer to the East.

It had an extraordinary effect on one, to fly suddenly out of the desert and the night into a whole world at prayer. It filled one with tremendous respect for those people down below. I felt humble before them.

Our machine must have looked to those simple, impoverished black people below like the quintessence of human achievement as it flashed broad wings over their unpretentious homes. Yet if we looked back at the night we had just endured, it was not difficult to realize how much greater than the knowing and the assurance expressed in the speed of our plane had been that great darkness of wonder and unknowing without. Were those simple people below by any chance saying for us the prayers that we should have been saying? Had it come to this, that we Christians needed the prayers of the heathen?

It was here, then, that Gordon had been killed. There was the place, on the steps of his tumble-down palace, where he came out calmly to his death. There his head was cut off, stuck on a spear and carried out to the screaming and yelling Dervishes.

That moment stays with us, for there faith met faith. That alone is how they meet. It is a law of the universe, it is a law like the law of gravity. Faith yields only to faith; faith begets, succeeds and replaces faith. Faith creates, all else destroys. Nothing else works. Our bright and glittering knowing by day induces an equal and opposite unknowing by night. But faith is knowing both ways.

> *It is the not-yet in the now,*
> *The taste of fruit that does not yet exist*
> *Hanging the blossom on the bough.*

It is this faith that I have always loved about this part of Africa. To me Omdurman and Khartoum are not distant places, but towns on the marches of my own Africa, for whatever the nature of the trees, Africa is all of the same wood and of the same interlocking pattern. Further, these particular places are essentially created by faith.

Over the river, just past three small feluccas on whose narrow decks more figures in white nightdresses were at prayer, we passed the place where two young naval officers, Hood and Beatty, had lobbed shells from their gunboat into the massing Dervishes. Both of them are now dead. Hood, a gallant, sensitive gentleman, went down with his flagship in 1916 during that other Great War, when a shell exploded in the *Invincible's* magazine. He went to his death as calmly as Gordon had done, refusing to leave his ship or to be rescued when others had to die. Beatty, a different type of man, who wore his spirit as jauntily as he tilted his cap over his eye, lived out his faith on the bridge of his flagship that day when he said: "There seems to be something the matter with our ships to-day", and made this signal—the last of the action—

KEEP CLOSER TO THE ENEMY

Close to the river, too, was that immense railway-line stretching back across the desert to Wadi Halfa. It, too, was an act of faith; Kitchener's faith in two junior lieutenants of the British Army, and their faith in themselves and the general plan and the feel of it all.

When I told the plumber that the line had been built by two subalterns with scores of uneducated, black workmen, he understood at once what this meant, because his experience and interests in life could readily assess the achievement. He exclaimed: "It would take a ton of brass hats and an army of sappers to do it now!"

Then there was Khartoum itself. We came down low over the housetops and we saw the streets, spread out on the pattern of a huge Union Jack as Kitchener meant them to be. What was that if not a symbol of the faith which moved at the back of his cool far-calculating mind? As a result, there to-day on the west bank of the Nile is Omdurman, the product of Dervish, of Oriental-Africanized faith, and Khartoum on the East, the product of Christian, of Western faith, staring at each other, with what seems like mutual respect in their regard.

We landed between the golf-course and the town just as the sun came up. A native immigration officer and a native customs officer quickly passed us through the controls. One look at the sky made it plain that they were anxious to get us away as soon as possible. The dust was already whistling across the aerodrome and pattering like hail against the windows.

We drove quickly through deserted streets to the Grand Hotel on the banks of the Nile where we were promptly served with a powerful breakfast. My companions, their senses still reacting to the violent experience of the night, ate what was put in front of them with a dazed, bewildered air as if they really did not know what they were doing. A meal consisting of paw-paws, large plates of porridge, fried Nile perch, bacon and five eggs each, roast potatoes

41

and tomatoes, toast, marmalade and steaming coffee, was set before them and consumed with impressive dispatch. I could not face such a meal in that heat and at that hour, so I went and walked around for a while.

I stopped to look at places I had known in the war. It was obvious that all memory of us had faded. Floating on the river in front of the hotel was still the same house-boat which used to take the overflow of senior officers from the main building. Now its empty windows stared blankly at some obscene Maribou storks standing in the dust on the far banks of the river, with their heads tucked into ruffled feathers. I walked to the house near the hotel where I had spent many happy days far from the war with books and comfort; but my friends had gone. There was a new name on the plate by the gate. The garden, however, still looked as English as a garden could possibly look there in that sun. This garden, it seemed to me, and the look on the faces of the natives had not changed in the least. Despite what I had heard and read, it was still the same frank, friendly, inquiring, manly look that I had always enjoyed so much after that strange, squint-eyed Egyptian glance. That look gives the lie to the people who say that there is something wrong in the relationship between the native and the European in the Sudan. It was always better there than anywhere in Africa; there is an essential rightness about it which is absent elsewhere.

I thought of my Sudanese camel-men in the war. I had been given very definite orders that when I got through into Abyssinia and reached the great Gojjam escarpment, I was at once to send back to the Sudan my camels and camel-men, who were civilians from Kordofan. I was told that at the foot of the mountains I would find mules and Abyssinian muleteers to take over my loads and go on with me. However, things turned out otherwise. When we reached the foot of the mountains we found neither mules nor muleteers. Furthermore our arms and supplies were desperately needed. We decided to disobey orders and to take the camels on into the mountains. As the camel-men were all civilians and I could not order them to go on, I asked for volunteers.

By that time they had all done as much, if not more, than they had ever contracted to do. A number of them were ill with malaria, dysentery and tropical ulcers; others had sores and festering feet. And worst of all, up there in the foothills they were miserable with cold at night. Some had pneumonia, some had bronchitis and all had colds and coughs. None of them had anything to wear but thin cotton smocks torn and tattered on the journey.

They were in such a state, in fact, that some of my European officers protested against my decision to take them on. An officer with me, who was killed a week later by an Italian bullet, felt so strongly about it that he refused to interpret for me. Nevertheless I had called all the Sheiks to my tent where we talked it over frankly and at great length. After many hours the oldest of them suddenly spoke up firmly: "Effendi," he said, "we have come a long way with you. We are far from our homes and we have done all that we promised to do. We are sick; we are cold; our feet are tired and full of sores. But I am older than any of these people here. I can remember what it used to be like before the Government came. If the Government wants us to go on, we will go on." This phrase "Before the Government came" stuck in my mind. I found the phrase most significant. Subsequently I came across it over and over again.

Now I looked at the people of Khartoum and exchanged a few polite words here and there; I saw them go about their humble occasions without fuss or compulsion; saw them lie down on the ground so confidingly and instantly go to sleep underneath those immense trees that had been planted by their shade-obsessed rulers as a matter of course in that desert where no trees grew before. And seeing all

43

this I could not believe that the phrase had lost any of its validity.

How I envied them their sleep just then. It is the best thing to do during the Sudanese day, which is no friend to man, dog or tree. Already the day was piling up over the town into a monstrous assertion of heat, dust, glare and aggressive power.

We were hurried back to the aerodrome. A few officials with their wives were there now to see the plane off. It looked as though it were a daily ritual for them, the moment when their homesickness had a brief, vicarious cure. They looked worn and rather listless. They watched us go with a wistful, condemned look on their faces.

In a few minutes, rocking violently, the plane was back in the sky, in the dusty, turbulent air over the town. But the morning before, at that hour, we had been in England and in the spring. That knowledge must have been there on our faces to be read enviously by those pallid exiles below.

Chapter Five

I HAD looked forward eagerly to the part of the journey we had now begun. We had to fly south-east from Khartoum over country I knew comparatively well and which I had not seen for several years. In particular I had hoped to see for the first time from the air some of the country which I had so slowly, painfully and rather precariously crossed with my camels on the way into Abyssinia nine years before. But I was to be disappointed.

Once in the air over Khartoum the pilot of our plane wisely put it at once into a steep climb. Even an amateur like myself could see that it was not the sort of day for hovering close to the ground, and that the sooner we got into steadier air the better. For a while I was able, despite the wind and the dust below, to distinguish a few landmarks in that featureless country, but very soon, as we steadily gained height, the land lost all character and coherence.

Little more than a mild, yellow, unrelieved glare stared back at me from the earth. Soon we had again the sharp sting of air in our nostrils that we had had the night before.

One of the elder women in the plane suddenly went very white, started to moan to herself, and had to be given oxygen. The plane flattened out and the engines got back to their more comforting deep-throated roar. We had stopped climbing, but even at that height the air, although not so agitated as it had been the night before, was far from steady. The machine kept lurching, staggering and dropping unpredictably. I do not think that anyone felt really comfortable, and many of the passengers were sick. The element of the unpredictable in the external circumstances of our flight now seemed to enter into the minds of the

45

passengers. They began to do things which they would not normally have done.

The men suddenly started drinking. Although it was only seven-thirty and although we had all just eaten far more than was good for us, bells were suddenly rung for the stewards, and beers, whiskies, gins, brandies and sherries were ordered, as if we were about to be served with lunch. One of the commercial travellers, while drinking a double brandy, began pulling letters and documents out of a case and tearing them to bits. I heard him say afterwards that he did not know what possessed him for he had destroyed several important papers.

The Army nurse said later: "I don't know what happened. I seemed to have a black-out and then came round to find myself sitting on the lap of a strange man, drinking a large whisky." The plumber, I am sure, did not usually have so much beer at that hour, nor did he normally chain-smoke in that manner. On solid earth the business man would not have swallowed so much whisky. And certainly he would not have stared so at strangers, particularly not through horn-rimmed spectacles placed, in such a precarious and unmilitary fashion, on the tip of his nose.

For a while something unexplained and irrational appeared to dominate the actions of all of us. My own reaction was to concentrate more than ever on what I could see of the world outside. With my maps handy on my knees, I continued to look down with fierce concentration as if I expected the haze and dust to vanish at any moment and a promised land to appear. After an hour or two I had my reward.

I noticed that the dust had gone and that a world of level, white cloud had appeared beneath us. Far to the east a peak or two of the formidable Abyssinian escarpments pierced through the cloud. I could not identify them from my map. The maps of Africa betray how young and incomplete is our knowledge of the continent. Beyond the

46

peaks on the horizon to which we were heading, and above this white, level world of cloud below us, I saw a tremendous array of curling, twisting and turning cumulus cloud. It stretched as far as the eye could see, like a battle formation at the twilight hour of the Nordic gods.

It was a most beautiful and impressive sight, but at that hour it made me fear for this lap of our journey In our kind of plane, with the load we carried, I could not see how we could possibly fly over those far-flung, those dense electric Himalayas of cloud, and through them we could hardly attempt to go with any degree of safety.

They were very like the great monsoon clouds that sweep down from Burma and Northern Malaya over the Bay of Bengal. Once, on an occasion like this, a pilot of a flying-boat I was in refused to fly into them because he had known a flight of five R.A.F. planes attempt it once, and only one had emerged intact on the other side.

Shortly afterwards I realized that the pilot of this aircraft must have reached a similar conclusion, for suddenly we changed course. Instead of flying south-east as we had been doing, the plane was now going due south, and for several hours we flew parallel to that great range of cloud. Nevertheless, without a split, a break, a pass or a valley appearing anywhere in its formation, it pushed steadily towards us. The atmosphere grew slowly darker, chillier and more ominous because of its grim encroaching presence.

Morning tea-time, that abiding, almost fanatical ritual of Southern Africa, was observed elaborately on the plane with trays full of fruit cakes, chocolate cakes, cream-sponge and walnut cakes, pastries rich with cream, with jam, custards, marzipans and icing, with half a dozen varieties of sandwiches, with fresh fruits and, of course, with cups of Nile-red tea. Just after all this had been consumed, at about noon, the clouds below us were suddenly parted and Victoria-Nyanza appeared.

Kampala and the airport were almost exactly underneath

us; a long way down but unmistakable, the blue-waters of the greatest of the African lakes, unrippled and serene, stretched away south of us as far as we could see, unimpeded by land of any kind. With the view I felt a rush of affection for Africa. Africa is great and majestic in all it does, there is nothing mingy or mean in its methods, no matter whether it is producing desert, mountain, lake or plain. One could, at the same time, almost hear the relief which filled the cockpit at that moment. The aircraft, losing no time, immediately did a determined and quick bank to the east, and put its nose into a long decline.

The range of cumulus came up dead in front of us. The pilot clearly intended to fly underneath it, now that he knew precisely where he was. The green hills and the green valleys, the well-watered succulent vegetation of this part of Africa lay there for our desert-worn and cloud-dazed senses to enjoy. But not for long. Wherever one looked, the horizon was black, purple-silver and pearl-grey with cloud. The far hills were already grey with rain and mist.

Up the valleys and down the plains, over mountain-tops and across rivers, the storms came striding towards us. Those lovely smaller lakes of the highlands of Kenya, whose deep-blue waters are so heavily burdened with sunlight and cloud and pink flamingos along their shores; those snow-capped towers of Mount Kenya; those snug homesteads and blood-red roads going from nowhere to nowhere through bush and plain, were now all hidden from view as completely as if it had been night. Bumping and driving hard through heavy rain, we hardly saw land again until some hours later we climbed with relief out of the plane at Nairobi.

I said good-bye to my companions at the aerodrome. From now on our ways divided. I had to spend the night in Nairobi and then take a smaller plane on towards my destination, early the following morning.

It is one of the more unjustifiable pretensions of our age

48

that it measures time and experience by the clock. There are obviously a host of considerations and values which a clock cannot possibly measure. There is above all the fact that time spent on a journey, particularly on a journey which sets in motion the abiding symbolism of our natures, is different from the time devoured at such a terrifying speed in the daily routine of what is accepted, with such curious complacency, as our normal lives. This seems axiomatic to me; the truer the moment and the greater its content of reality the slower the swing of the universal pendulum.

Let me give an instance. I could imagine a moment denied to a life as soiled as my own—a moment so real that time would come to a standstill within it, would cease to exist despite all the ticking of clocks that went on. I do not want to claim too much for this humble, this unwinged moment there on the aerodrome at Nairobi. But I must emphasize, as best I can in dealing with a reaction that is beyond the normal use of words, that there was more to it than a mere twenty-four hours measured on the clock. Somehow the barriers between all of us had been down, the masks over our eyes had been lifted and we had become genuinely and unusually well-disposed to one another.

I now found myself borrowing pen and paper from a reluctant and harassed immigrations officer in order to give to the plumber addresses of some of my oldest friends in Johannesburg. I also gave him a note of introduction to the managing director of a group of mines.

I exchanged addresses with the business man. We shook one another warmly by the hand and promised, without fail, to meet again. At the barrier his motor car was waiting. The business man pointed to his black chauffeur who was grinning with delight, his eyes shining with excitement: "Send me a telegram, any time. Doesn't matter how far, I'll send him to meet you," he said.

49

Chapter Six

AS I left the aerodrome by myself to go to the town I experienced a sense of anticlimax. I felt as if the day had suddenly been emptied of the meaning it had possessed in the morning. The reaction was encouraged in me by Nairobi itself.

I have never known Nairobi well and yet I have been to it often, over a period of many years. I went there for the first time twenty-three years before, with William Plomer[1] and Katsué Mori, the captain of the ship in which the two of us were travelling to Japan. I was there again on my own for a longer stay some years later. I was there in the war on my way out of Abyssinia. Once I spent three weeks in hospital there with malignant malaria. I had been there only eighteen months before on my way back from the Far East; on that occasion I had arrived there so exhausted after a wild and long flight by York that I had fallen asleep in a chair by the fire in a hotel lounge. But no matter how the circumstances of my visits, or my own state of mind varied, I have always had the same flat uninspired reaction to it.

As a town it is pleasant enough and comfortable enough, but frankly unworthy of the country around it. One must go outside it and climb the blue hills in the distance, or travel along one of those dusty roads leading out of it in

[1] Apart from feelings arising out of a life-long friendship with William Plomer I believe no one with any sense of the quintessential Africa can be unconscious of a very great debt to him. His was the first imagination to allow the black man of Africa to enter it in his own human right. Even the great and good Olive Schreiner saw the native primarily as a social and ethical problem. Plomer was the first to accept him without qualification or reservation as a human being. His stories of Africa are tremendously brave pioneer achievements and broke the first shackles in the European mind-forged manacles of Africa. Books like *Cry the Beloved Country*, or my own *In a Province* would not have been possible but for him.

50

order to get the feel of the vast and immensely exciting physical presence of the Africa by which it is surrounded.

Like so many towns of this century, Nairobi has discovered the deadly, the all too facile secret of growing without changing. Such places are the architectural equivalents of those earliest and simplest cells of organic matter which reproduce themselves indefinitely by the mere process of growing bigger and then dividing into two exactly similar halves. They are towns whose mounting sky-lines seem untroubled by doubt or imagination of any kind. Nairobi was no exception. It seemed to me unchanged, and left me rather indifferent.

And yet Kenya itself and its people are not of a substance to which one can be indifferent. They have between them the knack of rousing passions and excitements far beyond their own frontier, in a way unequalled in any other part of the continent. The people of Kenya appear to live in a permanent state of agitation, of frenzy, rage, rebellion and resentment, against various facts and circumstances of their daily lives. Much of this is understandable, because their circumstances are not at all easy, nor is their existence always pleasant. But over and above this consideration, there is something about the texture of life in Kenya which appears unrelated to fact.

It may be that the Europeans of Kenya are trying to live a fantasy. Perhaps they pursue, in the un-English setting of Africa, a dream of English country life which has long ceased to exist even in Britain. One feels that an important part of their lives is dominated by nostalgia. They are obsessed with a memory which is of no further use to them.

The many people in Kenya whom I know, like and admire, all have a queer, slight, but definitely somnambulistic air about them. They are not the lazy, pleasure-loving decadent creatures that so many people in Britain think they are. In fact, Kenya is full of brave, hard-working Europeans who, despite many disappointments, retain their sense of individual adventure. But they tend to behave at times like people walking in their sleep, and many of their excitements are dream excitements.

They themselves are the first to admit that they are a bit eccentric. They take quite a conscious pride in their eccentricity, and put it down, among other things, to the altitude. It is true that the Europeans on those far, blue-and-gold uplands come as close to being an air-borne, a sky-dominated community as is possible anywhere on firm ground in Africa, except in Abyssinia. And the Abyssinians, as I have good reason to know, lead lives dominated by fantasy. So perhaps there is something in what the people in Kenya say about the effect of altitude on European character. But there is a third factor that should be considered, which is everywhere overlooked in Africa.

We hear a great deal about the devastating effect that the European has on the native in Africa, but no one has ever stopped to inquire into the effect of the native on the European. The interplay of forces set in motion by that vast concourse of black, primitive people living so intimately with a small handful of white people. Those admirable women anthropologists, who examine year after year with such indefatigable ardour the tribal patterns, the sexual habits, the cats'-cradles of primitive Africans and the impact of European culture on them, could with profit and perhaps greater accuracy measure the effect this impact has had on their own patterns of behaviour. For it is by no means a one-sided business. Some of us who have been born and bred in Africa are well aware of it.

People like myself, whose first memory is of a large, black, smiling, crooning, warm, full-bosomed figure bending over his cot and whose friends for years were naked black urchins, know that contact between Europeans and Africans is, whether the individual wishes it or not, a significant, almost measureless two-way flow of traffic. The traffic can, with proper understanding and tolerance, enrich as well the life of the European. Or he can, with his own blind intolerance, divert and disorganize it to his own impoverishment and embitterment, as my countrymen do in Southern Africa.

I could easily make this the subject of an entire book. Similarly I am tempted to ask why do so many women of great intellectual attainments nowadays have this interest in anthropology, in primitive behaviour and in unearthing the buried cities of Africa from the dust where, as D. H. Lawrence once said so meaningly, we have buried with "the silent races and their abominations, so much of the delicate magic of life"?

But it would be going too far beyond my immediate purpose.

All I must do in justice to this image of Africa, that for good or ill walks like a sunset shadow by my side, is to draw attention to the fact that the fantasies of those few thousands of white people among millions of blacks are influenced to no mean extent by their contact with the primitive. One sees it in the records of European crime in the colony. There have been murders committed by Europeans in Kenya that have a singularly uninhibited, primitive, almost innocent quality about them. There have been feasts and celebrations there inspired not only by Claridges or the Ritz but also by the kraals of African royalty.

Quite apart from the abnormal ones, the so-called normal aspects of European life in the Colony suggest that conventional morality has lost some of its power, that people's appetites are given an importance and a licence they do not have at home. There is a love of eating and drinking, feasting and hunting, a love of collective excitement, of tribal agitation, of the unorthodox in dress, of leopard-skin waistcoats, cheetah tobacco pouches, of zebra and snake-skin hatbands, of crocodile shoes and hippopotamus-hide whips, of elephant-hair bangles, of animal-skin rugs on the floor and the heads of lion, antelope and buffalo on the walls, of excess of all kinds, that is in part the result of the contact with black people around. It seems as if the presence of the primitive and of people living far down in themselves and in time helps and encourages the Europeans to climb down from superior altitudes in themselves.

Nor is it an accident, I believe, that, like his black neighbour, the European leaves a very heavy, a disproportionate burden of the daily practical work to his women. These settlers' wives in Kenya are amazing. I raise to them a light, humble, European hat, officers' demobilization pattern, without snake or zebra skin round it, with great sympathy, respect and deference.

The point is that in Kenya one cannot for long escape this paradox. The country is full of people whose emotions and fantasies are most deeply engaged in their manner of living, and yet whose towns, like Nairobi, are completely without fantasy, emotion, character or colour of any kind.

After waiting for nearly three hours on the doorstep of the Norfolk Hotel, at last I got into the room there which had been booked for me by cable three weeks before. I had to wait because there were two desperate men in it who refused to leave because neither in that hotel, nor anywhere else in town, was to be had a room of any kind.

The two men would not move from the room and naturally I refused to budge. In the end policemen were called to dislodge them. At that stage I withdrew discreetly, as I had no wish to see my two gallant opponents fall back on such unprepared positions. The police, I believe, gave them a cell for the night, not out of revenge but out of compassion.

Meanwhile I wrote my name in the Hotel Register which resembled nothing more than a selection of pages from Debrett or the Navy, the Army and the Air Force lists. I then moved into my room where I was joined by two other men who had booked it six weeks in advance. The three of us agreed, after more argument, to share it for the night.

This set-back robbed me of all desire to rest. I set out at once to track down Peter Brinsley-White, an ex-cavalry officer who had been one of my guerrilla group in the war in the East.

He had an office in one of those midget skyscrapers which all towns in Africa, despite the surrounding open spaces about them, put up as an indispensable badge of their devotion to progress.

I found Peter a little older, less harassed, but except for his dress otherwise essentially unchanged since I had last seen him. Even in the jungle he had always been most fastidious and meticulous, almost too conventional about his appearance. But now he sat there by me, behind a most imposing desk with the latest American office devices, dictaphones, adding machines, inter-office telephones of white ivory all round him, dressed in bright green corduroy slacks, red silk socks, black suede ankle boots, and a red, yellow and black checked lumber-jack shirt rolled up at the sleeves and open at the collar. His hat hanging on the peg by the door had a vivid puff-adder's skin around it. His moustache was twice as long as when I had last seen it.

We talked long and enjoyably over many cups of sweet, thick red tea, and then Peter said suddenly: "I wish, old chap, I'd known you were coming, but I've got to go to this blasted meeting to-night. It's most important. It's absolutely vital, it's about those finger-prints, you know!"

At the word finger-prints I could not help noticing as he said it a well-known look of battle come into Peter's eyes.

"You know about them, of course," he added. I shook my head.

"But surely you do! You must be joking. I would have thought the papers in London were full of it. Surely *The Times* has told you all about it?"

I said I thought not, and as he looked so dismayed and unbelieving I asked him to tell me about it.

The entire country, he said, was in a passion about it.

55

Some two years ago the Legislative Council had passed a National Registration Bill with everyone's consent. Some two months ago when it was about to be put into effect, they had discovered it meant that Europeans, as well as natives, would have to have their finger-prints taken for the purposes of the registration.

"And, of course," Peter said, "we just won't stand for it. We're organizing. We've got chaps coming from all over the place. They're pouring into town. We'll make those bloody officials retract. It's just like them, slipping such a fast one on us. But we'll go to London, to Downing Street, to the Privy Council, petition the King, if necessary. But are you sure you didn't read about it at home?"

Poor Peter. I had never before, even in the worst sort of crisis, seen him like this; but I recognized the symptoms, and thought: "Whenever I am in Kenya there is something like this."

The first time William and I came to Kenya the country was in a passion about Norman Leys' book *Kenya*. We had great difficulty in getting a copy. We got it in the end from a man who, after first professing to be without it, brought it to us carefully wrapped in a mackintosh. He begged us not to tell anyone that he had lent it to us. Later it had been a "pyrethrum" scandal, and then it was the Indian vote. During the war it was a murder trial, for which such an assembly of distinguished witnesses was needed that even the Headquarters of the Army in the middle of Abyssinia had to surrender a quota of its staff-officers. Afterwards, the fourth or fifth time, it was amalgamation with the adjacent territories, and a host of other things. To-day it was finger-prints.

As I left Peter's office, I tried to retrace as nearly as I could the course of a curious search that William, Katsué Mori and I had conducted in the town twenty-three years before. Mori was convinced that somewhere in Nairobi he could buy bracelets made of lion's whiskers and he was determined not to go back to Japan without one. So on a hot, thundery afternoon in August, with a violent brilliant light pounding on the roof tops and ricochetting off flashing white walls and blood-red streets, the three of us had gone out from the New Stanley Hotel to search for a bracelet of lion's whiskers.

Our quest was not an easy one. We spent hours in shops, while Mori with the patient determination of his race and in the strangest of English cross-examined reluctant Europeans, Hindus, Sikhs, Parsees, Goanese, Singhalese, Kikuyu and Kavirondo on the subject of bracelets made out of lion's whiskers. Towards sunset an Indian in a small shop in one of the bazaars sold him a bracelet made of black-hair which he swore was lion's whiskers. To us there was nothing royal about them, nothing to show that they had ever shadowed the quick electric lip of a king of beasts, but old Mori was supremely happy. Proudly and triumphantly he held them up against the fading daylight. I wish I knew what they had meant to him, for one could almost see in the light of his slanted, child-of-a-sun-goddess eyes their supposed progenitor walking majestic and superb. It was as if the success was not Mori's but Japan's, as if the lion produced whiskers and paraded in the light of his eyes not for a man but at the behest of an emperor.

I walked down a street and noticed it was named after a man who had given us tea on the morning of Mori's great search. A little farther down the street there stood an impressive memorial to him. William and I had taken joy in a pamphlet of his on Kenya, particularly in the sentence: "The giraffe galloping on either side of my car, reminded me so vividly of pre-historic times." In those days he used to sell Nestlé's milk; now he was part of the history of the town, and no doubt in time would become pre-historic too.

And Mori, what was he now? Did he know what I had done to his countrymen in the war, what they had done to me, and what we had all done to one another? I think the

57

war walked the shimmering streets with us that day twenty-three years before far down at an inexpressible level of our minds. The pattern is continuous; and night and day, for all our aboriginal unawareness, invisible hands work at it without cease. Mori liked both William and me as much as a Japanese could like Europeans. No difference of idiom or lack of regard, but a sense of hurt, injured human dignity set us apart.

It was impossible to walk with him through one of the towns of our people without becoming aware that at every step something was hurting him, trying to make him feel, by contrast, inferior, getting at him through his colour and his race. He must have noticed, as we did, the looks the Europeans gave us, saying so clearly: "I wonder what that Jap is doing here with those fellows?" He must have noticed in the New Stanley Hotel that people registered inarticulate surprise at his being there in their midst. Instinctively they sat as far away from him as possible.

Then too there was the Governor of the Colony. A few months before Mori had carried the Governor with his following of A.D.C.s and secretaries in his ship from Mombasa to Dar-es-Salaam, and had refused to take payment for their passages. This very morning he had been to Government House for the fourth time to call on the Governor and again the Governor had been too busy to see him. It was no use explaining to Mori, as one might have explained to someone of one's own kind. He was convinced that he was deliberately being hurt because he was a coloured person. And in a sense he was right.

For days afterwards, I used to see Mori brooding, staring into the fierce Kenya distances as if he saw his answer coming from the far corners of the earth.

I am sure I need not elaborate, but I remember agreeing with William that "Chaps like Mori will counter this colour prejudice by a white prejudice; they will put a white hatred in its place."

58

Here in front of me now were the same streets, full of shops crowded with every conceivable produce of the African jungle. I thought how old Mori would have loved to raid and plunder them. The only difference was that there were more people, more Europeans; more Indians; more half-castes; more blacks; more, bigger and fatter motor cars. The proportions appear fixed and constant for the hunter as for the hunted. The Mori process goes on ceaselessly. Night and day the same injuries and bitternesses send eager, frantic hands to pick up the threads of the same sombre design.

While I was walking, the sun went down. The storms we had flown through in the morning provided a tremendous setting for this departure. I know of no part of the world which stages this daily drama better than this antique, this ancient, sun-drenched, sun-wise land of Africa.

Chapter Seven

AT four-thirty the next morning I heard a soft, but urgently persistent, African voice at my bedside: "Bwana! Bwana! Tea! Bwana! Tea!"

I had slept badly and spent most of the night, neither awake nor asleep, in that state which collects troubles from both the conscious and unconscious worlds. In the room next door, some men had played poker-dice all night. The dice still rattled as I shaved. My room-companions had come in late, full of whisky, still marvelling at its abundance and cheapness. I realized as I pushed my white mosquito net aside that I was beginning to feel rather desperate with fatigue.

For all the speed of our flying in what is universally regarded as God's free air, I felt imprisoned in my journey. I felt as if I was moving in a fixed, pre-determined groove down a dark, opaque shaft of time.

I came out of my room and on to the hotel doorstep, just as a red dawn came flashing up behind a ridge lined with very tall, very straight blue-gum trees. Their bark, as lovely and smooth as any young Nordic girl's cheek, went pink with the dawn. The spreading light clung like dew to their leaves. The street was empty. On a vacant, untidy lot some tattered black figures lay asleep on the dark damp earth.

Standing beside bags made of good, old English leather at the door of the hotel lounge and giving me suddenly the most genuine, cherubic smile of welcome, stood a man, a stranger to me. He was one of the biggest and fattest people I have ever seen, but there was nothing in the least repulsive about his dimensions. He obviously had a genius for being fat and a talent for being cheerful. He wore his size naturally, it fitted his temperament like a glove. It

reassured me in an odd way to see him there; to see someone in this town who obviously slept well at night. He was
wearing a pair of neatly pressed dark grey flannels, Eighth
Army ankle-boots, and a dark blue blazer with Guards'
buttons. He carried a topee in one hand and a fly-whisk in
the other.

"I take it," he said, "that you too are flying in this cargo-
boat?"

I said that he was correct if he meant the Bristol freighter
going south.

"Precisely," he answered; and then with a chuckle: "I
wonder if it has occurred to you that we are taking to the
air in a cargo-boat on Friday the thirteenth?"

It had not. But, as he drew my attention to it, I told him
that thirteen was my lucky number.

"I'm most interested," he said. "How could thirteen
possibly be anybody's lucky number?"

I explained that I was a thirteenth child, born on the
thirteenth of the twelfth month. If there had been a
thirteenth month I would have been born in that. I elaborated on happy coincidences of thirteen in my life.

"You astound me!" he said with such obvious relief that
we both laughed. "But being perfectly serious for a moment,
thirteen is *my* unlucky number. It haunts me, it pursues me
with bad luck. I stopped one in the war on a Friday the
thirteenth. My girl sacked me on the thirteenth. Even my
waist-line expands in multiples of thirteen. Whose thirteen
do you think is stronger, yours or mine?"

I said mine obviously because I was the older.

"Thank God," he exclaimed. "Do you mind then if I
stick close to you for luck?"

At the aerodrome we faced another of those great African
traveller's breakfasts, while the day spilled like a tidal wave
over the horizon. There seemed to be planes going and
coming every minute.

"Piccadilly Circus," he said, waving a piece of buttered

toast around. "The movement through here nowadays is quite incredible. There won't be room for a bloke my size soon."

From a nearby table a man, who had been staring at us, suddenly came over and said to me in German: "Have you forgotten me?"

I recognized a displaced person to whom I had given some slight help with his answers to the questioning immigration officers at Capetown about nine months before. But he was so changed, so much fatter and so prosperous-looking that I certainly would not have known him on my own. He had just flown in and was on his way back to Germany to fetch his father, mother, brother and his two sisters. He had done very well, he said, and was very happy. "I am in business in Johannesburg now," he added.

"What business?" I asked.

"Oh, business, very good business," he said.

When he left, I turned to my fat companion and said: "There goes a displaced person, no longer displaced," and told him the story.

"It's all very well, this displaced person business," he remarked with unexpected bitterness. "But please tell me who is not a displaced person nowadays? This is the age of displaced people. The world is full of people who do not belong anywhere in particular. I am displaced. You, I'm sure, are displaced. Africa is full of displaced negroes. They give it a long name here as if it were something peculiar to this continent, they call it detribalization. But plainly it is just displacement. Who could be more detribalized than us British out here in Africa?"

I looked at him with new respect, and asked him to tell me more. It was simple, he said, there was not much to tell. He had first come to Kenya during the war, liked it and had come back. He had been in East Africa five years now, and had to confess he would like to go back to England. But he couldn't. He had felt out of it on his last leave there.

His friends did not seem to know what he was talking about. He, on his part, hated "the lack of style, of elegance, of manners, the joylessness of life at Home". He said "Home" with such unconscious emphasis, and added, "And I found myself missing the black faces so."

He asked me about the theatres and the buses in London; the cinemas; the pubs, particularly the pubs round Cadogan Place where his people lived, about the weather and the spring. And he said: "I would love to be there now." Then he heaved himself out of his chair, stood up slowly with great effort, and surveyed the aerodrome with a look that went far beyond it.

Our "cargo-boat" came taxi-ing towards us. It looked an exceedingly sturdy aircraft, with a robust fixed undercarriage and broad, sturdy wings, but it did not please my companion.

"Bumps like hell!" he said. He looked about him and pointed to a dozen or so people walking out towards it, all with the same mass-produced mackintoshes over their arms. "See what I mean! No style! No composure anywhere. They can't even wait to be called to the aircraft properly but have to rush out there like a lot of sheep just in case they miss something, or are done out of something. That is your displaced rabble for you. A suspicious, uneasy, unbelieving bunch!"

They may have looked a bit anonymous, but I thought they were nice, ordinary looking sort of people. At that moment a loud-speaker summoned us.

We all climbed into the aircraft, strapped ourselves to our seats, and took off straight into the sun, leaving a trail of red dust over the aerodrome.

We circled the town, which was just coming to life. I remember in particular how very golden some bunches of bananas looked on the heads of a long file of native women carrying them to the market.

We rose over the hills just outside the town and swung

south on our true course. There was no sign of yesterday's storms, no hint of cloud, wind or dust in the sky. We could see clearly and very far.

To the north the 17,000-foot mass of Mt. Kenya stood up distinctly with a long feather of snow in the centre of its blue mitre. Far to the south-east, Kilimanyaro was humped and crouched along its 19,000-foot summit, under a far greater burden of snow.

I thought what an artist Africa is in the way it displays its great mountains. The greatest of them are never jumbled together as they are in Switzerland, the Himalayas or the Caucasus. They are set in great open spaces and around them are immense plains, rolling uplands and blue lakes like seas, so that they can see and be seen and take their proper place in the tremendous physical drama of Africa.

For it is a drama of great and absorbing interest, this continent of Africa, as we saw it that morning after the storm. It is a drama in the sense that the sea is one. I do not know of any country, except perhaps the far interior of Asia, which is, in terms of earth, of solid matter, so nearly the equivalent of the sea. There seems to be no end to it. One goes on for thousands of miles. One goes on until one's eyes and limbs ache with the sight and the bulk of it, dazzled by this inexhaustible repetition of desert, lake, escarpment, plateau, plain, snow-capped mountain, plateau, plain, escarpment, lake and again desert. And one almost thinks and hopes that there will be no more of it. But in the morning, across the next blue horizon, there is more. And what is stranger still, it is there as the sea is there, in a right of its own that is indifferent if not unfriendly to man.

One cannot fly over Europe, as I had done only forty hours before, and fail to realize how close the earth and man are to each other, how much and how deeply in one another's confidence. This land below us did not as yet care much about human beings. It was as D. H. Lawrence —with that strange intimate sense of his for the character, the personality almost, of inorganic matter—called it, "a continent of dark negation". The native, whose brown huts, thorn and mud kraals tucked themselves discreetly with a kind of implied fear and trembling into the shelter of the hills and ridges there below, may be closer to it than the European, but he too is not entirely at home. His spirit bows down before it, is over-burdened and exhausted by it. The only living things which look as if they really belonged to it are the wild animals. Between the animals and Africa there is an understanding that the human beings have not yet earned.

Over the Serengetti plain the pilot, out of goodness of heart, a desire to please his passengers and because it was such a beautiful morning, brought the aircraft down so low that we nearly touched the tops of the acacias.

"I wish he wouldn't do that," said the fat man, going quite pale: "I do get so sick."

As he spoke, the aircraft began to plunge and heave like a trawler off the Hebrides. We were indeed close to the earth. I realized suddenly that for a brief second I had looked almost straight into the antique eye of a large giraffe. It was staring at the plane over the top of an acacia tree with an expression composed equally of intense alarm and the immense curiosity of its species.

"That is why the bloody fool does it!" the fat man said with a groan, pointing to the giraffe and referring to the pilot.

Thousands of wild animals now came into view. Hartebeest, eland, zebra, impala, gnu, thousands of gazelle threw up their startled heads, and stopped grazing. If they were far away they just stared at the plane; but if close, first they bunched tightly together and then, as the aircraft came steadily nearer, they started desperately running in circles.

I found myself thinking of an incident in the war with the Japanese. At Leweeuliang in Java, when our light machine-guns on the left flank opened up on the Japanese infantry, they were completely taken by surprise. Instantly they had lost their heads and all conscious control. They had bunched just like those animals, and then started to run in circles screaming with voices that sounded as if they came not from their throats but from their stomachs; and all the while we continued to shoot them down.

When in doubt, it seems, when in fear, when taken by surprise, when lost in bush or desert and without a guide, the human, the animal heart prescribes a circle. It turns on itself as the earth does and seeks refuge in the movement of the stars. That circle, that ballet danced down there by light, fantastic antelope feet was magic once. But what use is it now?

Further on a furious rhino came charging out of a clump of trees. No circles for him to-day, no instinctive nonsense; the evidence of the noise of the plane is sufficient for him, or for any right-minded animal. There is no room for doubt. There is danger about and he will deal with it. We saw him disappear across the plain behind us, still charging the empty blue distances with undiminished rage, while his mate and her terrified young calf trotted energetically round and round a dark pool of water.

"That rhino," said the fat man, looking green, "reminds me of a bloke I knew in the army."

A short while later we saw a lion with a very dark mane. He got to his feet and casually looked upwards, then seemed to shrug his shoulders and to flop down again with an air of intense boredom. As far as one could see there was nothing but this plain with a few acacias spinning like tops in their own shadows, and the animals.

But soon we had to climb out of it. The sun grew hotter and the bumping increased and so we were sent back into the cool, blue sky. The detailed earth fell away from us. It became more and more difficult to distinguish the herds of native cattle, the kraals and the narrow red ribbons of winding footpaths and earth roads.

We flew over lakes, that would be considered big any-where except in Africa, over streams and long savannahs and over dry river beds which were great gashes of red, yellow and white in the earth. It looked to me, as it always does, more eroded and scarred, drier and less friendly than it had looked the time before.

After about three hours' flying, we came down at Tabora in the centre of flat, featureless bush country infested with tsetse fly. We trooped into a dark thatched room for the inevitable cup of thick, sweet tea, but the fat man did not come with us. He said good-bye to me on the aerodrome.

I watched him present his luggage to two enormous African servants wearing smart khaki house-coats. Their bodies seemed to purr with pleasure at his return. Then he climbed into a jeep with great slow dignity, pulled his topee firmly down on his head, and with the fly-whisk at his wrist, grasped the steering-wheel. And so he took himself and his love of style and elegance away into the bush.

We left Tabora within half an hour. I seem to remember listening at one moment to the keeper of the restaurant telling us that their telephone from the aerodrome to the little town was disconnected because a giraffe that morning had got his great, inquisitive head entangled in the wires. I remember thinking how ill and exhausted the man and his wife looked. The next moment, I was back in the air-craft, flying again over the same sort of Africa.

As the heat increased and as the day advanced with a shattering, irresistible brilliance, we climbed ever higher into the sky. Over Lake Tanganyika we were so high that the great hills round it looked flat and featureless, and the waters of the lake itself shimmered, vibrated, trembled and danced more like a mirage in the desert than a liquid substance.

I tried to look south for the outline of the plateau that I

had to explore, for it was not so very far away; but another great array of cloud, like that of the previous day, was marching up over the horizon. By the time we passed over Lake Banguewelo the heat and the glare had rendered the view as featureless, for all its brilliance, as a mirror with nothing to reflect. Even at that height one was aware of the great impersonal forces pressing towards an inexorable conclusion; one saw the point of a natural argument based on a logic of desolation. Only Africa can put it so clearly. To add to that feeling, great veld fires, vast areas of burning bush and grass, now began on every side to erect immense pillars of smoke, piling up towards the sky.

In the aircraft, meanwhile, we continued our routine. We had some more tea, and then we had lunch. We drank a hot tomato soup, had a choice of cold hams, beef, mutton, sausages, brawn and polonies, and then of tomato, potato, avocado and lettuce salads, and finished with cold trifles, fruit, cream and Roquefort cheese. People smoked and drank and exchanged commonplaces.

Sometime after one o'clock, we came down at Ndola in Northern Rhodesia. We had crossed a frontier without noticing it, for there is nothing like flying for showing up the artificiality of the barriers we set up against one another on earth. Africa itself takes even less notice than most continents of these lines drawn on the map. Africa hemmed in Ndola, pinned it down and kept it in its fitting European place as effectively as it had done to the other towns we had passed. Like them this town seemed from the air to have a look of pained surprise at finding itself where it was.

For me the place was notable mainly because the conversation that I heard at the aerodrome confirmed the impression I had had in the air. The rains had failed. It was desperately dry. The fear of drought was deep in people's eyes, in their blood and in their thoughts. A District Officer who joined us said that there would be a desperate famine among the black people before the year was out. Already

68

food was short, and there was a long way to go to the next rains, let alone the next harvest. I heard the District Officer assure his audience that these famines occur every three or four years. It seemed incredible that we could have been offered such meals over the heads of thousands who did not have enough to eat. This contrast is so elementary, it has such a long and dubious history, its injustice is so obvious, its dangers and the destructive thinking it breeds are so well known, that one would hardly have thought it possible for it to exist.

As we went on, the impression of desolation became sharper. We were going deeper and deeper into the southern winter. Here ground-frosts at night had joined the work of drought and heat by day. The earth took on a darker, a more unresponsive tinge. The smoke that came up at us from the fires below seemed fiercer and thicker. The afternoon wind, fitful and uncertain of itself, raised more dust among the bushes and trees than its effort deserved.

Lusaka, the capital, brought an unexpected area of green to our notice, it is true, but the chill impression remained as the afternoon deepened and the sun sank nearer to those koppies with which Southern Africa equips each of its horizons. And sadness crept into one's heart. It all looked so like the Africa, the plain, the Vlakte, which my countrymen in the Union called in the vivid speech of my childhood "Moedverloor se vlakte": the plain where courage fails.

Over the Zambesi the purple valleys were filled with mist; a veil of cold, frost-bitten air was being drawn over the scene. As the air became increasingly wintry, the sun found a hill and crept quietly and primly behind it, leaving a warm glow of satisfaction in the sky. It was a view and a moment with which I had so many associations that it was not difficult for me to imagine what the reaction to it was among the plants, the animals and the human beings down there. How keen would be the sense of forgiveness, of forgiving and being forgiven, which the hour of sunset confers on all living matter, and not least on the harsh day which has gone before.

We came down at Salisbury in the dark. I found myself taking part once more in a dreary battle for accommodation. Salisbury heaved and bulged with newcomers even more than Nairobi had done. It was friendly and well-disposed, but powerless in the face of this vast new human traffic which was assailing Africa. I had to share a room with three other men.

Next door once again a game of poker-dice went on for most of the night. At dawn a cup of tea was handed to me by a similar black servant, and it was all so like Nairobi, and had come about so quickly, that it took me some time to realize where I was. Before the sun had risen I was back at the aerodrome watching the mist lift slowly from the ground.

As I stood there, tired and feeling myself to be three-quarters fantasy and only a quarter real, I saw, as if it were a scene in a dream, a score of composed, very upright, neat, clean little girls, ranging in age from about seven to fifteen, in pigtails and identical school coats. They filed suddenly out of the door of the aerodrome building and walked tidily over to a large aircraft standing nearby. Quickly they disappeared inside, the door was closed and the engines of the aircraft roared into motion. As the machine came by me gathering speed, I saw a vague, perfunctory flutter of little white handkerchiefs from behind the cabin windows; the people round me answered them with an equally perfunctory flutter of larger handkerchiefs and the half-hearted waving of a few masculine hats. I heard someone near me say, "Yes, St. ——'s: good school, you know, better than we have here, and it's so easy nowadays to fly them to the Union."

The whole incident passed off without emotion, without tears or recognizable regret and even without a sense of the unusual, except the unusual degree of detachment with which it appeared to be viewed by the girls in the plane and their parents on the ground. But to me it was such an unexpected, such a surrealist addition to the traditional features of these wide African uplands that I found myself parodying a limerick:

> *"These are the young ladies called bright*
> *Who can all travel faster than light,*
> *They leave home to-day*
> *In a relative way,*
> *And come back the previous night."*

Soon afterwards my aircraft too was in the sky, heading east. All the morning there was mist between us and the earth, and it only parted just for a moment or two three hours later to let us glide down on the aerodrome at Chileka, in Nyasaland. I had my morning tea at Blantyre, 72 hours after leaving England.

I had travelled nearly 7,000 miles; I had passed from a spring of sunshine, of uncompromising and unending blossom into an early and barren winter. I had not, it is true, travelled faster than light and I had travelled in an absolute rather than a relative way, but I felt as if I had come back much earlier than the previous night, at some unfinished, unresolved moment far back in the past; and I was more relieved than I can express to have done with flying for some months at least.

PART III

ENCOUNTER WITH THE MOUNTAIN

"O the mind, mind has mountains; cliffs of fall
Frightful, sheer, no-man-fathomed. . . ."

GERARD MANLEY HOPKINS

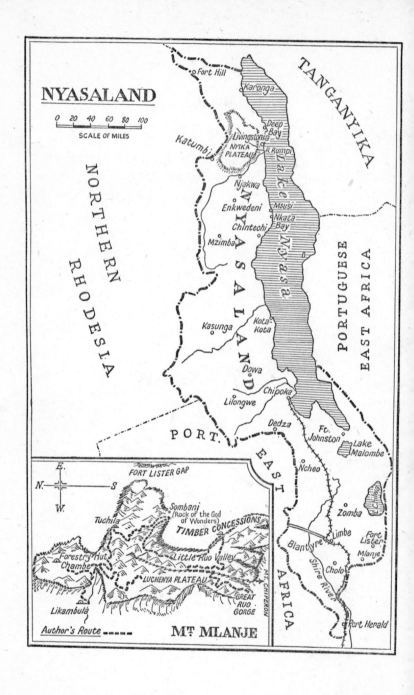

NYASALAND

0 20 40 60 80 100
SCALE OF MILES

TANGANYIKA

NORTHERN

RHODESIA

Fort Hill

Karonga

Deep Bay

Katumbi

Livingstonia

NYIKA PLATEAU

R. Rumpi

Njakwa

Enkwedeni

Chintechi

Mzimba

N
Y
A
S
A
L
A
N
D

Msusi

Nkata Bay

Lake Nyasa

PORTUGUESE

EAST AFRICA

Kasunga

Kota Kota

Dowa

Lilongwe

Chipoka

Dedza

Ft. Johnston

Lake Malombe

PORT.

EAST

Ncheo

Zomba

AFRICA

E.

N.   S.

W.

FORT LISTER GAP

Sombani
(Rock of the God of Wonders)

Tuchila

TIMBER CONCESSIONS

Forestry Hut
Chambe

Little Ruo Valley

LUCHENYA PLATEAU

Likambula

Author's Route -----

GREAT RUO GORGE

MT. CHIPERON

MT. MLANJE

Blantyre

Limbe

Fort Lister

Mlanje

Cholo

Shire River

Port Herald

Chapter Eight

IN Blantyre, the commercial capital of Nyasaland, I now found myself up against the same accommodation problem as in Salisbury and Nairobi. Blantyre and Limbe, its Siamese twin a few miles away, were in their small way as overcrowded and short of bedrooms as those other towns; and by experience less able to deal with the problem. Those other towns had a history of steady, energetic growth behind them; these places in Nyasaland had found their own leisurely, individual almost wilful way into the present, and were not used to this new scramble.

Before the last war, for people like myself, one of the great attractions of the Protectorate was its knack of being a quiet rule unto itself. It was one of the more neglected of the British territories in Africa. It attracted few of the attentions and none of the sensational publicity which some of its neighbours did. It roused little interest among tourists. The manly European heart, crossed in love, continued to show a marked preference for transferring its frustrated emotions on to the fauna of Kenya and Tanganyika. The League of Nations never grew particularly hot under its high international collar about Nyasaland. There, the problem of the European settler which so seriously troubled relations with the Colonial Office in Kenya and Northern Rhodesia appeared to be no problem at all.

Although there were close on two thousand Europeans in the country making a living out of planting tea, tobacco, coffee, trading and converting the African to Christianity, the difficulties they had with the odd thousand European officials who governed the country, and with their masters in Whitehall, were dealt with inside a tight and loyal family circle. The two-and-a-half million natives in Nyasaland, on

75

their part, seemed untempted by the growing African fashion of sending spokesmen or deputations abroad to appeal against exploitation by a white Imperialism.

The Protectorate, in fact, struck one as an unusually happy part of Africa, happy in the sense in which George Eliot defined a happy woman as being a "person without a past". I use "past" here not as a synonym of history. Nyasaland, of course, has a history. It has an exciting and highly individual history that bears comparison with most histories in the Continent. If anyone is interested in that remarkable, inspired mixture of motives, the desire to trade, to serve God and the Queen and to rid the world of slavery, which brought the Victorians to Africa, he can see it displayed before him, like a rare insect under a microscope, in the history of the Protectorate.

The Protectorate was undoubtedly one of the better products of those mixed motives. Its own native history was a recurring pattern of destruction from which the coming of the British happily delivered it. But what the Protectorate does not possess is a past for international gossip to feed on. For half a century world curiosity ignored it. The great and growing traffic of Africa passed it by. Stretched along six hundred miles from North to South, little more in reality than an extinct volcanic strip round the great lake which gives it its name, and well off the main routes of the continent, Nyasaland grew quietly in its own individual way, with its own colourful variations of the sun, mountains, valleys, plain and remoteness of Africa; a far country only for the devoted, the more adult and athletic tastes to enjoy.

But times are changing now, and people are pouring into the country. The stories I heard about hotel-keepers' troubles at the reception desk in Ryalls hotel on this Saturday morning of May 14, not only depressed me, but also filled me with alarm. I had to spend three months in the territory; winter was coming on. I decided that, as soon as possible, I would get myself a tent so that, if the worst came to the worst, I would at least have some shelter of my own. Meanwhile I gratefully accepted the loan of a back room, belonging to one of the permanent boarders who was away for the week-end and prayed hard that something else would turn up by the Monday. My accommodation problem, however, was about to be solved in the happiest possible manner for me.

I had with me a letter of introduction to Alan Macbean, the director of one of the bigger departments of the government. While my room was being prepared I decided to go to his office and present my letter in person. Though we had never met, our trails had frequently crossed in the past in other parts of Africa and we had a number of friends and acquaintances in common.

Blantyre is a small, ugly, commercial town. It has not had much time, and no reserves of wealth, tradition or local pride out of which to shape itself. About sixty years ago the government dealt it an unkind blow by setting up the official capital on the side of the huge mountain of Zomba, forty miles away, and so robbed Blantyre of a sure source of dignity and self-respect. Ostentatiously, pointedly and rather disdainfully, it was left to get on with its business, and however well it may have done it, it looks to this day rather ashamed of itself.

Fortunately this tentative little town hides itself behind the ample skirts of its surroundings, so the memory left with me is of a series of vivid but inadequate fragments. After my strange, precipitate flight from England we had emerged out of a narrow pass between substantial dark hills, mist still in their laps, and driven straight into the centre of the town before I became really aware of it. I was surprised when the driver of the car said suddenly: "Well, this is it!" I do not know what I had expected, but obviously nothing quite as drab and insignificant as these hunched, perfunctory buildings dumped by the side of a road full of dust.

In the main street itself we had to go very slowly to avoid

breaking the springs of our fat American car in the pot-holes. Behind us a thick, oily red dust rose up like smoke and spattered down like sleet on the trees, bushes, the glinting tin roofs and the sun-twisted wood of Goanese and Scottish shop verandas. The vegetation was grey and dejected with dust, the blanched faces of the whitewashed buildings smudged with it. The dust made many a black countenance a clown-like caricature of itself, and Indians and Goanese went turbaned and goggled against it. The sun made an unholy ally of it, and both sun and dust poured heavily, drunkenly over everything.

I admit, however, I had a more comfortable view of it now as I set out from the hotel for Alan Macbean's office. Away from that ugly, untidy centre, the town had more charm. The abrupt rises and falls in its wide background sheltered numbers of comfortable houses, all solidly built to an inoffensive office-of-works pattern. The houses gave on to gardens of a marked similarity. Each tried to have the same neat, level hedge round the inevitable lawn. I say "inevitable" because I believe, in Africa, the vision of an English lawn flies over the exiled British imagination like colours nailed to the mast of an out-gunned, sinking ship of the line. The lawns impinged on borders which grew European flowers of a sickly and outraged appearance. The only flower which seemed to do really well was the African zinnia. The lovely, effortless, uninhibited blooms, sizzling with colour and sun-fire like Catherine wheels at a fair, seemed to be sharing a joke of their own at the patient, determined nostalgia of the gardens about them.

The mist by now had gone from the dark hills round the town. Other and bigger hills, of a deeper blue, became visible and gave a suggestion of vast plains beyond them. The unflecked sky curved towards the dark earth with unimpeded rhythm like a long, Pacific comber speeding towards some lagooned land. The town and its gardens, the confused blend of Goanese and British suburbia seemed to

78

shrink to some vain and rather provocative gesture; to be no more than some very pink and white mouse rearing its head against the lowering, curved but as yet sheathed paws of an African cat. The image came to my mind unbidden and appeared confirmed by laughter which suddenly welled up like a spring around me.

I had not heard such spontaneous, pure and immediate laughter for years. I was turning down a road that had a halo of dust over it and was full of people doing their week-end shopping. Most of the few Europeans were in some kind of khaki, with set, sallow, lifeless, disillusioned faces under wide-brimmed hats. They climbed in and out of their cars with a listless, pre-determined air. I had the impression that they all longed for nightfall so that darkness and drink would help them to imagine themselves to be somewhere else. There were more Orientals than Europeans in the street and they, on the whole, were characteristic of a race which has a genius for appearing to be only half of what it really is. The Orientals all tended to have ascetic faces; finely made bones, delicate wrists and fingers; big, intro-spective eyes and a sensitive, gentle, defensive look. Their appearance, in fact, contrived to belie utterly the mercenary pursuits to which they dedicated their lives with such singular and indefatigable devotion. They had even less joy in them than the Europeans, and the laughter had come from neither of these, but from the Africans. These black people, overwhelmingly in the majority, carried the physical burden of the European and Indian day. They were, with few exceptions, dressed in rags and tatters which they wore not without pride and style. They talked with the greatest relish and animation. They were gay and laughed con-tinually. Their laughter seemed to come straight from some sure, inviolate source within where one felt they were un-failingly refreshed and had the habit of feasting with kings. Their laughter matched the sun, the curve of the sky, and the sombrely burning land and—and this is why I have lingered with it so long—it flashed like some inspired revelation of the future over that incongruous street. The impression was still vividly with me when I walked into Alan Macbean's office.

I was shown into it without delay by a black clerk who was extremely courteous but, unlike his raggle-taggle countrymen in the streets, was bowed down by melancholy. This learned, self-conscious gloom which higher education inflicts, almost without exception, on an instinctively happy people, is most noticeable.

Macbean, a man of about forty-five, sturdily but not heavily built, with wide, steady but not entirely happy eyes, came to meet me. His appearance was fastidious and he wore his clothes as if they were some distinguished uniform. Pipe in hand, he looked more like someone about to take his dogs for a run over a Scottish moor than a tried and experienced officer of His Majesty's Colonial service.

"But where is your luggage?" he asked at once.

"At the hotel," I told him.

"But you must come and stay with me," he said firmly and warmly. "I suggest you just pop over and pay your respects to the Provincial Commissioner's Office. We are a little sensitive here and appreciate these courtesies. Then come back here and we'll collect your bags and go straight home."

The Provincial Commissioner's Office was recognizable at once for the neat, white flagstaff outside it, flying a clear Union Jack, and for the whitewashed stones by the main entrance, brilliant under the sun like the polished skulls in a Dyak village that I had once seen. The African messengers, too, in their starched uniforms, were unmistakable.

The Provincial Commissioner was away but his deputy, young Charles Arbuthnot, received me on his behalf. He was not long out of the Army and was wearing white shorts and shirt. He sat at a desk of unstained African wood, a telephone at his side. The room was shaded against the light of the day which lapped, trembling like the clearest of water, at the rim of the window-sill.

Our greeting over, he startled me by saying suddenly: "You've come to do Mlanje and the Nyika, haven't you?"

My mission was confidential and I must have looked my surprise for he said quickly: "I heard from the aerodrome you'd arrived. You see, this is my district. It's my job to know what goes on in it, and no stranger comes into it without my knowing. When I saw your name, I remembered that London had asked us to help. I remembered it particularly because I know Mlanje. I love it. I often go fishing there."

I was delighted with the chance of getting first-hand information and asked him many questions. He answered them well and at length.

He brought out a map and showed me Mlanje. "A big, a terrific place," he said. People vaguely called it a plateau, but from the little he had seen of it, it looked more like a collection of sharp, jagged mountain peaks from seven to ten thousand feet high. They were supposed to cover an area of from 120 to 190 square miles, but they had never been properly surveyed. It was, he said again, with a sort of schoolboy emphasis, "a terrific, a wizard, a grand place." He knew one small end of it, a peak and a bit of plateau called Chambe, where the "forestry people" had a hut and depot. "Lovely there; like a glen in Scotland; clear streams with rainbow trout in them." He went there to fish whenever he could leave "this awful town". But there was a good deal more to it than Chambe.

There was another part of the mountain, with a track leading up it from the headquarters—the "Boma", he called it—of his opposite number in that district; there were two or three huts here also. In fact, an eccentric old lady (eccentric only in the Nyasaland sense, he stressed with a smile, because she thought of doing things that had not occurred to the majority), had kept some cows up there.

But by far the greater part of Mlanje was not known at all. In the old days, in the bad season, quite a few hardy souls had gone up to places like Chambe to escape the heat of a summer which had to be experienced to be believed. Nowadays, with cars and planes, of course, they preferred air-conditioned cinemas in Salisbury and Bulawayo. "Only one or two queer people" like himself went there for fun.

No, it was not difficult to get at. It was only about forty-five miles away, just off the road to Portuguese East Africa. The difficulty was not to get there, but to get up it, and once up it, to get round it. That would be "quite an expedition" and need careful organizing and stout legs.

He wished, with a genuine look of regret, he could come too. But, alas, too much bumf! Look at it! Trays of it! Crying shame! He would, though, give me a letter to Martin Boyd, his opposite number at Mlanje. He was sure Boyd would help to get me carriers. They would be the great difficulty. The natives did not like the place. The mountain was too cold, too wet, too misty, and too high and steep, and it frightened them in an odd way. Did I realize that it was the native legends about Mlanje that gave Rider Haggard the idea for *The People of the Mist*?

"There was something tremendous about it," as I would soon see for myself. He grinned at me like a schoolboy, but suddenly becoming serious, said with a plenipotentiary air that he thought I ought to go and see Peter Quillan, the Provincial forestry officer, as well. He lived at Limbe, only a few miles away. "A charming person" but a "bit of a fanatic about trees". He lingered over this rather as if for emphasis. I had a feeling that I was being warned. The pause, the hesitation, if any, was well-nigh imperceptible, but I felt it was intended to convey something.

He then looked me straight in the eyes and added: "In fact, all the forestry blokes are dead keen on Mlanje. They feel rather special about it. There's another young lad called Vance, who looks after the forestry end of the mountain.

He, too, is very keen, dead keen. The mountain means a lot to them, but I am sure you will get on with them all right."

I made a careful note of the "but" and said good-bye, grateful for the luck which had brought me to so intelligent and sympathetic an informant.

I found Macbean waiting patiently for me. His solemn black official was already in the back of the car, looking a bit like African chaos and old night.

"A spot of trouble at home," he said, pointing to the official, "so I am taking him along. Jump in."

The hotel seemed delighted to lose me, and within three hours of my arrival I was in what became for me, on the rare occasions I was to be in civilized surroundings, my home in Nyasaland.

Chapter Nine

A T the time of my arrival in Blantyre on this sunny, immaculate morning in May, Alan Macbean had been in Nyasaland about a year. Most of his career in the Colonial service had been spent in East Africa; twenty years or more of it in Kenya. I think he loved Kenya as much as a person with an inexorable sense of exile can love any country but his own. He did good and distinguished work there and left it with regret. He never told me, but I suspect that he left because of his children. He had two daughters. They were with their mother and at school in Scotland. Photographs illustrating their development from an East African cradle to a girls' college at home were discreetly but ubiquitously spread through the house: two charming, clean little Highland faces hung on every wall. Occasionally smiling, they were usually rather serious with something of that ancient, twilight, backward glance of the Gael. Their father had it too.

A few years before, the elder girl had recovered from a dangerous attack of infantile paralysis which had left her crippled. It had been a great blow to Alan. And it made him, a resolute person, determined that the best possible education that money could buy should make it up to her. When this offer of a government directorship in Nyasaland came along, he took it, not because he wanted to leave the Highlands of Kenya where he had been for so long, but because it meant promotion and more money. He had thrown himself into his new work with great energy and efficiency. His department, which had been one of the most backward, had quickly become one of the best.

There has always been something very moving about this quality, uniquely their own, that so many of the best

84

Colonial servants bring to their work. One realizes clearly that many of them have had no chance to identify themselves permanently with any part of their Empire. Irrevocably, they have had to uproot themselves from their own soil in Britain, and are never allowed to put down roots elsewhere. They have to make their work their home, although they must know that at forty-five or fifty-five, when they are forced to retire, the door of their own making will open and shut on them for the last time and leave them homeless. I am sure Alan was perfectly aware of what awaited him but, in the unavoidable, the cruel absence of a family life to which he was deeply attached, he too made his work his home.

The house in which he lived was for him little more than an outpost in his mind, a place in which to eat and sleep. With the discipline so characteristic of him, he observed all the civilized decencies. He made his house comfortable; furnished it with skill and not without taste; and made it for passers-by like myself a most welcome and endearing refuge. But I never felt that his heart or imagination was touched by it.

He left the running of it almost entirely to a remarkable Swahili servant Ali who had come from Kenya with him. His domestic staff consisted of Ali, a cook, a houseboy and a gardener, all black. No women were allowed in the house and Ali ran the staff with a hand of steel. He ran Alan, too, but rather as a nurse might run the eldest son of parents she respected and loved. Every day while I was there I heard Ali call Alan with his tea at five in the morning. "Jambo! Bwana. Your tea, Bwana. It is five o'clock." The deep voice spoke in Swahili, for Alan would not let him speak anything else.

At half-past five, Ali would be back at Alan's door, knocking. Getting no answer, he would go in and say: "Auck Bwana! Your tea now is cold. It is getting late. Surely the bwana can now wake up!"

85

At six Ali would be back, knocking again, with fresh tea. He would get no answer, walk straight in and say firmly: "You are doing wrong, bwana! This must now end. Here is fresh tea. It is six o'clock and what will your staff and clerks say if you are late. This is nonsense, bwana."

The "nonsense", the only English word he ever used in my hearing, always did it. With a great laugh and a heave Alan would be out of bed. At seven we had breakfast. At seven-thirty punctually Alan would be in the office. All through the day Ali ran the house with the greatest efficiency.

Frequently in the evenings Alan and Ali could be seen working in the garden together. It was a difficult garden, but between them they had grown the most wonderful beds of sweet-peas I have ever seen. The sweet-peas filled the hard, metallic air of Africa with a gentle, soft, nostalgic English scent. Every day I was there, Alan and Ali picked and arranged great, brimming bowls of them all over the house. Ali knew what those sweet-peas meant to Alan. He always called them the "English flowers" to me.

Whenever we left the house, Ali was there at the entrance to bow deeply and utter the Swahili farewell: "Kwa Heri, Bwana." Whenever we came back, no matter how late, at two or three in the morning, he was there waiting to let us in with great, good and dignified grace. He gave Alan something precious, something tender and human in his service that no other living thing did in Nyasaland, and I greatly respected him for it.

One of Ali's own, very special duties was to look after Argyle, a large, athletic young black cat Alan had adopted. Argyle was not only very handsome but also understood human beings and their speech to a remarkable degree. Alan would sit playing with him for hours, talking to him with Argyle talking back, with growls, miaows, flashing paws, electric quivers and strange curvatures of the spine. Alan would not eat until Argyle had his bowl of food put before him in a corner of the dining-room. The only subject on which he and Ali appeared to have differences of opinion was Argyle. Ali thought he was too harsh with it.

Alan had a tiny whip of string made. When Argyle interrupted the conversation at table, Alan would lean over and flick him gently with the string. Ali thought this went much too far. In the evening at dinner, the whip was in its usual place but the string had been replaced with streamers of paper. Alan had tried repeatedly to revert to string but Ali would not let him. These three were the real world of that house, these three and the sweet-peas in the garden; all the rest stood on the fringes of Alan's mind.

On the Saturday of my arrival, after lunch, Ali immediately went off to fetch the black official who had come along with us in the car. Through the windows I watched a great discussion taking place between the servants under the blazing sun by the kitchen door, a grave, solemn and detailed discussion. Later, Ali and the black official knocked at the door and came quietly in.

"Well, what is it, Ali?" said Alan.

"I will leave it for him to say," Ali answered, pointing to the elderly official.

"I am afraid, Bwana," said the official in a lugubrious voice, "I have grave trouble to report . . ." and then paused as if he dared not go on.

"Come on!" said Alan. "Snap out of it. What is it?"

"I am afraid, sir! There is a grave dissension in your domestic midst. Your house-boy accuses his wife of promiscuous infidelity. By some extraordinary coincidence she accuses him of the same thing."

He outlined the history of the quarrel in the most excellent, pedantic English. The quarrel, he thought, was beyond healing. They had all talked it over and agreed there was only one thing to do. Here Alan looked at Ali and Ali nodded. They were sending the couple to their village to get divorced. They had arranged for replacements in the meanwhile and he could assure the bwana there would be no more trouble if that were done.

"But, I say," said Alan, breaking into Swahili and talking to Ali. "Isn't that a bit steep? Aren't you going too far?"

"No, Bwana," Ali said emphatically. "It is the right thing to do. It is not nonsense."

"Well, you see to it, then, Ali," Alan said, and dismissed the matter from his mind in a manner which was most flattering to his black arbitrators. But he said to me later: "That old clerk of mine is a marvel. I get him to investigate all my labour disputes for me. He settles them all according to the customs of the land and it saves no end of trouble. But he is not a patch on Ali!"

Afterwards, because Alan wanted to buy a carpet, we got into his car again and drove over to an auction sale of second-hand furniture in the tobacco market at Limbe. Alan said Ali was always nagging him about his carpets, and plaguing him to get more. Besides, these sales were fun. Everybody went to them. They were held every Saturday. As there was no work to do, one might as well go.

"There!" I thought. "When there is no work to do, the homelessness comes rushing in."

Alan drove the car, a powerful American make, with great, impatient speed but immense skill; he drove it rather as I suspected he drove himself; as if he did not care for the journey and the machine, but wanted it over quickly.

At Limbe we found the whole European world at the sale. It was held in an empty tobacco shed with something of the atmosphere of the Caledonian Market about it. And how incongruous it was to see there in the heart of Africa, little heaps of soiled Victorian household things, outmoded Edwardian fineries, and in particular one large green-blue Japanese porcelain jar, with a vigorous and extremely elegant aspidistra in it. I confess I was astonished, and my imagination, when I thought of the immense tropical vegetation without, so stirred, that I stared at it as if it were the Livingstone, the Stanley of the botanical world.

In the end Alan bought no carpets. The prices and the colours were not right for him. His purse was too dedicated, his eye too fastidious. But we both of us met a number of old acquaintances, including a happy extrovert from Tanganyika who, with typical African disregard of time and distance, had thought nothing of motoring 1,300 miles to spend a week-end in Limbe.

The sale over, we drifted to the Club at Blantyre. European life in Nyasaland in its collective aspect, turns on a well-organized system of clubs, and the Europeans we had seen at the sale reappeared at the club-house.

We all spread ourselves in the sun on the club veranda and watched a team of European officials and business people play a team of Indians and Goanese at hockey. The setting was rather beautiful. The hockey match was being played on what was normally the cricket field. It was at the bottom of a deep bowl in the Blantyre hills. We sat on the rim and looked down on it. The grass below was of the colour and texture of English grass. Had there been a spire in the background one's imagination could easily have turned it into an English scene. But beyond, and above the deep well of angry light, the hills were unmistakably African.

I do not know why it is that the many and varied peoples of India should all have such a genius for hockey. Nothing we know about the Indian character, its extreme, ancient and subtle complexities; its profound mistrust of simplicity; its capacity for making the obvious mysterious and complicated, prepares one for it; but the fact is they have a talent and passion for the game that make them far and away the best hockey-players in the world. The Europeans of Blantyre were soundly and decisively whacked. The spectators, essentially European, were scrupulously fair. They cheered the two sides impartially. When the Indians came off victorious, they greeted them with a genuine, a warm burst of clapping.

They looked a good, unpretentious, pleasant crowd, not yet pulled out of proportion by Africa as were so many of their neighbours. But as I watched them I suddenly realized with a shock that they, and I, were all there, not because we really liked it, but in order to kill time. I have known the phrase all my life, but until that moment I honestly believe I had never fully appreciated its awful implications. I think it was meeting Alan, and the sense of the problem in him, that made me realize there were communities who deliberately set out to kill the time of which we all have so little. When the sun went down behind the hill and the damp, dark shadows welled up like a tide round the club-house, it was almost as if we had succeeded so well in our object that a faint, misty, smell of death welled up with them.

There and then I decided that I would not waste a day on my journey; I would get up and down that mountain, and over my plateau as fast as I could; and so out of Africa.

When we were back at the house that night, sitting in front of a large log-fire, Argyle purring on Alan's shoulder, his eyes tightly shut with heat and ecstasy, a smell of meat grilling on wood-coals creeping in from the kitchen, I told Alan how important it was for me to get my work done as soon as possible. He, characteristically, without hesitating, took Argyle off his shoulder, gave him to me, and without saying a word went out of the room and started telephoning.

"I have been through to Zomba and they will see you to-morrow," he said when he came back. "It will fit in quite well because I am playing golf. I have also rung up Boyd at Mlanje. He was just going to telephone you. He had already heard from the D.C. here. He will see you on Monday and make all the necessary arrangements. Now what about some food?"

I went to bed that night with a temperature of 103. Because I have had so much malaria in my life I took a large dose of quinine, but actually I was not at all worried about my physical self. I am physically very strong, indeed, would not have survived many of the things that have happened to me had I not been. I now had no doubt but that the fever would pass and leave my strength unimpaired. In fact, I only mention it because it seemed to me to have another bearing on my journey.

I have had fevers of many kinds in all sorts of places and circumstances, and I believe I can now tell when their origin is purely physical, and when it is not. Although I took quinine I was certain that my fever, this time, had no direct physical cause.

To me, one of the most striking things about fevers is their mysterious connection with our sense of time and space. It is almost as if one incorporates within one's own individual being all the time that has been and can ever be, and that fever is either the vehicle itself, or evidence of the means by which one is forced from one time context into another. The moment one's temperature changes from normal, one's self ceases to be contemporary. Before now I have emerged from serious illness with the conviction of having been in a time and a self anterior to the present, and the feeling has persisted despite my failure to analyse or define it. So I have come to believe that, in its most profound sense, our battle for survival is fought out at a level and in a spirit of which we have little conscious understanding. And what is particularly moving is that, when the battle is at its grimmest, all those rejected states of life from slime to tree-fern, from amœba to dinosaur, are thrown in to preserve the very thing that had found them wanting.

I think it is the submerged recollection of this great service, so selflessly rendered by less privileged forms of life, which gives the sick, on their journey back to normality, such a keen sense of having shared the mystery of all living things. It is from the heart of some such recollection that the world appears rounded and electric with meaning. The memory is like a sea beside which the reviving spirit walks, and from which it draws the grateful tears that fill convalescent eyes at the first sight of a bee tumbling a flower for honey, or a poplar trembling with delicious apprehension under the touch of a June breeze.

Heaven knows I do not want to confuse an experience which is already far enough beyond the reach of words, but I would be running away from what the journey meant to me did I not stress that in this place and time, or wherever it is that one goes with one's fever, it is almost as if the past, the present and the future move so close to one another that they become one. The past, truly re-captured, is time-future coming alive; time-present is a bridge between.

All I would suggest is that the future had begun to register a new design in my blood, and that the fever marked the beginning of its struggle for awareness.

Chapter Ten

THE following morning I felt most unwell but noticed that the sense of urgency which had come to me at the Club was keener than ever. I therefore got up early and went dutifully through the programme I had set myself and was grateful, as the day went on, to feel the fever ebb from my blood.

I paid my official calls, wrote my name in a book like a Stuart Bible at the gates of Government House, and was able to set off with a light and eager heart to see Martin Boyd, the District Commissioner at Mlanje.

The car was driven by a huge African who called himself Alexander Dougherty-Jackson Btahat-Labambekulu but who wisely asked me to use Jackson only. He drove with an ecstatic expression on his face, and obviously liked to keep moving. When we came over the hills at Limbe and I caught my first view of Mlanje, I told him to stop. He looked really hurt by the order. But one must stop when one sees Mlanje for the first time. I would always stop. It is one of the great views of Africa. Arbuthnot had not exaggerated, when he called it "terrific, grand, wizard". On this Monday morning it was particularly impressive.

There was not a cloud in the sky and I saw it so clearly and distinctly and in such detail, that it was difficult to believe that it was forty and not ten miles away. Between me and it there lay an immense, flat, featureless plain, burnt black, brown and gold by the sun; its trees and folds curled, withered, twisted, shimmered by heat and drought. Out of it all, Mlanje rose sheer. It stood up straight like a wall for six thousand feet, receded within itself a bit, and then soared sheer again for another three or four thousand feet. Twenty miles and more of it faced me across that

93

immense trembling plain, and I could see nowhere a break or gap which might suggest a possible way up. In that morning sun, it was dark blue, purple and gold, with a most refined, Schiaparelli-like stole of mist round the shoulders of its highest peak.

"Is the Bwana going to go up Mlanje?" Jackson asked me.

"Yes!" I said.

"Auck!" he said, and began to shake with laughter.

"Why do you laugh, Jackson," I asked, "and what does this 'Auck' mean?"

But he only laughed all the more, until I too was affected by it.

As we came nearer the mountain, it became greener and less blue. It was obviously well watered. A deep, dark gorge covered with dense forest, and ending abruptly against a two-thousand-foot cliff, came into view. The innermost peaks disappeared. We crossed a stream or two filled with clear mountain water, but the plain stayed with us. It was amazing how abruptly, like the walls of a Byzantine fortress, the mountain rose out of it.

Then we found ourselves driving through some big tea plantations, mingling the smug green of India and Assam with the shrill metallic hue of Africa. Within an hour and a half of leaving Blantyre, we stopped outside Martin Boyd's boma. We recognized it by the flagstaff and Union Jack flying over it. Both the building and flag looked rather insignificant and forlorn against the huge bulk of the mountain. Its perpendicular grey walls, glistening with water and splashed with moss, entirely dominated the plantations, buildings, and strips of luscious green at its foot.

I myself have always understood perfectly why people who live permanently among mountains find it necessary to endow them with personalities and give them human, if not Christian, names. This mountain had, at that moment, a great, grey, compelling Jurassic sort of personality, a character of ill-suppressed rage, a petrified brontosaurus-like grinding and gnashing of teeth, that made everything near it shrink and cower; it presented itself to my senses as a giant striding through time with the plain, like a mongrel, at its heels. I wished I knew what "Mlanje" meant.

Boyd, unfortunately, couldn't tell me, but in every other way he was most helpful. He received me charmingly, and what is more, helped me intelligently and with great good grace.

He had never been up the mountain himself, he said. It had never been possible. He asked me to look at the bumf on his desk, making a despairing gesture. How often I was to see that gesture in Nyasaland; how well I knew it all over Africa! Boyd had one of the largest, the most thickly populated districts in the country.

"I should be out among the people now," he said. "I should be among them all the time. But I can't for this bloody, this pointless bumf, that Zomba sends us. I have not time for essentials, let alone climbing mountains."

He promised that by Thursday, even if he had to empty his jail, he would get me twenty carriers to go up the mountain for a fortnight. It would be difficult, but it would be done. He promised to lend me his own tent and to get me a good personal boy and cook. He promised to write a letter to Dicky Vance, the forestry officer most concerned with the mountain; he had an idea that at the moment Vance, his young wife and a two months baby, were up the forestry end of the mountain. But he would locate them and ask Vance to help.

Then he looked at me, just as Arbuthnot had done, and said: "Vance is dead keen about trees, you know. He is a bit of a fanatic about forests and this mountain is all the world to him. But I think you will like him."

Again I felt I had been warned, but thought it better not to pursue the subject.

Boyd then took me off to his house, for a four-course meal.

I was continually being astonished at how well people fed in Nyasaland; at the good wines and sherries that accompanied the courses.

Suddenly, in the midst of lunch, the clouds came down and it started to rain violently.

"You want to watch that on the mountain," said Boyd, "the weather changes in a flash. You know, there is another ruddy great hill over there forty miles away in Portuguese East, called Mount Chiperone. When the wind gets up, as it does in a second, it brings heavy weather, usually in multiples of five days. We call them Chiperones and they can be the devil. For God's sake, look out for them up there on that peak."

I was to have tragic reason for remembering that remark, but actually, at the time, I did little more than register it lightly in my mind. I was more interested in the constant references to the forestry officer's love of the trees on Mlanje which kept reappearing in my official talks. As I drove away from the Boyds it occurred to me to go and call on Quillan, the Chief Forestry Officer for the Province. Near Limbe again I stopped the car on the same neck of hill on the edge of the plain; but how different now was the view of the mountain.

Black clouds from the Portuguese border were rolling over the base of Mlanje and soaring up like deep volcanic explosions round its flanks. The highest peak had spiked one of the darkest clouds and seemed to be whirling it triumphantly round its head; but, as I watched, a whole concentration of cloud rolled down on it and hid it from view. I then noticed a very curious thing; the clouds advanced no further over the mountain. They had in their possession one half of it, including the highest peak, and they seemed content to stay and consolidate their formidable position. But the eastern half of the mountain remained astonishingly clear and, as the afternoon deepened, drew lovely colours and tones into its keeping. It made the mountain appear divided against itself; one half of it dark and turbulent; the other bending a shining head over the evening.

The incorrigible Jackson, seeing me stare at Mlanje with a kind of hypnotized expression, was inspired once more to ask:

"Bwana! You really going up Mlanje?"

Again I said "Yes" and again he laughed as if he had never heard anything funnier. He was still laughing as we drove on.

Quillan was not at home, and when we were back again in Blantyre I said to Alan: "What is it about your forestry people that I should know? I have a feeling that I am being tactfully warned that my being here is not welcome to them." I went on to explain in detail how that feeling had first arisen in my talk to Arbuthnot on Saturday and seemed confirmed by Boyd to-day.

He told me to worry "nae bit" and rather generously and reassuringly said that I and the forestry "lads" had only to meet and all dangers of complications would vanish. But the fact is: Nyasaland is very small. In it there are no confidences in the real sense of the word, only misleading, half-confidences. Everybody knew I was coming and had their own versions about my object in coming. Alan thought the forestry officers were afraid I would either try and take Mlanje away from them or else make their plans for expansion on the mountain impossible.

"But I have not seen it until to-day, so how could I?" I exclaimed. "I have no ideas at all about the place."

Yes, he knew that, but there it was. Quillan and Vance were extremely good "laddies", but he thought something like that might be at the back of their minds. They were rather fanatical about Mlanje and, of course, I knew what foresters were!

"People, obviously, who can't see the wood for the trees," I interrupted with some vehemence, because I hate pre-judgment.

Alan burst out laughing and I had to join in.

"But seriously," he said, "why don't you go and talk to Quillan, he is the senior bloke."

I told him I had already called at his office on the way back from Mlanje that afternoon but had found him out.

"I am not surprised. He hates offices," Alan said. "He is out as much as he can because he really loves his trees and his work."

I did see Quillan, however, early the next morning. I was so determined to catch him this time that I beat him to his office, and, as Alan had prophesied, the meeting went well. I took a liking to him at once. It is not difficult to like people provided they have something in their lives that they themselves like. Liking begets liking. The difficult people are the great critics, the ones who cannot find anything in life to like.

Peter Quillan was not in the least of this sort. He was a big, strong, open-air fellow who enjoyed his work, who loved the country and, as I discovered afterwards, had a family to which he was devoted. But he was not free of suspicion of me.

There was one awkward moment, and that right at the beginning when he said brusquely to me: "Before we start, I had better say that I hope you realize the whole of Mlanje is ours and that we intend making it the finest forestry reserve in the country."

I said firmly that I realized nothing of the sort and that it was no concern of mine to realize it. My instructions were to give Mlanje a thorough look-over and, as his department was deeply interested in it, appeared, in fact, to be the only one that had ever done anything about it, I had hoped I would have their expert advice if not their help and blessing. I had no preconceived ideas about the mountain myself. I had never seen it, and the only plan I had was to go and live with the mountain for a while and let its nature impose its own plan, if any, on me. Besides, although I was not a forester, I was pretty keen about trees myself; not only did I like them and thought the world and Africa should have many more of them, but I was, in a sense, profoundly grateful to them. In the war the woods and jungles of Abyssinia and the East had often, for months, been my only home.

Thereupon Peter Quillan looked at me, I thought with some relief, and asked: "Would you mind if I came with you?"

I said I would be delighted, could not imagine anything nicer than going over it all together; and it would be the best way of keeping both ourselves and Mlanje fully in each other's minds.

Quillan revelled like a schoolboy given an unexpected half-day's holiday and asked eagerly: "When do we start and what would you like me to bring with me?"

I asked if Thursday would be too soon and he said: "My dear chap, I would go right now. I have been itching for months to lay my hands on that mountain again, and although I know it as well as anyone I have never done a complete round of it. By Jove! we are going to have fun!"

H

Chapter Eleven

I LEFT Peter Quillan feeling happier than I had done at any time since leaving London, and went out joyfully to complete my preparations for our expedition to the mountain. There is one thing in Africa that never fails to give me pleasure; getting out of the town into the country, particularly into unknown country. The physical fact of Africa is by far the most exciting and interesting thing about it. The tragedy is that it has not as yet produced the people and the towns worthy of its greatness. By comparison with its physical self everything else looks drab, commonplace and suburban.

It is fun, too, to match one's experience and imagination against the combinations, the enigmatic variations of necessity and circumstance which a journey through Africa can produce. It is rather like playing a game of chess against an opponent of formidable reputation. The opening move determines the end. During the game one uses all the pawns, bishops, knights and queen of one's imagination and initiative. The opponent, however, strikes back not only with mountain, river and lake, rain, wind and all the elements, but also exploits the inevitable distortions in one's innermost pattern, all that tends to accident and disaster inside oneself.

It is a good thing that neither Quillan nor I knew what we were playing against on this occasion, and I, for one, went from shop to shop in Blantyre with nothing but quickening anticipation in my mind.

First of all I ordered boxes to be made that were big enough to hold a forty- to fifty-pound load for each bearer. I then bought food sufficient for a three weeks' journey. Quillan thought we could do it in a week. But, suspicious always of Africa, and considering that neither Quillan nor anyone else had ever made a round trip of the mountain, I trebled the estimate.

I bought some superb hunks of bacon; coils of beef and pork sausages; tins of bully-beef, still the greatest of travellers' standbys, sardines, beans and peas; a bag of potatoes, plenty of rusks and biscuits, sugar, tea, coffee, cocoa, powdered milk, some tins of butter, a tin of marmalade, some tins of green figs and a tin of Cape gooseberry jam. I put in a few surprises for myself and Quillan, and, to make sure that they would be surprises, wrapped them in clean, but ugly, anonymous sacking. I put in two plum-puddings, a two-pound box of assorted chocolates, some dates stuffed with almonds and twenty-eight crisp Jonathans.

I put in a bottle of whisky for my guests and a bottle of cognac for the cold. I bought a good, wide but not too heavy frying pan, a water bottle, tin mugs and plates, knives, spoons and forks and a tin-opener, an electric torch, a couple of hurricane lamps, and a large coil of manilla rope. I had my own clasp knife and had borrowed a double-barrelled twelve-bore for which I now bought twenty-five rounds of buck-shot and twenty-five rounds of No. 5 shot. I packed three warm rugs; a trench coat with extra warm lining, a ground sheet, thick socks and stockings, a thick polo-sweater I had had for twenty years; a pair of hob-nailed boots and a pair of stout climbing shoes that had been made in Australia some years before. I took also a prayer-book, Shakespeare, *Modern Love*, and, of course, my sealing-wax.

I bought a small first-aid outfit, some M. & B. and Sulpha-guanidine; some quinine for myself and paludrine for the bearers. I was sure the bearers would be full of malaria and that the cold mountain air might bring it on. I even remembered that while I was at Mlanje the doctor had come in to report to Boyd a fatal case of blackwater fever. I bought a couple of bottles of peroxide of hydrogen because nothing convinces an African more that one's medicine is doing his sores good than this harmless disinfectant fizzing on his skin. That is a long way to winning his battle. I also took a large bottle of castor oil which all Africans love. I went amply prepared.

At dawn on the Thursday morning I said good-bye to Alan. It was raining and Argyle, much to our amusement, after coming with us to the front door, rubbing his back against my trouser leg for a moment and then putting one sensitive paw carefully on the wet front step, turned round as if he had been stung and scampered back into the house as fast as he could go.

On the way I stopped at the bakery in Limbe. The Greek baker was just taking his bread, lovely crisp, white Mediterranean bread, out of his ovens. The warm, homely smell of bread, charged with the world's oldest civilized memory, in contrast to the tang of the cold rain and damp earth outside, made the sleeping houses around look the most inviting places. I took eight loaves with shining gold crusts into my arms. They warmed me through my bush jacket.

At Limbe I picked up Quillan. He climbed enthusiastically into the car, loaded up with more provisions, bed-rolls, fishing rods and hurricane lamps. Just after eight o'clock we were at Likabula, the forestry depot at the foot of the mountain, some twelve to fourteen miles from Boyd's boma.

It was drizzling heavily. Only the base of the mountain was visible. But Boyd had been as good as his word. The twenty bearers and a personal boy and cook, a frail, asceticlooking African, called Leonard among other names, were there waiting for us. They had already divided into loads the tent Boyd was lending me. I noticed with some alarm that it was going to take six men to carry it and determined to get rid of it as soon as possible. We quickly distributed the remaining loads among them and sent them up the track in front of us. This part of our journey to the forestry depot at Chambe, Quillan said, would not be difficult. They could not go wrong. The difficulties would come later.

I stayed behind with him while he talked to his African officials at the depot. Although I was only a few yards off, a stream from the mountain nearby made such a noise that I could not hear what they were saying. The mist and drizzle swirled thickly round us, but I could feel the presence of the mountain behind it, breathing, as it were, over my shoulder. I hoped it would not be impossible to go up in this weather, but Quillan seemed to have no doubts; said that here he could find his way in the dark.

Just as we were about to start a native runner suddenly came out of the mist down the track towards us, saluted Quillan, and gave him a letter.

"Here!" said Quillan to me: "I think this is for you."

It was a letter from Dicky Vance, written in a large, open, impetuous hand, tilted somewhat backwards as if to put a brake on its obvious impatience.

"Dear Colonel: My wife and I have come up to the forestry depot here at Chambe for some days and look forward to seeing you here. We shall, of course, do all we can to help you and I have detailed someone to look for you coming over the edge and bring you here. Yours sincerely, R. Vance." The R. Vance was written quickly, carelessly, as if he did not much like signing his name.

Quillan and I then started our climb. It was easy to begin with and I was grateful, for sitting in ships, trains and aeroplanes had been no training for this kind of thing.

It was still and very quiet; the silence was the true silence of mountains, the silence of the incorruptible and abiding sound of streams, distant waterfalls and casual whiffs of air catching at the leaves of bamboo and tree. Heaven knows what sorts of monstrosities the unpredictable sun of Africa was brewing beyond this mountain of mist and cloud, but on our track we were unaware of its existence.

As the climbing was so easy, we talked as we went, or rather Quillan talked to me backwards over his shoulder as he led the way, turning round and pausing whenever there was a particular point to make. He talked well and had an immense sense of natural detail. He had spent all his adult life in the Colonial forestry service, in Nigeria, Nyasaland, Cyprus and now again Nyasaland. He had worked among all sorts and conditions of forests and trees, but I soon realized that his favourite forests and trees grew in this mountain we were climbing.

It seemed that Mlanje, from the forestry point of view, was unique. There was no other place like it in Africa or the world. It was indeed a world of its own, a very ancient, lost world of trees that grew nowhere else. These trees, he said, had been given the name of cedars, Mlanje cedars, because they looked to the uninitiated eyes like cedar. But they were not cedars at all. They were a conifer of a unique and very ancient sort, had their roots in the most antique of antique African botanical worlds. I would see them for myself soon, in fact I would smell them even before I saw them. Their scent, night and day, filled the air on the mountain; filled it with a heavy, all-pervasive but delicious scent of a lost world; of a time and a place that existed nowhere else.

Their colour, like their scent, was unique. It was green, of course, but like no other green; there was a sheen of the olive green of cypress, and the substance of the green of the ilexes of Greece and the Caucasus; the texture of the conifers of Columbia and the vital electric sparkle of African juniper. In the bark, in the veins and arteries of those trees, the sap, a thick, yellow, resinous sap of a specific gravity and density most unusual in conifers, ran strongly. If you laid your ear to a trunk, it was almost as if you could hear this vital, this dark, secret traffic drumming upwards, skywards, from the deep, ancient soil, the original earth perhaps of Africa, to the outermost, the smallest spike of a leaf, sparkling in the sun a hundred, even a hundred and twenty feet above. So full were the trees of this vital sap that it preserved them even in death; no insect, no worm, no ant would touch even the driest morsel of it. It was the only ant-resisting wood in the whole of Africa.

But when one threw it on the fire, as I would soon see, it was so full of life, of stored-up energy from another world, that it literally exploded into flame. It consumed itself joyfully and gaily, crackling explosively in flame with none of that lugubrious reluctance to burn of some other woods that Quillan could mention. And fire, unfortunately, had nearly been the cedars' undoing. Some centuries ago, when human beings first appeared in the plains round Mlanje, great fires swept up the mountain and burnt havoc through the responsive cedar woods. They, the Forestry Services, had come just in time to save the remnants of it.

There was still a good deal of forest left—enough for them to exploit in order to get the money to rejuvenate the species, but what I would see was a world of cedars in retreat, a world of unique and irreplaceable living trees, fighting a desperate rearguard action against fire and rapacious human beings, standing-to gallantly, night and day, without cease in the deepest, dampest and remotest recesses of the mountain. Surely I could understand why they were so jealous, so suspicious on the trees' behalf!

In this fashion we climbed for an hour. I remember I had just taken off a sweater and looked at my watch, when I heard the first yodel. It sounded for all the world as if it might have been in the Austrian Tyrol or any of the mountain slopes of Switzerland, and I asked Quillan if there was another party of Europeans ahead of us.

"Oh! No," he said, with a laugh. "Europeans don't come here if they can help it. These are departmental native bearers coming down with sawn cedar from above. They always call like that to one another, particularly when it is misty. You will soon see them. But it is a funny thing about mountains, they always make everyone want to yodel. We didn't teach these blokes. It is their own idea. It just came to them; a gift from the mountain."

He explained that they were so short of good wood in Nyasaland that they were cutting cedar at Chambe, sawing it up by hand and carrying it down the mountain, each length separately on the head of black porters.

"It is hell for them," said Quillan, "but they don't mind and we have got to do it. We make it up to them by feeding them and paying them as well as we can, but we don't like it. We intend changing it as soon as Vance finishes his road on top. At the moment we get more carriers than we can use, because there's a semi-famine on and they want the food."

Just then another yodel soared up like a bird close by. I became aware of a strange, thick, resinous, spiced, oily scent, and Quillan said: "Do you mind getting off the track, please."

There seemed to be a deep sheer drop on our right, so using saplings we pulled ourselves up on to a steep slope to the left of the track. I heard the pad-pad of heavily burdened feet coming out of the mist above, then someone breathing and puffing with every cell of his lungs, followed by a smell of human sweat mingling with the scent of resin, and a native balancing a heavy, thirty-foot beam of cedar on his head, came out of the mist towards us.

I thought it wrong, somehow, that laden and breathing as he was, he should feel compelled to raise his hand and say, "Morning, Bwana!" Besides, he was just on the edge of a precipice.

"He gets ninepence a day and some food for doing that," said Quillan. "I'd be damned if I'd do it."

From now on we passed dozens of carriers coming down the mountain at regular intervals. Quillan always took the same punctilious care to make way for them. We began to talk less. The track became steeper and we had to use our hands as well as our feet in places. One bit of it passed over a tremendous drop of smooth sheet rock, cyanite I think Quillan called it. The rock had a seventy-degree slope above us, but below it dropped sheer into the mist. We clambered across it from one precarious foothold of moss and aloe root to another.

At half-past ten we stopped to eat a bar of chocolate each. It was much colder, and I put on my sweater. The mist was thicker and blacker, had an English November look about it. At twelve exactly, three hours after our start, as we were going up a particularly steep part of the mountain, using our hands as well as feet in places, I heard dogs barking in the mist above us.

"Those are Vance's dogs. I expect he is coming to meet you," Quillan said, paused, and sniffing at the mist, added: "Do you notice something?"

It was that heavy scent. Every time the timber carriers went by I had smelt it, a scent that I had not come across anywhere else. But now it was much more confident and pronounced. I nodded.

"Cedars," he said, breathing the scent in with deep satisfaction. "Cedars, as I told you. We are near the top now."

He had hardly finished his sentence, when two vivid, streamlined, young ridge-back bitches came bounding out of a black cloud at us, gave one leap and a lick at Quillan—how they did it I do not know, because it was all I could do to stand upright there—and bounded back into their cloud again.

I heard the crunch of what sounded like heavy army boots, coming nearer.

A young man wearing an old King's African Rifles' slouch hat, a khaki pullover, officer's pattern, khaki shorts, thick stockings and boots appeared. He was not tall but built rather like the born mountaineer; medium height, broad shoulders, and sturdy legs. He had a frank, open face, grey eyes, rather hidden behind thick glasses, a prominent nose and a chin which looked as if it had been fashioned by experience rather than by an inclination to express determination. He had a deep, firm voice, entirely of a piece with his build.

Quillan introduced us rather as if we were meeting in a drawing-room and not six thousand feet up in the clouds.

"You have struck it unlucky. It's odd, the mountain doing this to-day," Vance said, not without the faintest tinge of something accusing in his tone, as if I were responsible for the change. "I don't know why Mlanje should do this to you. It has been fine here at Chambe up to now. Come on up to the house!"

"Up to the house" I found was another twenty minutes' climb and then a three-mile walk. But I enjoyed every moment of it. Vance and Quillan went ahead, talking the business of the mountain. I followed behind. When we got over the edge, it was half-past twelve with the invisible sun at its strongest, and the mist lifted to about a thousand feet above us. The peaks were still covered but the valley, the so-called Chambe plateau up which we had walked, became more and more open to view. I could see at once what Arbuthnot meant by saying it was like a glen in Scotland. It was utterly unlike the Africa we had left down below.

It was covered in lovely long rye, oat and barley grasses, gold-green and purple in their early winter colours. Through the valley on all sides, from behind folds, hills, and many slow gradual rises in its contours, flowed crystal-clear streams, presumably the rainbow trout streams of which I had heard so much.

At first I thought there were palm trees growing on the banks of the streams, but I soon realized that they were huge tree ferns, the last remnants of the great cedar forests that once had covered this valley too. The scent of the cedars themselves now was most marked. Soon I began to see them, as Quillan had so vividly described them to me: at first, in small clusters driven back into odd, remote nooks of the valley, but then, as we went deeper into the valley, there appeared in the central gash of it a real, dank, brooding, resentful forest of them. It was rather an awe-inspiring sight. They looked, in an odd way, prehistoric; lovely, but long before human time. I would not have been surprised to see a pterodactyl fly out of them. All round the edges their branches were festooned and heavily hung with long garlands and veils of lichen and moss.

"Aren't they wonderful!" Vance said to me in his clear, firm voice, proudly as if he had invented them.

He showed me the road he was making from the forest to the edge of the plateau in order to eliminate all heavy man-handling of timber.

"I slept with these blokes under the same blankets," he said, pointing at some black carriers going by bowed down with timber on their heads. "And I like them and hate to see them doing this."

"When? In the war?" I asked.

"Yes. Many a time in Burma," he answered. "I was with the West African Division, Nyasaland battalion, of the King's African Rifles. Arakan! Grand chaps."

"This is very beautiful, well-nigh perfect. Might be somewhere in Europe," I said, realizing it was a half-truth but not yet aware of the full one.

"Yes," he said, with a warm look that took in the whole valley. "Yes. It is absolutely perfect."

Quillan called us over to him. He was standing on a bridge which Vance had built in seasoned cedar of a lovely, Pacific pearl-grey colour.

"Why have you put these beams so far apart?" he asked Vance.

"To save the cedar," Vance said.

"Well, I think that is a bit unnecessary," Quillan said, not unkindly. "Spoiling the ship for a ha'penny-worth of tar. It will bump so when you get your tractor up here."

Vance's face did not change its expression. Yet one knew in that mysterious way in which changes in the internal atmosphere of human beings make themselves felt, that the remark had hurt him out of all proportion to its context and tone.

"I will alter it if you like," he answered in a level, even voice. "I was trying to save cedars, that's all. But I will change it if you like."

Vance had taken off his hat as he spoke, and the light cold air of the valley flicked at his fair hair. He looked suddenly fantastically young and hurt; far too young for the grey, old, pre-human world about us. It was almost as if I could see his grown-up mind reach far down inside himself, kneel and attend to the injury of some small lost boy. That done, it stood up, his adult chin took on its determined slant and he said again in that same suspiciously even tone, "I will change it if you like!"

"Oh! Good heavens, no! I was thinking of the future. I wouldn't do it again, though, if I were you," Quillan replied.

"Well! Shall we get along then," said Vance, looking past us at the farthest clump of cedars. "I think the mist will be down on us again soon."

I do not think Quillan was at all aware of what his remark had done, and he strode cheerfully on with the incident presumably erased from his mind.

But somehow I felt again as if the incident might be a kind of warning. It linked itself without conscious help from me with those veiled hints of Boyd and Arbuthnot. I felt that the mountain meant more to Vance than even Quillan, much less I, understood at that moment. I had a disconcerting feeling that my mere presence there was an intrusion in someone's most private and intimate world, and that Quillan and I were not walking along a freshly-made road on a wild mountain in Africa, but treading the edges, the actual matter of another human being's dream. And I found myself wishing suddenly that I had not had to come, and my heart went heavy with foreboding.

By the time we had inspected the road and admired the view it was close on three o'clock, and we were all glad to make a bee-line for the forestry hut.

It stood on a high grass-gold mound in the central gash of the valley. There was a wide, clear stream, and a darker fringe of immense cedars round the bottom of the mound. As we made our way slowly towards it, the afternoon light turned it purple and it looked rather like some kind of un-adorned velvet set in a crown of be-metalled cedars. On either side of the stream there were long slopes of golden grass, speeding away and up to where three miles farther on, perpendiculars of solid grey cliffs, smooth and shining like the bark of a blue-gum tree, rose two to three thousand feet above the floor of the valley. All round the cliff-tops the mist continued to sag heavily.

The hut itself was built of crossed-cedar beams, lath and plaster. It had a roof of cedar shingles, a little cedar veranda at the back, cedar floor-boards, and, I was to find, a few pieces of crude cedar furniture as well. It burned cedar logs whose flame and smoke added to the cold air their own variants of the generic all-pervasive scent. The smoke rose straight up for some hundreds of feet, wavered, and then curved slowly back on its course, until it looked like a feathery question mark stuck into the roof of the hut.

"What do you think of it?" Vance asked, pointing a proud possessive finger.

"I must congratulate you on having the only genuine Tudor building I have seen in Africa. It looks charming and absolutely right," I said, and was delighted to hear laughter break through in him again.

"By gosh!" he said. "You're right. It is a bit Ye Olde Hutte-ish, I must tell Val."

His wife, Valerie Vance, "Val" as he and Quillan both called her, had just fed her two-months-old baby Penelope when we arrived. The child was in a wicker basket asleep on the table by the fire whose light flickered over a puckered little face with tightly clenched eyes. The room was in a sort of twilight, warm and gay with the flame and explosive splutter of the burning cedar logs.

As we walked into it the warmth of it set my ears and face tingling. It was both dining-room and kitchen—there was only one other room in the hut. Val herself just then was cooking a meal for us over a large open hearth.

As she came to meet us, flushed with the heat of the fire, I thought how very young she looked, little more in fact than an attractive, vivacious schoolgirl. As she held her hand out to me the light from the door behind me fell full on her. She had the clear eyes and skin of someone who looked as if she had never lived anywhere else except in the hills. She seemed a deeply contented and happy person, but gave me her hand shyly and, I fear, with some apprehensive reservations that I couldn't fathom. Her greeting of Quillan was more confident but completely impersonal.

"You will forgive me," she said, in a pleasant, matter-of-fact tone, "if I go on with the cooking. Dicky's had nothing to eat since dawn and you too must be hungry."

"Can't you two get a servant to cook for you, Val?" said Quillan. "It is much too much for you. If you can't, I'll see that you get one at once."

Val stood up from the fire and turned round to give him a slow, shy but determined look, full of meaning, and said:

"I do not want a servant, thank you. Dicky has brought me several, but I don't want them. I do not like anybody cooking for my husband and my child except myself. I do not want anyone even to come in and sweep, and make our beds. I want to do it myself. It is just perfect as it is."

"That is quite true," Vance commented, as if underlining a basic law of life. "She doesn't like anybody else in the house."

Again that sickening sense of intrusion, but what could I do about it now?

Although they pressed me politely to pitch a bed with

Quillan in the room with the fire, I refused. As soon as we had some food, I went and pitched my tent on a level patch of grass about seventy-five yards from the hut and made myself as independent and self-contained as possible. But they insisted on my eating in the hut, and I had to compromise by getting them to take over some of my supplies.

That evening the mist left us. It was apparently a pure product of the sun, of the evaporation that the immense heat causes in the great plains below and its condensation in the cool air round Mlanje's peaks. But the moment the sun went, the mist scurried after it. And it was cold.

We all sat close round the fire and watched those lovely cedar logs burning with an eagerness that belonged to the world when it was yet young. Round about nine o'clock it began to freeze and the fire leapt with the same sort of little independent, purple flames, which make farmers in the winter in England exclaim: "My word! Look at that fire! It's going to freeze to-night."

We, or at least Quillan and Vance, talked about trees and forests and their problems, and Val and I listened. I was happy not to speak because I was tired. I preferred to listen and to watch.

Those two children, for so I thought of them, interested me enormously. I had never seen two human beings more complementary, more sufficient unto themselves than those two. She hardly ever took her eyes off him, except now and then to look at Quillan or me to see what effect her husband's remarks were having on us. He frequently would refer to her for confirmation, would stop half-way through a statement and say: "Isn't that so, Val?" or "You noticed it too, Val!" and so on. They never seemed to cease for a second being aware of each other.

When I got up at ten and said "Good night", Vance came some of the way to the tent with me. The sky was intensely black; pure black, if there is such a thing. The stars were unusually large and clear: so full of light that they seemed to be spilling it over pointed rims, as Vance would have it, "buckets-full at a time".

The night crackled and vibrated with their being; throbbed as it were with an urgent message, a quick, excited, electric, morse-code of stars.

"It looks," I said to Vance, "as if your stars up here burn cedar logs as well."

"By Jove," he said with a deep laugh: "I wouldn't be surprised if they do. Never thought of it. I must tell Val."

I could see, now that my eyes were used to the night, the dark outline of the peaks three miles away. They looked much nearer. How cold it was. I felt Vance shivering near me.

"I think you ought to go back now," I said to him. "It's much too cold and I am nearly there. Look!"

I pointed to where my tent, faintly illuminated by a hurricane lamp, was beginning to show up in the dark.

"Yes: I think I had better, but . . ." Vance began and paused. His teeth were now chattering. I was shivering myself.

"Yes?" I said, turning round to face him.

"I hope you won't mind my saying this," he resumed with an impetuous diffidence. "I hope you won't mind, but look, you are not going to take all this away from us, are you?"

"How could I? And why should I?" I said.

"I don't know," he said miserably. "I don't know, but the feeling seems to be that you might want to use Mlanje for something other than forestry?"

I reassured him as best I could. I said I had not seen Mlanje, had no preconceived notions about it, but judging only from what I had seen that day, it seemed obvious that whatever happened very special provisions would have to be made for the cedars and their rejuvenation. But it seemed to be a tremendous mountain and there might be room for other things besides cedars.

"It is big enough," he said sadly. "It's big enough! That's the trouble. But you know, anything else, particularly sheep or cows, would spoil it. They wouldn't belong. It should all be re-covered with cedars from end to end, as it once was."

I could almost see the earnestness on his face in the dark and I was moved more than I can say by his concern. I put my hand on his shoulder.

"Don't let us take any fences before we get to them," I suggested as gently as I could. "I am sure it will be all right. We'll see that your cedars are all right anyway. Now you had better get back. It is too cold for you here. Your teeth are chattering like a monkey's. Good night, and please don't worry."

I waited and shone my torch along the track for him until he was back in the hut. I don't know why, but I watched his sturdy, mountaineer figure disappear into the hut with some misgivings. Again I wondered why, ever since I had first discussed Mlanje in Nyasaland, sooner or later, some form of misgiving always arose.

As I stood there, I thought I heard a leopard cough in the cedars nearby. The mountain was full of them, Vance had said. That is why he locked up his two ridge-back bitches every night. There it was again, a startled, excited, almost involuntary expulsion of breath. It was unmistakable, and I loved it. It is one of the most exciting noises I know. I shone my torch along the edges of the cedar copse. I shone it all round the sturdy trunks and all over their patient, aspiring sides, up to their proud, brooding heads. I saw nothing and heard nothing, until the light of my torch near the top of one tree disturbed a bird of sorts, which flew up silently on exaggerated wings like a moth in candle-light. But the leopard, I am sure, was there, watching the night with jewelled eyes. I heard the dogs whimpering from the hut, they were uneasy too. Then came Vance's deep: "Quiet! Lie down, you two. Lie down!"

I went into my tent, drew the flaps round, fastened them tightly, went to bed, and was sung to sleep by the music of new heights in my blood, the rippling of starlight and crackling of frost on the roof overhead.

Chapter Twelve

I SPENT the following day, Friday, exploring the valley
round the hut. There were about twelve square miles in
all and I enjoyed myself thoroughly. I collected samples of
grasses, of soils, of plants, and had such a busy and interesting day that the time flew by. I got back to the hut after
sunset, to find them all round the fire, drinking great big
cups of steaming, hot tea. I thought both Vance and his
wife looked less apprehensive and their welcome was somewhat warmer.

"Vance," said Quillan, "is coming with us."

"That's grand," I answered, turning to Vance. "But
surely we can't leave your wife and baby here alone?"

"Of course he can," said Val quickly for him. "He has
never done a complete tour of the mountain. He should do
it. It is his job, you know, and he will love it. It is a grand
opportunity. If it were not for Penelope, I would come
too."

And she would have done. She had been with her husband on all his tours of the mountain.

But I was not happy about it. I did not and I do not
trust Africa all that much, and I said so. But they were all
three against me. Vance wanted to wait till Monday when
his foresters came back for duty from their week-end in the
plain below, and then we would set out on our big tour and
make a complete circuit of the mountain.

Meanwhile, on the Saturday and Sunday, Quillan and
I took a look at all the outlying, eccentric parts of the
mountain that would not come into our main circuit. We
went and had a look at the biggest of the mountain
plateaux, Luchenya, the place where an old lady, "eccentric
only in the Nyasaland sense", had once kept cows.

We set off at seven-thirty in the morning, climbed steadily out of our valley and along a ridge which brought us, about two hours later, to a narrow saddle connecting Chambe to the main Mlanje system. It was not difficult climbing, but there was one unpleasant place in the saddle where we climbed over smooth, sheet rock and had a sheer drop of thousands of feet below us.

It was at just this spot, Vance had told me, that once on her first exploration of the mountain, Val had felt suddenly overcome by exhaustion. What made her aware of her fatigue just at that particular moment she would never know, but the impulse to sit down at once was so compelling and urgent that she had to obey. It was thick with mist and rain. She could hardly see her own feet, but as she sat down a rush of wind from the cold peaks above tore the mist apart and she was horrified to see only two steps away on her track this sudden, this sly drop of thousands of feet.

The rest of the saddle was easy walking but it was barely a yard wide; a razor-back, with five-thousand-foot drops on either side of it, connecting gigantic peaks. Our excursion across it this Saturday was largely spoilt by mist. Luchenya was a good deal higher than Chambe and therefore much more favoured by cloud. Yet we collected some lovely wild flowers in all sorts of sheltered dells and valleys. Quillan and I came back with armfuls of them; white, scarlet, orange and purple gladiolus; lovely snow-white bell heather; deep, purple lobelias.

Two memories of that walk back through the mist remain always with me.

The first: how dark, militant, how resentful was the shade in those remote cedar groves through which we had to go. As one's eyes got used to that dim light, one saw everywhere the raw, bleeding, red, ragged places in their bark where the leopards came daily to sharpen their claws.

The other: our view of Chambe as we came out of the

mist over the ridge just before sundown. In that light Chambe, with its deep bowl of a valley, looked like the great bell of a wrecked ship cast upside down on a remote foreshore of time, and like a bell it gathered all its own sounds and silences together and hurled them backwards and forwards from one grey side to another in a steadily ascending spiral to the sky, until, from the rim on which we stood, they were so magnified and reinforced that they seemed to have lost nothing by the great distance they had come.

Suddenly both Quillan and I heard voices, European voices. Although we could distinguish no words, the conversation sounded so close that we stopped and looked round us. At first we could see nothing, but the voices went on in a tone and a manner that suggested a happy, untroubled domestic Saturday afternoon conversation. I could hardly credit my senses, but the voices were those of the Vances down in the valley, nearly a mile away, at the bridge where Quillan some days before had criticized the spacing between the beams of cedar. Vance had Penelope in his arms and Val was by his side. They stood there talking happily. We could not, of course, distinguish what they were saying but the steady drone of their conversation, the rhythm of their voices, mingling with the far-off sound of falling and running water, continued to suggest an unblemished and rounded moment in their lives. After a while Val took Vance's arm and slowly they started walking back to the hut, still talking steadily. They looked for all the world as if they were alone in Kensington Gardens on a Saturday afternoon instead of on a wild mountain top in Central Africa. I must admit I thought it a strikingly incongruous sight and I said to Quillan:

"You know they behave as if Chambe were their own private and personal suburb."

"Yes, I know," he answered, and smiled. "They do look thoroughly at home. You wouldn't think that less than a year ago she had never seen Africa and he only knew it very slightly. She came here straight from a Yorkshire Quaker home. We warned him not to bring a wife as we had no house for them and he would have to start life in a hut. He refused to come without her. I must confess I doubted utterly that good could come of it. But I am glad, I was wrong. It couldn't have been better, as you see for yourself. Only this morning Val asked me never to move them anywhere else. When I said we would have to in two years' time when Dicky was promoted, she answered disdainfully, 'Oh, that! We do not want to be promoted. Dicky and I have talked it over again and again, and we both want to stay here for ever.' It is rather wonderful, isn't it?"

Indeed, I agreed it was wonderful; and yet I had reservations, not perhaps so much on the Vances' score, as on Africa's unpredictable account. I am at heart too much of a nomad to trust and understand love of just one place, particularly one African place. I am sure one cannot love life enough; but I believe, too, one mustn't confuse love of life with the love of certain things in it. One cannot pick the moment and place as one pleases and say, "Enough! This is all I want. This is how it is henceforth to be." That sort of present betrays past and future. Life is its own journey; pre-supposes its own change and movement, and one tries to arrest them at one's eternal peril. As I listened to Quillan, I just hoped fervently that this most unsuburban of mountains felt about it all as the Vances did.

"If one lived here long," I told him, "I believe one would have to appease the mountain in some big way. I believe one would have to become a Druid of sorts and build stone altars and sacrifice live leopards on cedar coals to its spirit."

Quillan roared with laughter and said that often in the forests in the hills of Cyprus he felt if only he could pull the boots off the shepherds he would find that they had not human but goat's feet. And on that note we went down to the hut and the Vances.

On the Sunday, we spent the morning in the main cedar wood of the valley, and in the afternoon went fishing. Quillan caught seven rainbow trout, averaging about a pound apiece. The streams were very clear and it was so fascinating watching the trout pretending, at first, to be unaware of the fly and then rising to strike with incredible speed, that Quillan and I both forgot the time.

It was the cold that first made me realize how late it was and, looking up, I noticed the sun had just gone and darkness was bounding up from the plains below. We raced the cold and the night back to the hut, but before we started it was a race lost. It was so dark when we arrived at the hut, half-frozen, that the dogs from far-off barked at our hurrying footsteps. The Vances were both in front of an enormous fire drying napkins.

"I am glad to see you were not eaten by leopards," said Vance with a smile.

"Why specially to-night?" asked Quillan.

"Only because one of the foresters coming back this evening says he came face to face with a leopard right in the track through the cedars down there," Vance answered.

"What happened?" I asked.

"The usual thing," Vance said with a deep laugh: "they both fell back on previously prepared positions. In other words, ran like hell."

Triumphantly we handed Val the fish. She gave a small cry of surprise, said "How lovely", and then cooked them the Mlanje way in bacon fat with great streaky rashers and sliced potatoes.

That Sunday evening round the fire seemed a very warm, blessed, friendly evening. Things like fires and food, warmth and a roof over one's head, recover their original force of meaning on those occasions. We all ate too much, drank pints of hot, sweet tea, told one another funny stories and laughed as if we did not have a care in the world. But the night was the coldest we had yet had.

"It's going to settle fine for a spell," Vance said as he saw me out. "Look at Orion: I have never seen the Old Hunter so clear."

Chapter Thirteen

EARLY the next morning we collected our bearers, thirty in all now, with an old forester as guide, and set off immediately after breakfast. The last thing I did was to give my gun and cartridges to Val Vance because I did not feel happy about us leaving her unarmed. She blushed when I gave it to her, was obviously embarrassed, and took it reluctantly only because I insisted. She then came, the two bitches dancing round her, down to the stream with us.

It was our first really sunny morning. We sent the carriers on ahead with the guide. I took my keys and gave them to Leonard, my cook, telling him to have tea ready for us when we arrived at our camp for the night. We waited until the bearers were all across the stream and well strung out along the steep track on the far side, and then prepared to follow ourselves. Quillan and I and Vance last with his rifle-bearer.

Vance paused to say good-bye to his wife. I expect they were very shy, and in any case they were very young; but without looking or wanting to look, one felt it was not the sort of good-bye they meant it to be, was an awkward, brusque, self-conscious gesture quite unrepresentative of their feelings.

It was none of my business but, suddenly feeling sick at heart, I said to myself: "Dear God, I do hope nothing is going to happen to make those children regret their inadequate good-bye."

I record this knowing well that to anyone reading this in comfort, in cold blood, thousands of miles away, my reaction may seem odd, may even seem suspiciously like wisdom after the event. But I can only repeat truthfully that to my clear recollection these were my apprehensions at eight o'clock on the morning of Monday, May 23, six thousand six hundred feet up in the Chambe valley of the great Mlanje plateau of Nyasaland.

This precisely is how I reacted, and now, looking back, it confirms a suspicion that has grown up over many years out of my own troubles and disastrous mistimings in this mysterious business of living. Without looking for it, against all my training and upbringing, I myself have become increasingly aware of how little our conscious knowing pushes back the frontiers of our unknowing. In the forefront of our century all this parade of our knowledge, this great and glittering collection of demonstrable and ascertainable fact, throws no more light on our aboriginal darkness than one of Vance's bright cedar fires throws on the night round the peaks of Mlanje.

And yet there is a way of knowing which is at once underneath and above consciousness of knowing. There is a way in which the collective knowledge of mankind expresses itself, for the finite individual, through mere daily living: a way in which life itself is sheer knowing. So life is to me, anyway; a mystery in all its essentials, a complete and utter mystery. I accept it even gladly as such because the acceptance keeps me humble, keeps me in my little place; prevents me, as we used to say in the recent war, from being caught too far out of position.

And the future? I have been trained to think of it as something before me, something in the days ahead, and so indeed it obviously is. But there is a sense in which it is also behind us, in which it also is "now". I can only reaffirm that without looking for it or seeking it in any way, without any spiritual or theoretical axe to grind, as Vance said good-bye to his wife, I felt desperately afraid for them. And there, for the moment, I must leave it.

She walked back, lightly, easily up the slope to the hut, the light of the sun gay on her hair, and the two bitches running circles round her, and he followed us up the long steep slope out of the valley.

We climbed slowly up the way Quillan and I had gone on the Saturday. For the first time since our arrival, the whole of Mlanje had emerged into the full light of a clear African winter's day. The view from the top was immense.

We saw Lake Chilwa and across it for more than a hundred miles to a blue range of mountains in Portuguese East Africa. We saw the Zomba plateau, the massive Chirudzulu, the Blantyre hills and beyond, the elegant purple crest of the Kirk ranges. Then we crossed from Chambe to the main Mlanje side by the same narrow saddle ridge where Val Vance had so narrowly missed disaster, turned our backs on the plains and concentrated on Mlanje itself.

Here we climbed, slowly, up the side of a great, grey peak. I wondered again why Mlanje was ever called a plateau, for it seemed from this exalted position a collection of narrow ledges and valleys, poised on six- to seven-thousand-foot cliffs and dominated by a long succession of monstrous, grey peaks. We climbed for two hours. Our carriers spread and straggled out in the long, slowly, steeply ascending line in front of us.

How they did it with those loads I do not know. Unloaded, it was all I could do to get up. In particular, I was amazed at my cook Leonard, the frail ascetic-looking African from the malarial plain. With a saucepan, a frying-pan, kettle and bag of flour slung round his shoulders, he clattered and banged his way up as steadily and surely as the rest.

Just underneath the tip of the grey peak, we crossed over a thin shoulder and slowly came down once more on to a narrow ledge stretching for twenty miles in front of us, in the lee of a long line of massive, sheet-rock summits. To amuse ourselves, we tried to give them all names according to the impression they made on us: Nelson's Column; Little Pig With-back-so-bare Peak; Cocking-a-Snook Peak; Beer-Barrel-Point; The Admiral's Hat; Big-pipe-smoking Sioux

Chief; The Flappers' Downfall—because, said Quillan, that peak when it fell, like flappers when they fall, fell a long way and fell for good; and finally the Lion's-heart and the Elephant's Head.

In this manner we crossed deep, swollen river-bends, went through thick cedar groves, walked and climbed continually up and down. At three-thirty, when the sun was just drawing in behind the highest peaks, we came to a forestry hut at a place called Tuchila, about thirteen miles from Chambe.

A very old native forester was in charge there. He was a memorable old gentleman, with beautiful manners and the most serene, resolved expression on his face that I have ever seen. He said that, apart from Vance, we were the third group of Europeans he had welcomed there in thirty years. He lived there entirely alone. He had long given up visiting his descendants in the plain below. They never came to see him. His values were fixed for the last time. According to Vance he hardly bothered about his wages any more. Once in four or five months he would come over to Chambe to collect supplies. For the rest he stayed at Tuchila working in his garden, planting potatoes and being unreservedly content. That old man knew something really worth knowing, and I wished I had some way of showing him the respect I felt for him.

In the early morning, he led us up the flank of another grey peak, the Elephant's Head. We climbed straight into a blue sky between brightly-lit candelabra of tremendous, scarlet aloes. We climbed steeply for two hours, and then came out on a precipitous shoulder. Here the old man posed, without self-consciousness of any kind, for his photograph, and then said good-bye with great dignity, his hand raised in a Roman salute above his head. While we were resting with our bearers (who were getting to know us and gradually beginning to talk to us not as white strangers but leaders of their team), we watched the old man go down, without a single backward glance, to his home on the edge of a seven-thousand-foot precipice. The mountain looked very big and he looked very small, and I thought him unbelievably heroic.

From here we went on into a deep valley, called by the guide the Great Ruo. We nearly walked on top of a klipspringer which was obviously unused to this sort of invasion and therefore unprepared. It streaked up the peak with the speed and ease of an electric hare.

We went down into the valley. It was filled with smoke, because Vance's foresters were burning protective firebreaks round the cedars there. We crossed the far shoulder, climbed down into another, the Sombani, valley, and after six hours' continuous and fast walking and climbing in a hot sun, made our camp in a large cave overlooking the great Fort Lister gap in the southern hills of Nyasaland. The natives called this cave, "Rock of the God of Wonders".

We had climbed and walked in all eighteen miles. It was now bitterly cold and we kept a large fire roaring in the entrance all night. I slipped Leonard the first of my surprises, a plum pudding—to celebrate Empire Day. I was a day late remembering it but it did not spoil our enjoyment in eating the pudding, blazing with some of Quillan's Portuguese brandy.

The next day we traced our steps along the Sombani valley, crossed down an intersecting valley called Malosa, all presided over by the same colossal, grey, sheet-rock presences. They had brows like elder statesmen and looked profoundly engaged in the patient diplomacy of the elements and time. We were soon to have a demonstration of what could happen when they and the clouds put their heads together. With everyone's approval I christened them here, "Les Eminences Grises." They had become so real to us by this time that, as I did so, I had an urge to take off my hat and bow politely to them.

We walked down this wide valley below these grey

Solomon heads for some hours. It was the loveliest day we had yet struck and a wide blue stream kept us company for several miles. Its water was a perfect mirror to the sun and the sky. I had never seen the mountain more frank, more open and friendly both with nature and with us. It was for me a very happy morning. I was quite content to walk behind Vance and Quillan, who as usual talked forests, trees and mountains with unfailing zest. We got on very well together, but obviously I could only be on the fringes of their calculations.

Just before noon we climbed the inevitable far shoulder of a peak, crossed over it just underneath a wrinkled eroded and tightly-clenched old mountain face and came down into another valley called the Little Ruo. Oh, these remote unpeopled Mlanje valleys on their best behaviour on a sunny day; their surging, flashing streams and devout congregations of dark cedars worshipping at the foot of the great cliffs hard by, moaning a mindless, pre-human hymn of their own! They have to be experienced to be believed.

We raced the sun to the steep western rim of the valley, got there almost as soon as the sun did, and looked down in the long level light of the early evening on another far frontier of Mlanje. Here on the brim of the valley, built of wood and grass against an overhanging rock, was the hut of one of Vance's native fire-watchers.

We stopped to look at it and to get our breath. The fire-watcher was not at home, but the world about him was so entirely his own that he had left his precious bow and five delicately feathered, steel-barbed arrows, leaning non-chalantly against the entrance. At the side was a crude, stone trap set and ready with seeds spread for the birds.

Suddenly Vance went and pulled the prop out and at once the stone fell down.

"He'll come back and wonder for days what the devil happened to it," said Vance with a mischievously pleased school-boy laugh, and Quillan joined in with a perfunctory grin.

It seemed to me not only a thoughtless thing to do but, unintentionally, a betrayal of the unknown watcher's trust. I felt shocked by it out of all proportion to the importance of the material issue involved. Obviously no great practical harm would be done if the trap were left sprung, but somehow I found the incident impossible to stomach. Something was wrong in our set-up, we were off the true somewhere, if we could behave like that. My reaction had nothing to do with the ethics of the occasion; it was the discord that worried me. It jarred as I believe the first misfire, indicating a fault in some smoothly-running machine, must jar on the ears of an engineer.

I was stepping forward to try and set the trap again when an amazed "I say, look at that!" from Quillan, pulled me up short.

This fire-watcher had one of the world's great views at his doorstep. His hut was at least eight thousand feet above sea-level, and close on seven thousand feet above the plain below. Since the mountain fell away sheer to the plain, the whole of Portuguese East Africa was at his feet. However, what had now raised Quillan's interest was not this superb view but a desperate battle between an eagle and a buzzard carried on in the soft evening light.

When I first saw them they were about a thousand feet above us, locked together, and falling fast. At the point where they had first closed for battle a puff of feathers had exploded in the blue-gold air like a burst of ack-ack fire. They fell from above us, and were nearly level with us, before they disengaged their talons and regained their ruffled wings. Then up they went again, watchfully circling each other. In the cold, mellowing light we stood below, bearers and all, holding our breaths with a curious excitement, as they drove each other up. The buzzard was the first to reach the height it sought. Suddenly it shot up, did a loop, and came down on the eagle once again, beak, talons, wings and all.

There was another burst of feathers as the birds fell. They shot by us at a tremendous speed and then, far below us, the eagle broke free and fled. The buzzard made no effort to pursue it but rose impressively to a tremendous height on one of the great currents from the plain, and then on calm, impassive wings floated away over the grey peaks behind us.

We had neither ideas nor theories as to what the battle had been about, but I am sure of one thing: had we been ancient Greeks, whose manhood would not be dishonoured by tears nor by the pouring out of libations to the gods, then we would have taken a different interest in the encounter. I could almost hear the Homeric rendering: "Just then Zeus, the all-powerful, sent a buzzard to defeat the eagle as a warning to the sorely-tried Odysseus that greater perils lay ahead," and so on. But we had not the mind for such fancies. We had walked and climbed twenty miles. So we pushed on as fast as possible down the far side of the mountain towards our rest, and, for the moment, I forgot all about the fire-watcher and his sprung trap.

Just below us, on one of the spurs which rose up from the plain like a flying buttress supporting the immense, Gothic flank of the mountain, we climbed down on to the thickest and darkest cluster of cedars we had yet seen. The light of the sun struck a cold, steely sparkle from their erect tops. They looked suspicious even of the intentions of a most noble and generous evening. Once among them, it became quite dark. Quillan, Vance and I joined hands and could hardly get our arms half-way round many of the trunks, nor could we see a trace of the blue of evening above.

We had hardly entered the forest when I heard from far away the harsh, grating noise of mechanical saws. It really was a heart-rending sound and shattered that beautifully poised moment of evening-fall with its violent hysteria. Vance and Quillan both looked instantly ashamed of it, and hastened to apologize.

They said they had been unable to prevent it. This part

of the mountain had been taken from their control. The
shortage of wood in the country was such that the government had given some Europeans from the plains a concession to cut timber here. The only thing to be said for it
was that it produced more money for rejuvenating the
species elsewhere in the mountain. But they hated it, and
wanted it stopped.

I was convinced, as I listened to those two, that the trees
knew what was happening to their kind in that area. The
noise was so obviously the voice of destruction, and besides,
death was in the very air they breathed through their fine
dark leaves. Their characteristic scent, which lay so heavily
on the air, here had an extra tang to it—the smell of the
sap, the honey-gold essence of freshly felled, warmly carved
and still bleeding cedars.

We slept that night in the tiny log hut of the half-caste
manager of the concession. No European would face the
lonely life on the mountain except at an exorbitant wage;
no native was educated and expert enough; so, as often
happens in Africa, the half-caste was the inevitable compromise.

This half-caste, however, had an unusual quality about
him. He was a tall, good-looking boy with regular, sensitive
features and a pair of big, well-spaced dark eyes. His name
was Fitz David St. Leger and he had a neat, carefully
clipped, cavalry moustache on a quite un-negroid lip. I was
told that his father, an ex-officer of the Greys, was still alive
in the plain below, living with a black wife and a large
brood of chocolate children. He was, everyone said, a man
of great charm and distinguished appearance. About twenty
years before he had won the Calcutta sweep and tried to
begin life afresh in Europe. He had even married a European wife. But no miracle of money could save him from
Africa. Within a few months he was back, swearing that he
could not endure pale-faces, particularly pale-faced women.

This son of his must have modelled himself on his father

or some other ancestral memory. He seemed an intelligent, capable boy, with something of the cavalry subaltern in his bearing, but so vulnerable, so hopelessly, unfairly and basically vulnerable that I could not see him ever making the most of his qualities in that British-African world. One imagined him, for the rest of life, drifting from one weary compromise to another, living a sort of twilight existence between two worlds.

And he was much nicer to us than we deserved. He turned out of his hut the moment we arrived. He quickly had his bedding rolled up, and he told us to use an enormous cast-iron bath that he had brought up the mountain with him. I tried to get him to stay and eat with us but in vain. He raised his soiled white topee, bid us a polite, strangely old-fashioned "good evening" and went off to spend the night in a hut with his natives.

I think I enjoyed that night less than any of its predecessors. As we sat in our greatcoats, huddled round a pathetic table made of petrol boxes, our conversation just missed being tediously argumentative. At times I felt as if some outside force beyond our immediate awareness was deliberately trying to set us quarrelling. Also, the hut stood hard by an enormous pile of golden cedar sawdust, and the smell of warm cedar sap was so overpowering that I felt stifled by it. For a long time I couldn't sleep and my mind tended to return ceaselessly to the trivial discords of the day.

I was relieved when morning came. One of the first things I did was to go and thank Fitz David St. Leger for his hospitality. I was amazed when I held out my hand to him to see him draw his arm back. He flushed under his dark skin and said, "I am not clean enough." When we did finally shake hands, he did it awkwardly as if his own was burning. Vance and Quillan, I noticed, watched me with embarrassment and did not follow my example.

Chapter Fourteen

THEN, on that Friday, May 27, we climbed back on to the highest edge of the Little Ruo valley, about eight thousand five hundred feet high. There Quillan and Vance decided to take a short cut to our camp for the night and to send our bearers round the long, easy, known route with our guide. They did this because there was some unknown country in front that they thought we should see. As we stood on the rim, talking it over, in a cold breeze and under a grey, morning sky, I noticed far away in the plain below the lumber camp, the top of Mount Chiperone covered in cloud. The wind was blowing off it towards us and the weather was rapidly building up round it.

In a flash I remembered Boyd's warning to me in his house at Mlanje: "For God's sake, when that happens on the peak, look out."

So I said to Quillan and Vance: "It looks to me as if there is a Chiperone on the way. Don't let's take any chances! I don't like short-cuts anyway. My experience of mountains is that the longest way round is the shortest way there."

They turned round, regarded Chiperone solemnly, for a moment, looked at each other, nodded, and then Quillan said: "It is only a bit of morning mist. It will clear up soon. We'll be in the camp in an hour or two and can spend the afternoon resting. I think we can all do with it."

Because they were the experts on the mountain, because it was their mountain and their mountain's weather, and because I have been trained to give priority to what appears to be reasonable, I stifled my instinct and said no more. But if the future had an origin other than in itself, then I believe it was born in that moment. Our decision was a bad decision, it was the wrong decision. Wrong begets wrong, starts a chain of accident and disharmony in circumstances which quickly develop a will of their own. These circumstances exact their own logical toll and must run their time to the bitter end, before the individual is able to break free of them again.

We sent our bearers on their way, kept only Vance's own gun-bearer with us, dropped quickly into the valley below, crossed a wide stream and started up on the other side. We climbed hard and fast. It was eleven o'clock exactly when we came out on the rim close on nine thousand feet. We sat down, ate a piece of chocolate and prepared to admire the view.

Almost directly underneath us was the greatest of Mlanje's many dark gorges, the Great Ruo Gorge. The water of the Great Ruo river itself plunged down the top end of the gorge; fell with a wild, desperate, foaming leap into an abyss, thousands of feet deep. We could not see the bottom of it. On either side it was flanked by black, glistening, six-thousand-foot cliffs, tapering off into grey peaks nine thousand feet high. The whole of the gorge rustled, whispered and murmured with the sound of falling water, which at every change of mountain air would suddenly break over us with a noise like the sound of an approaching hail-storm.

"You see that clump of cedars just beyond the fall," Vance said, "our camp is there. We shall be there within the hour."

As he spoke the mist came down. He and Quillan said it would soon lift. We waited. We got colder and colder. The mist rapidly thickened. It began to drizzle. At eleven-thirty we decided to do the best we could. The sun had vanished, the wind had dropped. Neither Vance, Quillan, I, nor, for that matter, any living person, had ever stood before where we then stood. In the sunlight one stone is very like another; but in the mist on Mlanje they were undistinguishable. Because of that terrible gorge we could not go further down until we were past the head of the waterfall. So we set out along the peaks, keeping as near to their crest as we could.

Worst of all, the mist halo lay like a blanket over the noise of the fall. Not a sound came up to us. We had not even a whisper from it for guidance. The silence was really complete, except for our breathing, our boots squelching on the wet grass and moss or crunching on stone.

From eleven-thirty until four-thirty—and we had been going since seven without rest—we went up one peak and down into a bottom, up the other side and down again.

At half-past four the rifle-bearer said: "It is no good, Bwana; we are lost. Let us make a fire and wait for it to clear."

I said no. I knew it was no mist. It was a Chiperone and it came, so Boyd had said, in multiples of five days. We would be dead of cold before it cleared. I added, "At all costs, we must go down now. The night is not far off. We must get into a valley and then we can consider the next step."

So slowly down we went, down those steep, uneven slopes of Mlanje, listening carefully for the noise of falling water. But the whole mountain had gone as silent as the dead.

We slid and slithered in a way that was neither prudent nor safe. Suddenly at five the mist began to thin. The gun-bearer gave a tremendous shout. A warm golden glow was coming up to meet us and in a few minutes we were in the tawny-grass bottom of the Great Ruo itself, three miles above the gorge and four miles from our camp. We got to our camp at nightfall and the mist changed into a heavy, steady, drumming downpour of rain. The bearers were already in and Leonard had prepared our little mud-and-straw native hut. We lay down by the side of the fire in the middle of the hut, a great glow of gratitude inside us. We were too tired to speak for half an hour or more, and listened to the violence of the rain.

"It is a Chiperone all right now," said Vance: "the point is, how long is it going to last?"

Our camp was a disused, discarded lumber camp, the huts which had originally housed the native timber carriers. Once again, as often before in Africa, I thanked Providence for the African hut-builder. These insignificant-looking, brown beehive huts one dashes past by car or train in Africa are amazing. Considering the poor material, the lack of scientific equipment and research, the lack of education of their humble builders, they are works of genius. Although the rain now pounded down so violently, not a drop came through the ancient thatch.

When we had recovered sufficiently, we went round to inquire after our bearers and found them, also under dry roofs, cooking their dinners round crackling cedar fires. They were a happy and cheering sight.

We told Leonard to stay with them in the dry. We did not want him splashing round in the wet, trying to wait on us. We went back, dried ourselves out thoroughly, and did our own cooking. I made a kettleful of hot coffee which we drank very sweet, laced liberally with my medicinal cognac. The cognac was a great improvement on the Portuguese brandy and a welcome and complete surprise. It was precisely the anticipation of moments like these that had made shopping in Blantyre such fun, and I drew a glow of reassurance from this slight justification of my planning.

We ate in silence. I myself was too full of an unutterable sense of well-being to attempt to speak. I think the others perhaps felt something else as well, for they both, particularly Vance, looked somewhat reproved by the experience of the day. Then silently we stretched ourselves out beside the fire, with a good heart, to sleep.

But I was too tired to sleep at once. I lay with my ear close to the ground and listened to the rain drumming down on the mountain. Among those vast peaks there was no other sound than this continuous, violent, downpouring of the rain. There was no light of stars or far-off reflection of town or hamlet; only the dying glow of the cedars from a dying world of trees. The night, the mountain and the rain were woven tightly into a dark pre-human communion of absolute oneness. No leopard, pig or antelope or elastic mountain gazelle would venture out on a night like this. It is precisely against moments like these that the leopards bury some portion of bird, bush ape or pig, and leave it near their holes and caves. The summons riding the mountains with such desperate dispatch was not for animal or human hearts. But it was as if the earth underneath my head was slowly beginning to respond to this drumming, this insistent beat of the rain; to take up this rhythm of the rain; to answer this ceaseless knocking at its most secret door, and to open itself to this vast orchestration of its own natural, primeval elements, to begin to quicken its own patient pulse, and deep inside itself, in the core of its mountain, its Jurassic heart, to do a tap-dance of its own. Whenever I rose in the night to make up the fire there was the rain and this manner of the rain; and when I lay down again there was this deep, rhythmical response of the earth.

We woke finally at five and talked over the day while waiting for the kettle to boil. Our plan originally had been to go over the top of the mountain in the direction of Chambe. But we found now that our experience of the day before among the peaks on the far side of the Ruo valley had made us all decide in the night against any more adventures in the clouds while the Chiperone was blowing. In this way the previous day influenced our behaviour. Our guide well knew the way over the top and, had it not been for that short-cut, I do not believe we would have changed our plans.

Vance now said he knew an easy way down off the

mountain which led to a large tea estate at the bottom. Quillan said he knew it too, it was the old timber carriers' track. It was steep, but cut out in the side of the Great Ruo gorge and clearly defined. We could not go wrong. Only it meant abandoning the last part of the trip and that, he thought, would be a pity for me. I said firmly, "Abandon." Vance then decided to go ahead to the tea estate and get a truck to take us round by road to Likabula. With luck, he said, we could all be back on the mountain at Chambe that evening.

With our last eggs I made him a quick omelette for breakfast, and sent him off in the rain. Quillan and I followed slowly with the carriers.

We set out at eight but the rain was so thick and violent that there was only a dim, first-light around us. We went slowly. The track was steep and highly dangerous. On the left of us, only a yard or so away, was that deep cleft down to the Great Ruo gorge. The bearers too had great difficulty with their loads. They had to lower themselves down from one level to another by cedar roots and help one another down perilous mud precipices.

As we went down, the noise of falling water all round us became deafening. Whenever there was a slight lift of the rain and mist, the half-light, the mepacrine gloom on the mountain would be suddenly illuminated by a broad, vivid flash of foaming white water leaping down the face of smooth black cliffs, thousands of feet high. We had to shout in places to make ourselves heard.

Moreover the mountain itself, the very stones on which we trod, the mud wherein we slid, seemed to begin to vibrate and tremble under this terrible pounding of water. At moments when we rested, the ground shook like a greaser's platform in the engine-room of a great ship. This movement underfoot, combined with the movement of the flashing, leaping, foaming water in our eyes, and driving rain and swirling mists, gave to our world a devastating sense of instability. The farther down we went, the more pronounced it became, until I began to fear that the whole track would suddenly slither like a crocodile from underneath my feet and leave me falling for ever under the rain and Mlanje's cataclysmic water. It needed a conscious effort of will to keep me upright, and I found this all the more difficult because of a new complication that was arising. I began to feel as if my very senses were abandoning their moorings inside myself.

Luckily this stage of the journey did not last too long. Two and a quarter hours later our track suddenly became easier and broader.

Quillan said, "We'll soon be off it now."

We came round a bend in the track and there, to our surprise, was Vance. He was sitting at the side of a fast stream of water which was pouring over the track and had evidently held him up. He was joining some lengths of creeper, of monkey rope, together.

"I didn't want to cross this stream without a rope," he said. "I have been up and down this stream as far as possible and this is the best place to try it. It doesn't look difficult. Do you think this will do?"

He handed me his rope of creepers.

"No! Certainly not," I said, and looked at the stream.

Its beginnings, above us, were lost in the mist and rain. Then it suddenly appeared out of the gloom about a hundred yards above, charging down at us at a steep angle, and finally, just before it reached us, smashing itself up behind a tremendous rock, deeply embedded on the side of the gorge. Somewhere behind the rock it reassembled its shattered self and emerged from behind it flowing smoothly. For about twenty yards it looked a quiet, well-behaved stream but, on our left at the track's edge, it resumed its headlong fall into the terrible main Ruo gorge below us. I now went to this edge and looked over, but the falling water vanished quickly in the gloom and told me nothing.

Only the ground shook with the movement as my eyes and head ached with the noise.

I came back and found Quillan lighting a fire.

"Our bearers are nearly dead with cold," he explained. "They'll crack up if we don't do something. Two wood-cutter blokes died here of exposure two years ago. But if I can get this fire going for them in the lee of this rock, our chaps will be all right."

The rain poured down even more heavily than before, and it looked darker than ever. The shivering negroes, the bamboos bent low with rain, the black rocks, were like figures and things moving in the twilight of a dream.

Again I went and looked at the stream above. Vance appeared to have chosen rightly. The stream was swollen but did not look dangerous at that point, particularly with a good rope. Higher up it would have been hopeless.

"I tell you, Dicky," I said. (It was the first time I had called him that and I don't know why I did, except that we all suddenly seemed to be very close to one another.) "I tell you what, Dicky. We'll take all our ropes, you knot them together and then I'll go across. I am bigger than you."

"I don't think that is necessary," he said. "I know the way. You don't. And with a rope it will be easy."

We joined up the ropes, tested the result in every way, pulling it, leaning on it. It seemed tight and strong. We took Vance's valise straps and added them to the end, just in case. I then tied it round Vance's chest with a knot that couldn't slip. I made sure it could not tighten and hinder his breathing.

As I tied it I said, "Dicky, are you sure you are happy about this and know how to do it, for if you are not I would much rather do it myself?"

"Of course I know," he said with a deep laugh. "I have done it scores of times in Burma. And I must hurry. I want to get those poor black devils under shelter as soon as I can."

"Well, remember," I said, "keep your face to the stream;

always lean against it; go into it carefully and feel well round your feet with your stick before you move."

He took up the stout stick that we had cut for him. I called Quillan and two of the bearers. Quillan and I took the rope. I braced my feet against a tree on the edge of the stream, just in case, but I was not at all worried.

Vance waded in. The water came about to his navel. He went steadily on for some distance then, to my bewilderment, turned his back slightly on the stream. It was the first deviation from plan.

He took another step or two, stopped, suddenly abandoned his stick to the stream and yelled to us, "Let out the rope!"

It was the second deviation from plan. I was horrified. What the hell was he up to? Before we had even properly grasped his meaning he had thrown himself on the stream and was swimming a breast-stroke. As was inevitable, the stream at once caught him and quickly swept him to where it foamed and bubbled like a waterfall over the edge of the track. The unexpected speed with which all of this had happened was the most terrifying thing about it. Even so, Vance had got to within a foot of the far bank, was on the verge of reaching it—when the water swept him over the edge and he disappeared from our view.

Quillan and I were braced for the shock. As we saw it coming we both shouted for the bearers, who rushed to our assistance in a body. The rope tightened in a flash. The strain was tremendous. Vance's body, no longer waterborne but suspended out of sight, below the edge of the rocky track, with the weight and stream of water pouring on top of it, strained the rope to the utmost. Yet it held.

I think it would have continued to hold if the angle and violent impact of the water on the body had not now with incredible speed whipped Vance along the sharp edge of the rocks, swung him from the far side over towards our bank and chafed the rope badly in the process. It still held for a second or two. We worked our way along it towards him—were within two yards of him—when the rope snapped.

At that moment we knew that he was dead. Anyone who stood with us in the black rain, amid those black cliffs in that world of storming, falling, rushing, blind water, must have known that he was dead. Quillan turned round, lifted a face to me naked and bare with misery, and said hoarsely, "What to do, now? He is dead, you know!"

I nodded and said, "Please take a search-party as far as you can, Peter, and see what you can see."

He immediately set out. I called Leonard and some bearers and started to undo our baggage. It was obvious we could not cross now. We had lost all our rope; we had lost one body with a rope, we could not risk losing one without a rope. Nor could we stay there.

Quillan was back almost at once. I was not surprised. We were, as I have said before, on the edge of the Great Ruo gorge.

He shook his head. "Not a sign, not a hope. He is dead and there is nothing we can do now except to see that these fellows don't conk out."

He indicated the bearers.

We called them all round us. They were cold and terribly shaken by Vance's death. One old man was crying and they were all shivering as if with malaria. We told them to dump their loads and to start back up the mountain to the huts we had slept in the night before. A moan of despair rose up from them. They said they wanted to sit by the river, wanted to make a fire and wait for the sun. But I knew that that only meant that the spirit had gone out of them, that they had given up hope and were resigned to do no more than sit down and die in comfort.

It was then that Leonard, the puny plainsman, the sophisticated native from the towns, stood up, unsolicited, and lashed them with his tongue. I don't know what he said, but he insulted them into some shape of spirit.

We distributed all our own and Vance's clothes among them. That cheered them. They began to laugh and to tease one another, at the sight of their companions in tennis shirts, grey sweaters too big for them, in green, blue, red and grey striped pyjamas, and my own green jungle bush-shirts with their red 15 Corps flashes still on them.

I expect it was an incongruous sight in that world of rain, falling water and black, impersonal rock, but I did not find it at all funny. It seemed to me to fill the cup of our misery to overflowing. I expect whatever gods sit on this African Olympus might well find it amusing to kill a young man of twenty-eight in order to dress up some of the despised, ubiquitous outcasts of their African kingdom in silk pyjamas in the pouring rain. To me, just to kill was bad enough; to mock the kill an intolerable perfection of tragedy. I came near to joining in Quillan's tears at that moment, but fortunately I got angry as well, so angry that I believe if my strength had matched my rage I could have picked up the whole of Mlanje and thrown it over the edge of the world into the pit of time itself.

I walked up to the bearers in anger such as I have never known and told them, by look and gestures, to get the hell up the mountain without delay. In that mood, Quillan and I got them up the steep, slippery sides of the gorge that we had come down only a few moments before.

At half-past twelve we were back in our camp of the night before; we started a great, blazing fire and dried ourselves. The warmth and the sight of fire and smoke effected an amazing revival of spirit among the Africans. I was discussing with Quillan a plan for going out myself through the Fort Lister gap to fetch help, leaving him there with the bearers because he knew the language, when the oldest forester spoke up and said: "You can't do that, Bwana. It is too far. But I know a short way over the top that will bring us to Chambe safely by sundown."

Quillan asked them all if they had heard what the

143

forester said, understood, approved and were prepared to follow him implicitly? They all said emphatically, "Yes!" It was the only thing to do and they would do it.

By one o'clock we were climbing back up the peaks behind our camp, into clouds and into rain which seemed more violent than ever.

Peter Quillan was at his best. He was firm yet patient with the bearers, steadily urged them on, but it could not have been easy. He was heartbroken, and from time to time I could see he was in tears. He was deeply attached to Vance and was blaming himself bitterly for the accident. I did my best to comfort him. I couldn't see how he was to be blamed at all, and if he were, then what about me? He, after all, had not been worried by a sense of the future. It wasn't he who had lain awake at nights half stifled by a sense of death and listening to the dark drummer of Africa beating-up the weather round Mlanje. But as I comforted him and we slowly forced the bearers up the black peaks in front of us, I too was sick at heart and desperately tired.

Without any preliminary training I had been scrambling round these monstrous peaks from dawn until sunset for nine days, and I could now hardly lift my legs. Heaven knows I was fit, my lungs and spirit were all right, and my rage with the mountain and its gorge spurred me on. The problem was purely mechanical. My legs and feet were so abused that the muscles rebelled and would not react instinctively. It seemed to me that all my reflexes had gone. I had to treat each step as a mechanical and separate entity in the movement of my body. I could move only with a deliberate, calculated, conscious and determined effort of will. At one moment I thought seriously of retiring to the huts lest I should not be able to continue, and so should bring disaster on the others.

Quillan was amazing. His forester's muscles were intact. He cheered and helped me on by word and example. When, afterwards, we told people of this journey over the highest and wildest part of Mlanje they would hardly credit it. But on the day of Vance's death we did nearly twenty miles' climbing. I hope never to do such a journey again.

For two hours after leaving the hut we continued to climb, at the steepest of angles, into deepening cloud and rain. Our guide, the old forester, in his rags and tatters, dripping with water, was unbelievable. He climbed at our head with his stick held in one hand in front of him. Every now and then he parted the grasses with it, peered at them intently, or tapped a stone, listening carefully to its ring, and then changed direction to the left or the right; but he never faltered. Over and over again the rain and mist completely hid him from my view. It was dark, it was black; even at the best of times it was grey all around us.

After two hours, as far as one could judge in the mist, we seemed to pass right over the top of a peak, and our course began to drop slowly down. The relief to my muscles was timely.

Quillan offered me some whisky and water. I do not drink spirits as a rule, but I accepted gratefully and pushed on with renewed energy. At four o'clock, we suddenly came out of the mist and rain; we walked through it as if it had been a wall. At one minute it was raining; the next we were in the sunlight looking down on the long ledge by Tuchila.

We climbed down there as fast as we could. We had seven miles to go before we reached that razor saddle, and unless we got there before dark we should be unable to cross to Chambe and shelter.

We got down easily enough, but getting up and then down the river gashes and finally up again on to that high steep shoulder by Chambe was for me a bitter and protracted agony. However, we got to the ridge where Val Vance was nearly killed, just as the sun went down.

It was a frightening sunset, a sort of cosmic schism of light and darkness. On our left was that immense, dark pile of rain, turning and wheeling constantly over the bulk of

Mlanje, wheeling in such a manner, with such fantastic contortions of cloud shapes, that to my tired eyes it looked as if the devils of death were charging up and down those peaks on phantom, skeleton chargers. Yet to our right lay Chambe with a golden afterglow of sunlight on it, untroubled and serene, as if it had never known death or disaster of any kind. Less than a fortnight before I had seen Mlanje from afar at just such an hour, in such a way with this same pattern of fair and foul, dark and light, on it. Had the same pattern also been in me?

Chapter Fifteen

THE bearers, climbing for once without loads of any kind, were by this time a long way ahead of us. We had realized this would happen and had warned them not to arrive at Val Vance's hut before we did. We were concerned that their looks would betray our tragedy to her. We now found them waiting for us huddled together silently on the slope above the stream at the bottom of Chambe. The sense of tragedy was back with them too, and as we reached them they crowded silently round Quillan and me, peering anxiously at us. We told them to keep very quiet and fall in behind us.

The first stars were out; the night symphony of Chambe was tuning in.

"Oh! I do hope," Quillan said in great distress, "the dogs won't bark and bring Val out!"

But the dogs did not bark. The hut was deathly quiet, might have appeared deserted if it had not been for a dark plume of cedar-scented smoke on the sky and a flickering glow behind the window. As we walked by it, we saw Val sitting in front of the fire, among Penelope's napkins, her hands in her lap. Framed in that small square window it looked like the subject of a Dutch Interior full of warmth, security and domestic calm. She had not, as yet, lit the lamps and was sitting there in the firelight in a dream of her own.

We opened the door. Val jumped up and came towards us with a look of glad surprise and said happily: "Oh! How very nice. Somehow I did not expect Dicky to-night."

On the mountain Quillan had said that he felt he ought to break the news to Val as Vance, after all, was his officer, but this was too much for his shattered heart. He broke down and buried his face in his hand, while the two bitches jumped up round him, licking his neck and head.

So I took Val by the arm and said, "Val, dear! Hold on to me for a minute, and please listen carefully to what I have to say. Dicky is dead. He was killed this morning."

"Oh! No," she said. "Oh, no! Oh no!"

"Yes, Val," I answered, "he is dead. I am so sorry, so dreadfully sorry, but there is not any possibility of a mistake. He is dead. We saw him killed."

She looked at me and it was as if I saw, far down in her eyes, all their days together go out, one by one, like a series of candles. The image of Dicky, alive, seemed to me to leave her; it was wrenched from her like the topmost leaf torn from a high tree by a fierce blast of wind and sent falling down, vainly fluttering to retain its height, down below for good; down, down, and out of the sunlight of her mind, for ever.

For a moment then, I do believe, she too died as Vance had died, and life, as we normally understand it, stopped abruptly within her. It was as if I was looking right into a heart suddenly emptied of meaning. I saw something rounded and whole suddenly become such sheer, utter and black nothingness that my own pulse missed a beat at the horror of it. And then the tears welled up and spilt. I do not know what I should have done if she had not cried. I thanked God for sending those tears so urgently needed. I thanked God, and as I saw her crying bitterly like a child being born, she too seemed to come alive again. I put her gently in a chair by the fire and let the flames of those ancient cedars, older even than human tears, wrap their antique warmth about her.

That night Quillan and I did not leave her alone for a moment. We put mattresses in front of the fire and made up beds for all three of us. When she ceased crying for a while we talked to her. First, I told Val in detail what had happened, while Quillan dried out our things, for we were wet through and half frozen. He then made some food which no one would eat, saw to it that Val fed Penelope, and himself changed the baby's napkins. Then he came and told Val everything that had happened and I took over the domestic details.

After a while we all lay down by the fire, Val between us. But we none of us slept. We talked to Val incessantly, for the moment we stopped she began to shake with spasms of tearless sobs, as people do when they are really physically too tired for more crying.

The talking helped and she asked us many questions. I told her the truth as I saw it without reserve or qualification. I spared her no details where she asked for them. I respected her questions as carrying the seeds of their own healing, however brutal the answers may have appeared to my reason.

One of the most pathetic things about us human beings is our touching belief that there are times when the truth is not good enough for us; that it can and must be improved upon. We have to be utterly broken before we can realize that it is impossible to better the truth. It is the very truth we deny which so tenderly and forgivingly picks up the fragments and puts them together again. Miserable as I was, I took heart from Val's instinct not to flinch from any aspect of the horror brought about by us and the mountain.

Indeed, so pronounced was this instinct in her that that night she tried to relive with us every aspect of her relationship with Vance. For instance, she turned to me and asked quietly, like a very small girl:

"Did you think Dicky was handsome?"

"No, Val!" I replied. "He was not handsome, in the way most people mean it. But he had a very nice face."

"What do you mean by a nice face?" This was said not impatiently, but with an obvious longing for precision.

"Well, his eyes were big and well spaced." She nodded,

and I went on, "And they had an open, honest, but rather hurt and puzzled expression in them."

"So you noticed that too," she said with a desperate catch at her voice. "You see, he was so hurt as a child. Nobody seemed to care much about him. People looked on him as a failure. They were so horribly patronizing about him. Even here on the mountain tiny things could hurt him terribly. But I was going to make it all right for him. He said already it was so much better. I meant him never to be hurt again"—and she started crying again.

I went on quickly. "Then he had a very good brow, Val, and a broad forehead, and pleasant colouring. His nose and chin were a bit too long and determined to give the whole of his features the regularity that we call handsome. But the general effect was very pleasant and boyishly sympathetic."

"Yes! But you have not mentioned his teeth," she interrupted. "They were not really good, and what about his figure?"

"He was not tall enough to be imposing, but he was sturdy, strong and well proportioned, and I liked his voice a lot."

"I don't know if you are altogether right," she said slowly, talking from very far back in time and her mind. "He had rather a funny face and a funny, odd, boyish body. But, do you know, there was not a thing about him, not a hair on his head or a tooth in his mouth that I wanted any different. I loved every bit of him as he was. Oh, Dicky!" and there she was, back in the present, crying bitterly. Presently she stopped and said:

"Oh! You should have seen us together on this mountain. We were so happy."

"But I did see you," I said.

"No, you didn't," she answered fiercely. "You only saw us when there were other people about, and that spoilt both it and us. Oh, I could talk to you for a year of the lovely things we did alone up here, in quiet secluded places on this mountain." She paused. "We never wanted anyone else except Penelope."

She looked up at Penelope's basket still on the table. It was the first time she had mentioned Penelope, and my heart leapt at the sign. She paused again then, and said in that remote voice: "You know what women say about child-birth? Well, I just don't understand it. I have never known such delight as having Penelope. There was not a moment, not a second of her birth that was not sheer utter joy to me. I just wanted to go on and on having more children for Dicky. We were so *whole* together. Oh, God, how can I ever become reconciled again to being only a half for the rest of my life?"

I wished that I had had with me then some of the giant intellects, some of the great addicts of pure reason. This age, which is uniquely of their creation, has an answer for everything. But I must confess that I had no answer acceptable to the intellect. I had only a blind faith in Val's, as in all our tears. I had only a blind faith in our keeping together, closely, like sheep on the bitterest night of winter, and humbly committing our helpless knowing to the deep mystery of life.

At three o'clock in the morning our throats were so dry from talking and general strain, that words would hardly form themselves. Val was so exhausted that I believe if we had had just one aspirin to give her she would have fallen asleep. But she had none. It was so characteristic of her and Vance and their absolute trust in the mountain that they had no medicine of any kind in the hut; not even an aspirin for themselves or dill-water for Penelope. My own medicine, of course, was dumped with all the baggage in the bottom of the Great Ruo gorge. Long afterwards Quillan, talking about our vain search through the hut for medicine, said to me:

"Even I would not trust Africa and Mlanje that far."

After one of these searches for medicine I went out, for a

moment, to the night. Above us the stars were bright, particularly Orion, Vance's "Old Hunter", high above Chambe Peak, prancing, with uplifted club, after the swift game of heaven. But away to the west, over the gorge, there were no stars, only that wheeling, twisting, turning, diabolic world of cloud. It was one of those suspended moments of reality when the universal pendulum is slowed down and the seconds, it seems, will not pass. I would have, had it seemed any good, reversed the last plea of the damned Faust and called on the horses of the night to hasten, to hasten, and bring up a rose-fingered dawn.

When I went back Val was still dreadfully becalmed and awake in her agony.

At half-past four Quillan went down to the foresters' huts, to fetch me a guide. We had agreed that he would stay with Val, get the natives to pack up her belongings and my tent, while I went to fetch help. Val was now so tired that she did not even hear my good-bye.

I pushed back the dogs who tried to come with me, patted them on the head, shut the door and stepped outside. There was just a faint lighting of the sky behind Chambe's own peak.

It was bitterly cold. We stepped out briskly. Fortunately my physical body had not needed sleep to be rested. We crossed the stream, treading Orion and the Milky Way underfoot, and quickly passed the cedars which, in their ancient resentment and deep disdain of men and their mission, stood still without even a rustle or a whisper.

We went as fast as we could down Vance's road, over his bridge, over the far edge and down the track. Dawn broke to reveal that same schism between light and dusk, fair and foul, over Mlanje. Half-way down we heard the first yodel and soon met the bearers coming up for their daily load.

At eight we knocked at the door of the house of Mrs. Carmichael, a friend of the Vances', who had a small tea-estate next to the forestry depot at Likabula. Down there the sun was already shining on her garden and I shall never forget the scarlet of the poinsettias as the early light caught them. At the end of their long golden stems they burst on the blue and gold of the still morning air like pistol shots, disintegrations rather than fulfilments of the brightest red.

A native in a spotless white coat, so white that it hurt my tired eyes, came to the door, showed me into a room full of books, and said Mrs. Carmichael was coming at once.

Suddenly, as I sat there, through the open doors and windows a succession of cats of all sizes and shapes and colours came bounding into the room. I sat up with a shock. At first I thought I had fallen asleep and was dreaming, but as I counted thirty-one of them, and they all began begging for my attention, whining, miaowing, curving their spines, rubbing their shanks against my feet, jumping on my chair and waving their tails under my nose, I realized that I must be awake.

What my tired eyes were seeing was no disorder of my outraged senses, no midnight fantasy, but early morning on a tea-estate at the foot of Mlanje. And it seemed a needless, a derisory addition to the heavy adjustments my sense of reality had already to make. I had been on the go for thirty hours. In that time I had gone down the mountain, into that gorge, up it again, then done twenty miles over the top, and now twenty miles down it again, and all without sleep. Suddenly I resented the cats. It was all I could do to prevent myself from jumping up and putting my boot to them.

In desperation I looked over the arched backs and waving tails at some of the books. The first shelf began with all the volumes of Havelock Ellis' *Psychology of Sex*, and finished up with a book on sex symbolism by Kraft Ebing.

My heart sank again. I said to myself: "Dear God! Everything you wish but not that! Please to-day send me people who are normal. Solid young men in tweeds and handlebar moustaches who, should they suddenly find themselves in Kubla Khan's harem would read their *Times* first and finish their pipes before they so much as raised an eye to one coy beauty!"

Happily, at that moment Mrs. Carmichael came in. She had obviously just got up and was still in a dark blue dressing-gown. I was reassured at once by her appearance. The cats stopped miaowing the moment she appeared. I told her at once what had happened.

"Oh God. I was always afraid of it," she said, deeply moved. "I knew it would happen. I knew it. They just had something like it in them."

Her remarks helped me immensely. I could not, then, see why, but, in the days that followed, her remark often returned to me.

In five minutes she had dressed and we were in her big American car. I stopped at the depot just long enough to send some foresters with a stretcher up the mountain to fetch Val Vance. Then we drove at great speed to the boma at Mlanje. Within a mile of Likabula we passed once more through the wall of the Chiperone and from there on were back in the rain and the whirling mist.

Boyd had left Mlanje but his successor got on to the telephone at once. The doctor was sent up to meet Val Vance. While I shaved, the police were organized. Those small European communities in Africa in moments of disaster close their ranks at once without forethought or hesitation. Everyone stopped work.

By nine I was going up the mountain through the mouth of the Great Ruo gorge with a large search-party. At eleven o'clock we were on the bank of the stream Vance had vainly tried to cross twenty-four hours before. There was our discarded baggage, black with rain, on the opposite bank, the rope of creepers that I had made Vance discard and the burnt-out ashes of Quillan's fire.

It was astonishing what a difference it made to one's

reaction standing on the other bank, with a safe line of retreat at one's back. For a brief moment the sky lightened while we stood there. The place assumed the false, concentrated and exaggerated innocence of the truly wicked. But when I raised my eyes to the dark slopes behind and to the hidden peaks, and listened to the storm of noise raised by the falling water, I knew the mountain was unchanged and indifferent. It was as if the whole of Mlanje had been dematerialized and transformed into a kind of Tartar music, riding high, wide and diabolically handsome across the darkened steppes of heaven.

I turned my back on it for the last time without regret and joined in the search for Vance's body. As I and Quillan had expected, we found nothing. After a long, hopeless search, I went back to Blantyre and was with Argyle and Alan late that night.

I spent the Sunday helping Peter Quillan to organize Val Vance's affairs and booked her an immediate passage by air to England. It was not difficult because everybody wanted to help. Val was staying with the Quillans. Mary Quillan told me that the first night the doctor had had to give her three injections before she could sleep. She was a gallant girl.

When I went to say good-bye to Val and told her that we had not found Dicky's body, she said instantly: "I am so glad. I would prefer to think of him always there. He belonged to it."

"And you, Val, when you get home what are you going to do?" I asked her.

She didn't answer at once. She looked at Penelope on her lap, touched her cheek very lightly and then, staring out of the window into the rain and mist outside, said in a far-away voice: "Stay there for a bit and then come back to the mountain."

I knew then that she had turned her dangerous corner. On the Monday I spent the whole morning doing Val's correspondence for her. It was my only chance because I had to resume my own journey at dawn on Tuesday.

In the afternoon and evening I sat by the fire in Alan's study writing a long technical report on my expedition to Mlanje. The fire was a fire of Blantyre wood and it burned in a lugubrious way so unlike the eager, gay, to-hell-with-you flame of the cedars.

I recommended in my report that Mlanje should be left to itself, to its mists, to its split weather, and to its cedars. I knew that, even had they known of my recommendation, those dark, resentful, desperate trees fighting for their antique being, would not have thanked me. But I knew that Vance would have done.

PART IV

BEYOND THE MOUNTAIN

"It seems to me that people's private and personal lives have never mattered as they do now. For me the whole of the future depends on the way people live their personal rather than their collective lives. It is a matter of extreme urgency. When we have all lived out our private and personal problems we can consider the next, the collective step. Then it will be easy but before it will not even be possible."

LETTER FROM INGARET GIFFARD

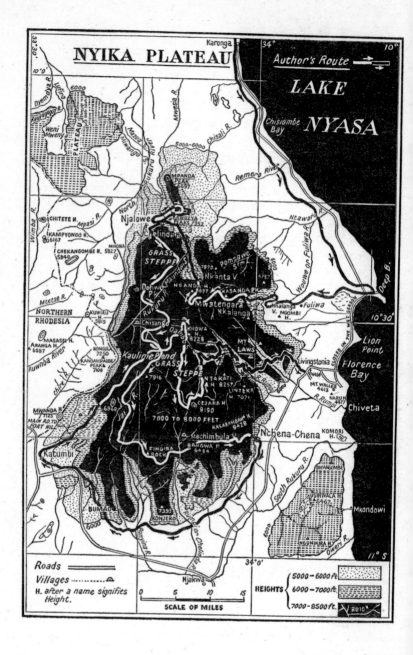

NYIKA PLATEAU

Karonga

Author's Route →

LAKE NYASA

Roads ═══
Villages ……
H. after a name signifies Height.

SCALE OF MILES
0   5   10   15

HEIGHTS {
5000 – 6000 ft.
6000 – 7000 ft.
7000 – 8500 ft.
}

Chapter Sixteen

IN order to get to the scene of my next task I now had to travel almost six hundred miles north, from one end of Nyasaland to the other. I had intended to go by road, but found on coming down from Mlanje that the people responsible for my travelling arrangements had taken a seat for me in an aircraft chartered to fly two extremely distinguished senior soldiers to the North. I was up and ready to leave at dawn on the Tuesday morning as arranged, but, as I listened to the rain and watched the mists swirl round Alan's sweet-peas, I knew we should not get away that day.

The weather that had contributed with such unnecessary and diabolic generosity to Vance's death was steadily thickening, and spreading from Mlanje far into the surrounding countryside. I was told on my return that the clouds did not disperse for thirty-five days. If, while waiting for the Chiperone to clear on Thursday, we had made the fire in the Ruo gorge as Vance's gun-bearer had advised, or if we had made it on Friday as our own carriers had wanted, then, obviously, we should all have died.

The plane did not go on the Tuesday, the Wednesday or the Thursday, and, by the time I had unpacked and re-packed again on Thursday night, I was a complete joke to the whole household. Yet, however anxious I was to go, my tired body was glad of the rest, and my mind was grateful for the chance to have Vance's death out with myself.

I found that I returned continually for comfort to two things: Mrs. Carmichael's remark, "It was in them"; and what Val had told me about Vance's childhood when we talked the reluctant seconds out that night by the fire. I do not want to harp on all this unnecessarily, but it was important to me and I cannot just pass it by.

From the moment Vance was killed I had blamed myself bitterly, though not for the actual accident. I think it is clear that there is a point at which all outside responsibility for an individual ends and the final event concerns him and his fate alone. Vance was twenty-eight, a soldier mentioned in dispatches in Burma, and an expert on the mountain. I do not believe that we were doing anything irresponsible in letting him attempt to cross the stream. From the moment he entered the water the game was between him and the mountain he loved.

It was rather in our being there at all, that I felt my share of the responsibility lay. Firstly, if I had not come out to Africa, Vance at that moment would in all probability not have been on the mountain. Secondly, if I had refused to let our party take the short cut from the lumber camp, we should not have been in the gorge either. Then again I had had all the time an uneasy feeling about this trip. I had left England in a mood of resentment and had always been in a divided state about Africa. Supposing my own conflict about it had been resolved, could I have ever got entangled in a set of circumstances so disastrous as those on Mlanje?

My instinct was to say no; that a split in ourselves produces a split in the pattern of our lives, creates this terrible gash down the middle, this deep, dark Mlanje gorge, through which disaster runs and the devil drives. Accident and disaster without feed on accident and disaster within. The design of our outward life, from its minutest detail up to the atom which we put in our latest bomb, reflects and confirms our deepest and most private purposes.

I will give only one example. The world to my mind has never been fuller of finer thinking than it is to-day. I never pick up a paper, magazine or book, be they in Japanese, French, Javanese, Russian, English or Twi, and fail to be struck by the fine thoughts, the idealistic feelings, the noble sentiments they express. Yet, though all the contributing writers appear to be merchants of man's finest feelings, has there ever been an age that, considering its lights, has done worse things than this one, with its class hatreds, race hatreds, colour prejudices, world wars and concentration camps? Has there been another age that, knowing so clearly the right things to do, has so consistently done the wrong ones?

I doubt it; and because I doubt it, I feel it is important as never before to get our private contribution to the split clear in our minds and, as far as possible, to close the gap in ourselves in every detail of our lives.

There was another curious point on the mountain. I had been afraid, and it had been for Val Vance that I feared and for her that I had taken precautions. But all my vigilance had been needed for ourselves; it was at our side, not hers, that disaster was creeping up. That too seemed typical of our age and its inheritors. Was it not the private equivalent of our public passion for effecting in others the cure we so badly need ourselves? Industrial England had once had a passion for converting the Africans of Nyasaland to Christian ways, which passion had increased in almost mathematical proportion to the un-Christian state of slavery in its own factories.

I could not help feeling that if I had been an utterly whole person that day in the gorge could never have existed.

Again when Mrs. Carmichael said, "I knew in my bones this would happen. They had it in them", she had shed a new light on the inner situation, as Val had done when she told me of her husband's past. Now I saw the real significance of Val's remarks about Vance's childhood. He had never been happy or even spasmodically at one with his home. He had always felt that he was rather looked down upon. This was no grown-up fantasy on Val's part. She had known Vance as a child, and could remember that even then people had never really understood him, or appreciated his qualities. It had always infuriated her to see him so underrated and held back by the opinion of quite inferior men.

After the war he had returned to marry her, as he had always wanted, and at once brought her to Mlanje. There for the first time he seemed to blossom out, and to be living in a free way of his own making. That is why they were so happy there, and, she hinted, why they liked to be alone. The presence of outside people, however pleasant, tended to revive in their lives the pattern of a past they had hoped to be done with for good, brought back responses and reactions of a discredited inferiority no longer their own. For she too had not had the happiest of lives until their marriage.

It had been perfect for them on the mountain. There, and in themselves, they found everything they had ever wanted; and in this perfection they meant to live till the end. She almost gave me the impression that they were refugees from their own past, thinking they could rid themselves of the problem of their lives by changing their location; believing they only had to go far enough away and they would leave their problem behind them. How little those unfortunate children of life knew of the hound of unfulfilled nature within the blood that is for ever on our trail, ready to aid and abet the dark fates without.

Now I shall never know any more detail about the life of that brave, upright young man; but it seems to me certain from what I know already, that sooner or later there was bound to be a reckoning between himself and his nature which I could not influence, save as an instrument of the inevitable. On Friday at ten-thirty in the Great Ruo gorge of Mlanje the unpredictable in himself and the unpredictable in the mountain, the split in himself and the dark gash in Mlanje met and became one.

When I reached this point I felt better. I do not pretend that this is a final solution. I am sure that to a heart and an awareness less clouded than my own there must be much more to understand. But I myself could take it no further. After all, one can never take anything far enough. If one is lucky one takes things as far as one can. This I had done, and a limited reassurance was mine. I needed it too; indeed I shall always need it. That moment in the gorge has become a part of me. I shall have to live with it to the end of my life. Nor is it the only moment of its kind. There have been quite a number of other moments equally grim. Of these I need say no more now, except perhaps that they have a habit of all massing together and presenting themselves to my senses at the most unexpected moments; waking me up at midnight, making me hesitate in my steps across a crowded street, or perhaps just making me stroke the head of a neighbour's dog with unusual tenderness.

When they do that it is necessary to relive them again in some way, to look them squarely in their eyes, to take them by the hand in an avowal of a sad friendship, and say "How are you now? Better? Is there anything more I can do for you?" and at a shake of a dark head, to reply encouragingly before continuing on one's way, "Perhaps it will be better next time. Perhaps it will pass." This does not sound much. But it is all one can do, and it helps even if it does not cure.

At least having got so far in my mind I was able to sleep. I had my first good night for some time.

I woke to see the rain still coming down. At half-past nine I was suddenly summoned to the aerodrome. It appeared that twelve miles out the sky was lightening, though round me there was no sign of it.

I got to Cheleka to find the pilot in consultation with the meteorological officers on the aerodrome. Archie Gordon, a young South African from Grahamstown, was very much worried. He was already three days overdue. He was getting angry messages from his superiors in Salisbury. They were, this private charter firm, a new pioneer organization struggling for a living and could not afford to annoy their clients. In addition, the two distinguished soldiers had become awkward and were also urging him not to delay another instant.

The pilot obviously did not like the idea. He told me he had already had a nasty experience coming through from Rhodesia on the Monday. He had then taken a grave risk for the sake of "the firm", as he loyally called it, but had not minded it as he had been alone.

As he approached Blantyre he had seen this extraordinary pillar, this dark turning, revolving, spinning pillar of cloud over Mlanje and the surrounding country. At seventeen thousand feet in his little single-screw plane he had given up trying to get above it. He had no ground control at Chileka to help him down. He had just trusted to his luck and his reckoning and put the plane's nose down into the cloud. He said it was as black as night and as turbulent as hell inside, but his luck held and he came down slap bang on the aerodrome. But it was not a risk he would ever like to take again.

As I listened to all this I had an uncanny feeling that once again I was in a workshop of Fate, so that when he turned to me and asked appealingly in my native Afrikaans what I thought of it, I said clearly: "Look, you must on no account take what seems too great a risk to you. If you think as a technician that the risk is too great, I would let no power on earth make you change your mind."

"But aren't you all in a hurry?" he said—relieved, I thought.

"I am not in a hurry to kill or be killed," I replied. "Whether you think we should not go or should go, I will trust you implicitly. I will back up any decision you take, to the full."

He seemed enormously cheered by this and said he would just go up for five minutes and see what it felt like "on top".

While he was up, the two generals telephoned from

Blantyre. They were at the hotel. Was there or was there not to be a flight? If not, why not?

The duty officer replied that it was still uncertain. Very well then, they would wait at the hotel and wanted the pilot to telephone them, as soon as he came down.

"I don't like it at all," said Gordon when he did so. "It is all right for the moment here but it is piling up, and bearing down fast, all round the place."

He spoke on the telephone, put the receiver down, with a very sour South African schoolboy face, that made me warm to him, and said: "Those two old Donners[1] don't like it. They want to go, and want to see me at once."

"Never mind," I told him. "You do what you think is right, and all will be well. Besides, the war is over and no one will thank you for killing two such distinguished soldiers, though they might be prepared to overlook the death of a half-colonel."

It was still raining in Blantyre. The two generals were sitting by the fire in the hotel lounge. They did not look pleased. One was General Brere-Adams, whom I knew from the Far East and for whom I have the greatest admiration and affection; the other, General Braidie, whom I hardly knew. Waiting, however, had got on their nerves and neither was at his best.

When the pilot told them politely and with great—I thought, almost exaggerated—deference, that he did not think it was wise to take off, General Braidie, the General I did not know, stood up, thrust his hands deep in his pockets, tapped the ground with his right foot, looked straight past the pilot with a shiny eye, and said: "Oh! Yes. So I have been told too: the whisky in Blantyre is better than in Salisbury, and there's plenty of it!"

General Brere-Adams, the one I knew, softened his re-

---

[1] Donner, literally thunder, is the Afrikaans equivalent of the Australian "Bastard". It can be either a term of great affection or extreme abuse. On this occasion, I do not think it was a term of affection.

mark with a smile and a sly upward glance from essentially friendly eyes, but it was to the same point: "Is she so very nice? Is she dark or fair?"

I was getting increasingly angry at all this and said firmly that I thought they were being extremely unfair to the pilot. It wasn't easy for him to say "no" to two such distinguished people, whom he obviously wanted to please, and what he needed was not their arm-chair judgment but understanding. Besides, I had been out at the aerodrome, spoken to the weather officers myself, and there was no doubt that flying anywhere would be a risky business. I spoke with some warmth and annoyed General Braidie, who snorted at every sentence I spoke, and was very rude to me afterwards. But we did not fly.

At lunch I told the two Generals not to count on my sharing their charter any more. I was going to make arrangements to go north at once by road. I did not tell them so, but I had seen enough that day of the sort of considerations, the flippant, irrelevant considerations, which could determine flights of the kind we had been trying to make. Africa jerks the European out of his own true centre and makes him accident-prone. I was glad to be out of it.

To my surprise General Braidie too said he had enough of the aircraft and could he join in with me by road? Between us we managed to arrange for a car to take us north the following morning, and for the first time I felt completely free of the cycle of events which started a week before with that unfortunate short-cut over the Ruo Valley of Mlanje.

Chapter Seventeen

THE main road north from Blantyre to Fort Hill and Tanganyika is long, broad and normally dusty. but there was little dust on the southern end of it that Saturday morning as we piled all our gear into a station wagon and set out on our journey. Our party consisted of General Braidie, a foreman-joiner for a vast development prospect up north, a bricklayer foreman, and myself.

The car was grossly overloaded and danced like a frightened horse from one end of the slippery road to the other. The black driver called himself Lincoln, and was at once christened Abraham by the bricklayer foreman, who was fresh from the army of occupation in Germany. This driver quickly lost his nerve and asked in rather plaintive Swahili if I wouldn't like to take over. So I did.

Luckily about fifty miles from Blantyre we passed out of the mist and the rain, and we could see the cloud standing like a wall over the land away to our right. The station wagon, however, continued to be tricky on the steering and I had no time for sight-seeing. Yet the general impression of the country seen through the wind-screen or from snap glances to right and left, was very beautiful.

Africa communicates its own enormous sense of relief to one when it shakes itself free from towns, and the ease with which it now unfolded its great vistas of bush, valley, hills and plains was most exhilarating. I felt like singing and even General Braidie seemed inclined to step out of his specialized view of himself and others.

At half-past twelve we were climbing out of the great Shire Valley, the deep depression along which Lake Nyasa empties its surplus water. We went through Ncheo, on the flank of the long, blue, elegant Kirk ranges, just at one o'clock. It was market day and the bazaars were full of natives dressed up in their brightest colours. There is no skin in the world for showing up colour like a really black one, and these people of the foothills are not only born black but burnt blacker still by the intolerable and fanatic sun of the Nyasaland summers.

Seldom, I thought, had I seen red so red, yellow so yellow and green so green, as in these cloths which the natives of Ncheo wrapped around themselves like Roman togas.

The women walked demurely behind their men, with that trance-like motion produced in them by the necessity for balancing the heavy earthen jars on their heads. They were vivid, eager creatures. The sly passing glances they gave us out of the corners of their eyes were gay and bright with awareness of their sex.

"Gosh, sir," I heard the foreman-joiner say to General Braidie: "it is a good thing the sun is not out, or those colours would strike you blind."

Outside Ncheo we climbed up on to one of the higher spurs of the Kirk range, pulled up by a large spreading acacia and had some lunch.

It was very beautiful. We saw the southern end of Lake Nyasa looking like the sea with a beginning but no end to it. We saw the whole of Lake Malombe and the vast Shire depression, lapped by a deep tide of winter-blue light. It was an orchestration of blues, almost of Whistler Battersea blues, and looked empty of human beings and terribly indifferent to them.

The road then took us on to the wide, towering plains of the Angoni highlands. Here spirals of spinning dust impelled by a cold south-west wind patrolled the roads and tracks. Again the background was an immense forlorn blue, the foreground lion-coloured. There were plenty of black figures in rags and tatters about, walking from nowhere to no obvious destinations. They looked so homeless that the view quickly resumed the forlorn, abandoned quality of the depression below Ncheo.

On these plains I always feel a private disappointment. The people who inhabit them are of Zulu origin, the descendants of one of the terrible Chaka's impis. They mutinied and raided north on a venture of their own, plundering bare an immense track of Africa, from Zulu-land to the southern shore of Victoria Nyanza. They are utterly unlike our Zulus in the South to-day, having none of their robustness of body and spirit; they seem shrunken and cowed as if to them, too, this part of Africa had brought no joy, only deception.

Here were our first koppies too, the stragglers from those isolated hills of stone which are such a feature of the vast central plateau of Africa. They added their own touch of aloofness to the scene. And it got cold, very cold.

We passed round the foot of the broad flanks of the freak-ish outcrop of Mount Dedza, but dared not go into the village because it was getting late. Going as fast as the dancing station wagon would let us, we got to the hotel at the little provincial capital of Lilongwe just as the sun, pink with cold, went down behind a long line of green and white thorn trees.

At dawn on Sunday morning we swung back into the road to the north. There was a crisp, frosty dew sparkling on the bleached grass; and a halo of honey-gold hung round the acacia-tops. The scene did not change much. What was remarkable was this quality of "unendingness".

One would climb out on a rise, round a hill or cross a river, expecting it to have changed, for it had looked the same for hundreds of miles, but there it would be, repeating itself with the same blue, melancholy satisfaction.

We passed no cars and saw no European, except at one bridge, where we found a Greek planter sitting with a gun in his hand. He looked yellow with fever and rather desperately ill. There was, he told us, all around there, a lot of sleeping sickness.

We drove like this from dawn until four in the afternoon, and all the while my companions seemed to me to be changing somewhat. They seemed to be acknowledging instinctively the great pre-eminence, the absolute priority of the physical fact of Africa, and the relative unimportance of human beings in the scheme of things around us. They became very quiet, depressed and stared continuously with defensive eyes at a landscape that offered no easy assurances. In that mood, at four precisely, we drove into Mzimba, the capital of the northernmost province of Nyasaland.

We spent the night with Charles Drackersby, the District Commissioner in Mzimba. He was out when we arrived, but Jock Standing, the resident engineer of the great Tung Development scheme in the Vipya highlands at Msusi, where the General was going, met us and took us straight to the D.C.'s home. I now gathered from him that we were none of us going to be very welcome at Msusi. John Grantham, his manager, had said firmly when he heard of our coming that he would tolerate no more impositions from London.

It all sounded very depressing there in Mzimba on that blue Sunday afternoon. If John Grantham really wouldn't help, it would be serious for me. I should have to retrace my steps all those hundreds of miles to Blantyre, plan again and start out anew. There was obviously nothing I could do as an alternative in Mzimba. The so-called towns on the map, strung out like beads on a red and black necklace, were not only getting farther apart, but desperately small.

Mzimba, in fact, was not a bead so much as a small seed, a mustard seed of administrative faith, on a thin and rapidly diminishing string of civilization. It consisted of no more than a dozen European bungalows, hurriedly built of unburned brick; a few Indian stores, an old boma waving a defiant bright new Union Jack at the black bush around;

an old commissioner's house with a few impudent poinsettias and purple bougainvilleas to distinguish it, themselves only a slight variation in the prevailing winter-blue theme of the atmosphere. For the rest it was idle to ignore that Africa was reasserting itself with increasing confidence, with a certain air of dark, sullen triumph.

Meanwhile I wondered what Drackersby could do to help. He got back at five: apparently he spent all the time he could in the bush. He was burnt black by years of service under the Nyasaland sun and had a wiry, out-of-doors look. Before he came over to us, he slowly opened the boot of his car, pulled out a small dead buck, and threw it down on the veranda of his bungalow. Apart from a polite greeting, he hardly spoke to us until he had cleaned his guns. That done, nobody could have been pleasanter or more interesting.

As far as I was concerned, however, Drackersby said nothing to encourage me. He had the same complaint about the lack of understanding in the capital, the same grievance that people like Grantham and himself were having too much asked of them. He didn't know what the hell London was about, sending me out in the winter. Didn't they realize it was cold in Africa?

"You won't get any natives to go up the Nyika with you," he said. "If you do, you will probably kill them, and yourself."

I winced inwardly at that. I myself had told him of the tragedy at Mlanje. I don't think he knew how deeply he had hurt me. For a moment the whole of that tragic Friday came back to me, and I could only say quietly: "Surely the cold is only relative. I always prefer the cold in Africa to the mud."

I honestly believe he had never thought of that, and was taken aback. He gaped at me with some surprise for a moment and then snapped: "Anyway, relative or not, you won't get any Africans to go with you."

171

He must have thought differently of it in the night, however, for he gave me the next morning a letter to the Chief Katumbi, whose people live near the foot of the great Nyika Plateau. The letter was very much to the point, and asked the chief plainly, in the name of the government, to help me.

"He will get you bearers if anybody can," he said. "But do not bank on it."

I left Mzimba at ten o'clock and drove straight into another cold, overcast day of expanding blue. About twenty miles out the bush fell away from us and the road began to twist among grey, elegant hill-tops, covered only with grass. The relief to the eyes was immense. For nearly a hundred miles the jeep, purring like a kitten, took us through highlands which had something of Scotland about them, but they were unmistakably African in their dark valleys dense with black, lichen-festooned, shrunken trees.

After driving fifty miles I saw one red brick house and farm buildings, obviously European. I thought their little settlement looked dreadfully hemmed in, pinned down by Africa, and I wondered how it would ever stand up to that sort of siege.

On the way I passed the cattle: I noticed they were grazed in a tight formation with three sturdy black men armed with long, broad spears, standing guard over them. They and their masters were the first living things I had seen for fifty miles, an island of threatened animal life in a sea of grass, trees, stone and grey hill-tops.

I travelled almost another fifty miles before I saw another living soul or human habitation of any kind. If it had not been for some lonely buzzard slowly circling the grey sky with geometric precision, I should have thought the land empty of animals too.

When I drove up at four, John Grantham, the General

and Jock Standing were talking in a group outside Grantham's house at Msusi. But for the black, lichen-strewn jungle all around, I could easily have taken the patch of clearing that was Msusi to be somewhere in England. Grantham's little house and the four other houses around were all built of near-red brick, with tall, sloping thatched roofs. There were rambler-roses growing up the porch of Grantham's cottage, violets against the walls, a garden in front full of lupins, foxgloves, antirrhinums, sweet williams, London Pride and carnations. The grey mist which smokes over everything in winter there on the summit of the Vipya highlands added to the European effect.

Grantham himself could only have been a product of the British Isles. To my astonishment he immediately held out his hand and in a pleasant civilized voice said: "Come on in! I have kept some lunch for you. I believe you are someone whom I can really talk to about Africa, and not be misunderstood."

The next thirty-six hours were for me some of the most pleasant I had spent in Nyasaland. We discovered we had known each other many years before when, fresh from the 1914–18 air-force and Cambridge, he had come to plant cotton in Zululand. The last he had heard of me was a report that I had been killed in action against the Japanese.

In these twenty-four years John Grantham had done many things, but as he sat by the fire with Papillon, his black spaniel, on his knees, he said that, varied as they had been, and however different from what he had planned, their effect had all been the same—to take him deeper and deeper into Africa.

The cotton experiment had been a total failure, as I knew. After that he had tried his hand at farming in Southern Rhodesia. That had gone well until the girl he was going to marry, climbing a koppie on his farm one day, scratched her knee on a rock, contracted blood poisoning and died within ninety-six hours.

Nothing had gone right after that. He went ranching for some years in Northern Rhodesia. A succession of droughts finished that phase of his life. His capital was exhausted. The outlook was dismal.

Then the war came and, of course, like all the rest of us, he joined up, rose to the dizzy rank of regimental sergeant-major in a reconnaissance unit, and finally was blown up by a mine in his armoured car in North Africa, and forced to leave the Army. Then the Nyasaland Government claimed his services, and in due course he was sent to start this big Tung experiment in the heart of the misty, un-populated Vipya. It was a job after his own heart. He was alone, except for the black labour he could raise. The Africans knew him, liked him, trusted him, and came to him readily, far more of them than he could use. All the clearing of the bush, all that eighty miles of road over mountain-top, and through valley and jungle, was all his own work. He had enjoyed it, but now the place was getting too crowded. He already had three other Europeans, and more were coming. He couldn't stand that. Africa was where he wanted to live and die, if, he grumbled, it did not get too crowded.

And yet there was a tremendous paradox in all this. And in so far as the facts of my journey imposed a theme on it from within, this paradox is most relevant to it. This is why I have sketched Grantham in detail here.

All the texture of his mind, the weave of his spirit, the very dream he was living on the Vipya, that high country, which smokes with mist as its native name implies, was essentially European.

Every detail of the room in which we sat testified to this. Over the fireplace were stuck picture postcards of Suffolk and its villages. There was also an old ticket to the members' enclosure at Newmarket, and a torn-off London theatre ticket. The guns, bright and clean in the rack; the fishing rods with their many flies, and dozens of others from the

British Isles, all delicately and temperately coloured; the port; the sherry decanter filled with Bristol Cream; the barometer; the spy-glass; the books and the smell of dogs, were all part and parcel of a European approach to life.

The point of it all, so it seemed to me, was this. People like Grantham could no longer sustain Europe; they needed, in a manner which is not yet clear to me, the support of Africa; the presence of black faces and black natures confirms their vision, their old, essentially European dream. It was as if, by losing themselves in Africa, they re-established the solidity and significance of the European in themselves.

As far as detailed help for my own journey was concerned, I found Grantham had lived for five years at the foot of the Nyika, the plateau which I had to look over. He had never been on it—"a hell of an expedition" he said. But he knew all the native gossip about it. They were terrified of it. It was high, it was misty, it had tremendous encounters with rain and thunder. It was cold, and was said to be completely uninhabited and rather sinister.

If one listened to the natives talking about Nyika one always heard about some tragedy connected with it. They would say, for example: "You know old Bathikutha? Well, he is no more. He tried to go over the Nyika three days after the last moon. The clouds came down and he has not been seen since."

They also believed there was a large snake living in a small lake on top of it. If one could touch its tail when one was ill, this cured one instantly, but if one went there for no good reason, the snake caught and carried one off to its hole in the bottom of the lake.

Yet they did sometimes go to hunt on the fringes of the plateau by day. They said it was full of game. He thought he could get me bearers from Katumbi's people. He would give me a letter too, for Katumbi. What was more, he would present me with his own personal jeep, Peaches, his own native driver, and his own hunting boy, Patrick, one of the Katumbi's own people who would recruit bearers for me. His stores, he said, were nearly empty since the lake steamer which brought them to Nkata Bay, about seventy miles away, was grossly overdue. But I was most welcome to what he had. He only wished he could come himself, but with such a crowd about he had no time. I did understand that, didn't I? And now, when was I last in Zululand?

Chapter Eighteen

I LEFT Msusi by jeep in a thick, blue mist thirty-six hours after my arrival on the Tuesday morning. We all sat in front. Once back on the road to Fort Hill we went really fast. We passed through several small native settlements, and everywhere the population came to attention, as it were, when we went by; bowed if they were old, raised their hats if they had any, and then brought them down to hang respectfully in their hands by their sides.

A hard, cold wind tore down the road outside Enkwedeni. We went straight into it at forty-eight miles an hour, and left a high column of dust rising in the air behind us. We were off the highlands now, had done with physical eccentricities like the Vipya, and once again there began the prevailing African theme of bush, plain, river and lone blue-hill, until suddenly, about sixty miles away, I saw the Nyika.

Everything at that distance looks small, and yet I found my pulse quickening at the view. There was a sort of Rider Haggard, a King Solomon's Mines, a Queen of Sheba touch about it. A massive, long, blue escarpment, a wall of solid, unbroken mountain rose sheer out of the land and lost itself in the clouds. This wall became bigger, more precise, but did not change. Still its cloud-capped blue towered unbroken in the forefront of our vision. Only at Njakwa—another native township nearly seventy miles further on—we were nearly at the base of it, at last.

Hard by Njakwa, we crossed the rumbling Rumpi. This was my first encounter with a river that rose somewhere in the clouds above, on the Nyika. It cut a deep gash through the fifteen-hundred-foot hills around Njakwa, and we drove straight up along the Northern flank of it, and on towards

177

Katumbi. Here we were too close to the hills to see the great wall of the Nyika, but our senses were perfectly aware of it in the background. Our eyes knew it from the colour and texture of that dense concentration of cloud to the north, our noses from a certain tingling in the nostrils, our ears from a singing in the drums, a sound almost like the purring of a large purple cat near at hand, and our bodies from a mounting excitement in the blood. So abstracted were we that at midday we nearly ran over a long, elegant, naked black body stretched out in the middle of the road.

I saw it first, and shouted to Peaches to stop. He managed to do this just at the body's feet. It did not move. We all three looked down in amazement over the top of the wind-screen, on a lovely young, black, female body, stark naked, in the road. At first I feared it was dead, but then noticed it was breathing deeply and was asleep. Peaches, who was roaring like a lion, leapt out of the jeep and shook it angrily. Slowly it sat up and rubbed its eyes, and then out of them looked a young woman who, quite undismayed, began making advances to Peaches. Patrick and he had to carry her off the road, where she continued to invite us to join her with looks, smiles, wriggles and other gestures. I have never seen anyone of her sex so completely and so happily drunk at that hour of the day.

Patrick explained that the harvest was on, and people always drank like that at harvest-time. He shook his head. It might be difficult to get bearers after all.

As we drove into the native town of Katumbi and stopped outside the Chief's court-house, the entire popula-tion seemed to drop what they were doing in order to pour out of their huts and run towards us. Their curiosity was quite unashamed but most friendly. They did not see a white face every day and were determined to make the most of mine. They pressed round the jeep and commented on my physical appearance: "Did you ever see such coloured hair?" "How big his nose is!" "Look at his eyes.

His cheeks are very red! Is he angry, you think?" "How much do you think that coat of his cost?" and so on endlessly.

Meanwhile I sent Patrick to see if the chief, the Umfumo, was there. He came back with one Patrick Kawonga, the clerk of the Umfumo's court, a handsome young man, pleasant, polite, but again with such a melancholy expression on his face that I knew he must be very well educated. I was not mistaken. He told me in clear, precise English that the Umfumo was away but that he would deal with the situation as best he could. I thanked him and decided there and then not to return to Msusi or Nzimba but to go straight on to Karonga, the northernmost province of Nyasaland, leaving Patrick behind me. I had come prepared to do that if necessary. I also had with me a letter to the D.C. there, and Alan had asked me to call on his Veterinary Officer at Karonga, a Michael Dowler, who would help me.

I took out my map and studied it carefully. This was not difficult. Facts, reliable facts, on maps of this part of Africa are few and far between. Karonga was too far for that day, but my eye fixed on Nchena-Chena, the Agricultural research station at the foot of the Nyika, about thirty miles from the Rumpi Gorge. The officer in charge of it, Colonel Henderson, was an old friend of Grantham's. If he was away, I would either sleep on the road or try and cadge a night's lodging at Livingstonia, another twenty or thirty miles further on, and the greatest of Nyasaland's mission stations.

At a quarter-past five the jeep drew up outside Colonel Henderson's house, Nyasaland Office-of-Works emergency pattern. The evening was closing in rapidly. Behind the house, almost from the kitchen doorstep, the land gathered itself together steeply, and rose covered with forest like a dark, blue-green wall seven thousand feet high, sheer into the cloud. All round about was the sound of falling, running water, and now more strongly than ever I had a sense that behind the wall of mountain and beyond the cloud, a gigantic purple cat was purring and purring with an incurable smugness and satisfaction.

I could not on this first close contact with the Nyika understand why it should be thought sinister. Mlanje had given me the creeps from the start by its quality of ill-suppressed prehistoric rage. The feeling here was different, not friendly, just utterly self-contained and satisfied.

Wherever I had met Henderson I should have known him for what he was, a soldier formed in the 1914–18 war. When, as a mere boy in the late Edwardian world, he first went to Sandhurst, it had been his ambition to make a career of soldiering. The war cured him of that. He had joined the Agricultural department of Nyasaland. He had made two blades of grass grow where one grew before—and I use that phrase deliberately because Swift's sentence from which it is taken was nailed like a flag to the wall over his desk.

Henderson, too, knew the Nyika. He had, years before, laid down an experimental pyrethrum plot on the lip of the plateau, just behind his house, eight thousand two hundred feet up. The soil was fertile. He had grown crops equal to the world's best, but in the end let the work lapse because he could not get the Africans, for whom it was done, to go there.

"I don't know what it is," he said, "but they will not live on the Nyika at any price. It is, as far as we know, completely uninhabited."

He was gloomy about my finding bearers to go with me. The harvest was on. It was cold, the old story. He thought I was wasting my time going to Karonga, the people of those hot plains would go with me least of all.

I made up my camp bed in Henderson's office that night, but before going to sleep, went outside to look at the mountains at the back. I could not see them, but again I felt their presence deep in the nerves of my body. I sat there for quite a while on a stone, being aware of them, and listening to the sound of infinitely falling water. Then, for the first time since my arrival in Nyasaland, I heard African drums warming up. I could see no fires, but everywhere in the black bush around the drums began. The tap-a-tap, tap-a-tap-tap-tap would break out in one place and then be answered in dozens of others near and far. As the night went on the drumming gathered speed, density and power. The darkness vibrated with its urgency. The sound of it, the purring of the great purple cat behind the clouds and the beat of my own heart harmonized so well, that I was soon sound asleep.

The next day we started early. The road moved all along the base of the Nyika itself. On our left was that sheer wall of mountain, its head buried in cloud; on our right a deep depression cut by the Rumpi and Rukuru rivers, and on their far side again was another chain of massive mountains. It presented everywhere a solid, unyielding, unbroken front that was quite unbelievable. I could see no obvious way up —in fact it looked as if there could not be one. Yet my task was concerned with the unknown summit. I noticed that native cultivation did little more than touch the fringe of the base of the Nyika. It was too steep and too densely covered with rain-forest even for native hoes.

An hour later we began climbing a flat-topped hill of about four thousand feet, which suddenly barred our way to the east. We climbed down and out of two deep valleys cut into its sides by the Rumpi—another Rumpi—and the Mwanana Rumpi, and by a series of steep hairpin bends reached the top. There I made Peaches stop, and looked back.

We were high up now and the Nyika looked twice the size it had looked from below. In order to appreciate the greatness of these mountains properly, one must oneself have achieved a certain height. Below there is no standard of comparison, but once one is some thousands of feet up the vastness of their scale becomes apparent and takes away one's breath.

For thirty miles, as far as I could see, there was nothing but this unbroken wall of mountain, standing on the tip of its toes on the edge of a great depression, its head in the clouds.

Only opposite me, where the two new rivers emerged, was there a tremendous split in the mountain wall which went back as far as I could see, hemmed in from rain-forest base to glistening grey cloud-tops.

Away to our right and on our own level, lay the great mission station of Livingstonia. To our mountain-, plain-and bush-fed eyes, its neat, red-tiled roof-tops and great cathedral walls rising above the acacia and brachastygea fringe of the horizon, it was an astonishing sight. It looked a brave, if terribly small, European gesture, a small clenched fist shaken at the world of giants around.

I had always wanted to visit it but felt I couldn't do so until some of the "ifs" were removed from my task. So regretfully I told Peaches to drive on.

Three miles further we came over the top and started going down. Then the sun suddenly came out. We were emerging from underneath the umbrella of cloud that lay on the mountains. We rounded a corner and saw Lake Nyasa. I have seen it many times from the air, from far-off mountain-tops and remote passes in the hills, but I had never been so near.

Three thousand sheer feet down there it was, that miracle of so much water in the midst of so much land. Indeed Lake Nyasa is a sea rather than a lake, and when one has said that, there is, as about the sea itself, nothing further to add which is neither an anti-climax nor bathos. Only on that morning it was a singularly gay sight. Very blue and sparkling in the sun, and with the far blue summits of the great Livingstone range, on the far eastern side about fifty miles away, pressing like Alps around, there was about it something of the Mediterranean in the spring. Away to the south, as far as the eye could reach, there was just blue water and nothing else. High as we were, we could hear the waves pounding the shore, as if they were indeed sea-waves. We started down eagerly towards the lake.

The road dropped down the face of a three-thousand-foot cliff. It was cut into the mountain side in a series of desperate zigzags. There were twenty-three of these inclines, each half a mile long; and when we looked up from below, our descent and, still more, the construction of the road itself, seemed an almost impossible feat. Yet that road was not the product of modern engineering. It was a product of missionary faith and zeal, built many years ago by believing amateurs with the help only of unskilled, unbelieving Africans.

At the foot of the escarpment the road swung away sharply to the north. We travelled slowly because it was so broken. For sixty miles it followed close by the lake shore on our right, whilst on our left was the wall of the Nyika, its cap of grey cloud still pulled down firmly about its ears. But as the plain between water and mountain widened it seemed to swing away in giant strides to the north-east.

It got hot. At first the country was thickly populated and desperately over-cultivated, but afterwards for most of the way it was nothing but shimmering grey bush, pale with sunlight on its long white thorns, and only splashed with colour where it showed a baobab tree or two, like a birth-mark on its sallow cheeks. It shimmered, trembled and danced incessantly in the heat, and it was deathly silent whenever the shrill cicada hymn to sun and thorn would allow it. At four in the afternoon, the Nyika well out of sight, we drove into the native town of Karonga.

An immense crowd of black people was surging over the landing strip in the centre of the town. Drums were beating, people singing, shouting battle cries and blowing shrill whistles. All over the place, independent bands and teams of natives, with baboon tails and leopard claws tied round their middles in all possible varieties of jungle fantasy, danced, leapt, swirled and stamped their feet, roaring deep down in their stomachs with a mad, ecstatic abandon. Neither Peaches nor I knew what to make of it.

We might have been alarmed, since the commotion and noise were terrific, but for the fact that nowhere was there a policeman or a uniform of any kind to be seen, and that the black people who were not actually dancing, leaping, shrieking, beating drums or ceaselessly blowing whistles, were dressed in the favourite flaming colours of their best clothes. Then suddenly I saw three topees, three European heads, floating like the corks of a fishing net on this heaving sea of twelve thousand black, prancing figures.

No one appeared to have noticed my arrival. I got out of the jeep and went among the crowd. The noise was deafening, but it was the sweetest-smelling, the cleanest African crowd I had ever been among. I suddenly felt how lovely it was to be among so many people and no longer sitting silently in a prancing jeep, holding myself back from a too great awareness of the aggressive, disturbing physical quality of Africa. The feeling warmed me through like wine, gave me a feeling of being a sort of ancient mariner walking among a goodly company.

I slowly made my way to the three topees. When I got near, I saw that they were deeply concerned in a tug-of-war. Two of them, nice-looking, clean-shaven Englishmen, in spotlessly neat khaki shorts and shirts, were directing operations, whilst a third, with a long, lean, sensitive face, grey eyes and a small cavalry moustache, his hair perhaps just a shade too long, was sitting at ease rather nonchalantly on a shooting stick and just watching them. The glow, the smile, in his wide grey eyes, however, belied his nonchalant pose of his body. A very tall African of about six foot eight was helping the other two. He was wearing dark suede shoes with plum-coloured stockings, fine navy shorts, a yellow silk shirt and green silk muffler. He had a gold watch on his wrist and a Livingstone-Stanley topee in his hand.

The two teams were keen. They faced each other like Angoni Impis going to war. The crowd was wildly excited. Both sides pulled with such a will and the crowd roared such encouragement that thrice they pulled apart a rope the size of a ship's cable, and to everyone's huge delight the two teams landed in a heap in the dust. It was a wonderful laugh that followed. It rang out absolutely instantly and spontaneously, like a loud peal from a bell hung in that blue sky over us. I felt like beginning to dance myself.

Suddenly I heard the older of the two Englishmen say to the other, in an agonized voice: "For God's sake, Jerry, go and hide the prizes quickly! We shan't get a decision. We have no thicker rope."

"Can't we give them all prizes?" asked Jerry, hesitating.

The other scratched his chin and said, "It's rather a lot of money, you know. I'm not sure I can afford to spend any more. . . ."

"Don't let us worry about that," said Jerry, now dead keen, "I would like to come in fifty-fifty with you."

The man on the shooting stick seemed the least engaged, so I went over to him, introduced myself, and asked for Michael Dowler.

"I am Dowler," he said. "I am delighted. I have been expecting you. Come and meet the others. What do you think of our family?" he added, as we shook hands. "We have given the whole town a day off—King's birthday, of course."

Chapter Nineteen

I SPENT the night with Michael Dowler, in his house on the edge of the landing-strip, now empty, black and silent. Because of the damp and the heat the house was built on two floors like the old-fashioned, lake-side houses, and was closed in from head to foot with mosquito wire netting.

The lake was close by. The moment we stopped speaking, the noise of the waves on the shore, a short, choppy, lapping noise, like the sea on an East Coast Channel beach, came in through the wide open doors and windows behind the mosquito netting, and spread throughout the house. The house itself smelt strongly of bats. Dowler carried on an intermittent war against them, but they were prolific and determined. Their smell, no matter what he did, penetrated everywhere: an acrid, ancient smell which touched, inside oneself, some fearful, obscure instinct beyond experience and knowing. Every now and then there would be a rush of their wings in the dark outside, followed by a burst of high-pitched squeaking, almost too sharp for human ears to bear. And all night long there was the sound of native drums: people drumming by the dark lake shore, drumming on the outskirts of the town and far back in the bush, which was now quite dark, with ranks closed tightly against the night and its arrows of stars.

Dowler was a bachelor. He was a man of about thirty-five. He was sensitive and loved civilized things—music, books, good food, and comfort. His house on the lake bore eloquent testimony to all this; but, if he wanted civilization, why come to Africa? He lived by the great lake with a certain royal abandon. He had four handsome, well-dressed African servants, who were obviously devoted to him and he to them. He watched over them with a solicitude remarkable in one so young. The more I got to know Michael, the clearer became my impression that he gave these children of African nature the consideration and affection he would have liked to give his own dark, unfulfilled self, only centuries of so-called European civilized values prevented him from doing this. We all have a dark figure within ourselves, a negro, a gipsy, an aboriginal with averted back, and, alas! the nearest many of us can get to making terms with him is to strike up these vicarious friendships with him through the black people of Africa.

We talked late into the night alone on the veranda. Michael assured me he had always wanted to go on the Nyika. It drove him nearly mad to wander up and down the low, hot, malarial plains at its base, infected with sleeping sickness, and month after month to watch the cool, purple flanks of the cloud-capped wall, feeling unable to escape up them. This was just the opportunity he wanted. Alan had made him free to do as he pleased, and if I would let him, he would love to come with me. The great question was bearers. But he himself was out in the bush most of the time and was therefore known to them far and wide. They seemed to like him and trust him. He never had any difficulty getting any. Would I let him try to raise a party for us?

I agreed to this as it made good sense. I would spend one day with him to complete arrangements and then hurry back to Msusi, pick up my tents and supplies, and rejoin him as quickly as I could.

We were up early the next day. Below on the lake shore the sun shattered the night and coolness in one quick blow. At one minute it was dark and cool, and the next the sun came roaring like a lion over the top of the far, purple Livingstone range on the eastern shore of Nyasa, and at once it was light and hot.

Before breakfast Michael had his two headquarters

askaris, Harneck and Karramba, summoned to his room. They were two young yet old soldiers, both of the King's African Rifles. Harneck was a good, solid, handsome peasant type, a stout African yeoman who, Michael said, could be relied on absolutely, though he was slow and too gentle. Karramba, who had something mercurial, almost Latin or Spanish about his appearance, was quick, clever, and brilliant, but a little cruel and at times not at all reliable. Michael kept them both because together they made a whole; apart they were inadequate. In a few minutes they had their orders and were packing up to set out into the bush for bearers.

"I have given them five days," Michael said, "to get us forty-five bearers."

After breakfast we got into Michael's car and drove fifty miles along the road by the lake to call on Bwamantapira, the greatest of the African lakeside Chiefs, whose authority stretched far back into the foothills of the Nyika itself. We came to Bwamantapira's village late in the afternoon. I do not know if he understood a word we said to him. He was dragged almost to the door of his small mud bungalow by a young wife and two handsome little black boys, and stood there in a daze, a fat, handsome man, swaying on his feet, dead drunk, agreeing amiably to all we said.

The dark overtook us on the way back, but it was preceded by a clear and unbelievably tender twilight. Michael had been out in the bush with his gun when it came. He had stopped to go after some guinea-fowl we had seen flying back from the lake to roost in golden trees. They seemed in the sunset glow to be covered with blue and silver sequins, with little scarlet scimitars over their dainty heads. The moment I saw them I knew Michael would not be able to resist following them. He was gone about twenty minutes. Meanwhile I sat by the side of the road and listened to the night symphony of the bush tuning up.

Fifty yards away a little duiker doe stepped out of the

bush, looked at the car for about a minute, with the most arch and innocent surprise, and then stepped delicately back into the bush. Ten minutes later a large lion with a long black mane, walked out purposefully at the same place and, without looking right or left, disappeared into cover on the far side. Near at hand three Franklyn partridges rose up in noisy hysteria. High overhead an eagle flew slowly by on ponderous wings, the pink afterglow burning on its feathers and glinting off a long silver fish in its talons. The night birds, lakeside frogs and crickets, gathered the scattered sparks of sound together and sent up into the silence a flame of evening song and praise. I was sorry when Michael ended the moment by stepping quietly out of the bush.

I told him about the lion. "Oh!" he said, with hardly a show of interest, "I expect it must be that fellow I nearly ran down with the car, just about here, the other night."

We dined that night with the District Commissioner, Peter Gracey, and his wife Joan. The light had gone long before we reached their house. As we walked through long lake grass up the track, to a shrill crescendo of night and water noises, we could see from far off their house-boy at the entrance waving a lantern to guide us. As we approached we heard a new sound—a sound of European music. The Graceys were playing their gramophone. It had a remarkable tone, and as we came nearer still we distinguished clearly the St. Matthew Passion of Bach.

I was instantly and profoundly moved by it. Not only was it so completely unexpected, but in that setting it sounded such a true, unfaltering statement of what is best in our complex European system of values. As I listened to the singing getting louder I felt that Bach's Passion was almost our justification. It seemed to give meaning to our being there by the dark lake, near the heart of that man-indifferent continent.

The voice of the crickets and the noise of the bush appeared to recede before the ordered advance of that silver, clear and unambiguous sound, and the night to let the great chorus rise unimpeded to the stars.

We sat talking with Peter and Joan Gracey far into the night. I could write much about them and the life they led in Karonga. I would like to dwell on the detail of their lives, but one more incident must be enough. At some moment in the evening, I think it was after we had been listening to a gramophone record of T. S. Eliot, and those lines which, although written about a Cambridge in America, always remind me so much of London that they send a stab of homesickness through me:

> *"The winter evening settles down*
> *With smells of steaks in passageways.*
> *Six o'clock.*
> *The burnt-out ends of smoky days. . . ."*

I then said to Gracey: "As I came up the track, listening to Bach on your gramophone, I could not help wishing that Livingstone too could have heard something like it when he walked by here."

He looked at me sharply for a moment and said: "I expect he heard the same thing, in other ways."

He went on to say that the more he knew the African, the more impressed he was by the fact that when Livingstone died his bearers carried his dead body for hundreds of miles through hostile, dangerous country to the coast. It was a deed so remote from their normal state of being that he never ceased to wonder at it. Years ago he had met a very old native who remembered seeing Livingstone standing in the lake washing. When he lathered his head, the old man said, they all ran away because they thought he was a wizard taking his brains out. Yet with all that sort of superstition and ignorance about him, Livingstone captured their imagination to such an extent that, dead, he still urged his servants on. This was the real measure of the quality of his greatness.

Certainly, as I listened in my bed that night to the waves on the shore, and recalled my first sight of the lake, I could understand as I had never done before how Livingstone could be both such a God-drunk and lake-intoxicated person. Having looked that wide land full in the face and seen those waters in their great frame of mountain and incalculable sky, it is not hard to realize how a search for them could easily be identified with a search for God.

I left Karonga before dawn the next day. As we now knew the road, we travelled fast, Peaches and I taking turns at the wheel. At four in the afternoon I was back at Msusi. Grantham was away with the General, but had left his house warm and open for me. I picked up my tents, blankets, cooking pots, ropes, petrol and food supplies. The jeep looked like a Christmas tree on wheels.

The next day we left again at dawn, and slept the night at Deep Bay on the lake with a hospitable trader at the depot of the African Lakes Corporation. We were back in Karonga soon after 9 a.m. and found the first bearers coming in.

Michael was delighted with the way things seemed to be going. The five days were not up until the following evening, but already eleven sturdy young bearers had come in and were being fed in the kitchen yard, seven of whom he knew from previous journeys in the bush.

We spent a busy day organizing our loads.

In the afternoon I did a round of the few small Indian stores in Karonga. I bought up almost their entire supply of blankets as well as a good quantity of salt, which we intended using as money in the hills, where it is very scarce.

Just before sundown Michael and I walked to the lake shore through green-gold papyrus grass shoulder-high and tasselled with seed. As it swayed in the slow breath of the evening air it seemed to spike and splinter the light between us and the sun.

The lake, in spite of its dense population of crocodiles, was full of black people washing. Some young girls, after coming out of the water, started to dance on the shining foreshore. They carried scarlet, yellow and brown wraps which, as they leaped and ran, they wove and unwove round their slim naked bodies. Some long, heavy, dug-out canoes, those black ships of Africa, were drawn up high on the beach, and several fishermen sat beside them in the amber light mending their nets, serenely continuous in their antique occupation. The waves of the lake pounded briskly, and urgently, at their feet, but they worked on unheeding.

Far away across the blue waters, on the threshold of Tanganyika, the mountains were purple and gold, their volcanic crevasses running full to the brim with the lava of the sun. It might easily have been a moment set for a meeting between Nausicaa and Odysseus on the Mediterranean shore, but, alas! it had to serve only as a moment of farewell in my own frantic little coming and going.

When we got back to the house, thirty bearers, all young and strong, were there. They made a good sight round their fires that night, and their lively conversation scattered a certain excitement on the air.

But there was a slight set-back the next day. Karramba came in just before lunch, dead-drunk, and with no bearers. I thought Michael's slim frame would burst with rage. He fined Karramba a month's pay, de-moted him, and straight away sent him on a fifty-mile journey to Bwamantapira with a letter asking the chief to produce ten more bearers for us by the following evening.

We put Harneck in charge of our thirty-five bearers, and gave him one of my guns and some ammunition. We distributed two blankets to each man. They had not expected it and their delight was real and deep. They spread the blankets in the sun, waved them about their heads and filled the air with girlish cries of delight. It was astonishing, the sensitive, maiden-like sounds these husky black bodies suddenly emitted.

Michael then ordered them to take up their loads and with these on their heads and their hands swinging free, one by one they marched out of the yard with a glad will, fell into a single file, singing in a well-calculated rhythm to their long strides, and passed out of sight, the dust raised by their feet rising like a swarm of golden bees into the afternoon air.

We followed on by car the next day and joined them at Deep Bay not far from Bwamantapira's village. The old Chief himself was on the roadside to meet us. He had made an effort to sober up and stood with two red-hatted messengers of his court, waiting erect with immense dignity. He had great charm, knew it, and used it effectively on us. He had received Michael's message, and said we could count on him to produce bearers early the next day.

We camped that night by a heavy, black tree. I have seldom seen a tree of a thicker and darker green. It was full of bats and it seemed deeply dyed with their essence, and drenched and dripping with their smell and matter. But it stood on the only level ground, so we had to stay near it.

We had a wonderful view of the lake. It made a perfect deep bay here, with the bush standing tiptoe in the lake surf. Not far out from the shore five sharp pinnacles of rock, stained white with bird droppings, burned with a dull phosphorescent glow all through the night. We heard the lake all night long, and at one moment a posse of hippopotami who went huffing, puffing and snorting by to raid the native gardens inland.

Our bearers were tired. They had come fifty miles in about thirty-six hours. But we insisted on their getting into our camp drill at once. We made them pitch their tent, taught them how to make their tea, and rationed their rice and sugar. By eight o'clock the camp was fast asleep.

Chapter Twenty

WE broke camp at eight o'clock the following morning. Our bearers were still rather disorganized and we could not get going earlier. Bwamantapira's ten bearers arrived just as we struck tents. They came reluctantly, almost prodded on by the messengers of his court. They looked a sulking bunch so we allowed them no time either for feeding or feelings, but gave them their loads and sent them off ahead of us with the dependable Harneck and the rest. Trouble on these occasions, one knows from bitter experience, never occurs in front but always collects at the back.

The track now led us due west, through a low marshy plain, away at right angles from the lake shore. The Papyrus grass rose high over our heads and we had no view except an occasional glimpse of a purple wall of the remote Nyika.

It was hot, and we were glad to make the most of the moments when we had to stop to ask directions of passing natives. Our bearers were out of sight. Only Karramba, now thoroughly ashamed of himself, Michael's two servants, the cook and house-boy, draped in lamps, fats and pans, were with us.

At first we passed many natives, all sorts of small settlements of little mud and straw huts, discreetly and respectfully tucked into the shelter of some rise in the plain. But after twelve miles or so of steady walking all signs of settlement disappeared, and we saw no one. I was delighted when this happened, felt we really were on our journey and nearly sang for joy. I saw Michael suddenly give Karramba a cigarette and I knew he was feeling as I did.

After three and a half hours' steady walking we came out

of the grass and started a gentle climb on to higher ground. The bush came back, a pale, sallow, shimmering bush, full of sunlight and tentative apologetic shadow. From then on it stayed with us until about four in the afternoon, when we reached the fields and clearing of a little village, called Nkalanga. We had done about twenty miles from the lake shore and decided to call it a day.

The Umfumo of the village was already waiting for us, our bearers sitting expectantly round him, hopeful of our decision. He guided us to a magnificent level camping site under three vast, wild fig trees. There was both shade and space, and in a few minutes the loads were undone, the tents going up, the water and wood being fetched, latrines being dug, and the Umfumo himself came in to see what food his village would like to sell us. We said he was to find, if he could, an ox for the bearers. They had learnt their lesson well and the camp was organized much more quickly than the night before.

We were in the midst of our tea when the Umfumo returned, followed by a procession of women carrying trays of food on their heads, and these in turn were followed by an old man leading a young bull. Michael explained that it was extremely rare for the natives ever to have oxen, and began to bargain.

I say we bargained, but that is a hard word for what took place. As we looked at those thin, friendly, black faces, so delighted to have the monotony of their lives broken by our visit, neither Michael nor I had any desire to bargain. What we did was to instruct Harneck, the sober, reliable peasant, to agree with the sellers on a weight of salt, and then we doubled the quantity. As a result the village became, for that afternoon and evening, an extraordinarily happy place. Everywhere people suddenly started singing and smiling to themselves.

We bought fresh mealies, ground tapioca root, sweet potatoes and beans for the bearers, some eggs and a fowl for ourselves, and then slaughtered the bull. At least the bearers slaughtered it with a huge primitive delight. They leaped at it, pulled it down in the dust and promptly cut its throat without a squirm, smirk or shudder, feeling nothing apparently but a warm glow of anticipation at the meal in front of them.

While all this went on, I took my gun, some soap and a towel, and walked two miles along the track to the bed of the Fuliwa river. The sun was already behind the Nyika, the shadows were long and dark.

I could not see the Nyika itself for I was up against the foothills, but the river, the Fuliwa, or Wouwe as it is also called, rises there. Here it cut a deep gorge in the hills, and brought with it the cold, heavy, densely-packed air which so unmistakably came from high mountain-tops. The water, as I bathed, felt like ice after the heat of the plain, and although I told myself again that cold was relative, I was glad we had taken all those precautions for the carriers.

Somewhere up the gorge, so old Bwamantapira had told us, there was a track of sorts leading up to the Nyika. I could see no sign of it. It looked in that light as if our journey might be a desperate business.

I got back to the camp in the twilight, to find Michael feeding the Umfumo with castor oil out of a bottle from our medicine chest. He made a little gesture of mock dismay and said: "I can't give him enough. He has nearly finished the bottle."

The news that the medicine chest was out soon went round, and the bearers crowded in on us from all sides. This was to become a daily scene in our camp and I often think back on it with real pleasure.

Michael dressed all the wounds and scratches, and many ugly festering things as well on those bare feet, felt the pulses, and administered according to need paludrine or M. & B., Epsom Salts or aspirin.

The native faith in the magic of white medicine was

boundless, and at times they would pretend to be ill just in order to have some. Whenever a pretender was detected and sent away, the good humour with which he took his exposure was only equalled by the delight of the bystanders.

With the slaughtering of the bull and this administration of medicine round the fire, we felt that our journey to the Nyika began to acquire a spiritual as well as a material shape. It now possessed an idea and an emotion that belonged only to itself and which, however slight, would never exist again in quite the same way. It was a deeply satisfying feeling, and I said to Michael:

"You know, I think we shall be all right now. They are not a bad lot."

"I shall feel happier," he answered, "when we are deeper into the hills and away from all villages. This is the last one near the lake, thank goodness!"

"The test will come to-morrow," I told him, and described what I had seen of the gorge. "The only bearers who worry me a bit," I concluded, "are Bwamantapira's bunch; they look very dissatisfied."

He nodded and pointed to where one of the lake-side bearers, a huge, brawny, ill-tempered man, was addressing some of the others. We had already noticed him and christened him Jo'burg Joe.

"I don't think he will cut any ice with my Karonga lads, though. There are only ten of his bunch, and at a pinch we might scrape through without them," Michael said.

The sight of the camp as a whole was reassuring, too. The bearers had now formed little groups and were grilling their meat round large open fires. All sorts of visitors were coming in from around. The conversation was brisk and lively and the laughter gay and carefree. They recover very quickly from fatigue, these native sons of Africa. When they lined up for their evening pay, all trace of weariness seemed to have dropped from them.

Over dinner the bearers borrowed a drum from the

village. They discovered that they had one of the most famous drummers of the Northern Province in their midst —a man who had once drummed at a feast for seventy-two hours without stopping. He warmed up the drum, took his time and did a few trial runs on it, but nobody's heart was in it yet, and in Africa drum and audience must be as one. This drummer was obviously an artist; he felt instantly that his audience was not yet ready, not yet united within itself, and he made no attempt to force any real drumming on it.

Michael and I were eating outside our tents because it was still warm, and watched all this with interest. We were half-way through our meal when a black man stepped suddenly out of the bush and advanced into the flickering fire-light.

He was a strange-looking figure, quite different from the lake-side people. He was short, stocky, immensely broad-shouldered, with great muscles to the calves of his legs. He had broad feet with toes widely splayed apart. His clothes were in rags. He carried a large earthenware pot on his head, a long broad spear in the right hand, and had a fear-less, independent look in his eyes. His skin, even in that fire and lamp-light, looked a clearer black than any of our people's.

I heard someone exclaim: "Auk! A Mpoka."

A thrill of interest went through the camp. The talking stopped. Everyone looked at the newcomer.

"I think he is from the Nyika," Michael whispered, and shouted for Karramba, who came at the double. Then they started a long conversation, at the end of which Karramba told us that the stranger was indeed a Mpoka, and that he lived in the hills just underneath the lip of the Nyika. He had come down to sell a pot of honey: would we like it? The season had been bad in the hills, and he needed salt and food.

There must have been forty pounds of wild honey in that pot and he asked only ten shillings for it. Karramba wanted to bargain, but we waved him aside and gave the man fifteen shillings.

We inquired if he would like to stay with us as a guide, but he shook his head and with the same independent air stepped back into the bush and vanished.

A terrific buzz of conversation broke out at his disappearance. The Mpokas are the only real mountain folk in Northern Nyasaland. There are few of them, and some say that they are either a dying race or vanishing into the greater tribes of the plain. To this day they cling to the high ground where they were driven by the Angoni, Henga and Arab slave traders of a century or more ago. There they cultivate a few remote valleys with difficulty, and eke out a precarious subsistence by collecting wild honey and selling it in the plain below.

There is no honey like it, I believe. It has a royal, antique flavour, a wild, sharp, stinging, uninhibited sweetness all its own, and it finds a ready sale. For it the Mpokas are welcome in the plain, though they themselves are viewed with a somewhat superstitious awe. They are believed to possess magic powers, the secrets of life and death, and the ability to change themselves into hyenas and leopards. They are, moreover, the metal-workers and the armourers of that world. Their steel is locally renowned. All the Mpoka men carry magnificent long, broad spears, which are as much a symbol of their craft as a weapon for their defence. Still deep in the African heart is the belief that the gift of the metal-worker is a gift from the hands of ancient gods. Moreover, the mistrust the people of the plain feel for the unknown Nyika is inevitably projected on the Mpokas as well.

The Mpokas for their part have no love of the people down below. They resent and distrust them of old, and keep their distance with a jealous and revengeful suspicion. I do not want to exaggerate these things, but the sharp interest aroused in our camp by this visitation out of the night was most marked.

Even the cynical Karramba watched our visitor go with some disapproval, and, making a wry face, said loudly for all to hear: "He says we have a long way to go to-morrow and would have done better not to come."

The heart went out of the drumming after that, the fires were allowed to sink into their coals, and the camp soon slept.

In the early morning the Umfumo accompanied us to the Fuliwa gorge and showed us where we could cross on a tree felled over it. Our bearers went over easily, as though they had done it all their lives. The tree was grey with age and worn smooth with the rub of many feet. I hated crossing over. I never get used to that sort of thing, no matter how often I do it. Whilst anxiously seeking a hold for my feet, I find that glimpses of fast-running water far below make the task of balancing, with a rifle over the shoulder, seem almost impossible. I have never fallen over yet, but I always expect to do so at any moment. I waited until they were all across, and admired Michael's technique from firm ground. He got over his dislike of the process by putting Harneck in front of him and Karramba behind—presumably to catch him should he stumble. He would then put his hand on Harneck's shoulder, appear almost to shut his eyes, and walk slowly and unfalteringly, like a somnambulist, to the other side.

I followed after him with infinite care, trying in vain to look indifferent.

On the far bank we waved farewell to the Umfumo. He was a small, pinched person, with an inexpressible look of something beyond our understanding on his face. He looked sad, marooned and abandoned on the edge of the immense, shimmering bush. Then we started to climb and soon passed out of his sight.

The track, and it was the only one, so the Umfumo had

said, was at first a clearly defined footpath; but, a mile or two up the gorge, it trailed away into little more than a goat track, old, broken and obviously very rarely used. We climbed with the sun on our backs, and, as the morning advanced it became very hot and the bush thinned out so much that it scarcely protected us. Within an hour all the bearers sat down for their first rest. Michael and I sat among them, and talked to them.

They were cheerful, and better for their meal of the night before, but it was obvious to me that they had not got their second wind as yet. And we were only just in the mouth of the gorge; the worst was to come. We gave them ten minutes and started off again.

Within three-quarters of an hour they asked for another rest. The track was getting steeper, but as yet there had been no difficult climbing in the real sense of the word. I noticed that the sides of the gorge were encroaching upon us and that the sound of the Fuliwa, which we had not seen since crossing it, was becoming louder.

Half an hour later the bearers wanted another rest. They were breathing heavily and complaining of pains in their legs. They rested nearly half an hour this time. The river was now quite close, and roaring like a gale through the trees. We climbed steadily for about another hour and came to the stream.

The trees fell away from us, and we looked up two steep grass summits, rising high on either side of us into a sky so blue that it was almost black. About fifteen yards away the main stream went cascading in foam and thunder down the gorge, and on the edge of the track was a deep pool. The bearers dropped their loads and soon were all splashing in the ice-cold water. All this looked very attractive, but we were already biting deep into the day. No one knew when we should get out of that gorge; obviously we could not spend the night there.

I spoke to Michael. He called over his Askaris and we

got going again. Only Jo'burg Joe staged a demonstration. He was the strongest of them all but now he wanted a longer rest, and swore at Harneck. Michael instantly walked down on him and told him to take up his load. All the bearers had stopped and turned round to watch, with tense potentially critical faces.

Michael looked Joe calmly up and down as if he were seeing him for the first time. "Take up your load and do as you are told," he said quietly, as if there was no possibility whatsoever of further disobedience. Joe stood up and went on.

Things went better for a while, until we had to cross the river again. The far bank was a steep, grass precipice about five hundred feet high. We had to get up it. I felt desperately sorry for the bearers. It was hard work getting myself and my rifle up.

When they came to the top, they were exhausted. What was even more discouraging, we found ourselves on an isolated pinnacle, in a world of similar pinnacles, hemmed in by enormous grass-covered summits beyond. There was supposed to be a Mpoka village here, but we saw no sign of it, and the afternoon was beginning to level itself out.

We went painfully up and down four or five of the pinnacles, sank up to our knees in mud and slime at their bottoms, and struggled slowly out again on the other side. At about four, when we had only an hour and a half of daylight left, at last I saw in front of us not a pinnacle but a long grass spur, running gold and green straight into the sinking sun.

Our bearers were now staggered out in a long irregular line up and down the mountain. By agreement Michael stayed with the rear, and I went in front.

Thinking that one good example was worth more than all the exhortation in the world, I led with a sturdy, cheerful Karonga lad; I had several times helped him on and off with his loads, and his bearing had impressed me from the start. We went up this spur steadily. If one is to be a good example one must not stop; the secret is to go on, steadily, inexorably, on and on. The Karonga lad was all that and more. His lungs were heaving like a blacksmith's bellows, but he did not hesitate. He never once stopped but slowly went up and up and on. At five we climbed out on to the spur, the slope levelled out and we stepped along quite fast through some sort of tall gold rye grass. The nearest bearer was coming slowly along below us and about a mile behind. At five-twenty we suddenly came over the far crest of the spur, and there, perched close to us on the edge of a deep valley, was a little Mpoka hamlet of four huts, with sufficient level ground round it for tents.

I made my companion drop his loads, climb up a knoll and shout back the magic words: "People, a village, a village."

His clear voice raised a protracted echo, and then from far away came a glad, confused acknowledgment, passed farther and farther back into the distance. Just then the sun went down.

The village was called Mwatengara and the Umfumo, a fine-looking, sturdy young Mpoka man, in a scarlet beret, came tearing up the slope to meet me. His bearing was respectful, but he was too excited to be dignified. He took me by the hand and led me to the village and introduced me to his old father, who was so old that I would not like to guess his years. His eyes, once black, had gone blue and dim like those of a very old dog. He held on to my hand with both his own and would not let go, tears rolling down his cheeks.

I told the Umfumo that the real Government officer was coming on behind me and at once he set off at a fast, eager pace to meet Michael. I noticed there were only two other men in the village. The rest were all women and dozens of fat-bellied, naked, wide-eyed little children. The men had already sent the women to work. Shouting and laughing with excitement and delight, they were tearing down the steep slope to fetch water in the valley, bringing in firewood and setting out some of their meagre supplies of maize and beans for our food. Soon there were half a dozen fires going to guide the rest of our party in.

We needed those fires. Within half an hour of sundown the thermometer was only a few degrees off freezing-point. A cold wind began to blow down the valley from the Nyika. Michael and I were cold in our tents and put on our warmest clothes. He drank a couple of large brandies, I some of a refined Spanish sherry that he carried with him. When his cook brought us large mugs full of chicken soup and great helpings of chicken and rice, we were really ready for it all. It was our first meal since seven that morning.

We had come, I estimated, about fourteen miles, and climbed, not counting those heart-breaking pinnacles and other ups and downs, about six thousand feet. For our reward, here on our second day out, we were camping right in a great mountain gateway to the Nyika. But we had pushed our bearers dangerously hard. It was obvious, so intense was the cold, that we could not possibly have spent the night out in the gorge. Nevertheless they were at the end of their strength.

"We had better rest them a whole day here to-morrow," I said to Michael.

When we told them, a deep murmur of gratitude and approval went through the camp, and everyone continued eating with a new zest. But there was no drumming that night.

"This is a no-good village, Bwana," said Karramba, with immense scorn: "it has not even got a drum."

Even if there had been one, I am sure it would not have been used.

Chapter Twenty-One

I WOKE up the following morning feeling profoundly depressed. It was a lovely morning. As far as I knew I had had a good, if somewhat cold night. We had done well. I had gone to sleep in the best of moods. It looked as if nothing could now prevent us from getting to the Nyika, an event contrary to the ill-suppressed expectations of the experts and authorities on the area. The bearers were all in a good mood, laughing and talking with the greatest vivacity round their early morning fires. There was every reason why I should be rejoicing, but there it was: against all reason, and against my will and the evidence of my senses, I was possessed by this feeling of depression, which would not let me be.

As soon as we had finished breakfast we summoned the Umfumo and Harneck. I took my rifle, and Michael his cine-camera, which the Umfumo and Harneck carried between them, and together we descended into the valley.

To the west there were three peaks facing our camp across the valley: Nkalanga Head which did a sort of eurythmic half-turn straight into the air; Mount Charo, staid, solid, and dependable as became the central peak; and Kasanga Head which performed its own steep melo-drama on the left of the other two. They were all three just under eight thousand feet high. We chose the golden mean and went up Charo.

It was not a difficult climb. The morning was bright and clear, and whenever we stopped to look back, we had a fine view of the broken gorge and valleys through which we had come, the plain all of a tremble, and the sparkling blue waters of Nyasa far in the background.

In two hours we were nearing the top, and then suddenly

we were given a most effective illustration of the power of the African sun. We had just turned round to look back when, without warning, an enormous black cloud of twisting and turning mist materialized in the blue, and poured straight down on our heads. It was only ten o'clock on a winter's morning but already there had been time for the sun to draw enough vapour off the lake to wrap all those remote mountain-tops in a thick black shroud.

The Umfumo, his scarlet beret now going in front of us like a lit candle, seemed undismayed by the event, said it was always like that, and would clear by and by.

We were doing the last and steepest part of the climb when the mist came down, and I had reason to be grateful to it; for, though I could not tell why, my feeling of depression seemed to have translated itself into an unusual and sharp attack of vertigo. We were climbing along an almost vertical grass slope, about two thousand feet high. Had anybody slipped or stumbled he would, without doubt, have shot straight down to the bottom, for there was not a tree or boulder on to which to hold. As a rule I am fairly good on this sort of occasion; but to my dismay I was obsessed that morning by a feeling that I had taken myself too high and too far beyond my own strength and balance. Then, and to my great relief, the mist came down and removed all sense of height.

Once on top we sat down to wait for it to clear so that we could, as the Umfumo promised us, get our first view of the Nyika. Michael prepared his camera for the great moment. I put my compass at my side on Henderson's map. Harneck and the Umfumo sat, with the natives' instinctive good manners, behind and away from us, and talked ceaselessly in low, contented voices.

It was dark and very cold. An icy wind was moving with the mist over the summit. I lay down on my back in the grass. How sheltered one was, and how warm there! I snuggled into it as deeply as I could, almost like a Steenbuck, the antelope which so hates draughts and cold winds that it has become a great artist in finding shelter even in the bleakest of places.

I took out my little pocket-book to make a note of the height of Charo . . . and suddenly I saw that it was Sunday, and noticed the date. Then it was as if a large double barn-door in the granary of my mind burst open, and my depression tumbled out into the full light of day.

It had happened on a Sunday, a lovely warm glowing day at the foot of the ten-thousand-foot Goenoeng Gedeh in Java. This was its "forgotten" seventh anniversary. I, or rather the contemporary "I" on its own special mission to Africa, had forgotten, as it had done several times before. But there is that in our blood which does not forget so easily; our hearts and our deepest minds have a will and a way of their own, and there are anniversaries they insist on keeping no matter what our conscious preoccupations.

It was always so with me, anyway, and I was unspeakably depressed until I acknowledged and observed this grim birthday within myself. Once I had fully, openly acknowledged it, things were better. For here was one of those sad friendships I have mentioned earlier, and because it was more relevant to my inward journey than the time or the place through which I happened to be moving, I must again hold out a hand of recognition to it.

We were a small, it seemed a condemned, group of British and Australian prisoners of war in Japanese hands. We were in an old Dutch jail for desperate criminals, at the foot of the Gedeh, one of the loveliest of Java's many volcanoes. It was a Sunday morning after a night of rain; I was sitting in the sun, shaking violently with malaria, and trying in vain to keep warm, when the Japanese sent for the senior R.A.F. Officer, Wing Commander Nichols,[1] and myself.

[1] Wing Commander, now Group Captain, W. T. H. Nichols is still serving in the Royal Air Force which he joined many years ago as a boy. One day I hope to write a book about the prisons he and I shared and to make some acknowledgment of the debt that his country and thousands of prisoners-of-

When we presented ourselves they told us we were to parade a party of twenty-five officers, and N.C.O.s, at two that afternoon. That was all, nothing more.

Nick seemed relieved. I said nothing. I was certain I recognized the look in their eyes. I had been through it before, he had not. They were either going to kill us, or kill someone else for our benefit. But I said nothing, for I might be wrong. Only I prayed in my heart that if I were right my malaria would abate sufficiently for my shivering to stop. I would not like them to see me shivering and think I was afraid.

We paraded at two. I was still shaking violently with ague. We marched out of the gate through streets full of Dutch civilians pushing their children in perambulators or taking them by the hand for their Sunday walk.

We were marched four miles to a large sports ground. All the machine-guns were out; there were hundreds of troops about in steel hats, with rifles and fixed bayonets. Hundreds of others, too, were laughing excitedly and flocking to the sports ground.

Yes, I had been right. It was to be a killing.

I said a prayer, silently, that my fever, that terrible shattering malarial ague, might go. Instantly my body stopped shaking, and a lovely warm sweat broke over me.

"Look!" I said to Nick in utter and grateful amazement, holding out my hand. "My hand is quite steady now."

war owe to him. He was a great camp Commander. In the last war I saw courage of all kinds but none quite of the Nichols quality. It was almost a matter of routine with him. All day and every day it was with him, as much a part of him as the colour of his eyes or the shape of his head. Neither that courage, nor what is rarer still, his imagination, failed him or us in those long, grim, inarticulate years in Japanese prisons. When we were released I stayed behind in Java, but I happen to know that on return to England not one of our thousand odd British prisoners-of-war needed rehabilitation—so unlike the prisoners returning from other theatres of war. I hope that someone, somewhere, in the R.A.F. has said to himself, "This is most unusual. How did this miracle occur?"

He smiled with approval and answered, "Good show!" His understatement was very English.

Already there were a thousand Dutch officers and men drawn up on the sports ground, and a similar number of Ambonese troops of all ranks. We marched our party in between them and faced about. Just opposite us, twenty yards away, two bamboo stakes were dug firmly in the ground.

"Look, you fellows," I said, or words to that effect, "it's going to be an execution, so hold on to yourselves and be prepared."

"Yes," said Nick, "I needn't remind you chaps who we are, and why we are here. Stand fast!"

We then saw the victims. I do not know their names to this day, but the manner of their going deserves a recording, even if it now cannot help them. One was a Eurasian, one an Ambonese. They marched jauntily and firmly on to the ground. The Eurasian was tied tightly to the two stakes; the Ambonese was made to kneel down in the grass in front of us, almost at our feet, and his hands were tied behind his back. One's first reaction was: "Thank God, not two of ours," and then, "Poor bloody, bloody devils."

The black muzzles of a dozen heavy machine-guns swung over towards us. A Japanese officer walked up to the Ambonese, who had long black hair. The officer lifted up this hair from his neck and dropped it over his eyes. Then he stepped back, drew his sword, measured his distance, stepped forward again, and smoothed the Ambonese's hair again. He repeated this cruel business backwards and forwards five times.

On the sixth, he raised his sword, yelled suddenly, deeply from his stomach like a man in a nightmare, leaped forward and cut the head off in one blow.

All round us the Dutch and Ambonese were falling in dead faints.

"Stand fast, chaps," Nick said.

A loud speaker almost drowned his words.

"This man has been killed," it boomed at us, "because he has shown a spirit of wilfulness to the Japanese Army."

Three Japanese soldiers with fixed bayonets now lined up in front of the Eurasian. His body was stretched between the stakes as on a cross. Then the Japanese on the right uttered the same mindless, inhuman, aboriginal, solar-plexus scream as the first officer had done, and plunged his bayonet three times into the bound Eurasian, whose skin at the first plunge snapped like a drum. The next soldier, and then the next, repeated the performance; then all three turned about again, fell on their stomachs, and fired four volleys into the limp and sagging body of the Eurasian.

All this time our twenty-five men had stood fast, but the officer next to me, Ian Horobin,[1] though still on his feet, was dead to this world, a condition that did all honour to him. He, like the rest of us, was living out each last second with those two humble, nameless victims, and living them through with neither hope, nor pity, nor expectation for himself. But at the first bayonet-stab he winced, as though he himself had received the blow, and swayed on his feet. I put my arm round him and in that way managed to hold him up through the rest of the whole bloody business; and

---

[1] Ian Horobin, Conservative Member of Parliament for Southwark, when war broke out abandoned politics for service in the R.A.F. After the capitulation of the Allied forces in Java he made an attempt to break away and join me in the hills of Bantam; but, as a result of this, he fell ill, was captured by the Japanese and imprisoned. Because he resolutely refused to answer the questions put to him about me and other matters, he was sorely beaten-up and ill-treated by his captors and was in a very poor state of health when I too was bundled into prison with him many months later. But his spirit was indomitable and we all brought away with us a generous store of the wise and witty sayings with which Horobin enlivened our days in jail.

He wrote a most moving poem about this execution called "Java Sunday". We buried it carefully lest it should fall into Japanese hands. After the war I kept a company of Japanese prisoners digging for it for a week but we never found it again and alas, Horobin can neither remember it nor has the heart to re-write it. And in a sense this is not necessary. The poem is being lived out in another way, for to-day Horobin puts all his great qualities of mind and spirit unreservedly into the running of the Mansfield House University Settlement for Boys in the East End of London.

in this moment, for me, lies the real significance of that afternoon. For as I put my arm round Horobin, a stranger, in order to support him, I felt to my utter amazement, how near he was to me. There seemed to be no barrier between us; we might have been the same person under the same skin; and, in spite of the dreadful circumstances of the moment, a tremendous warmth and reassurance welled up within me, like wine and song. All sense of isolation, all my restless, seeking self, my desperate twentieth-century awareness of isolation and doom vanished. I was out of it all in a flash, and far beyond in a world of inseparable nearness. This, I knew, was true: this nearness of him to me, of me to him. It was the heart of reality. That was how we all were, close to each other, if only we would allow ourselves to be so. With a singing sense of deliverance from unreality, from the prison of myself and my surroundings, I resolved that in the years to come I would never forget this moment. I resolved that if I lived—and I did not really care then one way or the other—I would try and carry this moment along with me in all that I did. Then Nick put out his arm to help Horobin, touched me, and I noticed that he, too, felt equally near.

That night, back in prison, we found a gloom as deep as night waiting for us. At first there was tremendous relief at our return, but as the news of the execution spread, the conviction grew that we should be the next victims. We summoned all the men to our regular evening service, Horobin read the lessons, and spoke to them as though he were a prophet down from a mountain in Palestine. That helped, but they were still depressed. I still had malaria, and was shaking again with the ague that had returned as soon as I re-entered the prison, but I knew I must do something to help the men through that night and out of their gloom.

Africa came to my rescue. I talked to them about the animals of Africa for two and a half hours; about the bush,

P

the plains, the great free mountain-tops and immense skies, about a life that was a continuous trek, a journey without walls or streets to hem it in. The sense of doom, the transmitted memory of the killing in the afternoon, receded, thanks to that recreated vision of my boyhood in Africa, and before the night was over our jail rang with laughter over the antics of baboons and elephants, lion and rhinoceros. I had realized then how deep, how life-giving and strengthening was this vision of Africa in my blood; that possessing this, and my knowledge of our nearness to each other, I could travel to the end of the world and time.

Suddenly I sat up, on the top of Charo, with so keen a feeling of happiness and release, that tears came to my eyes. It was still dark. Michael was still at his camera, the Umfumo and Harneck still talking. I could not have been more than a minute or two, reliving that moment seven years before. But the good of it was mine. The rest receding.

I lay back on the grass: the mountain seemed to take a firm, a friendly grip of my back. It, too, felt unbelievably near and sustaining. It seemed as if through me and through its great, strong heart, and right down to the centre of the earth, ran the axis on which the wide world turned through space and time. I had a vision of the universe and myself, in which circumference was reduced to a mere mathematical abstraction, and in which all was Centre; one great unfailing Centre, and myself, in the heart of Africa, in the heart of the Centre.

Yet, if we were as close and near one to the other, what then kept us so obviously, painfully and dangerously apart? The man on the stake, the headless Ambonese, Horobin, Nick and I were conceivably near to one another, but what could have been farther from that one-ness than the Japanese? It seemed so clear to me that morning. The distance between them and us was the distance of their unreality; just as the distance between us all to-day is created by our unreality. Those Japanese did not know what they were doing. They thought they were doing something which they were not doing. They gave their victims a fine, romantic military funeral—and what more could men want? They thought they were performing their duty nobly, beautifully and justly. Yet they were doing the opposite and doing it because their awareness of themselves, and of life, was inadequate. For this unreality starts in an incomplete awareness of ourselves; it starts in the elevation of a part of ourselves at the expense of the whole. Then, out of this dark gorge which we have allowed to open up between the two halves of ourselves, out of this division between the Europe and the Africa in us, unreality rises up to overwhelm us.

Evidence is everywhere that the great tide of unreality is running full. The human being, the natural person has never had so little honour from life and from himself as to-day. He is imprisoned in theories, in petrified religions, and above all, strangled in his own lack of self-awareness.

There is murder about. The air is foul with the stink of rotting corpses. But murder does not begin on the battle-field. There, in a sense, is the least of it. The murder is in our hearts, in our deepest selves, and no vicarious adventures in the footsteps of Holmes, Wimsey and Poirot will let us off. The murderer is powerful and respectable. He has churches, sciences, trade unions, political movements and dictators on his side, and he does not know his crime. He has a clean morning face, is well-spoken, has good manners and fine clothes. He sits with the judges and their laws are for him. He is good at getting himself increased wages, more afternoons off, better houses and finer gadgets, which are more and more ingenious in order to disguise the triviality of the service they render.

There is no great harm, perhaps, in all this. But what of his brother on the other side of the fence, the dark Siamese twin on the other side of the gorge, the Caliban tucked out of sight on the stormy side of the isle, the despised African far behind these blue escarpments? We murder him or are murdered by him from time to time, but can we blame our dark brother? If we murder him for virtue, why can't he kill for survival?

For those who care to look, the sad, secret presence of this killing is in all our bright twentieth-century eyes. The Molotovs of this world, the multi-millionaire, the quick, intolerant Puritans and one-eyed surgeons carry the secret of their own urge to murder on their faces, for all their un-awareness of it. It is only unreality that keeps us apart, that kills and murders and composes hymns of praise of Siberian concentration camps and metropolitan profiteers.

Yet this need not be. There is room for both, for Ariel and Caliban, for Cain and Abel, there is room for all, without murder, at the Centre, in the heart, without cir-cumference. Could fair and dark, night and morning, but understand the language they speak to each other across this dark gulf of unawareness, they would fall into one another's arms and embrace.

I repeat, only this awareness is true. And in this moment of reality the human being is neither fearful nor cringing. He does not mind how much he is asked to do, or how dangerous it is, if only it is something single, whole, com-plete and sufficient for his full self. He is greater than any dictator, factory or trade union. He is a mighty and heroic atom.

Any vision of himself or of life which does not acknow-ledge this, either kills or is killed. For there, in the heart, man's own dark aboriginal courage makes him free, his humbleness before the mystery of his being brings aware-ness, awareness makes him whole and wholeness gives him love. But merely to offer him increased wages, religious, political and scientific soporifics is to breed more murder. Give him a horse, give him a spear and bring out the dragon!

"I think," Michael called out to me suddenly, "the mist is going to break."

I sat up and opened my eyes. Indeed it was less dark, and along the edges of the other summits the mist was beginning to lift, a silver light running like a pentecostal fire all along the sombre ridges. For a few minutes we had a view that uplifted us beyond measure.

World beyond world we saw, a tremendous, rolling, folding country, clean, golden, grass-covered, rising like some Olympian pastoral symphony to a dark blue ridge, an Atlantic roller of land, fifteen miles west of us. In all the folds there appeared to be water, in all the bottoms dark-green copses, but no sign of people or human habitation of any kind.

"Bwana," said the Mpoka Umfumo with a smile as if this was his own work. "The Nyika, but the best Nyika, it is on the other side of the ridge."

As he spoke the mist came down again. We waited, but it refused to budge.

Released from myself, my eyes looked round the summit and were held by a purple glow in the green-gold grass.

I got up and went towards it. The summit was covered with wild irises, with lovely, proud spikes of purple flower. Everywhere there were small, glowing, delicate, precise flames of purple. They stood erect and undismayed, heraldic in the mist and wind. The grave, lowered head of the African plateau could not have understood the vision of chivalry they evoked. For they seemed to point a way, to pre-suppose a flame without fear or reproach—or was that but another fancy of a fevered heart?

On my way down I picked an armful to put in our tents, and that night I dreamed a dream. I tell it here, not because I have a theory about dreams, but because as a child I was profoundly impressed one night when my grandfather read out to us that passage from Genesis beginning: "And Joseph dreamt a dream and told his brethren and they hated him for it." It seemed to me then that there was a lesson one could learn from dreams. Here it is for what it is worth.

I dreamed I saw my father and mother standing together smiling in our garden at home. I did not remember ever seeing them like that. It was morning. The sun was shining. They were admiring a rose. The rose was white and the rose was on fire.

Chapter Twenty-Two

THE dawn the next morning was one of the loveliest I have ever seen. There were a few clouds over the lake and these were soon in flames. Standing at the door of my tent in the cold, pure air, it looked as if a great fleet of ancient ships, their sheets filled with fire, were plunging forward to battle. A happy murmur rose from the fires where the bearers squatted on their heels; now well fed they were keen to be away from that cold, drumless, foreign Mpoka hamlet.

Michael ordered the bearers to take up their loads and start at exactly eleven minutes to eight. Karramba took the lead and they went slowly down into the valley and up the other side, through the immense gateway between Charo and Kasanga.

They seemed to me to be taking the slopes in too direct a fashion, too steeply. They would have done better, I thought, to make use of the contours, but I did not worry unduly, because their behaviour was characteristic of the African. His sense of distances is not ours, and in any case his life is so surrounded with difficulty and trouble, and ups-and-downs everywhere, that he does not really believe he can ever get round things. So he would as soon go through with them and get them over and done with as quickly as possible.

We climbed on slowly from one valley to the next. We came across a tiny hamlet of three huts where the bearers all quickly sat down to rest and drink water. Then a black cloud suddenly materialized in the blue above, and poured down into the valley. In a few seconds we were in a thick fog and bitterly cold.

Fortunately after a time the going became easier. The

mist spoilt our view but we were plainly no longer struggling up and down mountain crests. The Umfumo said we were going over the Eastern edge of the country we had seen from Charo—not the true Nyika, he was anxious to add, but part of the Nyika none the less. What we were able to see, though, was superb African Cotswold country, lovely grass slopes, steep certainly but wonderfully free of trees and stone. Only tucked into the corner of each fold was a neat dark green copse, a Druid circle of sombre wood. In each bottom was a deep, clear, still stream, and again no people.

We saw no game, but according to the Umfumo the woods were full of leopard and wild pigs.

We did about twenty miles in the mist and at half-past four in the afternoon found ourselves on the edge of another deep valley. There was no question of it being another fold. On our left I could just see the bulk of what was Nganda Head, a mountain 8,600 feet high, and the highest point on the Nyika; and on our right a dark mass rising into the mist, which, the Umfumo told us, was Wendenganga. According to my map we should now be in the centre of the Nyika; but that valley, that unmarked cleft between the two peaks, was certainly no Nyika.

We went steeply down into it for about two thousand feet, and came to a small hamlet called Nkanta. It consisted of four tiny mud igloos, not huts but little mud bee-hives, occupied by another dim old man, four strapping young women and an immense brood of children. They received us as if we were angels. The old man said he had not seen a white face for twenty years, and he followed Michael round like his own shadow.

We pitched our camp there for the night. The bitter wind was bearing down the valley. It was cold, and we had to drive the bearers hard to put up their tents before dark. All they wanted to do was to make a fire and get round it. However, we soon had the camp staunchly pitched and well pegged down, like a ship with battened hatches and iron scuttles clamped on, against the night. Before this, we had built enormous fires and issued generous rations. It was as well we did. It blew a gale before morning, and the temperature went down to within a degree of freezing-point.

The wind dropped with the coming of the sun the next day. We packed up early, and travelling along the valley did close on twenty-five miles. We passed two small hamlets, both of which turned out their one old man, their four or five women and broods of children, who danced round us, and sang and clapped their hands from one end of their clearings to the other. At each hamlet we stopped to exchange news and to leave a small present of salt. They were people who had no contact with the outside world whatsoever, and whose gratitude was very moving.

All the way, in spite of my map, this cleft not only persisted but widened. The flank of the Nyika on our left became sheer precipice with unexpected cliffs of grey stone round the top. On our right and behind us it swung away in a wide curve towards the distant lake. About four in the afternoon the left flank of the Nyika too was turned.

We had come, as far as I could judge, to its northernmost point, and there hard by was the village of Njalowe. I had been told it would be in the heart of the best of the Nyika. It was nothing of the sort. It was in the heart of the bush far down at its feet. But it was a real native village with quite a fair-sized population, and it gave us a tremendous reception.

The people of Njalowe must have spotted us coming miles away, though how they managed to do this I do not know. The Umfumo and his elders met us several miles from the village and escorted us. A mile out, a party of about a hundred women came down the track to greet us. There was no pretence about all this, nothing forced, they were really glad to see us; it was a spontaneous act of welcome.

As soon as they saw us they raised a clear, bell-like warbling, yodelling cheer and came leaping and dancing towards us. All the way into the village they danced ecstatically round us and sang improvised songs of welcome with flawless, unselfconscious, glittering voices, clapping out the rhythm on their hands. There was nothing, no reservation, no qualification, no forethought between the desire to sing and the singing, the process was continuous and immediate.

I was quite certain, for my part, that I did not deserve such a Messianic reception, but I enjoyed every minute of it. I was fully convinced long before they led us into the village that we were really welcome. It is worth walking and climbing a long way to have that feeling. It is a good, healing, human feeling, and helps to melt some of the ice, and the calculation in our cold, de-humanized, limited-liability twentieth-century hearts.

Our camping site was already prepared for us, and food, firewood and water were all being fetched. There was no need to pitch any tents except our own, because Njalowe is so low down that it was warm, out of the wind and mist, and even at that late hour flushed with the full rays of the setting sun. A busy market sprang up round us.

No sooner had the women and girls seen us to our camping site than they dispersed, running and laughing happily along the village tracks. They were soon back again. Very dignified and serious now that they had business to do, and carrying great baskets of produce on their heads.

They brought mealies, fresh, ripe and stamped; beans, peas, sweet potatoes, sour milk, fowls, eggs and tapioca roots. We bought food for our bearers; they bought food for themselves. I am sure Njalowe had never had such a market. Finally we bought a bull for slaughter in the morning.

We did this because I felt we could not move on until we had explored this unrecorded gap in the Nyika. I was desperately anxious to get on to the true Nyika myself, but the unexpected existence of this large wedge of unhealthy, low-lying, practically uninhabited country, in what I had hoped would be the northern end of the plateau, could not be ignored. Michael and I therefore decided that we would rest the bearers for another day and night and ourselves do some reconnoitring with the new Umfumo as our guide. We were quite certain that, with a bull to slaughter and eat, our bearers would come to no mischief in our absence. And also there was the drum.

When Michael and I came back from our bathe in a stream at the bottom of the village, Karramba met us with the news, that Njalowe had a drum, a real drum, famous for its responsive tone. It could either boom like thunder or record the fall of a feather. If we stayed another night, they could have a real dance and do some proper drumming.

On the far side of the wide gap or valley in which Njalowe stands, there is a mountain close on eight thousand feet high, called Nkawozya. It has an impudent look about it, and seems to turn up the nose of its summit at whatever is around it.

I decided that the first thing was to find out what I could see from the top. Accordingly Michael and I, and the Chief, set off across the valley soon after the first light, taking with us Harneck, the indefatigable peasant askari, who had struck up a great friendship with me.

The Chief carried a magnificent broad spear, and a beautifully made snuff-box, shaped rather like a musketeer's powder horn. He stopped from time to time to help himself and pass the horn round with a royal hand. I think he had some Arab blood in him somewhere, and he wore a cloth like the Javanese Kaiang round his head.

On the way he told us that for miles around there were very few people. They hardly ever saw anybody from the outside world. Karonga was their nearest town, but it was several days' journey along a narrow lost track through the bush and plain. Many of his young men had to go into the world outside to find a living, and they did not all come back, or came back perhaps just to get a wife and then went away again. His whole community too was getting smaller.

We walked in this way up and down the steep folds in the valley to the base of the main peak of Nkawozya, doing in all about nine miles, in two and a half hours. We then climbed it without difficulty in about an hour and a half. The view from the top was most rewarding, in fact told me all I wanted to know.

To the north was Mpanda, another impudent peak slightly lower than Nkawozya, cocking a snook at the plain towards Karonga.

The real Nyika lay to the south of us; its northernmost point was hard by Njalowe, and although we could not see into it, we could see its great wall running south as far as the eye could reach. It was clear that the following morning we should have to climb up the steep grey peak immediately behind the village (it was called Chelinda by the natives), and then at last we should be in the country we had come to find.

I took some bearings to make sure and told Michael.

He gave a mock groan and said: "Oh God! must we climb out of this all over again? You know, I am beginning to feel about it as Moses must have done about the Promised Land. We keep on getting tantalizing glimpses of the Nyika but we never really get on it. Do you think we ever shall?"

While I worked on my bearings, I sat in the shelter of a rock out of the wind. Michael, some distance away, took a hundred feet of film or more. The view was tremendous. According to my map there should be bench marks on Nkawozya, but I could not find any. According to the Chief no European had ever climbed Nkawozya before.

I was sitting apart from the rest when suddenly, close to my left ear, there was a tremendous swoop and flutter of

222

wings. An eagle brushed my head, seemed to snatch at my compass which was all a-glitter in the sun, thought better of it and sheered off.

"It's all right," I shouted to Michael who, startled, called out to me; "it's all right. It's a good omen. The time you want to be careful in mountains is when buzzards drive the eagles off."

On our return journey we heard every now and then, from far off in the camp, a roll or two on the drum. It was evidently being warmed up for the night. It is a slow and skilled task getting an African drum up to the right temperature and texture. Our drummer, who had such a great reputation to confirm, was obviously starting in good time and taking no chances. But what struck me particularly that day about the far-off drumming was its absolute appropriateness to its physical and human setting. I seemed to have missed that point in my past. But the drum is as appropriate to Africa as the elephant's trumpet, the lion's roar, the leopard's cough, or the first tap of thunder in a dry summer, on a parched and shimmering horizon.

We were back in camp just before sundown. It was full of activity and a recognizable party excitement. Everyone was being very nice to everyone else, and quite unable to sit still. Karramba was everywhere. The ox had been slaughtered. The bearers in twos and threes had raised little grills of green wood, and were getting the coals up underneath them for cooking their meat. In the centre of the bearers, talking happily to all and sundry, sat our Umfumo in his scarlet beret.

When he saw us he at once came over and explained gravely that he would have to leave us early in the morning. He had come as far as his knowledge went, and could not let his old father and his women stay alone any longer. We said good-bye to him with real regret.

Chapter Twenty-Three

AS the sun went down the women started coming in from the village. They wore their wraps now lightly folded round them and as they walked down the tracks, silhouetted against a bright red sky, they took on an ancient classic appearance.

Soon after dark the party began. I was standing with Harneck and a group of the bearers watching a large aeroplane, blazing with light in every window, coming up from behind and above Nkawozya. It was, I thought, the mail plane from Heath Row to Johannesburg; a machine that did seven thousand miles in thirty-six hours.

As we watched it go by, the stars became, for the first time, very distinct and clear. I was getting the native names for them when the drumming began in earnest. I was soon alone and I walked a little way up the crest towards the village so that I could see the whole camp at a glance. There was no dancing at first but only singing.

The singing was lusty and clear, with many voices in harmony, but it had, like all African tunes, an undertone of frustration and melancholy in it.

As far as I could make out they were singing about their lives, not as they had been once, or could be again, but as they were in their vast present, in their shimmering and parched monotony. They sang about their little fields of maize and corn, about how the women tilled them, and the pigs and baboons raided them till there was no sleep left for anyone in the villages, and no happy evenings round the drum, only a cheerless night-and-day vigil in the midst of their crops. And what for? So that their stomachs, those insistent, never satisfied stomachs, could be fed, and for no other glory or aim. And the drum at this point was the

224

stomach, was its solar plexus, its digestive system, its craving for more, more, more, its own blind, dead, monotonous means and end.

They sang about an African boy called Charlie to whom Capetown was magic, Johannesburg Eldorado, who left the village and never returned. They sang about their taxes, they sang about the Government they had never seen, they sang about us and this journey we had brought them on, and where and when was it all going to finish? Oh! the questions that drum asked, and did not pause to answer, but just went on and on bringing all back to its basic theme, this routine of birth, begetting and dying, set in the harsh, monotonous, parched routine of Africa, from which there is no escape and in which there is no change.

Life could be more and it could be less, it could be long or brief, it could go faster and it could be slower, but in its essence, in its heart there was no change, no hope of change ever, unless there could be—and could there?—some magic somewhere, some medicine that could redeem all?

If anyone wants to know the African heart he should listen to its drum as I did that night alone on the crest between the two frayed ends of my journey. It is entirely appropriate to its meaning. It, too, cannot change, it cannot alter its voice or tone, but by God, it can be fast or slow, loud or soft, long or short. It knows densities and rhythm but only one quality. It takes you so far, with a beating, straining heart, and then drops you and your excitement in the dust, because it cannot go beyond. But it can and does begin again.

I walked close and watched them dancing. In the flickering firelight the men and women, their dark faces absorbed in an expression beyond knowing, stood in two opposite rows. The drum began softly, and a quiver went through their bodies; the basic desire was born. The blood began to rise, to sing and thunder in their ears, the drum became their pulse, was in them, and set the hungry, the eager pace.

There was no pretence about it. There was no guilt, no sense of shame, only a great wide longing of the body to be one, to be free of the winter of separation; a longing of the fraction to be a whole. It was a necessity of the blood, and most innocent. The tiniest children were there, watching their fathers, mothers and sisters with wide-eyed approval, as they gave this orchestration by dance and drum of the physical movements of the sexual act.

When the excitement in the blood was so high that it could rise no higher, when the drum could go neither faster nor louder, this antique fever had its spasm. It was as if an electric spark leapt from one black head to another, a brilliant stream of lightning from one cumulus crest to another, and men and women leapt at each other, seized each other round the waist with frenzied hands, and went quickly, violently, like a tree shaking in a storm, through the motions of the act of love. And then the spasm left them. Was this all there was to it? Was there nothing beyond? After such frenzy was nothing changed? The drum died down to a low tap of slow despair. The bodies broke apart, shoulders sagged and feet trod a listless rhythm. A low musical wail, heart-rending to hear, burst from the bearers round the fire.

Time passed on. The fire in the heart, the glow of coals in the blood, sank low. Could it ever flare and flame again? The drum tapped on softly, hard to hear, but with the rhythm still just there. Black faces in the firelight stared sombrely, watchfully at their own flames of wood. The smell of burning meat rose like sacrificial incense in the dark, to appease what gods, what everlasting hunger?

Surely this could not be the end, this could not be all; they could and must try again. The drum rapped out a roll of warning, it drummed an imperious call to attention. The bodies became erect and then it all began once more. The same excitement. Perhaps this time it would be different. The drum went far, farther perhaps than drum had ever been before; the bodies twisted, the heart beat, as neither bodies nor heart had ever twisted or beaten before. It must be, it could be different. But was it? "Oh no! Oh no! Oh no!" the watching figures wailed round their burnt offerings at the flickering firesides. And again the prancing bodies, in the half-world between the night and the camp-light, fell apart, as if emptied of themselves, emptied of fire and hope.

This then is the great, the joyful and the tragic drama of the African's life: its glory and its humiliation. As far as they will take him, he follows the body and its interests across the gulf of our split natures into that dark country on the other side. He puts all his trust and faith in the splendour of his body, he encourages it to shake and convulse with desires of flame, and appetites so violent and clear that their satisfaction alone may become purpose and end enough. He is strong, brave, enduring and patient in their service, but at heart there is still this "Oh no! Oh no! Oh no!"

It is not enough, there is a hunger still that escapes, that will not be satisfied. There must be something else, something more to give it, but what and how and where? Perhaps there is magic. Ah, he has tried that, and goes on trying it, but in the end the circle rounds on itself, leads the old trail back to the devouring stomach, the beating heart, to the world below belt and navel.

He belongs to the night. He is a child of darkness, he has a certain wisdom, he knows the secrets of the dark. He goes to the night as if to a friend, enters the darkness as if it were his home, as if the black curve of the night were the dome of his hut. How the ghosts of the European mind are warmed with memories of the African's response to the night. He does not really care for the day. He finds his way through it with reluctant, perfunctory feet. But when the sun is down, a profound change comes over him.

He lights his fire, he is at once happy and almost content,

sings and drums until far in the morning. All would be well if there were not still this hunger. And what should he do about it?

We could tell him—we who have too much of the light and not enough of the night and wisdom of the dark. We could, but we will not because we are split against ourselves, we are infinitely prejudiced against the night.

Half the love we give ourselves would do for him; half for our bright morning selves, and half for him. It is enough for both: two halves for a whole, and the whole for both. Listen to his drum and listen to his wail, look how he goes with people like Michael and myself, cheerful, staunch, friendly and strong, on a journey he does not understand, to a place he distrusts. He would go anywhere we ask for half our love. There is no problem there.

It is an irony so characteristic of our basic unreality to blame the problem on him, to shoulder him with our fears and our sin, to call it a black, a native, an African problem. It is a striking, an effective, a plausible irony. But it is not true. The problem is ours; it is in us, in our split and divided hearts; it is white, it is bright with day. We hate the native in ourselves; we scorn and despise the night in which we have our being, the base degrees by which we ascend into the day.

I say this not to evoke an emotion, to prove a theory, or to score a point in a special plea. I say it because I believe it is a law of life. It is as much law as the law of gravity. Defy gravity and you break your neck; outrage this law and you break your heart and lose your soul.

Scientists and judges have not the monopoly of laws. Euclid was an intuitive pattern before it became a textbook; Lucretius produced the atom whole out of his heart before it was split in a bomb on Hiroshima. The wholeness and the split, both, are within us.

But we have come dangerously late to this new awareness. We do not understand that we cannot do to others what we do not do to ourselves. We cannot murder and kill outside without murdering and killing within. We turn our hate on to the native, the dark people of the world, from Tokyo to Terra del Fuego, because we have trampled on our own dark natures. We have added to our unreality, made ourselves less than human, so that that dark side of ourselves, our shadowy twin, has to murder or be murdered.

Already there is the smell of murder approaching far off in the sky over Africa. And this need not be, that is the pity of it. If we could but make friends with our inner selves, come to terms with our own darkness, then there would be no trouble from without.

But before we can close our split natures we must forgive ourselves. We must, we must forgive our European selves for what we have done to the African within us. All begins with forgiveness. Even the spring is a re-beginning because it is sheer, utter forgiveness and redemption of the winter and its murder of leaves.

Still the drumming went on. It did not vary except that each repetition became louder, quicker, more insistent, and the rush of man and woman at each other and then clasping of each other became more and more frenzied.

Feeling as I did I couldn't face my tent. I climbed higher up the crest. The night was very dark: there was no moon, no pallid, half-way house of sun and earth about with its cold mirrored unreality of reflection. The stars were exceptionally bright and clear. They, too, seemed to have taken up the beat of the drum. The sense of oneness which that drum could create between itself and all that belonged to the night passed all comprehension.

The Milky Way was superb, more like a track densely strewn with daisies than its usual blur of misty light. Orion, Vance's old hunter, club erect, jewelled belt tucked tightly into his slim waist, seemed to be prancing like a buck negro to the throbbing of the drum. Castor and Pollux, the heavenly twins, Alfa Centauri, Sirius, the watch-dog at that dark entrance through the Milky Way into the greater night beyond; our own Jupiter, Mars and the inevitable Plough were all there, spear, bow, arrows and blade in hand. And away to the south where lay the Nyika, the land of to-morrow, a dark, pointed peak cut deep into the night. It was a night so clear that I had no difficulty in recognizing the full line of the great head of Chelinda. Immediately over it hung the Southern Cross.

As a Cross, I know it is not perfect. It is not symmetrical. But to love only perfection is just another way of hating life, for life is not perfect. And now, as I looked at the Cross, it seemed to hang over the proud, sullen head of Chelinda like a legendary blade, a crusader's jewelled sword, or the great Excalibur itself, held reverently in prayer against the lip and brow of the night. It made of the darkness a way-side altar, a chapel at which the undubbed soul might come for its final vigil and dedicate a sword to the quest for a single grail. It was itself a Sword-of-all-such-Swords; but also it was a cross held over a world old in time, but new in the European heart.

And what does that mean? What does any cross mean? These shapes of crosses litter our horizons from birth to the grave, but do we know what they mean? Out of what tender wood, by what great carpenter, are they nailed?

We must shut our eyes and turn them inwards, we must look far down into that split between night and day in our-selves until our head reels with the depth of it, and then we must ask: "How can I bridge this self? How cross from one side to the other?" If we then allow that question to become the desire for its own answer, and that desire to become a bridge across the chasm, then, and only then, from high above on this far peak of our conscious self, on this summit so far above the snow-line of time, in this cold, sharp, selected moment, clearly and distinctly we shall see a cross. A gulf bridged makes a cross; a split defeated is a cross.

A longing for wholeness presupposes a cross, at the foundations of our being, in the heart of our quivering, throbbing, tender, lovely, lovelorn flesh and blood, and we carry it with us wherever we journey on, on unto all the dimensions of space, time, unfulfilled love, and Being-to-be. That is sign enough.

After that the drum can cease from drumming, the beating and troubled heart have rest. In the midnight hour of the crashing darkness, on the other side of the night behind the cross of stars, noon is being born.

Our last morning in the low country broke clear and fine. Our bearers and askaris, who had drummed and danced themselves almost to a standstill, set about trying to get ready for our journey. But Michael and I kept them at their work with such pitiless determination that we made an early start and got away before seven.

(The heart had been drummed out of the village too). No one saw us off except the Chief who came limping along painfully on a stick, complaining that the walk and climb up Nkawozya had been too much for him.

The track up Chelinda started immediately behind the village. It was very steep but we all had our climbing legs now and went up it with a will. Once I stopped and far below down in the plain I saw the scarlet beret, the young gallant headgear of our Mpoka Umfumo, a tiny point of red bobbing up and down in the sombre track of the valley on that long difficult walk back to Mwatangera. I would probably never see him again, but that beret and he were a part of me I could never forget, if only for their presence at that moment of release from the War on Charo.

That was the last familiar thing we saw. From there on we got deeper into country which was different from anything we had seen. At first our track was lined with Euphorbias Candelabra, a tree so-called because it holds up the arms of its branches as if they were sockets in which the candles of the day are put to burn. When we climbed out of their Byzantine presence we came into a place dominated by immense scarlet aloes which raised the sun like some Burgundian wine towards a madonna blue sky. They in their turn gave way to white and scarlet proteas; the proteas to heathers, pink, white and russet bell heathers, yellow and white everlastings, and purple lobelias.

At that stage we came to a new view at the top of the head of Chelinda. For all its proud lift it was a false head. The real summit lay farther back at the end of a long, steep grass slope.

A loud cry went up from the bearers when they saw this slope. I am afraid it was not a romantic cry for all it said was "Meat! Meat! Meat!" and it meant to convey that ahead of us there was something they would like shot.

Over the slope all kinds of antelope and buck and gazelle were getting up out of warm beds in the grass to have a look at us. They were obviously not accustomed to this kind of intrusion, and though they could not possibly approve of it, the fear they had of it was the general fear of the unknown and not specific to man. As we advanced towards them, they gave way and scattered until in time the whole skyline was broken by their lovely, keen heads and proud delicate necks. They looked much nearer than they were and I refused all entreaties to shoot, although, alas, we would have to shoot sooner or later for food.

I now took the lead with Harneck and we went ahead of the bearers so that I could be free to scout around. Michael came on with the main body, keeping as near as he could on a southerly bearing, which was not difficult. There were wide, well-trodden game tracks everywhere and they all ran south. I, still deep under the influence of my night on the crest, was thrilled to see how clearly and unerringly everything pointed south.

When we came to the place where the first antelope had stood up, its bed was still warm with the warmth of its body, and the grass spread like a magnetic field around where he had lain. There I suddenly became aware of a familiar, purple glow in the grass, the murmur as it were of a dark purple tide ebbing through the gold of the grass. Irises, the proud, erect flowers of chivalry, were everywhere. We walked from there, I reckoned, through ten square miles of irises. When this heraldic field of gold and purple ended we came to an altitude in which the grass glowed with the orange, red, blue and gold of wild gladiolus. Most lovely of all, enormous, single, white delphiniums shone like stars on all the darker slopes. In the background on the horizon were those beautiful, antelope heads still staring down at us. It was like some fine ancient tapestry suddenly come alive.

At about noon we were right on the top. At last there was no doubt, we were on the true Nyika, high above the low malarial plains, above sleeping sickness, east coast fevers and the paralysing maladies and parasites of the low country. We were so high that the air smarted in our nostrils; it was so keen and cold that we promptly put on our pullovers. But we had reached the summit. There were no more peaks to conquer, no more heartbreaking climbs up one steep valley and the next. We were on a real plateau; far as our eyes could see stretched a gentle, rhythmically-rolling country of grass and flowers. Round the edges other peaks rose out of the shimmering plain, giving us a keen sense of our exalted world; but they were not our concern save as additional ornament to the immense African frame of our view. South I could see for about fifty miles, then my view was blocked by cloud. But in the whole of the distance between there was nothing but this free, gently rolling country.

I wish I could describe the effect that view had on me, but I will say little more than that it seemed to me miraculous. It was so unlike anything else. It was deep in the heart of Africa and filled with the animals of Africa, and yet it was covered with the grasses, the flowers and colours of Europe.

Yet it was unlike any other colour I have ever seen: I expect, basically, it was a tawny gold, the gold of the leopard's rather than the lion's skin, but this gold was shot through with undertones of a deep blood red and a shadowy purple.

As I looked at it, I understood at once why I had felt below that there was a large, purple cat purring up there behind the clouds. It looked in its colours, its shape and its isolation, a contented, serene, and deeply fulfilled land. It seemed a place which, without human interference, had made its own contract with life, struck its own balance with necessity and nature. Beyond that I cannot go.

After tea Michael, Karramba and I, taking our rifles, walked about two miles down the gentle dale through which the Rukuru ran. It was about twenty minutes before sundown when, round a bend in the stream, we came to a large pool, blue into its deepest depths with the evening sky. On the slope above it was a big grey boulder. All round the pool the mud and earth were deeply cut with the tracks of game. We went up the slope and sat behind a rock and waited to see what we could see.

There was no wind any more. There was no cloud or mist in the sky. I have never known such stillness. The only sound was the sound of one's blood murmuring like a far sea in one's ears: and that serene land and its beauty, and the level golden sunlight seemed to have established such a close, delicate, tender communion with us that the murmur in my ears seemed also like a sound from without; it was like a breathing of the grasses, a rustle of the last shower of daylight, or the swish of the silk of evening across the purple slopes.

Suddenly Karramba touched my arm. We could hardly believe our eyes. A very big male leopard, bronze, his back charged with sunset gold, was walking along the slope above the pool on the far side about fifty yards away. He was walking as if he did not have a fear or care in the world, like an old gentleman with his hands behind his back, taking the evening air in his own private garden. When he was about twelve yards from the pool, he started walking around in circles examining the ground with great attention. Then he settled slowly into the grass, like a destroyer sinking into the sea, bow first, and suddenly disappeared from our view. It was rather uncanny. One minute he was magnificently there on the bare slope and the next he was gone from our view. But as if to confirm his presence, three black crows without a sound came and perched themselves on the summit of the slope above him. They seemed to be watching the place where he had vanished as closely as we were, tucking their dark heads deep into their midnight shoulders with solemn absorption.

We waited attentively. About five minutes passed: not a sound anywhere, except this remote music of all our being. I was lying with my ear close to the ground when I heard a new sound that made my heart beat faster: it was the drumming of hooves far away. It was a lovely, urgent, wild, barbaric sound. It was getting louder and coming straight for us. I caught a glimpse of Michael's face, shining with excitement. The drumming of the hooves came towards us from somewhere behind the far slope, like a great Pacific comber, like a charge of Napoleon's cavalry at Waterloo, and then out of the midst of this drumming, this surf of sound, there was thrown up like a call on a silver trumpet, or the voice of an emperor born to command, a loud, clear neigh. It was one of the most beautiful sounds I have ever heard, and it established itself in all my senses like the far silver fountain that I had once seen a great blue whale throw up on a South Atlantic horizon after a storm. Now, as the sun tinted the horizon, the wave of sound rose towering into the air and then crashed down on to the summit of the slope opposite us. A troop of about forty zebra, running as if they had never known walking, the rhythm of their speed moving in waves across their shining flanks, charged over the crest and made for the pool where the leopard lay.

I wondered how it was going to end. I could not believe a leopard would attack such a lusty group of zebra, although I had never seen a leopard behave quite as this one did, so frankly, so openly. At that very moment, the leader of the troop with his mane streaming from him like the strands of the Mistral itself, stopped dead. At one minute he must have been going at thirty-five miles an hour, at the next he stopped without a slither in his tracks, two fountains of steam shooting out of dilated nostrils.

The rest of the group stopped with him. Had they seen the leopard or seen us? For about five minutes we saw a group of zebra, not fifty yards away, in earnest consultation. I saw Michael raise his gun and then put it down again. He had, I knew, to kill one zebra because it was his duty to examine them for parasites. I saw him take aim several times but always he put his gun down again.

Meanwhile the consultation went on, soundlessly and ceaselessly. Some invisible, some electric exchange of meaning was going on between those vivid creatures on the darkening slope. They looked so heraldic, like unicorns who had just had their horns pared. They had beautifully marked golden skins, with black blazonings. For five minutes they stood, their steaming heads close together, and then somewhere in the magnetic depths of themselves, their meaning fused and became one. They whirled swiftly round and charged back over the crest straight into the dying day and we did not see them again.

"I am sorry," Michael said to me, breathing hard: "I am sorry but I just could not shoot: they were beautiful."

"I am glad you didn't," I answered.

We got up and walked back, and as we rounded the bend saw that it was not the leopard that had scared the zebra but the smoke of our own camp fires rising straight up into the still air like a palm blue with distance. The camp was just on two miles away, but even that was not far enough for the timid herd.

That night I had another dream. I record it for exactly the same reasons and on the same terms as the first one. I would add only that I dream often about animals. I have lived and been brought up in wild places and animals mean much to me. I dream particularly about horses and, in a way that I do not define clearly to myself, I am influenced by my dreams of horses. When they are thin, tired, thirsty, when I have to drag them along with me, I take it as a kind of warning; and when, as once in the war, I dreamt that I was actually carrying a horse of mine, I was really alarmed. This dream, too, was about a horse, but it was different. Here it is:

I dreamt I caught my horse in a field covered with irises. It was a large black horse with a white star in its forehead. It was called Diamond. It was a cross between a hunter and a carthorse; a fast and sturdy horse, a horse fit to carry a knight in full armour. It reminded me of my mare, Duchess, as described in Lilian Bowes-Lyon's lovely poems about her. I mounted Diamond squarely and we set off at a fast thundering pace across the purple folds of the Nyika. The wind and sunlight whistled through Diamond's mane. A feeling of strength and security came from the horse through the close grip of my knees on its back. I seemed as content as it is possible to be.

Chapter Twenty-Four

WITH this dream my journey in Africa really ends. It is true I spent another three weeks on that lovely plateau, but there is nothing new to say of it. Always it was there as I have described it, alone with itself, its grass, flowers, and animals, and no people except us. Every morning we rose early, shook the dew or frost off our tents and made our way until sunset across a new tract of our exalted land.

We spent two nights at the sombre pond or lake at Kaulime where the serpent is said to live. We did not see the serpent itself, in spite of the fears of our bearers, but I must record that I, Karramba and Harneck all three missed dead-easy shots at game hard by Kaulime, too easy really to be laughed away. When we came back our bearers shrugged their shoulders and the Drummer said: "But Bwana, don't you know there is a powerful Mankwala, mighty medicine in that pond?"

I realized how wise I had been not to shoot earlier on. The light was clearer than I had imagined. I paced the distance to where I had first shot at the buck. I had thought it was a hundred to a hundred and twenty yards. It was six hundred and fifty paces away. And I tell this story against myself because it shows how pure and clear the air was over the Nyika, and how full, easy and generous its distances. I am not a bad shot, but it took me five days before I shot my first game.

Every day we saw that warm, electric flicker of flame of game moving in the distance—heraldic zebra, roan antelope with horns like Saracens' swords, and giant eland with purple coats and immaculate white dew-laundered socks. Every morning, even when one did not see them, one knew that the great bronze leopards of the Nyika, with their Assyrian profiles, sat by the edges of their Druid circles of wood sunning themselves and drying the dew off their whiskers; and every evening without fail the great African sun, as it went down far away in Rhodesia, left its light standing like an archangel on the horizon with wide outstretched wings gathering the world to its breast.

For about a fortnight we moved like this through uninhabited country, and then came down one evening in the dark mist at Nchena-Chena.

But we were not finished yet. We had to go back into the vast Rumpi cleft of the Nyika, before we were finished.

One day Harneck and I did a thirty-two mile trek. We went to the western edge of this new world and looked down immense precipices, and over a black valley for about a hundred miles of peak beyond peak stretching far into the blue Rhodesias. We came back and drank some water at the source of the great Rukuru river. We stalked some zebra but had to abandon our stalk because a lion on the same mission scared them as soon as we scared him; then, as the sun began to sink, we made for our camp.

At that moment I had my first and only difference of opinion with Harneck. Our camp was out of sight, indeed we had no idea where Michael had pitched it. Harneck, swearing he recognized Michael's foot-prints, wanted to follow one set of tracks, I another. It seemed most unreasonable for me to be arguing with a native born and bred to tracking. But I had had my lesson on Mlanje. I preferred to be the cause of my own mistakes and I insisted on going my way. Half an hour later we came on to a rise and saw the camp, perfectly pitched on the banks of the young Rukuru.

Two nights later we camped for the last time by the magic pond, dark and tragically still under the night sky, and so full of reservations that the bearers could hardly bear to look at it.

From there we did, although I say it myself, a remarkable and praiseworthy journey into the immense and extremely difficult Rumpi valley. Our carriers were beyond praise. They did some terrible climbs, loaded to the full, through deep gorges along vast precipices without a man falling out, and a week later, at two o'clock in the afternoon, we climbed out of our last valley and looked down on the shimmering red roofs of the Mission at Livingstonia.

We camped that night on the road, and in the morning said good-bye to our bearers. It was the last good-bye and made me very sad. It is always like that with journeys. One is as sad at the end as at the beginning; the reward lies in between.

The bearers, too, looked depressed, and as they walked by us down the red, dusty road to their home, I thought their farewell was deeper than usual, that ancient greeting: "We see you, Bwana! We see you."

"Aye! I see you," I called back: "I see you. Hamba Gahle. Go in happiness."

Michael stopped, suddenly tapped a cigarette impatiently on his case, lit it, looked at me and said: "And you? What will you do now? Will you ever come back?"

I said I didn't quite know. For the moment my work was over. My instinct was to get back as soon as I could to take up my own personal life where the war had interrupted it ten years before. It seemed to me by far the most important thing in the world to do: to begin trying to give to myself the wholeness, the singleness that I so wanted life and the world to have. But who could tell, I might be back. Africa was deep in me, and in the past sooner or later it had always brought me back.

I did not say so to him then, but the truth was that Africa was with me whether I came back or not. For years it had stood apart from me: a dark, unanswered, implacable question in my life. It was that no longer. I felt that I was not leaving it, but taking it with me. I might even be able to give some of it to Europe, to the Britain that had given me so much. For the sort of journey that Michael and I had just done never really ends. Where the body stops travelling, the spirit takes over the trek; but sometimes they work together and then one visits unknown, unexplored places. For me the greatest journey of all was on the move in Europe, and I wanted without delay to add what I had of singleness to it in order to help it on its difficult way.

I then had to leave Michael by the roadside with his servants already packing up. He was tired and looked thin and rather wan. For nearly a month he and I had walked and climbed from sunrise to sunset without a day's rest, and I knew he needed it. So I had volunteered to go to the Mission and telegraph for our cars.

The Mission was about eight miles away. It was a bright, sunny day and, after the Nyika, the two-thousand-foot climb up that hill was child's play to me. At the top I turned round to look back. But there was the old familiar cloud over the top of the plateau, hiding it utterly from view.

I walked as fast as I could to a little post office that was all of a tremble in the lake-side sun. A black postmaster gave me a telegraph form and a strange, attentive look. I caught a glimpse of my face in a small mirror. It was burnt black by the sun, but was the clear fresh colour that is never seen in the hot, malarial plains.

Quickly I wrote my telegrams. The little Morse machine started ticking busily before I was finished. Among other telegrams, I sent this: "All done and hastening home."

VILLA DES ÉLÉPHANTS, LA NARTELLE
and LA PONATIÈRE, ISÈRE, FRANCE

MADE AND PRINTED IN GREAT BRITAIN BY
EBENEZER BAYLIS AND SON, LTD., THE
TRINITY PRESS, WORCESTER, AND LONDON